M000104845

SLICES OF GOD

To Joe:

Wishing you all the best.
I hope you benefit from
the read.

SLICES OF GOD

Strange, Dimensional, and Fractal
Perspectives on God and the Cosmos

S.F. AUGSBURGER

Achronos Media

Slices of God
Strange, Dimensional, and Fractal Perspectives of God and the Cosmos
Copyright © 2013 by S.F. Augsburger

Published in 2015 by Achronos Media
Nicholasville, Kentucky, USA

Printed by CreateSpace

All rights reserved. Printed in the United States of America. No part of this book may be reproduced in any manner whatsoever without written permission, except in the case of brief quotations embodied in critical articles and reviews.

Key words: God, cosmos, strange, dimensional, fractal, paradox, iterations

Cover created in FractalWorks ©.
Illustrations created in DenebaCAD ©, FractalWorks ©,
and Microsoft Excel ©

Special Permissions

American Pie
Words and Music by Don McLean
Copyright © 1971, 1972 BENNY BIRD CO., INC>
Copyright Renewed
All Rights Controlled and Administered by SONGS OF UNIVERSAL, INC.
All Rights Reserved   Used by Permission
Reprinted by Permission of Hal Leonard Corporation

Vincent (Starry Starry Night)
Words and Music by Don McLean
Copyright © 1971, 1972 BENNY BIRD CO., INC>
Copyright Renewed
All Rights Controlled and Administered by SONGS OF UNIVERSAL, INC.
All Rights Reserved   Used by Permission
Reprinted by Permission of Hal Leonard Corporation

M.C. Escher's "Rind" and "Drawing Hands" used by permission. Copyright © 2014 The M.C. Escher Company-The Netherlands. All rights reserved.

ISBN-10: 0-692-46835-8
ISBN-13: 978-0-692-46835-7

10 9 8 7 6 5 4 3 2 1

Acknowledgements

I am forever indebted to my wife, Beth, my daughter, Rebecca, and my son, Jonathan, for their support, ideas, feedback, and editorial assistance throughout the fifteen-year journey developing this book. Most of all, I am thankful that they believed in the goal and in me.

I am also grateful to Minnette Hostetler, David Augsburger, Myron Augsburger, Fred Augsburger, David Swartz, Reid Thomas, and Art McPhee for their input, their patience, and their encouragement.

Last, but not least, this book would never have made it without the editorial assistance I received from Owen Burkholder, Justin Barringer, and Susan Samples.

Thank you.

To Beth

Table of Contents

Pre-Phase

Imagine being free to express doubt and disbelief without being promptly condemned and ushered to the gates of hell by those who robotically enforce the consequences of such abhorrent behavior. Imagine a heaven that rejoices in questions that undermine its very existence. Imagine a Deity who delights in intellectual processes that formulate its nonexistence as well as its existence. Imagine being thrilled when evidences usher out old concepts and announce the arrival of fresh ideas. Imagine newness being not only welcomed, but also anticipated, greeted with uninhibited excitement and celebration.

This book offers a journey and opens the door to such newness. It boldly explores fresh ideas that enlighten, contradict, replace, and even substantiate old theological concepts that religions exhaustingly attempt to maintain. It permits intellectual processes to confront the inconsistencies and incompleteness of religious assertions. It paves the way to a world that envelops the God concept, but freely resigns religious constraints. It recognizes that we have only slices of information to work with, and that our task is to merge them into larger composites that go beyond our preconceived notions of who God is and what the cosmos is all about.

For most of my life I have carried around a nagging intellectual uncertainty that resists the absoluteness of the religious doctrines I inherited. How can so many others in the world be so wrong while I carry around the baggage of theological correctness? Something simply did not add up. Once I began to acknowledge this exhaustion and uncertainty, doubts and questions that had been buried deep inside from years of repression surfaced with eruptive force . . .

"Who put God into power?"

"Why is there so much pain and suffering?"

"Can God hear me?"

"Does he, she, or it even care?"

"What kind of God plays sadistic tricks on humans, sending to hell those who didn't get the whole salvation thing *quite right*?"

Better yet, "What kind of loving God ordains some humans to fill hell?"

"If scripture is so inerrant, why do we jump through such elaborate hoops to explain away all the inconsistencies?"

"Why was I tormented as a kid, believing one moment that I was going to heaven, only to find myself in the next moment convinced that I was headed to hell?"

"Oh, and what about all those unanswered prayers? Who is to blame? Did I not have enough faith, or is God simply indifferent?"

"If we truly believe God is infinite, how is it that we have come to pretend to know so much about God?"

While the experience of regurgitating these questions was frightening at times, it gradually grew into one of freedom: freedom to ask fearful, ugly, and difficult questions. Now, instead of dreading the retribution of an angry God for such disrespectful interrogations on my part, I live with an enduring image of a Teacher who smiles at those who dare to ask *forbidden questions*. I eventually found answers to some of the questions. Others simply melted away in insignificance. Some remain suspended in time.

Seeds of Change

I grew up in a Christian home. My father was a pastor in the inner city. The environment was multi-ethnic and fairly ecumenical. Each one of us was part of the *ministry*, so to speak, with responsibilities ranging from cleaning the church to playing the organ during services. It was a family affair. But not all was well.

As a boy I wrestled deeply with the aforementioned questions and doubts. I was instructed to rebuke them. After all, scripture says, "Resist the devil and he will flee from you."[1] I did, and after many years the questions went away . . . deep into my inner soul.

One Saturday, in my mid-forties, one of those old questions came raging to the surface out of nowhere. It completely caught me off guard. Instinctively, I began the old incantations to rebuke it *and* the Devil, the *father of lies*. The discontinuity of what was happening hit me: "If God knows all, then He, She, or It already knows the questions buried deep inside. Why not get them out?"

I stepped outside, gritted my teeth, looked up to the sky, and said with an angry tone, "Who gave you the right to be God?" I waited to be struck by lightning.

Obviously, I wasn't. Instead, I was given an answer, an overwhelming answer that we will return to later on. Suffice it to say for now that I was overwhelmed with freedom and a very strange peace.

Resignation

Not long after I had hurled my question to the sky, I went on a weekend getaway with some college brothers, reuniting and catching up on life. During the course of that weekend it became apparent that our beliefs had diversified significantly. Some had become more deeply rooted in a fundamentalist view of scripture; others had moved toward more relativistic perspectives. I listened (when I wasn't preoccupied with the changes stirring within).

Finally at one point, while sitting around the fire, they turned to me and asked, "What do you think?" Unbeknownst to me, the process had already started. It was then that I realized that the staunch positions I had held so deeply were beginning to melt. The freedom I had experienced that fateful Saturday was growing; it was spreading into deeper regions of my soul. All I could say was, "I am letting go of my dogma and starting anew. Nothing is too sacred to reevaluate."

I left that weekend with more questions and fewer answers than ever. Seeds had been planted: seeds of doubt, of inquiry, of determination to explore and find

---

[1] James 4:7b; NIV The Bible, *New International Version* (Grand Rapids: Zondervan Publishing, 2002), unless otherwise specified.

answers to the surfacing questions. I gradually let go of my beliefs and began wrestling with the doubts. I entered freedom.

A Journey

I have been on this quest for more than fifteen years so far. This book is an outcome of that process. It is, however, only an intermediate stopping point: a stepping-stone. The journey will continue. In fact, I now believe the journey *is* the destination.

For the record, I do not doubt the sincerity of the religious expressions I was a part of the first forty-some years of my life, nor their importance. They, too, were stepping-stones in the process. I simply regret taking so long to experience the freedom of asking questions and seeking answers: the freedom to move across the *river of discovery*, jumping from stone to stone. Strangely, it wasn't until I freely abandoned my beliefs that I discovered what I truly believe.

Tools for the Road

It may be helpful for you to become acquainted with some of the tools that have shaped my journey. Some were old and rusty, having shaped my early worldviews, yet timeless in their ability to address the roots of knowledge and understanding. Others, though introduced centuries ago, were new to me.

My first tool of choice was science. I believe in the scientific method and in scientific data. The implementation of scientific inquiry and the interpretation of available data are fundamental processes that cannot be ignored by religious pursuits. The God concept and the physical world are too intertwined to be compartmentalized. Science, and in particular quantum mechanics, was a crucial tool in this process.

Imbedded in scientific inquiry is the discipline of mathematics. One of my most revered historical characters is Sir Isaac Newton. Newton not only contributed to our understanding of the physical principles that govern the universe, but he also contributed significantly to the development of calculus. Calculus utilizes observed data, particularly data of motion, to make valuable predictions. While it may be hard to grasp how mathematics could possibly address the God concept at this point, I trust you will come to see its importance along the way.

My work as a biomechanical engineer, which blends science, mathematics, and technology to study human motion, introduced dimensional analysis to the process. Dimensional analysis, as a biomechanical tool, combines numerous, and sometimes conflicting, two-dimensional camera views into one three-dimensional perspective. Similarly, as a philosophical and religious tool it is quite helpful (though often uncomfortable) as it merges diverse and paradoxical views into unifying, higher dimensional perspectives.

Obviously, I could not leave scripture behind. Though I have studied scripture for most of my life, my scope and understanding of it has expanded significantly. It has grown beyond the closed canon I grew up with: the Bible. I recognize that definitions of scripture vary widely, but for the purposes of this book *scripture* is a subset of *special revelation*, consisting of seasoned and authenticated sacred writings. Many of these texts are recordings of special revelations such as miracles, visions, dreams, prophetic utterances, and God incarnate. You will encounter some of the scriptures I have come to embrace as we wander.[2]

Last, but not least, is a tool some intellectuals are not so comfortable with: mysticism. I am a mystic: an intellectual mystic. For some, the terms "intellectual" and "mystic" represent an irreconcilable discontinuity. For me they represent openness to intellectual processes and mystical encounters, allowing each to impact the other. While it may not be the most intuitive combination, it is a most powerful tool. Many of the solutions at which I arrive, though they may be intellectual in nature, come through times of contemplation, meditation, and what I refer to as *mystical listening*. I will share some of these encounters with you throughout this journey.

The Format

The book is divided into five sections, or Phases, as I call them. While they uniquely convey progression of thought and development, they are also

---

[2] A point of clarification: I use the term "we" extensively throughout this book to refer to all of us who are on a journey, who are coming to terms with our questions and doubts, yet are determined to wander on, relentlessly seeking answers.

significantly interdependent. None stands unconnected to each of the other Phases. Interdependence permeates the process, for it permeates the cosmos.

The first Phase is introductory, discussing the current state of religion, common pitfalls in belief systems, misuses of data, and unsubstantiated conclusions. It then moves into an anticipatory stage, looking forward with great hope to new destinations and the processes necessary to move in those directions.

The second Phase examines the strangeness of the cosmos, the mathematics of the God concept, the ramifications of infinitude, creation and evolution, the brokenness of our world, and the need for resolution and personal transformation.

The third Phase delves into quantum mechanics, extra dimensions, time, chaos and contradictions, dimensional approaches to truth, our dimensional restrictions, and time-independent perspectives.[3]

The fourth Phase examines the strange mathematics of imaginary numbers, the deep beauty of fractals, and their implications on our beliefs.[4] We will see that the interconnectedness of all things *is* the structure of the cosmos.

The fifth and final Phase brings the ideas together by evaluating the vision and clarity of thought processes used in the previous Phases. It permits quantum mechanical principles to address the issue of unanswered prayers, calls for compassionate living, and leaves us with a call to continuously process, always moving from precept to precept.

You will discover as you progress from Phase to Phase that I love parables. I delight in conveying hard-to-grasp concepts through creative narratives. What is more, the process of writing such stories facilitates *my* understanding: I learn as I write. I have written six narratives of a young man on a quest to explore, meet significant individuals, and discover answers. You will encounter the *Narratives* as they surround each the five Phases of this book. These narrative wanderings put meat on the concepts discussed herein. I hope you will have as much fun reading them as I did writing them.

---

[3] If you don't know what these terms mean, don't worry; I will explain them later.
[4] Ditto.

And Now for the Journey . . .

I am delighted you chose to join me. I hope you will enter this quest with questions, honesty about your doubts, a willingness to diligently pursue answers, and an excitement for what we will discover together. The cosmos is full of mystery and begs us to ask because we want to know, to seek because we want to find, and to joyfully anticipate surprises along the way. And now for the journey . . .

Phase 1

Introductory Perspectives

1.00

The Narrative

Perplexed, he knelt in the damp debris next to the rock. No simple geological fracture produced its sheer faces, for there were signs of artistic effort in its smooth facets and sharp edges. He brushed away the leaves and dirt to reveal an inscription that read,

> *Listen!*
>
> *Is is not and IsNot is*
>
> *Many are one*
>
> *One is many*
>
> *Seek to understand!*

Time seemed to slow down as he stood there, fixated on the rock and its message. *Was it intended for him?* He shook his head, surfacing. *Surely not!* With deliberate effort, he tried to avoid its challenge. *It could be for anyone! Or everyone! What has it to do with my mission? After all, my mission is noble.* Trivial riddles would only distract him from his purpose.

Turning from the rock, he continued down the path through the woods. The sun was in front of him and to the left, casting lengthy shadows from the trees. The leaves, past their prime, were loosing their grip on the trees, and quickly covering the path. Autumn was coming to a close. He hoped his mission would be complete before winter set in. Surely, it would only take a week or so.

Weary as he was, he found himself walking carefully, but with some haste in the approaching dusk. He wanted to find a place to rest before nightfall. The journey felt as though it had taken forever; and yet, it strangely seemed as though he was moving outside of time. His purpose was, after all, timeless.

The woods cleared and the path began to wander through a meadow of tall grass. Below, in the valley to the west, he could see the village. He had been told of its location and quaint nature. Many a traveler returned again and again, once introduced to its strange aura.

At the village's entrance, an elderly man was leading sheep to their stalls for the night. The Elder was hunched over, face to the ground. "Pardon me," he said to the Elder. "Would you know where I could stay for the night?"

The old man replied without lifting his head, "Listen Inn."

"OK," he said, "I am listening."

"No," said the gentleman, "Listen Inn! You will want to stay at Listen Inn."

"Oh, I am sorry, sir. I thought you meant . . ."

"Not to worry, young man. It's not the first time I have been misunderstood. It happens again and again."

"Where can I find Listen Inn?"

"Go straight into town," said the Elder, directing him to follow the main roadway into the center of the village where the inn had been welcoming travelers for centuries.

Entering the inn, he rang the bell on the front desk. "Can I help you?" called the innkeeper, as she entered the foyer.

"Uh, yes, do you have a vacancy?"

"Allesa Horen's the name, since you asked. Welcome to Listen Inn."

"I'm sorry. Nice to meet you, Ms. Horen. I'm Fritz Streuner."

"Please, call me Allesa. And yes, I do have a vacancy," she said with a coy smile. "Up the stairs, to the right, last door on your right. Breakfast is at seven o'clock."

As he picked up his knapsack and headed up the stairs, Allesa noticed his limp. "Can I get something for your leg?"

"No, I'm fine, but thanks," he replied.

His weariness prevailed over the discomfort in his leg. He drifted off to sleep quickly. Few dreams chased him this night. No shadows, just rest.

If not for the school bell's piercing ring outside his window, he would have slept through the morning. He sat up and moved to the edge of the bed where he noticed steam rising from a basin on the nightstand. A jar of ointment and a few fresh bandages were next to the basin. He smiled, remembering his refusal of help the night before. He gratefully, yet painfully, cleaned the wound and applied the ointment and bandages. He was a quick healer and knew he would soon be back to normal.

Anticipating the length of the journey ahead of him, he hastily dressed and packed his knapsack. Nothing was going to slow him down now, not even pain.

"Can I get you coffee?" asked Allesa, as he sat down at the last available table.

"Please."

"Eggs and toast?"

Fritz enthusiastically replied, "Yes!" He had not had much to eat since leaving the kind elderly couple who had graciously taken him into their home earlier on his trek. The warmth of their words still echoed in his head. Fritz knew he would get it right. Besides, here he was, on his journey! He could smell the . . .

"Here you are," Allesa said, placing the plate of warm food on the table.

"Oh, thank you," he said, looking into her eyes. "By the way, thank you for the ointment and bandages. How did you know?"

"Oh, I am familiar with such a wound," she said. Seeing his knapsack was ready for travel, she sat down at his table and pointedly asked, "Where are you going?"

"I am headed to Dimen Castle."

"Dimen Castle! What a journey you have ahead of you!"

"Is it far?"

"Listen," said Allesa, "It can take longer than you think, but I am sure it will be a good pilgrimage."

"A good pilgrimage?"

"Yes."

"You've been there?" Fritz was intrigued to meet someone who knew his destination personally. "Tell me about the castle. Is the lord of the castle friendly? Is the castle as spectacular as they say it is?"

"The castle is quite spectacular, and its lord is an amazing man. But it is the journey that will be the most rewarding," Allesa said with a faint smile.

"The journey will be that enjoyable?"

"Oh, do not misunderstand me. I am not saying it will be easy. I am saying it will be rewarding."

"Do you think I will get to meet the lord of the castle?"

"Oh, yes, you will meet him." After a short pause, Allesa said, "Listen . . ."

Fritz cut her off mid-sentence, "By the way, I wanted to ask about the name of the inn. Why Listen Inn?"

Sighing, she said, "I will tell you, but you will have to listen to my explanation."

"I'm listening," he replied, stuffing his mouth with toast.

"The name reveals, first of all, that to understand, one must listen to hear the meaning. Secondly, it admonishes all who enter its doors, to listen, always listen. To understand, one must first listen."

"Understand what?"

"You, my friend, are not listening."

Fritz, looking offended, retorted, "Yes, I am."

"Yes," she replied, "with your physical ears, but not with your inner ears. If you were, you would hear it."

"Hear what?"

"Precisely," she said. "If you were truly listening, you would hear many things. All things speak! The rocks you climbed over to get here, speak boldly! The waters echo their voice. The plants you nonchalantly stepped on, sing! The animals you sent running for shelter as you stumbled through the woods, speak, and, surely, hear far more than you ever will!"

"I *want* to hear," Fritz said sincerely.

"Well, that's a start," said Allesa. "You must find a quiet place."

"I have been in many quiet places, and still haven't heard the things of which you speak," reflected Fritz.

"Then," said she, "there is one quiet place you obviously do not visit."

"Where?"

"Inside," she softly murmured.

"Inside what?"

"Inside yourself!"

Fritz put down his coffee, as puzzled as he was when face to face with the inscription on the rock. Allesa continued, "When you are finally able to quiet the noise within, quiet your thoughts, and quiet your needs, then you will hear."

He stood and reached for his knapsack. "Thank you for the lodging and the breakfast." Leaving a tip on the table, he excused himself, and headed toward the door. In the doorway, he turned and said, "I will try. To listen, that is."

She nodded and said, "Then you already are."

He smiled as he passed the fresh fruit and flower stands in the open market, and paused, straining to hear something audible coming from a table of neatly stacked apples. *Oh well*, he thought, ruefully.

At the edge of the village, he encountered the Elder who tended the sheep. "Pardon me, sir," said Fritz, "Do you know the way to Dimen Castle?"

"Of course I do," said the Elder. Face to the ground again, he raised his right arm and pointed north. His skin caught the morning sun and reflected jagged light off a roughly sealed wound.

Fritz, seeing the scarred arm, couldn't help interjecting, "How did you injure your arm, sir?"

The Elder eased his arm back inside his cloak, raised his head, looked Fritz in the eyes, and said, "Never mind that. Go down to the river and follow its edge. The water will eventually turn away from the road. When you come to the fork in the road, turn toward Isnot. There will be signs. Once you make it to Isnot, they will direct you to Dimen Castle."

"How long of a journey is it?"

"It depends," said the Elder.

"Depends on what?"

"If you get in a hurry, and are not paying close attention to the signs, it will take a long time. A very long time. But, if you carefully watch your walk, you will do well.

"Oh, one more thing," said the Elder. "Avoid going to Is. The people from Is always lie, but the people from Isnot always tell the truth."

Strange, thought Fritz. *Strange, indeed.* Why could he not get a straight answer from the Elder? How could a journey of a fixed length take one person a very long time and another less? Traversing a fixed path always takes less time if the traveler moves with haste. After all, the Elder did say the road was marked with signs. He was confident of his skills as a navigator, and quickly dismissed the warnings. Winter was coming, and he wanted to be back home by the first snowfall.

The road was level and smooth, meandering along the river's bank. The sound of water rippling around and over the rocks reminded him of Allesa's words. Were there voices he had missed on the first leg of his journey, voices that spoke, but whose sound fell on deaf ears? Surely he wasn't deaf, at least, not completely. She did say he could find these inner places, places where the sounds, the voices, and the echoes could be heard. It was a journey unlike any he had ever considered taking.

Why not? Why not make it two journeys in one? The thought had never crossed his mind before. His first intent, to make it to Dimen Castle and back before the first snowfall, was reasonable, and would not necessarily be hindered by a secondary venture. He could move quickly, and learn to listen to unfamiliar sounds along the way. It might even be entertaining and lighten the journey.

With his purpose intact, he tried to listen as he walked. It was an awkward challenge. He couldn't get his mind off Allesa's words. She kept referring to the noise, *the noise within.* How could he distinguish the difference between *the noise* and the sounds he needed to hear, *the voices*?

Fritz was so busy addressing these tough questions that he failed to notice he was walking in tall, dry grass. Where had the path gone? Where had his attention gone? Quickly turning around, he retraced his steps to the path. He remembered the Elder who warned of such digressions. Fritz would not discard such advice so quickly again. But the words of the two, Allesa *and* the Elder, were both good words; yet, in tension. One encouraged *listening*; and the other, *observation* of the signs to come. *Careful attention to the external, yet quiet within? Is that even possible?*

1.01

Our Current State

The universe is a symphony of wonder and beauty, simplicity and complexity, elegance and extravagance. Yet those of us living here in the miniscule sector we call *home* wrestle with fear and survival, discontinuity and incompleteness, life and death. We feebly reach for something beyond this small space but remain firmly entrenched.

We humans live for what we do not see and die for what we do. We fight for what we want to believe rather than live into the strange, dimensional, and fractal nature of the cosmos and the symphonic entities we were intended to be.[5] We live in a state of discord.

Dis-chord

Imagine, if you will, attending an orchestral performance of Johann Sebastian Bach's *Brandenburg Concerto No. 2 in F Major*. This particular orchestra is known to have members who are quite opinionated on the topic of Bach. Some are quite adamant as to which scores of the concerto best represent Bach's intentions. In their pursuit of the purest form of representation of the Master, they limit themselves to these scores.

The conductor raises his baton and the audience is hushed. Then all hell breaks loose. Scores from the beginning to the end of the concerto are played simultaneously! The din is overwhelming. Yet, the musicians do not flinch. They each *know* they are playing the *right* score. The conductor feverishly taps his

---

[5] Fuller explanations will come.

music stand. The members, however, are not even looking at the conductor. Some look at other performers angrily for being on the wrong page! The chaos continues.

This scenario sounds preposterous, but in reality plays itself out every day on earth. It is what we have done for millennia. Music that would otherwise overwhelm us with beauty, if played symphonically, is now a most displeasing sound. We depreciate variation rather than pursue truth in harmonious relationship. We have failed by letting our complexities divide us rather than use them to build a larger and more complete symphony that pursues truth without hesitation.

This is not simply a religious problem. We are fragmented philosophically, racially, politically, scientifically, geographically, economically, and culturally. Still there is beauty in the fragments. It is found in giftedness, in perception, in color, and in tradition, among other diversities. Can the pieces play in harmony once again? I believe they can. I believe our call is to *resonate* in diversity. Diversity *is* the symphony.

Grand Illusions

Illusions interfere with the music. I am, however, one who lives without illusions. Except, of course, for the belief that I live without illusions. Strangely, as I admit to this illusion, I acknowledge that many illusions infiltrate my perceptions.

As a boy I was transfixed with *All Is Vanity*, an 1892 sketch by Charles Allan Gilbert (Figure 1). At first glance there is a woman beautifying herself in front of the vanity mirror. But by stepping back (or squinting) the larger picture tells a very different story. To a certain degree it reminds me of legalism. When viewed up close it gives the impression of being disciplined, working towards a goal, and following the right path. From a distance, or perhaps an eternal perspective, however, it may shrivel our spirit to the point of death.

What other perspectives are deadly illusions? There are some we hold onto with a vengeance, *knowing* we see reality. What about religion? How illusory is our understanding of God and how such beliefs are to be lived out? Is the belief in God's existence one grand illusion? Is the belief in *Not-God* one such illusion?

Some theorists believe we, as a human race, "will evolve" out of these illusory tendencies. However, problematic questions arise from such claims. If evolution explains all, then why has it led us to a place where we must be enlightened so as to rid ourselves of religion? Why would natural selection lead us to religious formations in the first place?[6] It is quite an anomaly of natural selection that one of its outcomes would be to question its own efficiency in explaining the presence of mysticism and religion.

I am not the first to ponder this. Atheistic evolutionists have been addressing it for some time. Richard Dawkins, in *The God Delusion*, says, "Religion is so wasteful, so extravagant; and Darwinian selection habitually targets and eliminates waste."[7] He acknowledges the tension between the assertion that natural selection should have gotten rid of religion, and the fact that it did not.

Richard Dawkins in *The God Delusion* and Eckhart Tolle in *A New Earth* expound on the virtues and elegance of the evolutionary process, that evil and a dualistic view of right and wrong are but temporary stages in a very elegant process. All this is said hoping to renew our trust in natural selection's eventual overthrow of evil. But if evolution is as elegant as these theorists claim and if we are the products of such an efficient self-governing process, how is it that so few have been informed and the rest lack such knowledge? What inefficiencies in the evolutionary process have kept most of us out of the loop?

I believe it is a profound illusion to insist that we are in the process of evolving out of what religious peoples call *evil,* and will eventually arrive, even if it takes millennia, at a higher state, free from such inadequacies. First of all, nowhere in the evolutionary code is it written that we should *ever* know *what* we are going to evolve into. Knowing the outcome of the evolutionary process is contrary to natural selection itself! Secondly, how is it that these theorists have come to know what *the best thing we could evolve into* looks like? Where did they get the idea of *good* or *better*?

---

[6] Though theorists, such as Richard Dawkins, attempt to address this question, their answers leave me empty and longing for more.

[7] Richard Dawkins, *The God Delusion* (New York: Houghton Mifflin Company, 2006), 163.

Figure 1. All Is Vanity

We do not know that we are going to evolve into something greater than our current state, one without *evil*. For all we know we will evolve into something far worse than we currently are.

Is the belief that we are going to evolve and rise above our current state an improvement over religious illusions? Or is it just another illusion? I have to admit that religions have wrought havoc over the millennia and one could argue that atheism is an improvement. Richard Dawkins seems to think so, pointing a finger at all the wars that have been waged in the "name of religion." At the same time he also claims that no wars have been waged in the "name of atheism."[8] I have heard claims to the contrary. In my lifetime alone wars have been waged by atheistic regimes with great devastation. Clearly, religion is not the only illusion with which we struggle.

Thomas Merton wrote, "We have become marvelous at self-delusion; all the more so, because we have gone to such trouble to convince ourselves of our own absolute infallibility."[9] It seems that we need illusions to cope. We use them to rationalize away our ignorance. Jesus said, "He who says he has no sin lies."[10], [11] His words could be paraphrased, "He who says he has no self–deception is most self–deceived." The worst of the worst of illusions is that we possess none!

We are enveloped by illusions of completeness, of consistency, of inerrancy, of absolutes, of clearly defined right and wrong. But if we live surrounded by so many illusions, how do we discern their presence in our lives? Where do we start? Perhaps we start at the very beginning.

Trunks of Truth

Many of us live our lives convinced that our beliefs are formed by and attached to the *trunk of truth*. This is an illusion. The *Tree of Knowledge with Pseudo Trunks* illustration shows various starting points for the development of such systems. We

---

[8] Ibid., 278.
[9] Thomas Merton, *The Seven Storey Mountain* (Orlando: Harcourt, 1948), 224-25.
[10] 1 John 1:8-10.
[11] I must here inform the reader that I am not an academic exegete. While this work is academic in some regards, it is not so in an exegetical fashion. I routinely perform context and comparative translation exegeses, though they are not included herein. My confidence in the appropriate use of such texts is evidenced by their inclusion. Furthermore, while some academic exegetes shy away from proof texting for notable reasons, I will present arguments further into the book in support of the appropriate use of stand-alone texts.

all start somewhere on the tree (Figure 2). And while we frequently convince ourselves that we started at the trunk of the tree, we most likely started on a pseudo–trunk, created by a collection of experiences, preferences, and religious input. Even if all of the data we see ahead of us is real, it can lead to a limited system of belief if we insist that our pseudo-trunk is the real deal. We may think that we are at point A, but in reality may only be at D or E.

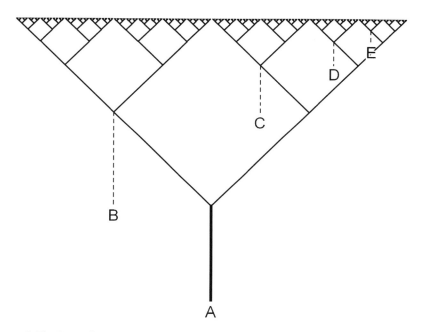

Figure 2. The Tree of Knowledge with Pseudo Trunks

Let us put some meat on the illustration. Assume, for the sake of discussion, that the following designations fit some of the trunks on the tree. A - God is. B - There is no God. C - God is, but you cannot know him, for he is too removed. D - There is a God, and it is possible to know him, but I do not care, nor does it matter. E - There is a God, it is possible to know him, I want to, but I am not important enough for God. Notice that most positions use some of the same information that other pseudo-trunks use, but limit their field of view.

Before starting this journey my view of God was not the most pleasant one. There were many troublesome issues. Some still remain. It was when I realized that I might possibly be on a pseudo-trunk that I knew I had to go back down the tree, down as far as possible, and reconstruct my system of beliefs. I acknowledged that even the assertion that "God is" could be a pseudo-trunk! Admitting that I may never get to the trunk, I continue to work my way down the tree, hoping for a fuller view.

The *tree of knowledge illusion* can express itself in certainty. While scripture admonishes its followers to *know* the hope they worship, such knowledge easily morphs into an illusion of knowing God fully.[12] When we believe that we *know* God fully, we efficiently box God in. Likewise, when we *know fully* that God does not exist, we box God out. Either way, we construct perspectives built on pseudo-trunks.

I See It All

Quite some time ago a friend of mine was granted an interview with a major software company. The interview went very well and they offered him the job. To celebrate, a number of us went to the Seattle waterfront, ordered some fish and chips, and sat down to hear about the interview. My friend talked about the questions he faced in the interview. One question in particular caught my attention. The interviewer asked him, "Why are manhole covers round?" My friend replied succinctly, "Because it is the only shape that will not fall through its own hole." The interviewer was very impressed. My friend launched a very successful career with the software company.

Later, I stewed over the question. Something about it bothered me. I couldn't quite put a finger on it. Then it hit me (not the manhole cover)! There is a ledge that the cover rests on, and its opening is a bit smaller than the cover. However, the reason manhole covers do not fall through their own hole is not because they are round! What keeps them from falling through the hole is that the cover's

---

12 Ephesians 1:18.

smallest diameter (or diagonal) is larger than the hole's largest diameter/diagonal. It is not the only shape that will not fall through its own hole! It may be the most efficient shape, but not the only one. A better answer to the software company's question may be, "Because we prefer more efficient round manhole covers." There are numerous shapes that would suffice. (Figure 3) They are not very efficient, having quite large rims for the covers to rest on, ensuring they do not fall through their own holes. But, they work.

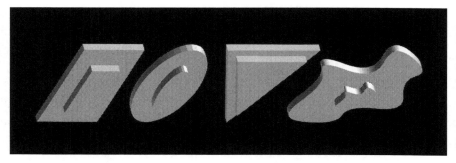

Figure 3. Manhole Covers

The software company and my friend were right in that a round manhole cover will not fall through its own hole, but also wrong in that it is not the only shape that fits that criteria. The real reasons have to do with economy and ease of removing and replacing the cover. Surely one would not want to manufacture one of the covers in the above illustration. However, what I learned is that we too easily claim to know exactly why something is what it is without pursuing underlying principles that reveal deeper, more complete reasons.

Some theories are built on shreds of evidences to formulate "truth," only to later be outdone by newer evidences. One such example pertains to theories developed on Neanderthal remains found in the mid 1800's. In an anthropology class that I took during my college years the professor waxed eloquently on the physical, mental, and cultural characteristics of the Neanderthal. *They were certainly bi-pedal, a separate, yet related species to humans, not very intelligent, probably communicated with grunts, having little to no speech, used very primitive techniques to survive, and walked hunched over.* This was all presented as *fact.*

Well, much of this description has changed, thanks to the Neanderthal Genome Project, conducted by the Max Planck Institute for Evolutionary Anthropology and broadcast by NOVA in *Neanderthals on Trial.* The analyses of DNA samples of Neanderthal bones indicate that most of previous claims were misled. They discovered that not only were the Neanderthals closely related to humans (cross breeding successfully with humans from Africa and other areas, leaving many of us with traces of Neanderthal DNA), but that they had *substantial language centers* in their brains.

I hope to be a person willing to uncover and consider things we *know* today that are built on fragments of information that, over decades of use, have become solid and unquestionable "truth." And when new evidences surface, I am determined to not turn my head, close my eyes, or argue that it just cannot be so. I want to keep an open mind: evaluate the data, contemplate its ramifications, and exhibit a willingness to adapt my stance to account for the new information.

In the following example, you can test your *see-it-all* skills, deducing the shapes of the four geometric pieces stacked on top of each other. (Figure 4) It is obvious that the top shape is a circle (or cylinder if you account for the depth). The shape below the circle is a triangle. Next is an elongated rectangle. Finally, at the bottom is a not-so-elongated rectangle. The assertion of such shapes could be convincing to a jury in a court of law. It could be convincing in the development of one's beliefs. However, unbeknownst to the artist (yours truly), a tad piece of evidence contrary to these assertions was left protruding out from under the circular shape, located at what would be 7:00 on a watch face. Once I discovered it, I decided to leave this tiny piece of serendipitous evidence to make the primary point! Are there tiny bits of evidences that are contrary to our established truths?

Because we believe we see it all clearly, we also believe we do not need to know any more than we currently do. Some may respond with, "We know just as much as we are supposed to know."

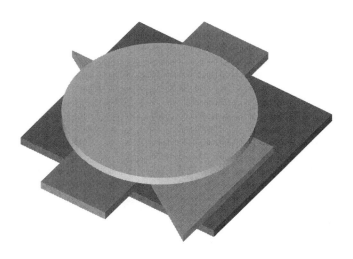

Figure 4. Hidden Shapes

If this is true, why do we investigate anything at all? We inquire why our car stopped, we go to the doctor to diagnose a developing medical issue, and read books such as this one. We do so to inquire and learn. For those who believe we were "designed," why would we be designed to want to know, only to suppress such a tendency?

The disciples of Jesus of Nazareth thought they saw it all, again and again. On one occasion they were certain they understood just how to perform Jesus' incantations to heal a young boy plagued by epilepsy. The problem was, Jesus was not around, and their ritualistic efforts failed. When Jesus arrived he said, "How long must I be with you until you see that you do not see it all?"[13] Did you *see it all* in Figure 4? Look again (Figure 5).

---

[13] Luke 9:40-42, SFA Paraphrase.

Figure 5. Hidden Shapes Revealed

Data Dogmatics

Collecting data (bits of truth) is one thing. Interpreting it is another. There are two common interpretation processes that work with the data: interpolation and extrapolation. Interpolation estimates data points between real data. Extrapolation projects data points outside or beyond real data. With evolutionary theories, interpolation estimates what took place between archaeological finds. With the issue of climate change, extrapolation projects what will happen beyond current climatic data. Each has its own hazards. Take, for instance, the illustration *Interpretations: The Data* (Figure 6). In this figure there are numerous data points that appear to be headed somewhere. With the exception of the one extraneous data point (the *outlier*), one can attempt to estimate what took place between the data points by interpolation.

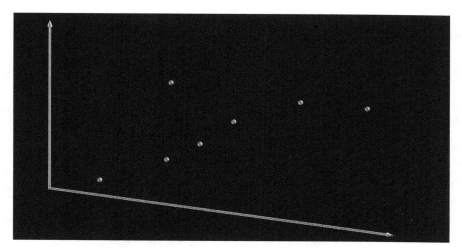

Figure 6. Interpretations: The Data

Why do we need to interpolate or extrapolate? In research we do so to find solutions to real-life problems, or to predict catastrophic events. In belief systems there are numerous motivations for connecting the dots. It may help us to understand life, explain the past, and predict the future.

Interpretation: A Third Order Polynomial Fit (Figure 7) illustrates a common interpolation technique used with numerical data. (A third order implies that the variable on the horizontal axis is put into an equation wherein it, its square, and its cube are multiplied by constants, with yet another constant added in to shift the data up or down accordingly, all summed up to fit the real data points.) This approach assumes, however, that the one data point that simply does not fit the curve is an *outlier*. It is acceptable in research to throw out a *high* and a *low* data point as outliers, primarily because we *know* there must have been some error in the data collection. Such outliers, for instance, can be pieces of dated archaeological finds. They can also be pieces of belief systems that just do not fit. We can see that this polynomial fit is clearly the best estimate of what took place between the *real* data points. Or can we?

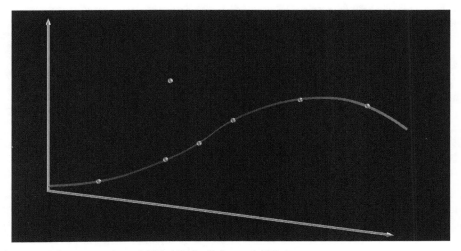

Figure 7. Interpretations: A Third Order Polynomial Fit

What if we are totally wrong in excluding the *outlier*? Are we forced to take the random approach to connect the data? Not necessarily. A mistake we easily make is to assume that we know which ones are the real outliers, if there are any at all. What if the phenomenon we are attempting to study transpired numerous times? We see in the illustration *Interpretation: A High Frequency Sinusoidal Fit* (Figure 8) that not only does such an interpolation fit the acceptable data, but also includes the outlier. Perhaps we have been too quick to perform our interpolations. Have we labeled some beliefs as religious outliers? What if, God forbid, there is an even higher frequency than what I plotted? Of course, I have not mentioned the possibility that all of the data points are outliers and that the real curve is not even close to the illustrated plots!

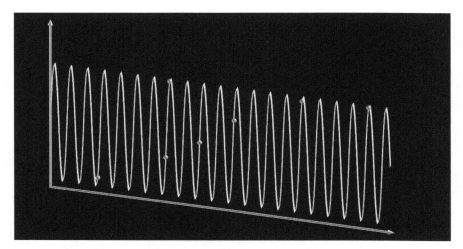

Figure 8. Interpretations: A High Frequency Sinusoidal Fit

Extrapolation is another story. Often we assume that our small timeframe is enough to project what will take place beyond. Sure, we can make good projections, ones that have great outcomes. But do I *know* where the previous data points were or that the trend will continue upwards? In the illustration *Interpretations: A Look at the Larger Picture* (Figure 9) we see that our comprehensive data may be but a tiny blip in a very different course of events. I know you realize that I have created these illustrations to conveniently make my points. But these tendencies play themselves out too frequently.

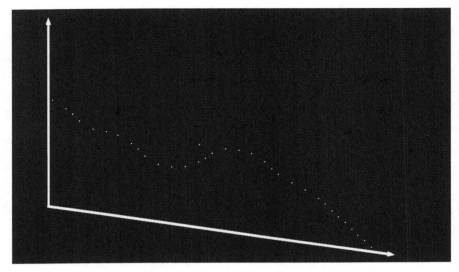

Figure 9. Interpretations: A Look at the Larger Picture!

Are belief systems subject to interpolation and extrapolation errors? I believe they are: we impose much upon our belief systems. We jump through elaborate hoops to explain away data (outliers) that do not fit our interpretation curve of preference. Furthermore, we work overtime to gather data points that do fit. The ultimate question is, "What will we do with ALL the data?"

It is tempting to assume that people of religious persuasion use different data points than non-religious people. While there are sets of data that each explains away, there are many data points both use. In *God and the World*, John B. Cobb, Jr. confirms this assertion, pointing out that frequently each side of the debate is convinced that their conclusion is not arbitrary and that they correctly used *all* the evidences.[14] We use not only the same data points but also the same limited processes.[15]

---

[14] John B. Cobb, *God and the World* (Eugene: Wipf & Stock Publishers, 1998), 118.
[15] We cannot, of course, assume all the data is in or available.

In Closing

Given the current state of human beliefs, we need sound reasoning. However, reason has gotten a bad name from its misuse. The problem with rational thought today is that it is rationalized rational thought. It is polluted with human wish lists. Rarely is it pure rational thought. Yet I am convinced that we must at least make attempts at identifying such rationalized rational thoughts in our processes, laying down the ones we are equipped to identify and picking up ones that are truly rational, even if outside our comfort zones.

1.02

Where We Are Headed

Given the current state of our existence, how can we possibly project where we are headed? Are we headed to some place we think we *should* be, or are we on a journey of letting go of our current constraints in order to simply move forward? I think the latter is a better and more achievable goal.

Given the finite scope of this book, we are headed to at least four inner places. 1. Where we identify and acknowledge our assumptions. 2. Where we accept and work at integrating all available slices of God. 3. Where we embrace paradox. 4. Where we resign our need for complete and consistent closures.

Assuming Assumptions

I believe all beliefs are based on assumptions. Assumptions are primary building blocks in the formation of organized systems, including science, politics, philosophy, and religion. Of course that statement in and of itself is also an assumption. Assumptions are not necessarily bad, but important to identify. Yet even identifying assumptions utilizes assumptions.

As I was leaving the grocery store one day, an Arab couple, dressed in full Muslim attire, was exiting ahead of me. An elegant elderly woman right in front of me turned to me and said, "If they want to live in our country they could at least dress like us and talk like us!" Without giving it a second thought, I replied, "Ma'am, if you carry that logic to its natural conclusion, then you and I should be dressed like and speaking like Native Americans." Surprisingly, she paused and then said, "Well, I guess you're right." She recognized her misguided assumption and its resulting narrow perspective.

While some assumptions are true, there are two common types of false assumptions: false negatives and false positives. A false negative assumes, for instance, that if a given type of event has not occurred in our small frame of reference, then it has never occurred anywhere. For example, if I, or anyone I know, have never witnessed a miracle, a false negative concludes that miracles do not happen. A false positive, on the other hand, assumes that if a given type of event has occurred in our frame of reference, it has always occurred in a similar fashion in all other frames of reference. If I have experienced a miracle, then miracles have always happened in all reference frames. Both can be misleading.

The God concept is based on sundry assumptions. So is the *Not-God* concept. To say either of the previous statements is not true is to cling to the assumption that one's sources of truth are correct and unquestionable. Some theorize that the God concept is an outcome, or effect, of insufficiencies left behind by the natural selection process. To some, spirituality is *all in our heads*, the result of certain neural portions of the brain that *create* the spiritual realm. Of course such psychological assessments are also *all in our heads*. Perhaps the need to explain away the God concept is also a residual insufficiency of natural selection!

One of the arguments for the nonexistence of God is that it is inconsistent for God to make laws, then to break them in order to intervene. Though this once gave me cause for thought, I now find it a bit humorous. Physicists today do not even know all the laws of *our* universe, let alone adjacent universes that may or may not intersect ours. And we pretend to understand *their* laws? How could we possibly know how two or more sets of laws interact to define what is "consistent" or "inconsistent" within the cosmos?

Assumptions affect and are affected by psychological filters. None of us has an "unfiltered" image of God or *Not-God*. If we think we do, we are probably living under yet another illusory assumption. Take God's gender for example.

Many theists believe God is male. Some base their beliefs on scriptural texts that use male terminology. Others have simply inherited a male filter. There are scriptural texts that open the door to other possibilities. One such text says that God is a father to the fatherless.[16] What then is God to the motherless? What is God

---

[16] Psalm 68:5.

to the childless? What is God to the spouseless? What is God to the friendless? What is God to the lifeless?

I believe God is far beyond our limited gender designations. On one hand, *She* laughs with us in our uncertainties and, on the other hand, *It* empathizes with our struggles. It is in this spirit and in this freedom (and given my personal filters) that I use *He*, *Him*, *Himself*, and *Father*. I believe God presents *Himself* mercifully in various forms: I *firmly assume* that God is all things to all people!

Starting Points

For most of my life I have assumed that my beliefs were formulated by God and for God. An Old Testament text reads, "Ask all the people of the land and the priests, 'When you fasted and mourned in the fifth and seventh months for the past seventy years, was it really for me that you fasted? And when you were eating and drinking, were you not just feasting for yourselves?'"[17] This passage begs two questions. Who are our belief systems for? What are our starting points for the formulation of such beliefs?

I have encountered belief systems that are admittedly anthropocentric, that start with humankind as the center framework and work out from there. Some philosophical and scientific systems fit this description. For most of my life I have been proud that my belief system was theocentric, being totally convinced that my beliefs started with God and progressed outwardly toward humans.

In more recent years I have become convinced that all belief systems, including the one I held so dearly, are more anthropocentric than we may want to admit. Religion, even though it attempts to start with God, starts with humans starting with God. Human beings paint a picture of God that starts with their experiential framework, establishing an image that works best for them, and label it, "God," their *starting point*. While "special revelation" (which includes scripture) may be the starting point for some, interpretations of these special revelations can be impacted by human experience and need, thereby making them *not–so–special*

---

[17] Zechariah 7:5-6.

revelations.[18] Admittedly there are many, including myself, who genuinely try to start with God at the center, but it is almost impossible. It is especially difficult in isolation.[19]

For those of us who attempt to start with scripture, we invariably meet up with the issue of inerrancy. For some it is of utmost importance that all scripture is totally inerrant.[20] It is quite interesting that the concept of inerrancy is only a recent trend. As a Christian doctrine it did not exist until the 1600's.[21] Yet we *function* as though this doctrine has been around since the inception of scriptural texts: since *their* starting points.

On the reverse side of the discussion are those who need scripture to be not so literal and not so inerrant. They *need* certain religious stories to be myth. Sure, myth abounds in the world, but to simply assign difficult-to-believe religious stories as myth is a very significant stumbling block in the pursuit of truth.

Marcus Borg refers to Biblical texts, particularly ones that are difficult to espouse literally, as *metaphor.*[22] While this may be the case for some passages, it is too easy to walk away from difficult passages with such a trump card. Furthermore, what *other* truths are metaphor? Are we to treat Borg's opinion itself as metaphor? Treating all scripture as metaphor is too easy of an answer for me. You certainly do not read anything in Dietrich Bonhoeffer's writings about metaphor (e.g. *Cost Of Discipleship*). He did not metaphorically suffer and die for his faith.

What other sources of truth can we turn to besides *special revelation* as starting points? The Bible itself proclaims that there are evidences of truth about God in nature.[23] That being the case, can we not explore *natural theology*? What is more, since all interpretations of religious texts are riddled with human experience, should we not acknowledge that *existential understandings* are valid

---

[18] "Special revelation" is used herein more broadly than "scripture." While scripture may consist primarily of seasoned, verified, tested, and agreed upon texts, special revelation also includes unusual and supernatural revelations, such as miracles, visions, dreams, or an incarnation.
[19] The need for community in formulating beliefs will be addressed more fully in Phase 4.
[20] It does, of course, depend on what one includes in their definition of scripture.
[21] Marcus J. Borg, *The Heart of Christianity: Rediscovering a Life of Faith* (New York: HarperCollins Publishers, 2003), 12.
[22] Ibid.
[23] E.g. Romans 1.

witnesses to truth?[24] You will see in subsequent chapters that *special revelation*, *natural theology*, and *existential understanding* will return again and again in a triune fashion to address our assumptions and to progressively develop our theologies.

Absolutes

While there may be *some* valid absolutes within our belief systems, systematic theology can easily and erroneously assume itself to be such an absolute. Karl Barth once said, "Is not the term 'Systematic Theology' as paradoxical as a 'wooden iron?' . . . Theology cannot be carried on in confinement or under the pressure of such a construction."[25] Broadly it is assumed that *solid* or *sound* systematic theology will never change. Are no new things ever to happen? Are new theologies never to emerge? When God says, "Behold, I will do a new thing," is he joking?[26] According to rigid systematic theologies, yes.[27]

It is beginning to sound as though there are no absolutes to cling to. But are there? First of all, if there were no absolutes, I doubt we would even be questioning their existence, not having an inkling as to "what in evolution" they would be! Secondly, if there were none, then at least one would exist: that there are absolutely no absolutes. Either way, we establish the existence of at least some absolutes. Plato acknowledged that if there were no absolutes, everything, including the details, or particulars of life, would be without meaning.[28] And, if there is no meaning to life, how is it we have come to know what meaning is all about?[29] The most difficult challenge of all is to distinguish between assumptions and absolutes.

I will never forget a discussion that my mother, who was extremely quick witted, had with a college philosophy professor. He had been expounding on the fact that there were no absolutes: "All is relative." My mother spoke up and

---

[24] I acknowledge that there are diverse meanings associated with *existential*. I simply use it to refer to experienced-based knowledge and belief.

[25] Karl Barth, *Dogmatics in Outline* (New York: Harper & Row Publisher, Inc., 1959), 5.

[26] Isaiah 43:19.

[27] I acknowledge that an academic exegete may insist that this passage has only to do with the ushering in of a new order by Jesus of Nazareth. We will see in Phase 4 that there are good reasons to believe that this is not the only explanation.

[28] Francis A. Schaeffer, *How Should We Then Live?* (Wheaton: Crossway Books, 1976), 144.

[29] C.S. Lewis, *Mere Christianity* (New York: HarperCollins Publishers, 1952), 39.

innocently asked, "Are you sure?" "Oh, yes," he replied. "Are you really sure?" "Indeed." "Are you absolutely sure?" "YES, I AM ABSOLUT . . ." He turned and stomped out of the classroom. As soon as we are convinced of the absence of one entity, we find ourselves proving its existence. Proving the absence of absolutes in our lives only substantiates their presence.

Slices?

Slices of God? Are we dissecting God as though we were in a biology lab, looking for clues to the structure and function of the *Supreme Being*? No. Are we dicing God up into bite-size pieces we can handle? No, though that is appealing in some respects. Cutting God into slices implies that we think we have a complete view of God! The primary thesis of this book is precisely the opposite: we have nothing to work with but slices of God.

Can we adequately put such slices together, constructing a greater understanding of God? Unfortunately, our humanness often gets in the way. We efficiently equip ourselves to believe in and live with only a few slices: little fragments we assume *are God*. We have stared at these few slices of God for so long that our sense of their nature being anything other than slices has gradually diminished to nil.

We need a reconstruction process to piece together slices that, individually, have wrought discord, war, death, isolation, and even the abandonment of the God concept. What have we to lose? What have we to fear? Some may argue that such an attempt to *reconstruct* God is idolatry. I argue that holding a few slices up for the rest of the unenlightened world to worship is the epitome of idolatry. We worship finite pieces of God. If God exists, wouldn't *he* want us to know more about who he, she, or it is?

MC Escher understood the concept of slices. In his *Rind* sketch he aptly illustrates the process I believe we need to employ. (Figure 10) One can clearly see he intended the rind to represent a person. However, if the rind were strewn on the kitchen counter, as if having just been removed from the fruit, it would not resemble the original image at all. Carefully arranging the rind portrays the entity it was removed from; not perfectly, but enough that we are able to "fill in the gaps."

Figure 10. M.C. Escher's "Rind" Copyright 2014 The M.C. Escher Company - The Netherlands.
All rights reserved.

So, who or what diced the God concept up into slices in the first place? Who cut the rind from the fruit? While this will be addressed more fully in Phase 3, for now we may want to consider it our doing. We dice God into pieces with our need and insistence that God is tangible and reachable, consistent and complete: and on our terms. In doing so we end up with only fragments of slices of God.

Insisting that *we* have the *real* slices of God, and others do not, is what religion does best. It is a mistake, and in many cases a fatal one, to assume that peoples from other faiths and cultures have not seen slices of God. Stories abound from cultures and traditions around the world that include such slices.[30]

For far too long people of faith have argued over such slices, instead of embracing the mystery of the slices of God with joy. Because of our need to systematize slices into our version of order and consistency, we are forced both to be selective as to which slices we will use, and to venture into exhaustive explanations as to why we exclude inconsistent, paradoxical, and even contradictory slices, continuing down the road to a view of God that is not only a slice, but perhaps a slice of a slice. Even if we are so disciplined as to ignore our own preconceived ideas about who God is and have the ability to approach all evidences with an open mind, the process of weeding through the slices presented therein is tedious, complicated, and difficult.

We live in a cosmos comprised of estranged fragments, yet drift through physical and spiritual space convinced we are complete. The denial of our fragmented nature is in itself evidence of the problem. There is so much more to this life than the illusion that we see it all. Our desires for answers dictate so. We would not be burdened with such an assortment of wishes if there were not more to be had. C.S. Lewis addresses this conundrum well in *Mere Christianity*: "Creatures are not born with desires unless satisfaction for those desires exists." Desires unfulfilled in this world point to an ultimate existence in another world.[31] Our desires are slices of more to come.

---

[30] I highly recommend reading *Indian Spirit*, by Michael Oren Fitzgerald. When I read it I weep for slices lost. When you read it you will see why.
[31] Lewis, *Mere Christianity*, 136-37.

Embracing Paradox

Paradoxes: one could spend a lifetime and beyond (assuming of course there is a beyond) attempting to resolve paradoxes and never make a single one disappear. We are plagued with discontinuities. We may come close to ridding ourselves of such paradoxes, but close is not good enough. G.K. Chesterton says in his biography of Saint Thomas Aquinas, "It is a fact that falsehood is never so false as when it is very nearly true."[32] This may be the case with human attempts to resolve paradoxes.

Theologians and philosophers have argued over paradoxes for centuries, all the while failing to resolve them. My personal journey into accepting them began with Douglas Hofstadter's *Gödel, Escher, Bach: An Eternal Golden Braid*. Close to the beginning of his monumental work he encourages the reader to "confront the apparent contradiction head-on, to savor it, to turn it over, to take it apart, to wallow in it," so that the reader might gain fresh insights into this strange universe.[33] Hofstadter demonstrates that paradoxes are an integral part of the cosmos: Bach capitalized on paradox in his compositions; Escher in his sketches; and Gödel in his mathematical proofs.

I believe our motivation to resolve paradoxes is rooted in distaste for tension. While some of us are seemingly equipped to deal with tension, many of us work tirelessly to make it go away. In doing so we live a contradiction. Our bodies, for instance, would drop dead without structural tension. Biological homeostasis (the antagonistic pursuit of chemical balance) is our lifeline. Within the realm of music, there would be no stringed music without tension. There would be no kettledrums in the orchestra. There would be no overhead lighting in the concert hall.

Paradoxes abound and come in many shapes and sizes. One of the greatest paradoxes comes from our understanding of light. Physicists have puzzled over the behavior and nature of light for centuries. If studied under one set of circumstances, light reveals itself as a wave of electromagnetic character. If studied under another set of circumstances it portrays itself as a particle: a photon.

---

[32] G.K. Chesterton, *St. Thomas Aquinas / St. Francis of Assisi* (San Francisco: Ignatius Press, 2002), 85.
[33] Douglas R. Hofstadter, *Gödel, Escher, Bach: An Eternal Golden Braid* (New York: Basic Books, 1979), 26.

These two qualities of light are contradictory, yet are the source of life on this rock we call Earth.

Religious texts are notorious for such paradoxes. In one text we find that truth will be hidden from the wise and revealed to babies![34] Perhaps truth is more simple than complex. In some texts we discover that if we want to live, we must die. To be the greatest, we must become the least. To keep anything, we must give it away. To hold on in desperation is to lose what is sacred.[35]

G.K. Chesterton raised one such paradox with respect to issues of faith and mysticism: "The whole secret of mysticism is this: that man can understand everything by the help of what he does not understand. The morbid logician seeks to make everything lucid, and succeeds in making everything mysterious. The mystic allows one thing to be mysterious, and everything else becomes lucid."[36] What do you seek? Comfort? Consolation? Escape from tension? No discontinuities? Understanding the complex? Many wise people have discovered that in order to make sense of our existence we must dive in and swim wholeheartedly in the waters of paradox. If we run from paradoxes we will most certainly end up coming round to meet up with them again and again. (Figure 11)

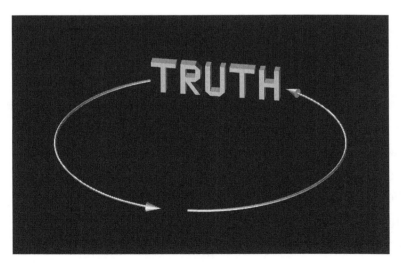

Figure 11. Running To & From Truth

---

[34] Luke 10:21-22.
[35] Appendices A and B have many such references.
[36] G.K. Chesterton, *Orthodoxy* (Colorado Springs: WaterBrook Press, 2001), 32.

So, whether we are running to or from paradox, we encounter truth eventually. It may, however, make the journey a bit more enjoyable if we choose to embrace paradox with courage and a resolve to understand as much as we can.

Closure

Closure: our need to have it all wrapped up in a neat package, signed, sealed, and delivered. Oh, and it would be nice if I could get it all at once and not have to worry about coming back for more. The need for closure is evident in all arenas. In his book *Closure: A Story of Everything*, Hilary Lawson argues that closure is a response to the brokenness of this world. Lawson says, "For we find ourselves in a world without certainties; without a fixed framework of belief; without truth; without decidable meaning."[37] While his synopsis is considerably fatalistic it is very accurate in summarizing our pursuit of closures.

Systematic theology, which is a form of closure, neatly organizes and "closes" issues that demand more processing. Good can come out of systematically exploring theology, but not by applying manmade closures or boundaries. Our profound leaning toward closure shuts out many theological surprises. The inclination to derive a tightly packed stream of logic that "God always follows" may be comforting, but it will also be very limiting.

Kurt Gödel, the Austrian American logician, theorized that no organized system, including mathematics, logic, philosophy, religion, and other such closures, can be both consistent and complete. If it is complete, it is so at the expense of including inconsistencies. If it is totally consistent, it is so at the expense of excluding inconsistent parameters, and therefore not complete. It is the nature of the cosmos! Demanding both consistency and completeness results in failure.[38] We will come back to Kurt Gödel again.

Closure is a double-edged sword. It is not failure if we acknowledge our tendency towards closure and work at accepting both a level of uncertainty and

---

[37] Hilary Lawson, *Closure: A Story of Everything* (London: Routledge, 2001), ix.
[38] We will see in Phase 3 that there are dimensional components to inconsistency and incompleteness in our domains that necessitate their existence.

change. While closure demands immutability and certainty, openness to God expressing himself as he sees fit at any place and time is quite another story.

Is our understanding of God not Gödelian? Why would God not present himself in a fashion consistent with the cosmos we claim he created? Why should we expect everything around us, including light itself, to be paradoxical and inconsistent, and our understanding of the cosmos incomplete, yet not our understanding of the Creator himself? The greatest irony is that we innately resist the very closure we seek once we realize it is riddled with paradox.

Why do we innately seek closure? Perhaps we sense something that once existed that is no more. Our desire for closure implies its existence. Join me in going to a new place, where we resign assumptions, embrace paradox, let go of completeness and consistency, and integrate slices of God.

1.03

How We Will Proceed

What is needed to proceed? How do we achieve a version of closure that we know is limited and incomplete, yet looks forward to change and progress, and is adequate as a map for our wandering here and now? I believe science and religion, if permitted to speak, complement each other and can form such a map.

It is not easy to develop new ways of thinking, new methods of processing. The resistance is strong. Limiting perspectives about religious texts often prevail. But how can we advance beyond our current dis-chord if we shut out any other input to our closures? Francis Schaeffer asserts, "A Christian holding the strongest possible view of inspiration still does not claim exhaustive knowledge at any point."[39] To refuse any authority outside of the Bible is to do just that.

If there are no authoritative sources of truth outside of the Bible (picking on the Judeo-Christian tradition for the moment), then how have other peoples seen slices of God without the Bible? How did the Magi from the East know to look for and find Jesus of Nazareth as a child? Apparently they used astrology. One could argue that they acquired such prophetic insights from the Jews during the Babylonian exile, but there is no astrological guide in ancient Judaic scriptures. There were clearly other sources of authoritative truth.

It is believed that Confucius said, "Do not do to others what you do not want them to do to you." Jesus came along and said, "Do to others what you would have them do to you."[40] Though Jesus' statement is in the positive sense rather than the negative (we will see in a later chapter that the two are intrinsically connected), it

---

[39] Francis A. Schaeffer, *Genesis in Space and Time: The Flow of Biblical History* (Downers Grove: Intervarsity Press, 1972), 35.
[40] Matthew 7:12; Luke 6:31.

would appear that Jesus quoted, or at least referred to, Confucius. Was Jesus acknowledging Confucius as a prophetic source of truth? If Jesus did not hesitate to refer to Confucius, why do we? Why not quote physics texts in a Sunday morning sermon? Why not bring mathematics into a lesson on the size of God?

Though he does not believe in the existence of God, Richard Dawkins, in *The God Delusion* says, "The presence or absence of a creative super-intelligence is unequivocally a scientific question, even if it is not in practice—or not yet—a decided one."[41], [42] On the other hand, the Dalai Lama refers to the notion that science should be the foundation for all knowledge as "scientific materialism." He insists that our existence is more complex than such materialism permits.[43] Is a balance between the two attainable?

In his biography of Saint Thomas Aquinas, G.K. Chesterton describes the saint as one who "was a very great man who reconciled religion with reason, who expanded it towards experimental science, who insisted that the senses were the windows of the soul and that the reason had a divine right to feed upon facts, and that it was the business of the Faith to digest the strong meat of the toughest and most practical of pagan philosophies."[44] Regarding his own journey, Chesterton says, "Reason is itself a matter of faith. It is an act of faith to assert that our thoughts have any relation to reality at all."[45] Aquinas and Chesterton argued that true reason and faith do not exist apart from each other.

In Hebrews 11:1 faith is described as the "substance" of things hoped for, the "evidence" of things not seen. Fermilab (a particle accelerator in Illinois) and CERN (The European Organization for Nuclear Research) are exploring the "evidences" of unseen subatomic particles on computer monitors. That sounds quite like faith to me. Both science and religion rely on *indirect evidences* to build systems of belief and/or scientific theory. What is faith other than trying to interpolate pieces of a puzzle that we have not been privileged to observe in its entirety?

---

[41] Dawkins, *The God Delusion*, 58-59.
[42] Though I do not fully agree with Dawkins, nor end up with the same conclusions as he, I do endorse a scientific approach that is too frequently left out of the God equation.
[43] His Holiness The Dalai Lama, *The Universe in a Single Atom: The Convergence of Science and Spirituality* (New York: Morgan Road Books, 2005), 39.
[44] Chesterton, *St. Thomas Aquinas / St. Francis of Assisi*, 30-31.
[45] *Orthodoxy*, 40.

A Trio of Methods

The physicist Sir James Jeans once noted, "The Great Architect of the Universe now begins to appear as a pure mathematician."[46] William of Occam (1284-1347) would have supported this conclusion. He was an English philosopher and theologian, working on knowledge, logic, and scientific inquiry. "He based scientific knowledge on experience and self–evident truths, and on logical propositions resulting from those two sources. In his writings, Occam stressed the Aristotelian principle that entities must not be multiplied beyond what is necessary. This principle became known as Occam's Razor: a problem should be stated in its basic simplest terms. In science, the simplest theory that fits the facts of a problem is the one that should be selected."[47] In commonly paraphrased terms, "All things being equal, the simplest solution is the best." Perhaps, in light of Sir James Jeans' quote, *the simplest mathematical solution may be the best.*

We will use science and mathematics to assess the existence and nature of God. This natural theology (NT) approach (though it may not be labeled as such in its purest form in academia) acknowledges that if God exists, there must be sufficient physical evidence in the cosmos to establish his existence.

Religious texts, or special revelation (SR), will augment the NT process. Textual criticism (the academic validation and/or invalidation of authorship, authenticity, and historicity of these religious texts) will be permitted to speak as an auxiliary input to the overall process. Textual criticism has contributed much to the analysis of manuscripts and validating their authenticity, clarifying the meanings of words and/or phrases, and their contextual application. It has its place, but it will be held in balance with natural theology (NT) and with *existential understanding.*

Belief systems rely on existential understanding (EU). They are experientially based. None of us can rid our beliefs (or disbeliefs) from existential influences. Even if I am convinced that my theology is not human-experience based, that my starting point is God and is absolute, in reality I start with me starting with God. I begin with my interpretations, my observations, and my experiences. They

---

[46] K.C. Cole, *The Universe and the Teacup* (Orlando: Harcourt Brace & Company, 1997), 10.
[47] Encyclopedia Britannica, "Occam's Razor,"
http://abyss.uoregon.edu/~js/glossary/occams_razor.html.

validate or invalidate what I ultimately refer to as truth, even when I am unaware of their influence.

Mythology is fundamentally existential. I believe mythology has its roots in real human experience, frequently explained in ways common to human understanding, and often in terms of *gods*. I am convinced that either there is mythology in scriptural texts (e.g. the Bible) or there is truth in mythology. I am somewhere in-between these perspectives. Either way, mythology sheds light on our understanding of where we have come from and perhaps where we are going in our belief systems.

Letting go of our assumption that special revelation (SR) is the primary (if not the only) source of truth, we will proceed by plunging head first into a river of NT (via science and mathematics), EU (experience, intuition, contemplation), and SR (sacred writings, special revelation).

Repressed Questions

To question is human. To pretend there are no unanswered questions is to deny our humanness. To refrain from asking questions, especially the difficult ones, is to live in fear and ignorance, or perhaps laziness. There are questions some of us are afraid to ask. In the spiritual climates that many of us grow up in there are some "givens" that simply are not to be questioned. In some cases, such as mine, some of these questions are deemed blasphemous. Why were we given such curious minds if not to ask questions? Do such questions truly threaten God?

Children innately ask difficult questions. It seems they are equipped to deal with the strange, dimensional, and fractal aspects of life. However, as we mature, we successfully bury such gifts. One child who asked poignant questions was Saint Thomas Aquinas. It is recorded that he was, "phenomenally silent, scarcely opening his mouth except to say suddenly to his schoolmaster in an explosive manner, 'What is God?' The answer is not recorded but it is probable that the asker went on worrying out answers for himself."[48] Oh that we would never stop asking such profound questions!

---

[48] Chesterton, *St. Thomas Aquinas / St. Francis of Assisi*, 55.

I no longer fear asking questions of, or about God. Only a finite, manmade god is so weak, so insecure, as to be threatened by such questions and respond in anger. The problem has more to do with religion than with God. Religion has built about itself walls so thick and rigid that no one dare ask, "Why?" In his book *Quantum Theology*, Diarmuid O'Murchu says, "Not infrequently, the very system that was intended to mediate divine life and create a climate of openness and receptivity has been the one that has alienated seeking souls from the wellsprings of hope and truth."[49] Religion can too quickly become an alienator to knowledge, inquiry, and process.

Since that fateful Saturday I alluded to in the Pre-Phase, numerous questions have found their way into my frail brain. The difference now, however, is that they have complete freedom to cause me doubt and intrigue, prompt intellectual wanderings, and even remain unanswered. I strangely find peace in knowing that I do not know.

An offshoot of the initiating question (*Who gave you the right to be God?*), with a significant, yet less challenging tone, is the question of *who* or *what* put God into power? Additionally, *is God real? Is "he" physical or not?*[50] I am not alone in wondering about the physicality of God. John Cobb in his book *God And The World* implies that if God is not physical, then he most likely is not real.[51]

Is there eternal purpose to humanity? Would the concept of "eternal purpose" even exist if it were not at play in our lives? Can we know what such a purpose is and how it unfolds? If there is no purpose, no meaning, how have we come to even ask such a question in the first place?

Oh, and what about evil? (Or should I capitalize that: *Evil?*) *Is evil real, or simply a manmade tag or excuse for the frailty and flaws induced by an incomplete evolutionary process?* Even if some theologians are correct, that "Satan" is only institutional evil, I still must question the origin of such institutional evil. Whether or not one believes in the presence of evil, there is another question that must be asked: *What is wrong with the world?* The dilemma such a question poses is that it

---

[49] Diarmuid O'Murchu, *Quantum Theology: Spiritual Implications of the New Physics* (The Crossroad Publishing Company, 2004), 79.
[50] Is God physical as we are physical?
[51] Cobb, *God and the World*, 68-69.

assumes we know what *right* is. Do we? And if we do, how did we come to know the difference between right and wrong?

Here is perhaps the most troubling of questions for many of us: *Why is there pain in the world*? Related to this: *How could a loving God allow pain and allow humans to inflict pain on other humans*? Though we will address these further, I must here state that I do not have, nor will I have, simple, consistent, and complete answers for these.

Then there is the issue of a messiah. I have had two messianic problems posed to (or hurled at) me by intellectual friends. First of all, "would be messiahs" are a dime a dozen. Historically it is reported that there have been a couple dozen Jewish messiahs; several dozen Christian messiahs (some purporting that they are the 2nd coming of Jesus); several Islamic messiahs; along with numerous other messiahs.[52] As someone who was raised Christian, why should I believe that Jesus was *the Messiah*?

Furthermore, I must ask: *Why do we even need a messiah*? Clearly there were divergent reasons for needing a messiah throughout Jewish history: some pushing for a political messiah, others for a socio-economic messiah, and some for a spiritual leader. Other religious groups had their own unique needs in a messiah. On another note: *If Jesus was the messiah, then why did he wait so long to come*? This is a valid question, and one I wrestle with. I am not satisfied with, "Because the Bible says so," or "I just take it by faith." I need more than that, and I am sure you do too.

Listening

Who am I? Why am I here? Who or what put me here? What will become of me? Even thought these questions have become sources of joyful inquiry for me, they amount to little use if I am not listening for answers.

The call to listen is a timeless and universal beckoning. There are great and powerful hidden things to be found in the still and the quiet. Even contemplation over a mathematical approach to the God concept requires such listening. One scriptural text says, "If any of you lacks wisdom, you should ask God, who gives

---

[52] Wikipedia, "Messianic Claimants," http://en.wikipedia.org/wiki/List_of_messiah_claimants.

generously to all without finding fault, and it will be given to you."[53] Yet even this *God-dispensed* wisdom requires listening. And listening requires silence.

The world we live in is not comfortable with silence. Most of us require conversation, games, and other sources of noise to cope. In all honesty, I easily fall prey to such tendencies. How is it that we have lost the gift of silence? In the *Gospel of the Redman* silence is revered as God's voice. "If you ask him, 'What is silence?' he will answer, 'It is the Great Mystery. The holy silence is His voice!' If you ask, 'What are the fruits of silence?' he will say, 'They are self-control, true courage or endurance, patience, dignity, and reverence. Silence is the cornerstone of character.'"[54]

Thomas Merton heard this voice: "We refuse to hear the million different voices through which God speaks to us, and every refusal hardens us more and more against His grace—and yet He continues to speak to us: and we say He is without mercy!"[55] It is we who have built soundproof shells around ourselves, blocking out the voice of *Mystery*.

Sometimes the *noise* is in our beliefs and lifestyle. We manage to keep ourselves so occupied with what *has been* said that we cannot hear what *is being* said. We have managed to fill our lives with other more satisfying sources of input: society, self, religion, advancement, pride, complexity, and possessions. Even in the midst of such noise, much can be heard if one dares to listen.

Obviously discernment is necessary, for there are voices that would love to distract us from our missions. Sometimes they are literal external voices that run us amuck. Such voices can also come from within. Only clarity of mind can discern who or what is speaking. Is it *truth*? Is it my selfish hopes of what I *want* to hear? There are times when the most misleading voices we can hear are our own. One scriptural passage says, "Test the spirit."[56] What is there to test if we are not listening?

---

[53] James 1:5.
[54] Earnest T. & Julia M. Seton, *The Gospel of the Redman: A Way of Life* (Santa Fe: Seton Village, 1963), 17.
[55] Merton, *The Seven Storey Mountain*, 143.
[56] 1 John 4:1.

Scripture calls us to "pray without ceasing."[57] I believe it also means, "Listen without ceasing." Without such listening we have little hope of expanding our understanding and opening our boxes.

Opening the Box

Children are excellent at opening boxes. They approach them with great expectancy. There is no inhibition to experiencing new things. Perhaps this is why scripture speaks so gently and reverently about children. They not only accept new things, but also anticipate them. Brennan Manning, in *The Ragamuffin Gospel*, addresses our inner child and its *former* openness to *new things*: "When our inner child is not nurtured and nourished, our minds gradually close to new ideas, unprofitable commitments, and the surprises of the Spirit."[58] Contrary to this tendency, he asserts, "If we maintain the open-mindedness of children, we challenge fixed ideas and established structures, including our own."[59] How wonderful it would be if we approached our theological boxes as children do, opening them with excitement and without hesitation.

If I were to paraphrase Jesus' words to the religious leaders of his time, it would be this: "Think outside the box." This message permeated his words to those who were convinced they knew the law, for they were also ignorant of it. If we think we absolutely understand, we probably do not! The most enjoyable thing granted to us is the permission to think creatively, imaginatively, spontaneously, strangely, and *outside of the box*.

As a child I delighted in the story of Karl Friedrich Gauss (1777-1855), a German mathematician, who as a youngster supposedly got into trouble with his teacher. He was held after school and, as punishment, was told to add all the numbers from one to one hundred. After a few seconds of pondering, he blurted out, "Five thousand and fifty!" The teacher, in doubt, proceeded to take quite some time to add up the numbers himself. Much to his amazement, he discovered the student was correct. He asked, "How did you do that?" The student, thinking outside the box, was sure that there was more than one way to solve the problem.

---

[57] 1 Thessalonians 5:17.
[58] Brennan Manning, *The Ragamuffin Gospel* (Sisters: Multnomah Publishers, Inc., 2000), 64.
[59] Ibid., 65.

He realized that the first and last numbers in the sequence added up to 101. He then realized that the second and next to the last numbers also added up to 101. There were fifty such pairs. Hence, his quick response of 5,050! Who taught whom in this scenario? Whose box was opening?

I doubt there are many religious peoples out there who enjoy Richard Dawkins (a very vocal atheist) as much as I do. Granted, I have to overlook what I think are illogicalities and contradictions, but his ability to poke fun at the pitfalls of religion is much needed. It would behoove us all to have a sense of humor about some of the absurd things we believe and do. He and I do not end up at the same place, but he offers a valuable look at the humanness of religions: our rigid boxes.

My rigid box experienced a crack soon after my mother's death. During that time, I received little to no recognition of my mother's death from the Christian community I was a part of. No cards. No flowers. There was a rare, "Hey I heard your mother died. Sorry." I must admit that I was quite offended by my Christian brothers and sisters. I rationalized that I was making too much of it and shrugged it off. That is until I received a *dissonant* phone call after returning to work. It was a gentleman I had become acquainted with while doing some computer programming. He is a Buddhist.

He asked, "What has happened?"

I replied, "What are you talking about?"

"Something has happened. I haven't been able to get you off my mind this whole last week. What has happened?"

I shut my office door and broke into tears. I told my friend of my mother's death. He offered consoling thoughts and caring words. After I got off the phone I sat pondering the beautiful dissonance of that conversation. It was dissonant because it was so far out of my Christian experience. It was beautiful because, unlike the silence of my Christian associates, it possessed harmonics of love and concern. My friend helped to crack open my box that day. He heard what a *know-it-all* faith had failed to hear. He was listening while others were not.

Are there limits to such an open box? Yes. Our neurophysiology does not welcome change. John Cobb, Jr. explains that our "bondage to the past and conformity to human expectations have inhibited (our) response to new possibilities of growth and service."[60] Change can be painful. Avoiding such pain is a natural response. Sometimes it is easier to sink our heads into the sand than to go through the pain and labor of thinking outside our comfort zones. We tend to prefer sand in our nostrils to fresh air in our heads.

If we believe we have an adequate understanding of the meaning of life and the cosmos, then we comfortably reside in small and tightly sealed boxes. However, there is too much mystery in life to settle for such encasements. Our boxes not only keep out the mystery, but the grace as well. Remember the manhole cover question? What if the manhole cover question was, "What does a child of God look like?" or "Who will fall through the hole into the great abyss called Hell?" Our *round/circular* theologies, with right-angled ledges may in fact keep us out of such an abyss, but they may also be false exclusionary criteria! Who besides God knows what other shapes and ledges will suffice. After all, do we truly know what grace looks like? Perhaps it is those of us who are convinced we do not need grace (or the ledge) that will fall through, regardless of the symmetry or perfection of our lives and theology.

If we move out of one box only to find ourselves in yet another box, the best choice is to open up and move yet again. The beautiful thing is that when one box opens, others will as well: "When the time is ripe for certain things, these things appear in different places in the manner of violets coming to light in early spring."[61] Look for the violets. They are bursting open all around us! Join them. Open up and bloom! It is a call to process.

Process and Performance

Opening boxes and blooming flowers—both call for and require a willingness to process. Nature *is* process, and it calls *us* to process. This call can be heard in the seasons and in the stars. It is witnessed in our curiosity to understand and learn. It can be seen in the ever-changing environments in which we live. It is a call to move out of our sedated states, out of our static systems of belief, and to process. This process is a continuous action toward refined understanding.

---

[60] Cobb, *God and the World*, 62.
[61] Farkas Bolyai in Hofstadter, *Gödel, Escher, Bach: An Eternal Golden Braid*, 92.

We so quickly forget the history of our theologies. For those closed to new theologies or even special revelations I ask, *Why did it take 1800 years for some components of Christian systematic theology to be formed?* Can the process really be over? According to Christian texts, scripture is *living. Living* means alive, animate, processing, active, growing, changing, dynamic, breathing, adapting, and yes, even evolving, as are we![62] Our theologies, not to mention our view of *what scripture is and is not,* is called to be dynamic, spawning more living entities.

Ralph Waldo Emerson once said, "Nature ever flows; stands never still. Motion or change is her mode of existence." Why would a God who is static, or *not in motion,* put all of creation into *motion?* Should we not also have systems of belief that are in motion? Theology is a growing entity. Theology is a *verb.*

One's theology may be as solid as a rock; however, my friend, rocks do not breathe. Brennan Manning in his book *The Ragamuffin Gospel* says, "paralysis of analysis" is at the root of shriveling spirits.[63] To remain alive, to stay viable, to exert positive change in the world, we must breathe. So it is with theology. Theological processing is unavoidably a call into discomfort, and even pain. The great German theologian Dorothee Söelle once wrote, "We must view with suspicion all theology that is pre-pain."[64] This is a testament not only to deep theologies like Dietrich Bonhoeffer's, shaped by persecution, but also to daily pains and stresses producing living and breathing understanding and change in us.

Some secularists are critical of theologies that change. Such systems of belief are seen as wishy-washy, ever guilty of situational compromise. There is a profound irony in this perspective. Secularists cannot have it both ways, espousing evolutionary mutations to adapt to stresses and change, while criticizing people of faith for the same process. Process *is* our nature, our existence.

Performance is the measure of our processing. Jesus spoke of performance when he said, "By their fruit you will recognize them."[65] Do our beliefs result in change? Do they produce fruit: positive and productive outcomes? Vern Poythress says in his book *Symphonic Theology,* "The acid test of whether particular people

---

[62] Acts 7:38; Hebrews 4:12; 1 Peter 1:23.
[63] Manning, *The Ragamuffin Gospel,* 110.
[64] Dorothee Soelle, "Pre-Pain Theology Quote," http://www.clayfirecurator.org/2011/04/someone-said-w-david-o-taylor-art-of-lament/.
[65] Matthew 7:16.

know something is whether they are able to use it in relevant situations. The person who claims to know something but who cannot apply it in an insightful manner may well know the words without having really understood. Knowledge is thus always knowledge in relation to other truths and situations of possible use."[66] If our beliefs are not producing relevant fruit, what good are they?

Wandering

We are all wanderers. Our journeys may be quite varied, yet we share a knowledge that seems to be innate: we are only passing through. Whether we believe in pre-existence, post-existence, both, or neither, we are still just passing through. Some have traversed many landscapes, while others are newcomers: newcomers by direction, not age. Parker Palmer writes, "Some journeys are direct, and some are circuitous; some are heroic, and some are fearful and muddled."[67] Whether your trek is an apparently positive one with great clarity of vision, hope for the future, and anticipation of the unknown, or an apparently negative journey with hurt, uncertainty, and lack of direction, I invite you to wander on.

My invitation is to purposefully wander, by thinking critically about issues of faith. It is an invitation to look at evidences for faith and to consider them carefully, applying sound intellectual processes with integrity. It is a call to think, a call to reconsider, a call to process. Working outside our comfort zones is the way of it. It is not my purpose to be right or correct, to provide another system of beliefs, or to simply construct a new box. Rather, I support the call to perpetually move outside our ever-changing boxes, boxes that are alive. We must never stop wandering.

---

[66] Vern Sheridan Poythress, *Symphonic Theology* (Phillipsburg: P & R Publishing Company, 2001), 46.
[67] Parker J. Palmer, *Let Your Life Speak* (San Francisco: Jossey-Bass, 2000), 36.

Phase 2

Strange Perspectives

2.00

The Narrative

Time floated by as the river turned away from the path's edge. All was well. It was just as the Elder had said. All the signs, so far, were very clear. For Fritz, there was a certain amount of comfort that crept in, comfort in knowing his gifts so well, comfort in having listened to the call to *listen*, and then, in turn, having listened so well to the Elder.

The trees that had beautifully lined the river's bank were disappearing behind him now. So, too, were the small river rocks that had covered the path. The path was now packed dirt, worn to a fine dust from many travelers. Surrounding the way were small cedars and briars. This was not, certainly, the most pleasant of trails to follow. Gradually, the flat land began to rise around the path. Soon the meadows were no more. In their place, hillsides turned into foothills. The path became a narrow valley and what lay beyond was now out of sight.

The path began to twist and turn, following the slopes of the surrounding hills. Fritz began to wonder if he would ever arrive at the fork in the road. This fear was mixed with thoughts of Allesa and the Elder. They were strange, but seemingly full of wisdom. As he pondered the two, he rounded another turn and saw the fork. It was unmistakable, thanks to the Elder's description. At that moment, a cold wind descended the hill that rose between the splitting trails and hit him head on, sending chills down his spine. Winter was closer than he had realized. But that was not the only thing troubling him now.

He stood gazing left, then right. There were no signs. There was no indication which way he should turn to head toward Isnot. Neither could he see beyond the hills. He was trapped; trapped by indecision; trapped by the knowledge that he could go the wrong way and never make it to Dimen Castle before winter.

The Elder had seemed so trustworthy, but perhaps Fritz's trust had been misplaced. Then again, maybe the signs were recently blown away. However, the wind descending the hill in front of him would have blown the signs back onto the path he had just traversed. There had been no such debris.

He felt colder in the midst of his confusion and indecision as the wind blew around his head and whistled in his ears. "What do I do now?" he asked himself as he pulled a scarf from his knapsack and wrapped it around his neck. He had come too far to turn back.

The whistling got louder, becoming too regular to be just the wind. It had rhythm. Suddenly he realized he would soon not be alone, for the whistling of the wind was mixed with the tonal whistling of someone coming around the bend of one of the forked paths. The echoes were too confusing to tell from which direction the whistling came. He waited, preparing to meet whomever it was from whichever trail they appeared.

The man was startled as he rounded the curve and saw Fritz. "Why do you stand here at this junction?" asked the whistler.

"I was told there would be signs to direct me to Isnot, but I have found none," explained Fritz, "Do you know the way to Isnot?"

"Why of course! I am from Isnot. Know it well! Just follow me," said the whistler.

Relieved, Fritz picked up the knapsack he had set down to rest his shoulders, ready to resume his journey. His nerves, however, were a bit unsettled. Perhaps, he was just recouping from the worry of not making it to Isnot in good time; perhaps, it was the cold settling into his bones; or, . . .

His thoughts suddenly shifted back to the Elder's words, "The people from Is always lie, but the people from Isnot always tell the truth." Clearly, the whistler was coming from one or the other of the two towns. Perhaps the Elder was wrong. He had been wrong about the signs. Surely, he could trust this whistling man!

Doubt, however, filled his mind. What if the whistler was from Is? If so, he would direct him away from Isnot, being a constant liar. But if he was from Isnot, incapable of telling a lie, he would direct him to Isnot. *How shall I tell one from the other, an Isian from an Isnotian?*

At that moment, he heard a voice from within saying, "*Listen. Listen.*" It was Allesa, or at least her words. He set his knapsack down and closed his eyes.

"Well, aren't you coming?" shouted the whistler.

"Just a moment," called Fritz, trying desperately to listen to whatever he was supposed to hear.

Moments passed and the whistler was growing impatient. Suddenly, a thought entered Fritz's mind. "That's it!" he cried.

"What's it?" asked the whistler.

Fritz looked into the face of the whistler and asked, "Which way would you go to get to your home town?"

"Why do you ask such a foolish question?" retorted the whistler.

"Answer my question!" yelled Fritz.

"OK, OK. There is no need to get all riled up. I will tell you. You would have to take the path I just came from."

"Thank you!" cried Fritz, as he picked up his knapsack and took off down the right hand side of the fork, down the path the whistler had just come from.

"Wait, don't you want to go to Isnot?"

"I do indeed," said Fritz. "And furthermore you are headed home to Is!"

"And just how have you come to know that?"

"You see," said Fritz, "If you had been from Isnot, you would have directed me down the path toward Isnot, since you would be unable to tell a lie. If, however, you were from Is, you would have directed me away from your home town, down the path to Isnot, since you would not be able to tell the truth. I now know the way to Isnot."

"Yes, but how do you know where I am from?"

"If you had been from Isnot you would not have said, 'Wait, don't you want to go to Isnot?'"

The whistler turned and continued down the path to Is, his whistling gradually fading into the wind. Fritz was so thankful that he had heard the voice within.

Now he understood, at least in part. The voice within probably spoke more often than he heard.

Picking up the pace, he headed toward Isnot with a new peace. He was mistaken to have doubted the Elder. There *were* signs along the way. The whistler was one of them. His tread lightened as he thankfully replayed the Elder's words, determined not to question his wisdom again.

The terrain, however, quickly turned mountainous. Fritz marched onward, focused on making it over the pass to Isnot in good time. Switchbacks aided his climb through the thinning air.

Near the top, Fritz could see signs of winter. Several inches of snow had already fallen. The thin air and the slippery drag of the snow impeded his gait. His resolve to make it to Isnot, however, was unwavering.

Isnot. *What a peculiar name! The town of Isnot surely is! Why then is it called Isnot?* As he approached the wide ironclad gates, he noticed they were locked. "How is one to get in to such a town?" muttered Fritz with a crinkled brow.

"Hey, you!" cried a voice from somewhere. "That is not the way to get in to Isnot." Fritz looked up to see the head of a child hanging out of a window in the wall. "Go around to the small door on the side wall."

"And who are you?" asked Fritz.

"I am Fremd," said the high voice. "Go around to the side door, and I will let you in."

The door creaked as it opened. "It has been a while since we had a visitor here," said Fremd.

Fritz, puzzling over the comment, said, "I would think many travelers would find their way to Isnot."

"Oh, many try, but get lost in the journey. Isnot is not as easy to get to as you may think. You should know that. After all, it was a close call for you too, Fritz."

It took Fritz a second or two to absorb the words. "Wait a minute," replied Fritz, "How did you know I almost didn't make it here? How did you know I was even coming?" Then it dawned on Fritz that he hadn't even introduced himself; yet, Fremd knew his name.

Before Fritz had a chance to push the point any further, Fremd quickly shut the door and hurried off down the street. "Wait," cried Fritz.

"Well, come on then," yelled Fremd.

"Where are we going?"

"Nowhere in particular. I just wanted to see if you would follow me."

"Wait a minute," trembled Fritz as both parties came to a stop. "I need to understand what is going on here. Why should I follow you without knowing where we are going?"

"Do you trust me?" asked Fremd.

"I don't know you," replied Fritz.

"Then why are you following me? It seems to me that I should be the one asking the questions!" smirked Fremd.

"I am confused," said Fritz.

"No kidding!"

"Seriously!" pleaded Fritz, "The only face I have seen is that of a child. I was brought in through a small side door. I was asked to follow someone I don't know to somewhere I know not. Isnot is not what I expected."

"Precisely!" said Fremd.

"Precisely what?"

"Look," sighed Fremd "Do you or do you *not* want to make it to Dimen Castle?"

"Of course I . . . Wait a minute! You knew I had a close call getting here. You knew my name without an introduction. You know I am headed to Dimen Castle. How?"

"Perhaps a good night's sleep and a new tomorrow will help it make more sense," said Fremd, softly. "Come, I will show you to your room."

Fremd led Fritz down a narrow walkway to a little inn. Fritz had to duck his head to enter the door. Fremd called into the dim entryway, "Ratsel, our guest is here! Take him to his room. Make sure he has plenty of blankets and firewood. I will check on him in the morning."

Ratsel, an old man, hunched over from a curved spine, led Fritz to a very small room, with a door even smaller than the front door. Fritz ducked his head again, turned sideways, and narrowly entered the room. "Fresh linens are on the bed.

There are plenty of blankets in the closet. The washroom is down the hall to the right. Ring the bell by the bed if you need anything."

"Thank you," replied Fritz. "By the way," he continued, "why do you take orders from a child?"

"A child?" snickered Ratsel. "You sure don't know much about Isnot, do you?"

"Well, he is a child after all, and you are an elderly man. I was taught that the young were to treat the elderly with great respect, not with commands."

"Everything is not as it seems," replied Ratsel. "I can tell you have more to learn from Fremd than I do!" he continued.

"You? Learn from a child?" asked Fritz.

"Everything is not as it seems in Isnot," Ratsel muttered as he left the room. "Get some rest. Fremd will be back in the morning."

From under the cover of thick blankets on a tiny bed, Fritz watched the flickering flames in the fireplace. Many strange places he had encountered. This, however, was the strangest of all. Questions filled his head. How could Fremd have known of his encounter with the whistler? It was apparent that Fremd and Ratsel knew he was coming, but how? They even had a room prepared. It was as though they knew him well. The questions continued as he drifted off to sleep.

It was early dawn when Fritz woke to hear Fremd and Ratsel talking down the hallway. "Well, Ratsel, I have news!" exclaimed Fremd.

"Tell me, tell me," replied Ratsel.

"The snowfall last night tied the longest standing record!"

"That's good!"

"No," replied Fremd, "that's bad. It amounted to twenty-one inches on the pass and three here in Isnot. We, my friend, are snowbound."

"Oh that's bad."

"No," replied Fremd, "that's good. We have enough food in storage to last the winter."

"Oh, that's good."

"No," replied Fremd, "that's bad. There is one more of us now."

"Oh, that's bad."

"No," replied Fremd, "that's good. We will have more time to spend with Fritz."

"Oh, that's good."

"I sure hope so!" laughed Fremd.

Fritz emerged from his room wearing the bathrobe that had been hanging by his door. Having heard the tail end of the conversation, Fritz asked, "So, is it good or bad?"

"Yes," Fremd jovially responded. He and Ratsel broke into laughter.

"Do you always make it a habit of listening in on other people's conversations?" asked Ratsel, continuing to laugh.

"Look," Fritz said with a furrowed brow, "I have to make it Dimen Castle before snowfall. I don't have time for such nonsense. I was told you would be able to tell me how to get there."

"Sure, it's just over the next mountain, but . . ."

Fritz cut him off, "Then tell me. I am leaving as soon as I dress and eat breakfast." Ratsel's face defied his aged appearance. For a second, he looked just like a child fighting back the urge to divulge a secret.

"I am sorry, my friend," Fremd replied soberly. "This may come as good news. On the other hand, it may come as bad news. It all depends on how you look at it."

"What?" responded Fritz impatiently.

"You might want to sit down. You are not going anywhere today. For that matter, you will not be going anywhere for the next several months," explained Fremd.

"Oh, yes, I will. I have a mission to fulfill. I want to fulfill it and be home before the first snowfall."

"Well, that is just the problem. You see, it snowed last night. And not just a little snow."

"How much?" asked Fritz.

"Twenty-one inches on the pass!"

"Twenty one inches!" yelled Fritz.

"Yes," interjected Ratsel, "And three here! Isn't it wonderful?!"

Fritz stared out the window, confounded. He was snowbound. Winter had arrived, and more snow would come. Months would pass before the winter snowfall would melt and permit passage over the mountain to Dimen Castle. No turning back either, they were locked in from all sides.

At noon, Ratsel called Fremd and Fritz to lunch. "What's for lunch today, Ratsel?" asked Fremd.

"Today we are having snow pea soup and humble pie."

"What's humble pie?" asked Fritz.

"You will find out soon enough!" replied Ratsel.

They sat down together. Fremd was served a very small bowl of soup and a tiny piece of pie. Fritz was served medium portions of both. Ratsel gave himself the largest portions of all. "Here in Isnot," commented Fremd, "the oldest gets more than he can eat and the youngest less than he needs." This seemed apparent to Fritz as he surveyed the servings.

Fritz finished his soup, slid his bowl aside, and took a bite of pie. He instantly coughed and sputtered, trying, bitterly, to swallow the bite of pie. "What is this?"

"It is clear that you are not ready for such a delicacy, Fritz. The time will come, however, when it will be the best thing you have ever tasted," promised Fremd.

Strange, indeed. Fritz noticed that Ratsel's bowl was empty and his pie gone. Fremd's food, on the other hand, was only partially eaten. "You told me that the eldest got more than he could eat and the youngest less than he needed. How then do you explain that Ratsel's portions are gone and yours are unfinished?" Fremd looked at Ratsel, then back at Fritz.

"Well, I guess it is time you learn more about Isnot. Come, let's go for a walk."

Fremd and Fritz bundled up for a walk in the freshly fallen snow. "Let's take the path around the town wall," Fremd said, cheerfully. Walking through the snow was easier than Fritz had expected. Dry and powdery snow did not cling heavily to boots.

They headed down the walkway towards the small door through which Fritz had entered. Turning left at the wall they began a stroll on the walkway that looped the town's interior. The wall to the right was tightly constructed with finely chiseled granite blocks, keeping light and wind from sneaking through its joints. To the left was an array of buildings, apparently constructed by the same mason that built the wall.

Fremd broke into a monologue. "In Isnot, the thing you expect the most is not. The thing that is not expected at all is. Large is small, and small is large. Old is young, and young is old. The past is not strange to us. Neither is the future. Sometimes the present is strange, but that is another issue. You see, Fritz, I am the oldest person in Isnot. Ratsel, on the other hand, is the youngest. Age and size, here in Isnot, are the inverse of what is known to the outside world."

"That explains Ratsel's behavior!" exclaimed Fritz.

"I beg your pardon," replied Fremd.

"Please do not take offense," Fritz continued, "but I have noticed Ratsel's childlike behavior on several occasions. I also wondered why he took orders from you. It is all adding up. And you, Fremd, wanted to see if I would follow you. No child wants to test a strange adult to see if they will follow them."

As they continued down the path, things strangely began to change. The town wall became disjointed. The buildings were much closer to each other. Some were even joined by the masonry. Puzzlement began to set in. Suddenly, Fritz realized where they were. Just ahead on the *left* was the small door he had entered when he first arrived. "Come on, Fritz, let's head back in and get something warm to drink," invited Fremd.

"But we were walking around the interior of the town. How did we end up out here?" Fritz looked back down the walkway behind them, but the curve of the wall blocked his view.

Fremd smiled, opened the door, and said, "Isnot is not without surprises!"

That evening, Fritz pondered the strangeness of Isnot as he peered out the window watching the snow fall. He would make the best of his stay here, trying to accept the strange character of Isnot as it was.

Days turned into weeks, and weeks into months. He had long given up his goal of trekking to Dimen Castle and back home within a couple of weeks. Somehow the goal seemed less important now. He would go to Dimen Castle, but not in such a rush. He was learning to accept the small, but strangely large, things in life. His large and noble goals were becoming insignificant. The enforced slow-down had its benefits.

Questions still remained. Yet, in the midst of such unknowns, a strange softening was happening. He was changing within. The strangest of all was his discovery that the pie was no longer bitter.

When the news came that the mountain pass was clear for passage, a tinge of sadness overcame Fritz. His new friends would remain in Isnot. He would go on. But the travels to come would be different. He would face them with a better understanding of life and of himself. He would try to carry the principles of Isnot with him beyond the mountain. Even if the outside world was not inverted like Isnot, he would carry some of its strangeness within.

"It is time to go," Fritz said sadly to Fremd and Ratsel. "What do I owe you for all your hospitality?"

Fremd walked up to Fritz, reached up, put his hand on his shoulder, and said, "You owe me an amount that you cannot count."

"Oh, I don't have much to give," replied Fritz.

"Well, there are two amounts that you cannot count. One is infinite. The other is nothing. I will settle for nothing," smiled Fremd.

Fritz hugged his friends and headed toward the small door he had come in through just months before. "Fritz, you cannot get out that way," called Fremd. "You can only enter by that door."

"But I thought . . ."

"Follow me," Fremd said, softly. Together they walked to the large iron clad gates. They opened easily with Fremd's gentle touch. "Take the northeast road over the mountain. When you are half way down the other side of the mountain, the road will fork. Stay on the northeast branch. It will lead you directly to Dimen Castle. Safe travels, my friend. Do watch your step. The road can be quite rocky."

As Fritz began the mountainous climb, he realized he was not limping. "My leg is not hurting!" he exclaimed to the trees and the melting snow. "But of course, that is what happens in Isnot!" His leg had completely healed during the months he was confined in Isnot; so had his misgivings about the delay. He traveled with the awareness that having been snowbound with his friends in Isnot was *not* coincidental. He was changed. "Life *is not* the same!" The words echoed off the surrounding slopes.

2.01

A Strange Existence

We live in a strange universe where not all is as it appears to be. What appears to be up may be down. What is in may be out. What is provable may be impossible to prove. Many have uncovered and proclaimed this strange nature, from the Buddha to Jesus of Nazareth, from Galileo to Newton, from Einstein to Hawking, from Chesterton to Barth. Then there was Kurt Gödel.

To examine Gödel's work we must start with Bertrand Russell and Alfred North Whitehead, who published *Principia Mathematica* (PM) in 1911, a monumental work aimed at providing a complete, consistent, and non-self-referential mathematical system.[68] Kurt Gödel, a young Austrian logician and mathematician, came along in 1931 and blew PM out of the water in a remarkable published paper. He revealed numerous problems within PM and argued that no system "could produce all number–theoretical truths, unless it were an inconsistent system!"[69] Imagine the reaction of the newly knighted Lord Russell toward this 25 year-old Gödel who declared that the formidable PM, created to rid itself of self-reference and inconsistency, was "in fact riddled through and through with formulas allegedly stating all sorts of absurd and incomprehensible things about themselves," says Hofstadter.[70] Gödel had discovered a myriad of paradoxes imbedded within PM. In particular, he uncovered numerous self-references, which Russell and Whitehead had attempted to avoid.

---

[68] A non-self-referential work avoids using itself to substantiate or prove itself.
[69] Hofstadter, *Gödel, Escher, Bach: An Eternal Golden Braid*, 24.
[70] *I Am a Strange Loop* (New York: Basic Books, 2007), 147.

Gödel's Theorem

Gödel's theorem has plagued many mathematicians, logicians, and philosophers ever since it was published. He revealed that any and all organized systems of thought cannot be both complete and consistent. If they are totally consistent, they are at the expense of excluding elements that would otherwise make them inconsistent. If they are complete, they are at the expense of including inconsistent elements. Gödel demonstrated that "provability is a weaker notion than truth," regardless of the system under scrutiny.[71] Truth is unprovable. Even Gödel's theorem is unprovable! "Kurt Gödel is unprovable not only although it is true, but worse yet, because it is true."[72]

Gödel & Theology

There are parallels between mathematics, logic, philosophy, *and* theology. They are all subject to Gödel's Theorem. First of all, if God does indeed exist, then there will necessarily be, in our limited views of God, discontinuities and inconsistencies. Secondly, the inconsistency and incompleteness that critical atheists claim invalidate the God concept are the very characteristics that validate truth!

If systems of belief are permitted to take their natural course with integrity, given Gödelian principles, there will be paradoxes therein. What some philosophical and religious theorists fail to recognize is that the presence of paradoxes does not indicate failure, but clarifies the limits of our domain. The greatest error of all, after we have explained away unwanted texts and evidences, is to convince ourselves that our beliefs are complete. They may in fact be totally consistent, but prescriptively incomplete. Paradox is not a guarantee that the development of such systems of belief had integrity, but if integrity runs its course paradox will be present.

Gödel, Escher, Bach

I must here acknowledge the role that Douglas Hofstadter's book *Gödel, Escher, Bach: An Eternal Golden Braid* played in launching my research. Hofstadter

---

[71] *Gödel, Escher, Bach: An Eternal Golden Braid*, 19.
[72] *I Am a Strange Loop*, 165.

revealed hidden links between the logic, drawings, and music of Kurt Gödel, M.C. Escher, and Johann Sebastian Bach. This "eternal golden braid" of strangeness permeates our existence. I must, however, point out one glaring inconsistency (said with a Gödelian smile) within GEB (the acronym Hofstadter used when referring to his book): that Hofstadter, a humble and devout non-theist, chose three theists who each saw and worked not only within this eternal golden braid, but because of it. What beautiful irony . . .

A Gödelian Postscript

At the beginning of this chapter I referenced *Principia Mathematica* (PM), the monumental work that Gödel found riddled with inconsistencies and self-references. You may recall it was co-authored by Alfred North Whitehead. As it turns out, Whitehead paid humble attention to Gödel's criticism. Most theologians today know Alfred North Whitehead as the *Father of Process Theology*. It is quite possible they know little of PM and the eventual outcome of Gödel's paper. Process Theology and PM are at two extreme poles. PM was founded on what mathematicians call closed-form solutions, which provide absolute answers: complete and consistent answers. There is no continuous processing. Process Theology, on the other hand, acknowledges what mathematicians call open-form solutions. These solutions, or equations, provide approximations that become the variables that are run through the process again and again, continuously refining the answer. Apparently Whitehead went through a transformation that acknowledged Gödel's theorems and eventually applied them to his own system of belief. His transformation resulted in *Process Theology*. This was a humble and exemplary response that points to anything but absolute answers: it points to a call to process. This is the strangeness of our existence. Having said that, let us continue with the God concept, enveloping a process that, in Gödelian terms, will be both inconsistent and incomplete.

2.02

Initial Cause

What brought about the existence of the cosmos? This very question assumes a definitive beginning. Perhaps everything always has been in existence, cycling over and over, without the need for a beginning. Much of the scientific community works exhaustively at avoiding the issue of initial cause (IC). While some adopt a *no beginning* stance, others keep moving backwards in time to bigger natural phenomenon to explain events such as the Big Bang. Some simply avoid the debate over a *beginning* altogether. Why? There are natural outcomes of assuming a beginning to the cosmos that result in unwelcomed conclusions for those who believe in complexity without a reason for its existence.

In Douglas Hofstadter's book he addresses this issue by focusing on the complexity of DNA, asking the fundamental question: how did all this get started? Did it start itself? That, of course, is unimaginable to Hofstadter. He concludes the discussion by diverting the focus to the wonder of complexity. He moves away from the dilemma, delaying a conclusive discussion on origins.[73] Diverting away from the difficult issue of initial cause is too frequent a trend.

Spontaneous Changes

Whether one believes in a beginning or no beginning to the cosmos, one fact is insurmountable: no scientific data exists that exemplifies an effect without a cause. This is evident from Newton's laws of motion to DNA mutations to electron transfers. In a journal article published in *Physical Review Letters*, E. Marinari says, "There is no evidence for spontaneous changes in nature, only changes without

---

[73] *Gödel, Escher, Bach: An Eternal Golden Braid*, 548.

known causes. The only remotely suggestive evidence is within the world of quantum mechanics . . . Even this is not understood well enough to state any proof of spontaneous changes in nature without a cause."[74]

Still some theorists attribute all that is to spontaneity, asserting that the cosmos simply emerged out of "primeval chaos."[75] Even if such an emergence did happen, *where did the primeval chaos come from*? Mathematical probability, let alone logic, does not lend support to a universe such as ours coming into existence of its own accord. Physicists estimate there are approximately 10^{100} atoms in the entire universe (that is a 1 with 100 zeros following it). The apparent order is so grand and the probability so miniscule that to espouse a *universe out of chaos by chance* casts a grim shadow on intellectual integrity.

Thermodynamics

The second law of thermodynamics states that the universe is continuously moving in the direction of increased disorder. (Notice that these are not scientific theories, but scientific laws.) This increased disorder is commonly referred to as *entropy*. The whole universe is undergoing entropy: the *whole* universe.

The issue of *existence* pertains not only to atoms coming together in arrangements to bring about complexities such as stars, planets, and life, but also to the existence of atoms in the first place. Even the *strings* that physicists purport to make up all sub-sub-atomic particles have complexity. Where did their complexity originate? Once again one could claim that this complexity always existed (though that still leaves me intellectually unsatisfied), but spontaneously bringing higher order out of disorder is still very problematic.

Brian Greene, in his book *The Fabric Of The Cosmos: Space, Time, And The Texture Of Reality*, assures us that even though our universe is driven to more and more disorder, stars and planets and life can still form from *pockets* of order. However, a "more–than–compensating generation of disorder" still dictates the

---

[74] E. Marinari, "Numerical Evidence for Spontaeously Broken Replica Symmetry in 3d Spin Glasses," *Physical Review Letters* 76, no. 5 (1996).
[75] Boltzmann in Brian Greene, *The Fabric of the Cosmos: Space, Time, and the Texture of Reality* (New York: Random House, Inc., 2004), 320.

overall trend toward cosmic disorder.[76] While this may appease some theorists on a local level (our universe) it does not address the existence of cosmos, nor the remaining order within the cosmos that is moving in the direction of entropy. What brought the *disintegrating order* about in the first place?

Cause & Effect

Our whole universe speaks of causation. "All things are subject to the law of cause and effect. This great principle knows no exception."[77] The scientific community has discovered no exceptions to this principle. The Dalai Lama states in *The Universe in a Single Atom: The Convergence of Science and Spirituality*, "Since we interact and change each other, we must assume that we are not independent . . . Effectively, the notion of intrinsic, independent existence is incompatible with causation."[78] While this may be a reverse argument, it is nonetheless an argument for cause.

I assert, based on the second law of thermodynamics, that any and all complexity indicates a cause. No-cause equates to zero complexity and zero complexity equates to nothingness. Furthermore, as pointed out earlier, no scientific data exists demonstrating any effect without an associated cause. It truly is that simple.

No Beginning

Some get around the initial cause issue by asserting that the universe has no beginning. There are very elegant arguments for this. I am not opposed to such a theory. Though *no beginning* is very appealing, such a cyclical existence cannot continue without energy input. Why the need for a continuous energy supply? Any loss of electromagnetic radiation is both a loss of energy and mass. One could argue that energy never escapes, but energy must be spent in order to keep energy and mass *in*. Any loss of energy implies eventual total loss of energy and mass, which implies that our universe will not go on forever. If it does not go on forever, the implication is also that it has not gone on forever. "*No beginning*" theories do not do away with the need for continuous energy input. Cause is still a factor.

---

[76] Ibid., 173.
[77] Carl Menger
[78] Lama, *The Universe in a Single Atom: The Convergence of Science and Spirituality*, 47.

Too Close to Examine?

Part of the problem with such pursuits is that we are a part of the very system we attempt to analyze. "Science cannot solve the ultimate mystery of nature. And it is because, in the last analysis, we ourselves are part of the mystery we are trying to solve."[79] While this is true, we can continue to explore and reason to the best of our ability, working diligently to move beyond our biases, scientific or religious, to gain deeper understandings of the nature of our existence. As an example, we have explored and come to understand so much about the human body in spite of the fact that we are confined to such bodies.

In Closing

Hilary Lawson aptly says, "Science can give an account of the causes of events in the world by reference to other aspects of the world, but it cannot give an account of what caused the world to exist, for the cause would have to be outside of the world."[80] Regardless of whether you are a millions-of-years evolutionist, a 6-day creationist, a nanosecond eventist, or an eternal cyclist, the common denominator is the inescapable issue of initial cause and/or continuous energy input. All scientific data points to a cause for every effect, and ultimately to an initial cause.

---

[79] Max Planck in O'Murchu, *Quantum Theology: Spiritual Implications of the New Physics*, 85.
[80] Lawson, *Closure: A Story of Everything*, 231.

2.03

Infinite Initial Cause

It was that fateful Saturday afternoon in my garage that got all this started. I had just recalled a question that had bothered me as a boy and finally decided to ask it of God, or whoever was listening. I wanted to know who put him into power: who gave him the right to be God. It was only moments after asking this question that it occurred to me that if in fact (or in miracle) he actually answered, informing me who appointed him God, I would quickly turn to that "whoever" and ask the same question. You see, it was a logical and foregone conclusion on my part that whoever put God into power had to have more power than God, or else he would have been incapable of ordaining him *God*. Then I realized that the series of questions would never end, assuming the series of individuals did not run out of patience with me and continue to answer my finite questions.

At that moment I acknowledged not only that every cause must have a cause, but also every cause is the effect of a higher order cause. Remember from the previous chapter, entropy (thermodynamics) dictates that each and every cause must be of a higher order of complexity than its effect. This principle is true because we live in a less than infinite state. It is mathematically, scientifically, logically, philosophically, and experimentally impossible for any entity to create or give rise to another entity that has more complexity than the entity that brought about its existence. Einstein knew this and asserted it by famously declaring, "God does not play dice." Douglas Hofstadter interprets this statement by saying, "What Einstein meant is that nothing in nature happens without a cause, and for mathematicians, that there is always one unifying, underlying cause is an unshakable article of faith."[81]

Taking It to the Limit

"Nature and nature's laws lay hid in night. God said, 'Let Newton be,' and all was light."[82] Sir Isaac Newton developed calculus at a very young age and applied it to the study of motion and gravity. Calculus is an extremely valuable mathematical tool, especially when calculating infinitesimally small or infinitely large limits problems. Limits equations assess the eventual outcome if a variable as the variable approaches zero, a finite value, or infinity. While the answers to such questions may seem trivial, the mathematical proofs are anything but simple. Newton's approach made such calculations plausible.

Infinite regression is essentially what I was doing that fateful Saturday, when I was asking the cause of the cause of the cause of the cause . . . where it came from. I realized I was posing a calculus problem. If each effect had a cause that was only a small fraction more complex than it was, where would I end up if I asked the question an infinite number of times? This was a problem for calculus. I grabbed my old calculus reference book and quickly looked up the equation. It is expressed in Equation 1.

$$(\text{Equation 1}) \qquad \lim_{n \to \infty} 1.0000001^n = \infty$$

These mathematical symbols basically mean that if I multiply 1.0000001, a number barely greater than 1, by itself an infinite number of times (which is *taking it to the limit*), the answer is infinity. In other words, each cause of a given effect is necessarily more complex than its effect, even if only by a very, very small value. If one were to ask each effect about the magnitude of its cause, continuing up the chain of more complex causes, one would end up with one and only one answer: infinity. In case you were wondering, the answer is the same even if the cause is

---

[81] Hofstadter, *I Am a Strange Loop*, 120.
[82] Alexander Pope.

only 1.0000000000000000000000000000000001 times greater than its effect. Calculus proves it.

Richard Dawkins, in his "Mount Improbable" illustration in *The God Delusion*, uses regress to explain why no creator or designer was needed to get us where we are today (since we got here ever so gradually, climbing a most improbable mountain in extremely small steps), but stops short of taking it to the limit at the bottom of the mountain. He ignores the dilemma of where the starting blocks came from.[83]

Mathematically the initial cause (IC) must be infinite; it cannot be less. Every effect must have a cause, and every cause must have a causal entity larger and more powerful and more complex than itself, even if by a minute amount. At the start of each and every cause-effect progression is infinity. Jean-Paul Sartre, the French existentialist philosopher pointed out that "a finite point is absurd if it has no infinite reference point."[84] We are not the finite entities we claim to be without an infinite reference point: an infinite initial cause (IIC).

Taking It to the Limit Again

Let us assume for a minute that evolutionists are correct: everything that currently exists evolved from lower states of existence, complexity and order. I have already referenced Richard Dawkins' "Mount Improbable," the illustration he uses in *The God Delusion* to show how order can evolve on its own, slowly inching its way up the mountain of complexity, rather than needing a creator to boost such order to the top of the mountain in six days. That is all well and good, but a problem other than an IC raises its head at this point. Evolutionists acknowledge that each stage of the evolutionary process emerges from a less complex stage. If this is the case, what was the level of complexity at the very start?

Well, you guessed it: calculus has something to contribute once more. If each previous stage was less complex, even if by an incredibly small amount, the mathematical outcome is expressed in Equation 2.

---

[83] Dawkins, *The God Delusion*, 121.
[84] Schaeffer, *How Should We Then Live?*, 145.

(Equation 2) $\lim_{n \to \infty} 0.9999999^n = 0$

Even if the degree of complexity for each previous stage of development was only 0.999999999999999999999999999999 times less, the answer is the same when taking it to the limit: *zero*. If Dawkins' "Mount Improbable" is correct (even though he does not take it to the limit), everything that currently exists came initially from zero complexity. That may not seem staggering, but let us look more carefully at the implications of such an outcome. Zero complexity, as yielded by the limit equation, equates to *nothingness*. Anything, even the simplest of all things, has a complexity greater than zero. Even a quantum mechanical string, the entity that physicists theorize is the building block for all subatomic particles, has a complexity greater than zero. If the total initial complexity of the cosmos were zero, there would be nothing. Not even the fabric of space itself would exist. Dawkins' argument to prove that no creator was needed inadvertently argues that everything came from nothingness.

Zero and Infinity

The two limits equations present confounding statements regarding the existence of the cosmos: either it always existed (requiring a continuous energy input) or it came to be from nothingness by means of infinity. For scientists to insist that complexity and order have risen out of the dust of the cosmos on their own is mathematically not an option. Equation 1, regarding initial cause, yields infinity as the cause. Equation 2, regarding complexity, yields zero as the starting point for the infinite initial cause. In a very real sense, these two values are on two sides of a very strange coin. Though some mathematicians insist that the inverse of zero is undefined, it is also thought of as infinity, and vice versa. Zero and infinity are at the root of all that is.

An Aversion to Zeros and Infinities

Scientists, especially biologists and physicists, avoid zeros and infinities at all costs. I hope you have been able to quickly assess why. Diarmuid O'Murchu addresses this phobia in his book *Quantum Theology: Spiritual Implications of the*

New Physics. He states, "Physicists seem to abhor infinities and have invented a questionable, scientific procedure called 'renormalization' to eliminate them from calculations. What in effect happens is that the experiment is so construed that all the infinities cancel each other out . . . Infinity must somehow be included in scientific research, not conveniently circumvented."[85] This "renormalization" refers to the process whereby physicists inserted mathematical terms into the equations (initially derived to explain the existence of the cosmos) in order to get rid of the infinities they produced. Philosophically they do not believe the very equations they derived! The implication of everything coming from nothing by means of infinity is a concept they simply do not accept. Ex nihilo!

The implications on this discussion are mathematically clear: zeros imply infinities and infinities imply zeros. It is no wonder such renormalization of the equations of the cosmos has taken place. If one believes that there is no infinite initial cause, what option is there but to manipulate the equations to make it go away? To see such astute academicians renormalize the equations in an effort to get away from the initial results is disconcerting. For many of them the only justification is simply that, "It simply cannot be."

Three Options

I believe there are three cosmic options to consider. Option 1: Everything existed for an infinite amount of time in the form of low complexity building blocks until those pieces were kicked out of their dormant existence to initiate the formation of the cosmos. Option 2: Everything that exists has cycled endlessly through big bangs and eventual collapses, reformulating complexity out of disorder and disorder out of complexity without end (though physicists are beginning to question the eventual collapse of the cosmos since its expansion appears to be accelerating). Option 3: Everything that exists came from zero complexity (in other words *nothingness*) by means of an infinite cause.

All three seem to be viable options *and* all three of them mathematically require an infinite input to either bring them about or sustain them. Option 1 and 3 obviously require an infinite initial cause. Option 2 requires an infinite input, one

---

[85] O'Murchu, *Quantum Theology: Spiritual Implications of the New Physics*, 184.

that could just as easily be labeled an *infinite continuous cause*. The IIC could just as well be the ICC!

Closing Thoughts

Reason, no matter how convincing, if limited in the extent to which it is carried out, is not in the end authentic reason, but a deceptive form of reason. Some escape the need for an infinite initial cause by claiming that the universe has always existed. If that is the case, it is infinite. Either way one cannot escape infinitude. What if, just what if, the IIC took nothingness and turned it inside out? What would it look like? Perhaps we are staring at it.

2.04

Infinite Initial Cause with Personality

Just as there is no scientific data available to demonstrate an effect without a cause, neither is there data to demonstrate the occurrence of an attribute or parameter in an effect that was not present in the cause. DNA mutations can result in changes in shapes, sizes, colors, and functions of a subsequent generation, but there will still be shapes, sizes, colors, and functions. Though many theorize the onset of new parameters, there is no data to support such claims.

Look at a piece of art. No sculpture comparable to the *Pieta* existed before Michelangelo sculpted it. Yet, it demonstrates no qualities that were not present in either Michelangelo himself or in the subjects he used to model its formation. Furthermore, when one studies a Rembrandt painting carefully, the master's signatures are evident. His unique inflections of the brush give him away. No effect possesses a property that its cause does not have. No field of scientific study has ever demonstrated one example to the contrary. The causes have the same essential properties as the effects. An effect may have a new combination of attributes derived from the cause(s) but will not exhibit a new attribute.

Evolution theorizes the rise of new and better attributes in subsequent generations. Did they come into existence on their own, or did they derive them from an ultimate cause, such as the IIC? As fully as current evolutionary theories are accepted, it is surprising that they are accepted without any evidence of attributes coming into existence spontaneously without cause or without being present in their predecessors. This pre-existing attribute criterion, or *PAC*, is an issue conveniently skirted by many theorists. Contrary to current theories, proven evolutionary changes involve mutations, but not different elementary building blocks.

Personality

If we follow this logic to its natural conclusion, taking it to its limit so to speak, then the IIC had to have personality.[86] Therefore it will hereafter be referred to as the *infinite initial cause with personality* (the IICP). We can theorize that personality came into being via a collection of experiences, relational neurological synapses, or some other random connectedness, but it sidesteps the pre-existing attribute criterion. The very fact that artificial intelligence theorists are working steadfastly to reproduce intelligence in the *ultimate machine*, is in and of itself evidence for this argument. Whether personality is simply a collection of ideas or not is ultimately irrelevant. The artificial intelligence gurus miss the point if they think they can prove spontaneous generation of personality by duplicating it in machines. Ponder this for a second: if the artificial intelligence community is successful at building personality into a machine, where did the machine get its personality? From its causes! The point is, regardless of *what* personality is, the IIC had to have had it! The question ultimately moves from "What is it?" to "Who gave it to us?"

A critic may say, "So you are telling me that early, very early, life forms had personality?" Though they may have, that is not what I am primarily arguing. The theory that early life forms in the evolutionary process did not have personality does not disprove the logic herein. I am arguing that somewhere along the line, whether early on, midway, or in later stages of the process, the IICP instilled personality into the effects.

Buddhists and Mind

It is very interesting that Buddhists attribute the existence of the cosmos to *mind*. The Dalai Lama asserts that "mind is the creator of the entire universe."[87] I see an intricate and amazing connection between this and an IICP. Either way, we

---

[86] For the purposes of this discussion, implicit in *personality* are also sentience, intelligence, and consciousness.
[87] Lama, *The Universe in a Single Atom: The Convergence of Science and Spirituality*, 109.

have an infinite entity bringing about sentient beings and everything else, including some beings that may not be sentient. As I have mentioned before, even if *all that is* cycles endlessly through iterations of big bangs and ultimate collapses, it does not take place without an IICP, or if one prefers, an infinite continuous cause with personality: an ICCP.

The God Concept

It may seem like a huge leap to move from the IICP to the God concept; however, I see little difference between the two, except that the *God* label is more restrictive, given the profound negative *and* positive preconceived images that it conjures up in the human mind. Throughout the rest of this work I will use the IICP and the God labels interchangeably with some reservation due to so many distorted images of God. Some may find the IICP label too impersonal. I intend quite the opposite, yet understand if it does seem so. I have used the acronym so much over the past decade that I am accustomed to it and feel at home with it, especially given its ultimate connotations. Perhaps it will grow on you too as we go along.

The Infinitude of God

The IICP is not only infinite, but strangely so. I used to think that the infinitude of God was just one of its qualities or characteristics. I grew up being taught about the omniscience, omnipotence, and the omnipresence of God as though they were unique characteristics. I now realize that the IICP cannot be the IICP if it is not infinite! All of the IICP's qualities and characteristics lie inside this infinitude. Every characteristic or quality of the IICP is infinite. Mathematically, it must be so.

We will get into specific attributes of the IICP in the next chapter, but for the moment let us assume that the IICP is merciful. How merciful is the IICP? Mathematically, the IICP is infinitely merciful. Scripture refers to the IICP's mercy as never ceasing.[88] While this could mean, "never stopping," the infinitude of the IICP implies something else: the IICP's mercy is all encompassing, infinitely so. Of course, so are all of the other attributes of God. I hope you see the irony in that last

---

[88] Lamentations 3:22.

statement: *all of the other attributes*. How many attributes of the IICP are there? Perhaps we are in error to *count* them. Once again, mathematically there must be infinite attributes.

The IICP is infinitely complex, yet infinitely simple. For me, to contemplate an infinite entity is on one hand impossible, yet also strangely simple: everything about the IICP is smoothly blended into one grand infinitude. It becomes irrelevant to discuss *parts* of the IICP, for each *part* is infinite. In a sense, there are no *parts* to the IICP. The IICP just is. It is quite ironic to me that Richard Dawkins, in his book, *The God Delusion*, concludes the same, by saying, "However little we know about God, the one thing we can be sure of is that he would have to be very, very complex and presumably irreducibly so!"[89] While he states this as an argument for the impossibility of such an irreducible entity existing, he essentially agrees with theists that the IICP is not reducible into finite parts.

All or Nothing

The IICP must be completely the IICP or not at all. It is not created. If it were, then the one who created it would be the IICP. To believe in the absence of an IICP is to believe in nothing. But nothing, as an entity, is something. Something must exist in order to recognize nothing. If anything exists, then the one to whom we owe it is the IICP.

This, my friends, is why I am so critical of closed systematic theologies.[90] Either we know everything about the IICP, in which case the IICP is not infinite, or we know little to nothing compared to the IICP's infinitude.

The Evolution of God

I must here clarify the difference between the evolution, or development, of the God concept and the evolution of the IICP. We are growing and evolving in our understanding (or at least I hope so) of who or what the IICP is and how it functions with respect to the cosmos. But to believe that the IICP itself is growing and evolving is quite another issue. Some theologies, particularly variations of

---

[89] Dawkins, *The God Delusion*, 125.
[90] Notice that I said *closed* systematic theologies. This book is in and of itself a systematic theology, but one that is open-ended, not closed.

process theology, propose that the IICP is changing and evolving. Variations of *open theology* argue that even the IICP does not know who or what it will eventually become. There are profound mathematical problems with both of these beliefs.

Infinitude implies immutability. More importantly, it implies no need for change. Those who believe that the IICP is evolving in a progressive sense deny the infinitude of the IICP, though perhaps unknowingly. If the IICP is currently anything it once was not, then the IICP of the past and the IICP of the present each have characteristics that the other does not. If this is the case, then neither the IICP of the past nor the IICP of the present are infinite. Mutability, whether by adding or taking away, implies a state less than infinite. If any entity *is* what it once was not, then it was not infinite then or now. The IICP cannot become the IICP. The IICP cannot become infinite. Either the IICP always was infinite, or never was. Both mathematics and thermodynamics assert this.

One of the problems with insisting that the IICP does not change whatsoever is that it implies that God does not think, for thinking is a process, and process implies change. Or does it? The IICP changing into something that it previously was not negates its infinitude. However, *changing* into something that it always was is still infinite. It is *infinite change* as opposed to finite change. Perhaps God is *all change* and infinitely encompasses all possible permutations. Strangely, infinitude does not imply a static condition. It implies anything but static! We cannot completely develop this theme here, but will come back to it in a later chapter on strange loops and in the next Phase on dimensional perspectives. For now let it suffice to say that mathematically it is bad news for both *process* and *open theologies*.

One or Many?

Here is where I may lose a polytheist or two. Mathematically there cannot be more than one IICP. If there were, each having characteristics that the other(s) did not have, then each of them would be missing some attribute or magnitude. None of them is total: none of them is infinite. Infinitude implies completeness and entirety. It truly is as simple as that. That, however, is quite different than having a complete understanding of the God concept.

Can there be more than one *finite* God? Yes, but they will indeed be finite. That last statement must be qualified. Such a finite entity is necessarily less than infinite with respect to the IICP; however, it could be *infinite*, so to speak, with respect to our finiteness. It depends *where* that particular infinity resides with respect to us. I am unavoidably getting into the next Phase here, but must acknowledge the quandary we are in.

The implications on a Trinitarian view of God are not to be taken lightly. If each of the Father, Son, and Holy Spirit has characteristics that the other two do not, then none of them is mathematically infinite. As pointed out above, infinitude implies completeness, entirety, lacking no attribute or quality. If there are three people in the room, each with qualities the others do not have, then none of them is infinite.

Before I lose all of you (realizing that I may have in fact gained a few for the opposite reasons!) let me point out that the story does not end here. We will discuss the issue of *where* infinity resides in Phase 3. It had to be brought up here and now though, for if one is to truly endorse the infinitude of the IICP, (though we cannot fully envelop it) these implications must be brought to light. For far too long *believers* have bought into these contradictory notions without allowing themselves to thoroughly think through them. I, for one, believe that the IICP wants us to process and struggle with these issues. Hang in there with me!

The Absolute Truth

The infinitude of the IICP has implications for the issue of absolutes. First of all, even without a mathematical treatise on the subject, if there were no absolutes we would not know there were none for we would not know what they were in order to identify their absence. Secondly, the infinitude of the IICP implies at least *some* unchangeability (notice the qualification that awaits further detail!), which in turn implies the existence of absolutes. This, however, is quite another thing from functioning as though we have the inside scoop on absolute truth. To claim to have a corner on absolute truth is to worship something less than infinite. Can anyone besides an infinite entity know such absolute truth in its fullness? We humans simply pretend to, thereby making ourselves gods. If we endorse the infinitude of the IICP we also envelop the humanness and finitude of our wanderings toward such truth.

The God Within

It is a current trend, though not a new one, to believe that *we are God*. This is quite different from believing that God resides in each of us. It is an affirmation that the total composite of us *is* God. Eckhart Tolle, in his book *A New Earth: Awakening to Your Life's Purpose*, says, "The Truth is inseparable from who you are. Yes, you are the Truth. If you look for it elsewhere, you will be deceived every time. The very Being that you are is Truth. Jesus tried to convey that when he said, 'I am the way and the truth and the life.' These words uttered by Jesus are one of the most powerful and direct pointers to the Truth, if understood correctly."[91] Why he stopped short of finishing Jesus' quote ("No one comes to the Father but by me."[92]) I do not know, except that it would have implied the unique divinity of Jesus.

We know that such thinking is not new, for G.K. Chesterton said in 1908 in his book *Orthodoxy*, "Of all conceivable forms of enlightenment the worst is what these people call the Inner Light. Of all horrible religions the most horrible is the worship of the god within. . . . That [anyone] shall worship the god within him turns out ultimately to mean that [they] shall worship [themselves]."[93] Friends, it sounds wonderful and feels good to think that *we* are God and that *I* am Truth, but it simply is not the case. Mathematically we are not infinite: we are not the IICP. It is indeed the worship of a finite god. As I have stated already, this is not to say that a small finite part of God cannot or does not reside in us. The presence of slices of God existing in each of us does not make God less than infinite. Remember, any number subtracted from infinity still results in infinity. But to insist that *we* are *it* is quite another story and very disappointing, for included in *we* is all the evil of the world as well. Simply stated, God is God and I am not. The IICP is the IICP and I am not.

---

[91] Eckhart Tolle, *A New Earth: Awakening to Your Life's Purpose* (London: Penguin Books, 2005), 71.
[92] John 14:6.
[93] Chesterton, *Orthodoxy*, 109.

Closing

There are those who argue we are nothing more than an illusion that perceives itself. I have already given arguments against such a position. However, even if we are such illusions, the logic still leads us back to an infinite initial illusionary cause with personality! Either way we are left with an inconceivable entity to ponder over. Yet to even say that the IICP is inconceivable is to acknowledge that a certain portion is indeed conceivable. To assert that God is entirely inconceivable is obviously a false claim, given that we know at least something in order to establish how little we know.[94] I have to chuckle when I hear people say, "Some day, when we get to the other side, we will see God in all his fullness." We certainly will see *more* of the IICP, but we will never see the IICP in its fullness. Why? The IICP is infinite. In order to *see* infinity, we would have to be infinite. Finite can never become infinite. But do not be disappointed: we may see more of the IICP than we can comprehend!

I truly believe that if there were no God, we would not know to even ask the question of God's existence nor be fully convinced that God did not exist. We would not know what was missing. For those who are convinced that God is a noninterventionist, I assert that even *that* knowledge would not be available to us if God were truly a total noninterventionist. For those who believe that *we* are God, well, it leaves me very disappointed, not to mention that it is mathematically problematic. The bottom line is that our humanness somehow or other needs to box God in (into something that we can get our arms around) or box God out entirely. Either way, God is there. The IICP is real.

---

94 Barth, *Dogmatics in Outline*, 38.

2.05

Attributes of the IICP

The infinitude of the IICP is the IICP's primary attribute. All other attributes derive from this essential and eternal nature. Attributes are *what* the IICP *is*, not what he exhibits. They are natural properties of who the IICP is, properties that flow without ceasing from the IICP. How many attributes are there? That is like asking how many stars can fit inside infinity. It may well be that not only are each of the IICP's attributes infinite (remember that infinity divided by any number is still infinity!) but that he also has an infinite number of attributes. Of course as I write these words I am creating a closure that boxes the IICP in, which is why many insist we cannot use words to describe the IICP. *But even my need to have a box to wrap my arms around is understood by such an infinite being.*[95]

Warped Perceptions

One common misconception of the IICP is that he is too big and too busy for little insignificant me. Ironically, a natural outcome of infinitude is to also be infinitely finite. If infinity cannot express itself in finite ways, then there is something that it cannot be, and is therefore not infinite. It is personable. Infinitely personable! It knows the number of hairs on our heads; it knows our names before we are born; it knows the number of days and seconds of our lives. This leads us to a primary attribute of the IICP.

---

[95] Are all the attributes of the IICP good, as opposed to evil? Is it possible that the IICP is infinitely prideful, greedy, or deceitful? Such negative attributes imply weaknesses and deficiencies. As such they are finite. The IICP is infinite.

Love-Compassion

Wading through the key attribute of love-compassion, one unfortunately warped by human experience, begins with two things. First of all, let us try to lay down our experiences of love. Whether they have been positive emotional and/or physical experiences, or negative ones, try to let go of them for a minute. Secondly, try dwelling only on infinitude. This vastness we call infinitude has no inadequacies to make up for. It has no psychological tendencies to human-like anger. It needs nothing in return from *its subjects*, so to speak.

Friend, when I practice this exercise I feel freedom from human emotion. I feel acceptance; no reason for rejection. I feel enveloped. It is a sensation I bask in. It is like lying on a sandy beach, soaking in the smell and sound of refreshing waves. Infinitude envelops us without need of anything in return. What else is that, except love-compassion?

Love-compassion implies a personal connection with the one that is loved. Some individuals doubt such a personable nature or that God is a person-like being. "Some theologians speak of God as transpersonal. Such language is useful, for we often think that the only alternative to 'personal' is 'impersonal.' But transpersonal is another option: it means 'more than personal,' not 'less than personal.'"[96] To question the person-like nature of God, or that God is personable, is to question God's infinitude. God is infinitely person-like and infinitely personable. Yet infinity has no needs of its own. This is precisely why the IICP *is* love-compassion. Anti-love is rooted in incompleteness. God is infinite; therefore God is complete, leading to the logical conclusion, that God is love-compassion. Needy love is not true love. True love needs nothing in return. It just is. *Needless* love is true love. It is God. It is precisely because the IICP is infinite that the IICP is infinite love-compassion.

I hyphenated love-compassion because it changes the love concept significantly. *Love* has become a warped concept in our world. Phrases such as, "I love pleasure." "I love food," and "I love myself" portray a selfish nature to love. The love of the IICP is not selfish. This is why I prefer to think of it in terms of compassion. The IICP is forever and always compassionate; forever and always love-compassion.

---

[96] Borg, *The Heart of Christianity: Rediscovering a Life of Faith*, 73.

Truth

This attribute almost goes without saying. There is no knowledge that is not inside infinitude. What it also implies is that there is no falsehood inside infinitude. There is no need for deceit. There is no deceit in the IICP: only truth. What is more, there is no truth that is not in the IICP. We intersect such truth by such a finite and narrow margin that we should cower in embarrassing humiliation at pretending to have *corners on the truth*. It is like having a corner on infinitude. The IICP is infinite; therefore the IICP is truth.

Mercy

Can we separate mercy from love-compassion? No. Love-compassion is merciful. Mercy is love. Mercy is steadfast or unchanging love. It is infinite love. To the IICP there are no such entities as the *unlovable*. Therefore, there are no entities out of reach of the mercy of the IICP. The IICP's mercy never fails. It reaches to the highest heavens and extends to the lowest hell (assuming there are such places!). No one or anything is out of reach of this infinite mercy. The IICP is infinite; therefore the IICP is merciful.

Faithfulness

Infinitude never changes. The IICP's love never changes. The IICP's truth never changes. The IICP's mercy never changes. This is faithfulness. The IICP is faithful. Sure, we lose sight of this faithfulness given our confines to space and time, to pain and suffering, to the brokenness all around us, but friends, let not the appearance of faithlessness dissuade you from living inside this infinitude. I am not flippantly passing over such discontinuities, and will come back to the issues of brokenness, pain, and suffering.

Justice

I grew up with such a skewed sense of the justice of God. It seemed forbidding, cruel, and angry. Infinitude is anything but these. When seen in light of the infinitude of the IICP, justice takes on a very different meaning. If the IICP has no inadequacies, such as I exhibit when I get angry, then his justice is based on our needs, not his![97] God's justice is for our good, not his. God's justice comes out of his infinite love. He wants what is *best* for us. That is justice. If we reject it, he does not force it upon us. That too is justice.

Humility

It may seem counterintuitive to attribute humility to God, the *infinite initial cause with personality*, but it is a derivative of infinitude. Ponder for a minute the roots of humility's counterpart: pride. Pride sticks out its chest, raises its nose, and boasts of its accomplishments. Infinitude has no need for such displays. It needs no attention drawn to its accomplishments. No inadequacies are present to drive the antithesis to humility. The IICP exhibits true humility, not false humility as we so often display. True humility does not hesitate to state what it has done or accomplished, but does so to benefit the listener, not to prove a point, not to boast. Profound and simple humility flows from the IICP.

Enough God to Go Around

As a child, it bothered me to ask God for anything or ask him to spend time with me since there were so many people in the world with much greater needs than my own. This perception clearly was not based on the infinitude of God. I was not taught that God did not have time for me; it was my lack of understanding of infinitude that held me back.[98]

The infinitude of the IICP is such that there is always more than enough to go around. Remember, any finite value subtracted from infinity still results in infinity. A.W. Tozer is quoted as having said, "An infinite God can give all of Himself to each of His children. He does not distribute Himself that each may have a part, but to each one He gives all Himself as fully as if there were no others."[99] Friend, do not think the IICP has no time for you. The IICP has an infinite amount of time just for you.

---

[97] Notice that I subconsciously associated God's justice with anger. That in and of itself says more than any other words can! Though scripture does refer to God being angry at injustices, confusing anger with the justice of God is a common misconception.
[98] I apologize for sounding like I now understand infinitude! I obviously do not, but simply imply that it was not on my radar for most of my life.
[99] A.W. Tozer in Ben C. Ollenburger, *A Mind Patient and Untamed: Assessing John Howard Yoder's Contributions to Theology, Ethics, and Peacemaking* (Telford: Cascadia Publishing House, 2004), 218.

On and On

We could go on and on and on, listing more and more specific attributes of the IICP. The IICP is alive. The IICP has no flaws. The IICP is intelligent. The IICP is all-knowing. The IICP is everywhere-present.[100] The IICP is all-powerful. The IICP is pleasure, infinite pleasure! The IICP is cause and effect. The IICP is all possibilities. The IICP is all change. The IICP is free-thinking.[101] The IICP is infinite, therefore the IICP is.

No Religious Texts Needed

Have you noticed that I have not used any religious texts in deriving the attributes of the IICP? Ultimately no religious texts are needed to assess and/or derive the attributes of the IICP. They can all be derived from infinitude.

Human Impossibilities

I remember times when I pondered the question, "How could God permit horrible things to happen to innocent lives?" as though I had more compassion than God seemed to exhibit and that God was acting with harshness and a lack of compassion. It was not until the infinitude of God was so impressed on me that I began to realize that I cannot be more loving than God. I cannot be more merciful than God. I cannot be more truthful than God. I cannot be more just than God. *I cannot be more compassionate than God.* If I feel compassion and mercy towards those labeled by some fundamentalist as damned, then God feels infinitely more mercy and compassion than I. What is more, he not only *feels* it, he *is* it and *acts* on it. Strangely, my worries began to fade away. It is impossible for humans to have and act with more compassion than God does.

---

[100] This is problematic for some theorists, given that it implies God is also in hell. While I have issues with human understandings of what hell is or is not, you will see in upcoming chapters that I believe God is also capable of self-imposed limitations: infinitely so.

[101] Free-thinking, by the way, is an attribute that causes me to believe that the IICP delights in our free-thinking, even if our free-thinking leads us to the point of not believing in the IICP. To imagine the IICP delighting in us not believing in its existence, assuming we have processed with integrity, is truly infinitude at its best!

Summing It Up

Love-compassion is the ultimate attribute. One who exhibits compassion *is* God-like. One who does not exhibit compassion is not God-like. One who exhibits true humility is God-like. One who desires truth and is faithful in the pursuit of it is God-like. One who extends mercy, especially to those who do not deserve it, is God-like. The IICP by any other name, whether Allah, Jehovah, Being, The Almighty, Great Mystery, Mind, Waheguru, or Essence, is still the IICP.[102] What is more, any and all human constructed images of the IICP will necessarily be incomplete and inconsistent due to our finite constraints. If anyone is convinced otherwise (that their image of the IICP is not misconstrued) then either their god is finite or *they* are infinite, and the latter is surely not the case. Regardless how humans warp the IICP's image, it is still love-compassion, truth, mercy, faithfulness, humility, and much more. The IICP . . . is.

---

[102] All this is not to say that perverted images and names of God do not exist. They certainly do. And as you will see in subsequent chapters, neither is it to say that God never presents himself in definitive ways for definitive purposes.

2.06

Where Is Infinity?

Infinity presents a conundrum of sorts. In many respects it is indefinable and, as such, is difficult to determine *where* it exists. In a mathematical sense, it is an expression of the number of possible numbers. But where does such a number exist? Infinity is nowhere and everywhere.

Math may be helpful here, starting with a discussion regarding the end of the number line. Is there an end to the number line? If one were to reach such an end, what would exist beyond it? Such a discussion is reminiscent of our discussion on infinite regress in a previous chapter. We end up going just a little bit further, and a little bit further, forever. So, according to calculus and the process of taking the limit, the reality is that the end of the number line does not exist. Infinity is not at the end of the number line. It is a mathematical recognition of a never-ending line. Anything less than infinite, even slightly less, cannot arrive at infinity by going farther on the number line. It is not there. Then where is it?

Another strange place to look for infinity is actually between the integers on the number line. To illustrate, let us choose two numbers adjacent to the midpoint between 1 and 2 on the number line. Two possibilities are 1.4 and 1.6. If we wanted to find two numbers even closer to the midpoint we could choose 1.49 and 1.51. Likewise, we could refine our choices even more by choosing 1.499 and 1.501. For that matter, two numbers even closer to the midpoint would be 1.49999999 and 1.50000001. Yes, my friend, we can continue to get closer and closer in a similar infinite regress, never arriving at the two closest numbers to the midpoint between 1 and 2. Infinity is not just a very large number "at the end of the line." It is also a very long process leading to a very small difference between two adjacent locations. Infinity lies not only beyond the number line, but also within it.

Infinity Is a Verb

As I have shown, infinity does not exist at the end of the number line, but neither does it exist between any two adjacent numbers on the line. It is the never-ending process of going either direction. Infinity is an indication of eternal movement. It is, in a very real sense, a verb. It does not reside at any given location, yet it is everywhere and it is ever-moving.

The beauty of pursuing limits in calculus is that they represent a way of expressing the outcomes of processes that never end. I must here clarify, that what Sir Isaac Newton and others developed in calculus are not misled attempts to arrive at infinity, but real answers to what would otherwise have been infinite processes. These scientists and mathematicians recognized the infinitude of the process. They understood the nature of infinity: it is a never-ending process.

Infinitely Close

Having established that infinity does not end at a particular place, let us discuss one more of its discontinuities. Imagine being stranded on the moon in a capsule without the energy necessary to leave the moon's surface. The Earth and all its resources are within sight. The distance between the moon and the Earth is known to be 384,400 kilometers (238,900 miles.) This is not an infinite distance. Or is it? The possibility of returning to Earth is out of the question. There is no way to get there. It might as well be an infinite distance away. In fact, as I argue now, and also in Phase 3, it is more than *practically* infinitely far away, it *is* infinitely removed and out of our grasp. It is one thing to talk about points on the number line that are infinitely headed outward or infinitely inward, but quite another to talk about a point that is not even on the number line! It could be a point infinitely close to the number line, yet to the points trapped on the line it is infinitely removed. It is outside the bounds of connection. It is a location, a real location, but inaccessible. It is infinitely close.

In Closing

As we have seen, infinity can be very close and very far, unreachable by us either way. Such discussions are not trivial. They lay the groundwork for discussions to come. One could ask, "Where is the IICP?" The answer may be, "It is infinitely far away." But if that is the only viable answer, then how is it that we can even contemplate the existence of an IICP? Perhaps the IICP is also infinitely close.

2.07

Evolution vs. Creationism

If the IICP exists, being both infinitely far and infinitely close, then discussions on the origins of the cosmos and life itself are significantly impacted. Did the IICP bring all things into existence, from the grandeur of the universe down to its minute details, or did everything come into existence of its own accord?

Evolution, or self-directed natural selection, has a strong contingency of supporters. However, there are some difficult hurdles to overcome if one is to endorse evolution as it currently stands. What is the origin of evolution? Where did natural selection get the idea of *order*? How do we know it will continue to progress in the direction of improvement?

Richard Dawkins, in *The God Delusion*, asserts that natural selection is an improvement over *design* (creationism) precisely because it avoids the problematic question, "Who designed the designer?"[103] He argues that design demands infinite regress in its justification (which to him is to be avoided at all cost), yet does not admit to the need for infinite regress in justifying the existence of the initial building blocks that natural selection used to climb his "Mount Improbable." He fails to take his process to the limit, thereby avoiding the bottom of the mountain.[104] He is certain that natural selection is "the only process ultimately capable of generating complexity out of simplicity."[105]

But where did natural selection get the idea of complexity, or *order*? Dawkins claims that imbedded within natural selection is a drive toward order. Where did that drive come from? Why did some random chemical event produce the RNA

---

[103] Dawkins, *The God Delusion*, 121.
[104] Ibid., 121-22.
[105] Ibid., 150-51.

necessary to replicate itself via cells? Brian Greene, a prominent physicist, admits that ordered states are indeed rare and demand an explanation.[106] It is precisely this explanation that we seek.

Attributes of Humankind

Evolution struggles to reasonably explain several human attributes. The Dalai Lama, in his book *The Universe in a Single Atom: The Convergence of Science and Spirituality*, points out that a Darwinian approach to our existence fails to explain the presence of altruism and self-sacrifice.[107] This caring for one another, whether displayed by humans, primates, dolphins, or other species, is difficult to imagine emerging from a competitive process such as *the survival of the fittest*. Darwinism also fails to explain the presence of sentience, pain, and pleasure.[108] That humans know they exist and seek fulfillment of this knowledge is astounding. While easily explained by some evolutionists, this reality evades such trivial attempts to push it under the rug.

Humans have another distinctive characteristic that separates us from the rest of the animal kingdom: creativity. G.K. Chesterton sarcastically stated in his book *The Everlasting Man*, "Monkeys did not begin pictures and men finish them; Pithecanthropus did not draw a reindeer badly and Homo Sapiens draw it well. The higher animals did not draw better and better portraits . . . All we can say of this notion of reproducing things in shadow or representative shape is that it exists nowhere in nature except in man; and that we cannot even talk about it without treating man as something separate from nature."[109] Where did such creativity come from? Natural selection does not alone account for it.

On The Flip Side

On the flip side of the origins coin, are creationists who claim that everything came into existence in six 24-hour days, 5,000 years ago. There are many problematic assumptions built into this *young Earth creationism*. Let us start with

---

[106] Greene, *The Fabric of the Cosmos: Space, Time, and the Texture of Reality*, 165.
[107] Lama, *The Universe in a Single Atom: The Convergence of Science and Spirituality*, 112.
[108] Ibid., 115.
[109] G.K. Chesterton, *The Everlasting Man* (San Francisco: Ignatius Press, 1993), 34-35.

genealogical records. Many interpret the genealogical records in the Bible literally, as consecutive records of the history of humankind. In Francis Schaeffer's book *Genesis in Space and Time: The Flow of Biblical History*, he points out, "Before the turn of the century, Professor William Greene at Princeton Theological Seminary and Professor Benjamin B. Warfield following him maintained that the genealogies in Genesis should not be taken as a chronology."[110] He asserts that, "Prior to the time of Abraham, there is no possible way to date the history of what we find in Scripture."[111]

The Bible does not claim that the Earth is 5,000 years old. What is more, the Bible does not claim that only one "day" lapsed between the creation of the heavens and the earth and when God said, "Let there be light." Neither does it claim that there are no gaps in the genealogical accounts. The Bible does not claim to be exhaustive truth.[112]

Our expanding universe, as observed by astrophysicists, presents a dilemma for young Earth creationists. The data, along with basic velocity equations, leads to the conclusion that the universe is 14 billion years old. We can see light that emanated from stars that are millions of light-years away. How can this be in such a young universe?

Another troublesome issue in the Genesis account of creation lies in the time lapse between the creation of Adam and the creation of Eve. In between, Adam supposedly named all the species of livestock, the birds in the sky, and all the wild animals. He did all this in addition to working and taking care of the garden? There are roughly 15,000 species of birds and mammals on earth. If he named all the species at a rate of 10 seconds per species, it would have taken him at least two days, assuming he did it non-stop, day and night. According to Genesis chapter 2, all this, plus caring for the garden, was done before Eve was created. Yet according to Genesis, she was created on the same day as Adam. It simply is not realistic.

For an IICP, the question is not whether it could have been done in 24-hour days, but rather was it? Infinitude does not have limits, but has choice. The

---

[110] Schaeffer, *Genesis in Space and Time: The Flow of Biblical History*, 122.
[111] Ibid., 124.
[112] One of my editors, J.B. Barringer, astutely pointed out that some scriptural texts, especially at the end of the Gospel of John, precisely claim that the Bible is not exhaustive truth.

Hebrew word that is commonly translated as *day* in the Genesis creation account is elsewhere in the Old Testament translated *era*. But, to get caught up in this debate misses the primary point: I believe that Genesis chapters 1-10 are poetic. One may even label them *prophetic poetry*. For instance, Genesis 3:14-15 is clearly a proclamation of God's judgment on sin and his intent to set aright the resulting devastation. Yet it is clearly written in poetic prose. Will literally crushing a serpent's head resolve all sin and evil? Reading the Genesis creation account poetically does not take away from its beauty and importance, rather it adds to its significance.

Shared Problematic Issues

There are a couple of problematic issues that both evolution and creationism share. The first is the assumption that our current state of being is the first and only iteration, or the *first time around*, so to speak, for life and order on this planet. Surely creationists have wondered why the earth was "void and without form" in the Genesis chapter 1 account. Would God intentionally create something so distorted? Or was it left over from the destruction of the previous iteration?

Evolutionists make a similar assumption. Remember the discussion on misled interpretations from data in the chapter titled *Data Dogmatics*? I have to wonder if fossil finds have been such data points. Do we really know that one smooth continuous flow of natural selection is the only and accurate interpretation? What if the fossil records are a mixture of data from a dozen successions of development and demise on Earth?

Secondly, there exists the *insurmountable* problem of something coming from nothing. Evolutionists would deny that such a problem exists, but as I have shown in the calculus limits equations, and as applied to Richard Dawkins' "Mount Improbable," the problem exists inescapably for both sides of the argument. Creationists have an easy out by claiming that God spoke everything into existence *out of nothing*! Atheistic evolutionists simply deny that nothingness was ever a state of being.

G.K. Chesterton wrote in his biography of Saint Thomas Aquinas, "In a word, the world does not explain itself, and cannot do so merely by continuing to expand itself. But anyhow, it is absurd for the Evolutionist to complain that it is unthinkable for an admittedly unthinkable God to make everything out of nothing and then pretend that it is more thinkable that nothing should turn itself into everything."[113] The tension between the two is not insignificant. Neither side has more answers than the other. We cannot literally interpret the Genesis account of creation without running into difficulties. Can we trust the data that science gives us? Even if we can, something is still missing in current evolutionary accounts of our existence.

The Data

One complaint of scientific dating methods is that they exaggerate the age of the materials being tested. Not all dating methods err on the side of overestimating the age; some underestimate. For instance, if one were to arbitrarily subtract ten times the margin of error from the results of such dating methods, the results are still so many orders of magnitude beyond 5,000 years that the discussion becomes pointless. The bottom line is, there is an insurmountable quantity of data indicating that the Earth is close to 4 billion years old. I believe this data. The methods used in dating, not only the Earth but the universe as well, are tools we have been granted in order to understand the cosmos. I believe we live in a very old universe.

A Driver

I have to admit that I react in a negative way to the "Truth Fish" swallowing the "Darwinian Fish," an attachment commonly displayed on the cars of some 6-day creationists. But I also react to the "Darwinian Fish" swallowing the "Ichthus Fish" (the symbol of the early Christians and adopted by creationists). Even if evolution, or Darwinianism, is truth, it is still finite truth; it is limited truth with many missing pieces. Perhaps ultimately truth will still swallow *it* up. But so it is with creationism stories as well. Ultimately truth will swallow everything!

Both theories leave me empty. Things happen too quickly in 6-day creationism when one carefully evaluates the data. But everything evolving of its own accord,

---

[113] Chesterton, *St. Thomas Aquinas / St. Francis of Assisi*, 159.

springing forth complexity out of nothingness, is totally contrary to the laws of thermodynamics and mathematics. What are we left with?

For all things to come into being and progress as they have requires an energy input. I find it helpful to visualize a *driver* reaching into our domain and pushing the Darwinian fish along. Yes, I believe Darwin was on to something. If one compares the sequence of creation in Genesis with Darwinian progression, the parallels are uncanny. The difference is in time and energy. Hence I propose that the ultimate Darwinian driver, the IICP, drove the process.

John Polkinghorne, a preeminent thinker and writer on the convergence of science and religion, affirms in his book *Science and Religion in Quest of Truth* that God does indeed act in a general fashion via the natural laws set in place, but that there is also the "possibility of specific divine providential action" in the evolutionary process.[114] This divine process is consistently displayed throughout the cosmos. Whether it was the *hand* of the IICP or a *voice* spewing forth strings of *complex energy*, all that is came to be and progresses by means of the IICP: the infinite driver. (Figure 12)

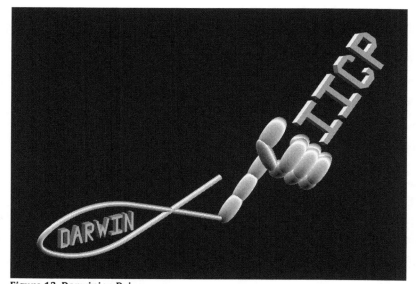

Figure 12. Darwinian Driver

---

[114] John Polkinghorne, *Science and Religion in Quest of Truth* (New Haven and London: Yale University Press, 2011), 83.

A God of Process

A common thread throughout both the creation narratives and evolutionary theories is that they both speak boldly of process! Forgetting the time frame for now, let us focus on the process. Whether 6 days or 6 billion years, the most confounding thing of all is that an IICP took any time at all to bring everything into existence. Regardless of the process, the miracle is that God took *time* to do it! It was a process! The IICP could have blinked an eye (assuming it has one), or nodded its head, or snapped its finger, and everything could have been instantaneously in place. Even a nanosecond (0.000000001 seconds) is an eternity to the IICP. Why take so long! One thing both creationists and evolutionists agree on is that it took time. Even if one does not agree on how much time, it still took time. That to me is the most confounding fact of all. Why bother to bring all things into existence by taking time? For that matter, why do so at all?

I believe the IICP led with example: infinity took time to create. He still takes time for all creation. This example is a call to process: it is a call to iterate. Throughout sacred writings God has revealed himself as a God of process. The process has always been as important, if not more, than the product. God seemingly has never been about an instantaneous product or solution. The prospect of God using an evolving process is reflected in the God of the Bible, the Koran, and other texts as well.

Closing

Neither creationists nor evolutionists have the corner on the origins market. To a degree I fault both sides for assuming they know the whole story *and* for thinking they completely understand the process. While it is speculated that Charles Darwin gradually shifted from theism to an agnosticism, I find it quite interesting that he appears to have ended up somewhere between the two extremes, believing in a Creator, or at least divine driver, for the very process he proposed.[115]

---

[115] Charles Darwin in Robert Finch and John Elder, *The Norton Book of Nature Writing* (New York: W. W. Norton & Company, 1990), 166.

For some, the speed of the process is proportional with the magnificence of the creation. But to G.K. Chesterton, "The ultimate question is why they (the processes described herein) go at all; and anybody who really understands that question will know that it always has been and always will be a religious question; or at any rate a philosophical or metaphysical question."[116] Even the mathematics that I have used this far in my arguments for an IICP raise such metaphysical questions. There is so much more to the story than either creationists or evolutionists espouse.

---

[116] Chesterton, *The Everlasting Man*, 25.

2.08

A Broken World

You may be a theorist who claims that we are not a dualistic world of good and evil, but that we are evolving our way out of the current paradigm and on into a better state of humanity. You may believe that we are in a world of brokenness, one with both good and evil. I suppose you could be one who has never thought through the state of the world to the point of deciding which it is. Regardless of your position, something is wrong. In the words of G.K. Chesterton in his book *Orthodoxy*, "The real trouble with this world of ours is not that it is an unreasonable world, nor even that it is a reasonable one. The commonest kind of trouble is that it is nearly reasonable, but not quite. Life is not an illogicality; yet it is a trap for logicians. It looks just a little more mathematical and regular than it is; its exactitude is obvious, but its inexactitude is hidden; its wildness lies in wait."[117] Such a perspective is reminiscent of our friend Kurt Gödel!

Perhaps I could be persuaded to believe that we are evolving out of such a state if it were not for the lack of an adequate explanation as to how we got here in the first place. Just as theorists have difficulty explaining the presence of religion, they also have difficulty in explaining the presence of *evil*. Some insist that evil (though most theorists do not like the label) is simply a "dysfunction as a form of collective mental illness."[118] Even if this were the case, how could such an elegant process as natural selection result in such a dysfunctional state?

The world has a fixation with the anomaly some call *evil*. I have yet to hear an adequate explanation of human fascination with horror. Where does it come from?

---

[117] *Orthodoxy*, 117.
[118] Tolle, *A New Earth: Awakening to Your Life's Purpose*, 8-9.

How did we arrive at such an elegant state, yet delight in our own destruction? I doubt we are capable of construing such gore in the theater without some innate knowledge of evil (not non-pleasantries, but horrific evil). Diarmuid O'Murchu says in *Quantum Theology*, "We humans have become a cosmic anomaly. We rape and pollute the very womb that nurtures and sustains. We have become a dysfunctional family, blind to our own addictions, heading headlong for self-destruction."[119] Why? Even if evil is nothing more than a dysfunction, its origin still evades evolutionary theorists.

Regardless of the labels we choose (evil, horror, darkness, sin) something is wrong with the world. G.K. Chesterton astutely said, "Whatever else men have believed, they have all believed that there is something the matter with mankind."[120] Chesterton goes on to argue that such broken states have not gradually evolved, nor are we gradually evolving back out of them. "According to the real records available, barbarism and civilization were not successive states in the progress of the world. They were conditions that existed side by side, as they still exist side by side."[121] I believe Chesterton was right: the world is broken.

The Origin of Brokenness

Given what is apparently an innate knowledge of God (the IICP) and our apparent brokenness and separation from such a God, I am led to conclude that we were once close to this entity. This separation may in fact be at the root of disbelief in God for some: if we are not close enough to sense God, God must not exist. Such a conclusion may be misled. Perhaps if we are not close enough to sense such a God, there is a separation.

I believe something catastrophic happened somewhere in our past. Even if we completely ignore religious texts, we come face-to-face with that something through streams of logic. What was it? Perhaps our ability to ask such questions holds the answer: we are free entities.

We are clearly beings that choose. I established earlier that we have no unbroken attributes that the IICP does not have. I believe the IICP gave us what he

---

[119] O'Murchu, *Quantum Theology: Spiritual Implications of the New Physics*, 114.
[120] Chesterton, *The Everlasting Man*, 53.
[121] Ibid., 62.

has: the freedom to follow the IICP. We have that freedom. It is a gift. What is more, I believe we as a human race did in fact choose to follow that example to the core: we chose to follow ourselves alone as though we were God. We replaced the IICP with the *god within*. The irony is that only God can do both: follow himself by recognizing his own sovereignty and dwell within himself. It was in error that we, given the same choice, chose to follow ourselves.

According to the Biblical record there were more than Adam and Eve present on earth at the time of what I call the *Great Rebellion*.[122] The Great Rebellion affected everyone. Brokenness may have entered by one person, one group, or the whole human race, but it took down our entire existence and separated us from God just the same. No more walks in the park. As you will see in Phase 3, I believe the ramifications of this deviation have impacted the very dimensions we exist in. They may have even impacted evolution.

I believe evolution, driven by the IICP, was a very elegant process. But I also believe it too is now broken. I believe natural selection is broken as a result of the Great Rebellion. Sure, it continues in a small fashion, producing moths of different colors, along with other adaptations, but these are but *faint reflections* of what natural selection was in its grandeur. It is possible that survival of the fittest may *not* have been the mantra of the evolutionary process for millions and millions of years. Now, however, we *are* left with a dog-eat-dog brokenness.

If God knew we would choose our own way, why give us such freedom? C.S. Lewis explained in *Mere Christianity* that not only does freewill make evil possible, but it also enables us to know love, goodness, and joy.[123] Evil is the result of any entity choosing to become less than they were meant to be. We chose such a state.

We were formed in the likeness of the IICP. This *driver* who led us through our formation left its mark on us. The most ironic mistake some theorists and philosophers make is to assume that *we are God*. That was the assumption that got us in the fix we are in! We are no more *God* than there is the absence of dysfunction in the world! No, we are not God, but do we have his signature. As broken as we are, we have his imprint on us.

---

[122] Genesis 4:8-16.
[123] Lewis, *Mere Christianity*, 48.

Warped Slices

We possess slices of God. If we did not we would have no idea what slices of God are. This *God slice* may be no more than the knowledge of God. It may even be *goodness* within us, waiting for the right moment to emerge. It is in character with the strangeness of the cosmos that we were created in the IICP's image, which includes the ability to go our own way. That is both a beautiful and a dreadful gift. Ironically, part of that image includes the right to reject that image.[124]

We reject the image when we choose to follow ourselves and not God. If we had continued following God we could have done both, because following God is also following ourselves following God, which is what God does. He perfectly follows God by following himself. When we follow God, we follow ourselves following God. The mistake we made was following ourselves following ourselves. To have perfectly stayed in his image we would have perfectly followed ourselves following God and perfectly followed God by following ourselves following God. We were intended to live in God's image.

Perpetuating the Problem

We perpetuate our brokenness via sin. Eckhart Tolle provides a clear understanding of sin in *A New Earth*, "Sin is a word that has been greatly misunderstood and misinterpreted. Literally translated from the ancient Greek in which the New Testament was written, to sin means to miss the mark, as an archer who misses the target, so to sin means to miss the point of human existence."[125]

I believe there are several ways we miss the mark. The first was initiated when humans decided to advance themselves on their own terms. We do so still. It is a place as much as it is a condition; it is a location of brokenness. It is not an intermediate stage in an evolutionary process leading to a greater place. It was a *backward evolutionary move* on our part, one away from the *driver* who was leading us forward. In this light sin is our condition; we are in a broken state. We missed the mark when we decided to walk away from the target.

[124] For the record, I also believe all of creation, the whole cosmos, bears God's image, his signature. It will become clearer how the whole cosmos is struggling with the effects of human choices. It bears God's image nonetheless.
[125] Tolle, *A New Earth: Awakening to Your Life's Purpose*, 9.

In a second sense, sin is comprised of the things that hinder us from being all that we can be. To this end, Eckhart Tolle and other self-improvement theorists provide clear and helpful methods of getting out of depths of failure and moving on to be all that we can be. Such self-improvement efforts can be quite effective in spurring us on to become better people. We need such helpful advice, encouraging us in our journey. But there is more to the story.

In the final sense, such efforts on our part do nothing to translate us from the broken world we live in (that narrow line we ended up on) back onto the plane of God's original intent. Eugene Peterson implies in his book *Leap Over A Wall* that the more we attempt to fix ourselves, the less we become who we were intended to be.[126] Mathematically, such attempts leave us where we began: still in a broken world, infinitely removed from the IICP.

In this latter sense, sin may simply be *attempting restoration on our own terms*; not the self-improvement efforts referred to earlier, but restoration from the line to the plane. We lost a major part of what we were. Now we lust after things that we think will complete us, restore us, and put us back into the state we were intended to be in. But, still we do it on our own terms. The very things we do to overcome the problem only serve to hold us there. Sin is, in a sense, self-induced neuropathy. It is like drinking water that leaves us thirsty.[127] We can be better people, live successful lives, have wonderful families, be productive in work, and give back to society, yet still thirst.

We Need a New Paradigm

There are some theorists who insist that we need a new paradigm, yet also argue that we are not *broken* as such.[128] If we are not broken, why are we putting so much effort into becoming *all we can be* and *moving beyond our inadequacies*? Why does nature have a survival instinct? Why not simply step into the inevitable and die?

---

[126] Eugene H. Peterson, *Leap over a Wall: Earthly Spirituality for Everyday Christians* (New York: HarperCollins Publishers, 1997), 217-18.

[127] John 4:13.

[128] Eckhart Tolle in *A New Earth* and Richard Dawkins in *The God Delusion* argue that the world is evolving out of the limited state it is currently in. What some would call brokenness, they seem to think of as intermediate stages in a very elegant and continuous evolution. I simply believe it is broken.

Yet we instinctively fight death and pursue life. Many still look for the *fountain of youth*. We do not want to die; we fight to survive. We prolong facing the unknown, or even the known. To me these are evidences that we long for something beyond this narrow line we call *existence*.

We need a new paradigm. Religion alone is not leading us there. Religion is part of the problem.[129] We need more than manmade efforts to solve the brokenness of our world. What is more, we are not going to evolve our way out of this conundrum. The very fact that we humans imagine a world without pain and evil is an indication we miss what once was. John Lennon's song *Imagine* was not a dream: it was a memory. Martin Luther King, Jr.'s dream was also such a memory. Mahatma Gandhi saw visions of this past. These memories call us to a new paradigm, one strangely old and familiar, with traces woven into the fabric of the cosmos.

I believe most of what humans do is aimed at restoration. From acquiring material things, to seeking pleasure, to publishing self-help books, and exploiting each other: all are aimed at self-restoration. We live our lives obsessed with finding the missing pieces. Most efforts are ineffective. Some are counterproductive. They may address little bits of pieces that are missing, but not the hole in our souls. We so desperately want to be completely restored. Instead, in our pursuits of restoration, we are sidetracked by our own efforts. We are our own worst enemies. We need a new paradigm, something that goes beyond the limits of evolution and efforts to restore ourselves. We are broken.

---

[129] If you are looking for a fuller explanation of this claim, it is the subject of the next chapter.

2.09

Religion

Religion is an expression of the brokenness of humanity. It is an effort to move beyond our brokenness. The problem is, however, the more we try to restore ourselves and move beyond the brokenness, the more broken we behave. We believe that our efforts are pure and right, yet exemplify through our fruits that we are still as broken as when we set out to fix ourselves. Is it due to our finiteness that we fail so miserably?

On the flip side, it is an error to assume that finite beings cannot please an infinite God. We are a subset of his existence; an existence he created. Why would he not take pleasure in this subset? Surely this infinite God longs for our restoration. Yet one way or another we end up getting in the way of such restoration.

At The Root of Religion

Religion is the natural outcome of human tendency to either deny or defy the infinitude of God. This denial may be willful or subconscious, but it is denial nonetheless. In a sense it is an organized rebuttal of God's eternal essence. It is a limited human measure, an illusion of having a grasp on the infinitude of God. It is a *form* or *structure* without power to transform.

There are at least three ways we deny the infinitude of God. One is to argue that God changes over time. If there are characteristics that God now has that he did not previously have, then he was not then, nor is he now, infinite. The second way is to argue that our understanding of God is complete. This puts us on an equal level with God. In this paradigm since we are not infinite, neither is God. The third way is to argue that our understanding of God cannot increase. We cannot know more than we do now. This claim denies the infinitude of God by rendering God incapable of communicating and teaching us more than we already know.

In summary, the first method, *process theology*, argues that God changes, our knowledge of God is not complete, and that we can learn more about God. The second, *complete theology*, argues that God does not change, our knowledge of God is complete, and that we cannot learn more about God. The last, *agnostic theology*, takes no stance on God's immutability, claiming that our knowledge of God is incomplete, and that we cannot learn more about God. All three perspectives deny the infinitude of God. A fourth option, which I refer to as *progressive theology*, argues that God does not change, our knowledge of God is not complete, and that we can learn more about God. We will return to the concept of progressive theology later on.

Atheism

Let us state the aforementioned definition of religion once again: religion is the natural outcome of human tendency to either deny or defy the infinitude of God. In this light, atheism is very religious. It suffers from the same limitations as the rest of the religious world. In some cases it can be just as fundamentalistic and extremist as theistic religions. In the case of some prominent atheists, it is even evangelistic. Kurt Gödel has shown us that the more we try to avoid an incomplete or inconsistent system, the closer we come to being part of such an incomplete or inconsistent system. So it is with atheism. It is, in the end, another finite religion. It too is under the delusion that it is not a finite religion.

Religion: Foreshadows of Transformation

There is another way to view religion. I believe religions are foreshadows of ultimate transformation, knowledge, and relationship with God. Most are misrepresentations of the infinitude of God, but their significance lies in the foreshadowing of transformation. Religion is humankind's attempt to know and get right with God. Redemptive transformation, on the other hand, is God's solution: building a relationship with humankind and making us right with him.

Simply ridding ourselves of religion only yields another religion. The process of destroying idols can quickly become a new idol. Arguments that *failed religions* are proof of the non-existence of God are as weak as arguing that there is no such thing as parents because the children are misbehaving. Arguably there has to be more. Why would we yearn for transformation if it were not possible?

Religion, when understood as foreshadowing ultimate transformation, is quite another story. God speaks and relates to religious peoples precisely because he understands our finitude. In infinite grace God speaks to us. *God wants a relationship with us more than we will ever want one with him.* He can and does answer the prayers of religion in spite of religion. That is the most profound thing of all: *God, even though hindered by religion, uses religion to relate to us nonetheless.* He uses religion in spite of religion. What a strange existence. What a strange God!

2.10

A Godly Intervention

Human efforts at self-restoration can in fact improve our day-to-day functions; they may even improve our lives to the point of impacting others in a positive way. However, nothing we do to restore ourselves can move off the line and any closer to living on the plane we once had access to. In fact, our attempts to do the latter only make things worse: they result in religion. We need a Godly intervention.

Messianic Themes

Mythologies, including Greek, Judaic, Eastern Religious, & Native American mythologies, are filled with deities taking on the form of human flesh. As I have discussed before, mythology is fundamentally built on either real human experiences and/or innate knowledge. We innately realize not only that deities can take on human form, but also that it must be done for the restoration of humankind. If there were no such need, these myths would not abound. Some interpret the volume of messianic myths from diverse cultures and various eras as proof it is not a viable option. I believe the volume of such myths only confirms this messianic need. The probability is too great to ignore: an ultimate reality drives such beliefs.

Humans have an instinctive need for God-incarnate, or God-become-flesh. Millennia of manmade idols confirm that we need something finite we can wrap our arms around, understand, and pray to. We cannot see the IICP, so either it is not there, or it is infinitely inaccessible. However, I have shown that it is *there*. But where is *there*? Since it is not easily accessible in our domain, it must be at infinity.

We need a go-between, one to span infinity for us: we need a God-become-flesh, a *GBF*.

Restoration can only come from infinitude: from God himself. It is beyond anything we can accomplish of our own doing. On human terms it is preposterous to think of God becoming flesh in order to restore humankind. Yet it is humanly impossible to transverse the infinite chasm to reach God. Only the infinite, the IICP, can accomplish this task. The only way to get close to and know the *infinite extension of ourselves* is for this perfection to come to us.

It is also important to consider God's reasons to become a GBF. Karl Barth wrote, "So great is the ruin of the creature that less than the self-surrender of God would not suffice for its rescue."[130] But why would God step into our world? Perhaps the question is backwards. Why would he *not* step into our world, why *not* become a GBF? I believe that God, being infinite, desires our restoration more than we will ever want to be restored. This love drives the GBF.

We are so limited by the finite, yet need the finite. We need a finite representation of God. Our idolatrous tendencies demonstrate this need. Questioning the need for a GBF is in a strange way a confirmation of that need. We need God to become flesh precisely because we are so broken that we do not see the need ourselves. It is precisely because we cannot wrap our heads around infinity that we need infinity to wrap itself around us in the form of a GBF. If the infinite is truly indescribable and beyond words, then we need flesh we can wrap our heads around: we need a closure, a Godly closure.

Redemption

What is the price of such a GBF? Though not arguing for a GBF, it is intriguing that the Koran refers to being *bought* back by God.[131] *Bought* implies a price. What would God pay for our restoration? What would it cost him? How would such a transaction take place? Who would *receive* the payment?

Throughout nature the theme of salvation can be seen. A Killdeer plays lame, moving away from its nest, to save its young, risking its own life. A lioness goes to

---

[130] Barth, *Dogmatics in Outline*, 116.
[131] The Koran as translated by John Medows Rodwell, *The Koran* (New York: Bantam Books, 2004), IX:112.

battle to save the pride. Swat teams lay down their lives to redeem a hostage. The firefighters on 9/11 paid the ultimate price. Why give up our lives for the sake of others? Only one answer suffices: instilled in us is the drive to save people. This comes from the ultimate drive to save: the IICP.

There is no doubt that we need the IICP to accomplish redemption. C.S. Lewis wrote in *Mere Christianity*, "But unfortunately we now need God's help in order to do something which God, in His own nature, never does at all—to surrender, to suffer, to submit, to die." [132] This observation is quite consistent with the strangeness of the cosmos. But, why suffer and die?

Some theologies insist that a worthy offering must be made to appease God's wrath for the brokenness of the world. Some forms of this penal substitutionary atonement theology are only a few hundred years old and have more recently come into question. It is my belief that cause and effect were confused in the formation of substitutionary doctrine. While blood being shed may be an outcome of such restoration, it most likely is not the primary objective. In cases such as this we too easily assume pertinent scriptures are *prescriptive* rather than *descriptive*. For instance, there are Biblical references to the GBF that mention suffering, bloodshed, and dying. [133] However, such passages are quite descriptive, not prescriptions of a bloodthirsty God. Such bloodthirstiness does not match infinitude, for infinitude has no such need.

Rather than viewing the Old Testament sacrificial traditions as efforts to appease God, I believe they were *foreshadowing acts* of the natural cost of the redemptive mission of the GBF. They were not for forgiveness, for there are plenty of examples in the Old Testament where forgiveness was granted because of contrite hearts, not sacrifice. The best example is in the Psalms where David cried, "My sacrifice, O God, is a broken spirit; a broken and contrite heart you, God, will not despise." [134] The infinite GBF will ultimately suffer and die in the process of rescuing humanity. How and why such suffering will take place will be addressed more fully in Phase 3. Suffice it to say for now that death is strangely a prerequisite to life.

---

[132] Lewis, *Mere Christianity*, 57-58.
[133] Isaiah 53.
[134] Psalm 51:17.

For the sake of discussion, if one were to assume for a moment that Jesus of Nazareth was that GBF (we will come back to this in a later chapter), he described himself as the *Good Shepherd*. In one of his parables he talked about a shepherd leaving ninety-nine sheep that were safely in their stalls and going out into the night to rescue one lost sheep.[135] *This* is the redemption and restoration that the GBF offers. It is not a bloodthirsty redemption, though the shepherd very likely scraped his shins on the rocks and tore his flesh on briars in an effort to rescue the sheep. I clearly do not believe in a *somebody-has-to-pay* doctrine, but rather one wherein the shepherd rescues at any cost: an infinite shin scraping. Blood is a consequence of such restorative love, not a prerequisite.

The latter kind of redemption is motivated by grace. I must admit that the strangest concept of all is grace. By its very existence it is strange, for it defies all human logic. Why go out of the way to rescue and restore beings that chose to go their own way? Humans tend to treat each other *in-kind*, doing to others as they have done to us. God, however, in grace, acts *out–of–kind* or contrary to *in-kind*. The irony is we are so utterly dependent on grace that even our need for grace is revealed to us by grace.

One Will Do

We need a GBF, a redeemer, regardless of culture, religion, and time. Multiple redemptions negate the infinitude and effectiveness of any of those redemptive efforts: they imply incompleteness. To need redemptive missions for multiple periods of time implies the inability of the infinite to traverse time in any direction except forward. Time is *our* handicap, not the IICP's. Anything less than one complete redemption is less than infinite. There have been many messiah types over the centuries that were less than infinite. We are in need of an infinite solution. Infinitude is singular.

We cannot limit the way in which God chooses to reveal the GBF. It is his purpose, his choice, his time, his place, and his means to rescue humankind. It is most certainly *not* prescribed by manmade religions. The entity must be one, or it is not infinite. Just as the myths of a worldwide deluge abound around the world,

---

[135] Luke 15:4.

so do myths of the GBF. But whether local or global, there was one deluge. So it is with the GBF. Myths do not numerous infinities make!

How Much of God Do We Need?

The solution's origin makes it infinite, not its size. Using the plane-line analogy again, if it comes from God's domain (the plane) and confines itself to our limited line, it is an infinite solution. In a very real sense, God, being infinite, is already here, though not in the flesh. We need him to become a GBF. Only infinitude can infinitely and perfectly subject part of itself to finitude.

Rest Your Doubts

I acknowledge that some may doubt the processes leading to my conviction that we need a GBF, attaching my logic and its outcome to subconscious remnants emerging from my Christian upbringing. While I acknowledge that it is impossible for anyone to completely empty themselves of the imprints of their upbringing, I am not content with such a source of doubt for several reasons. First of all, such questioning inadvertently implies that all belief systems, no matter what processes were employed to derive them, were simply inherited, thereby minimizing the intellectual integrity that brought each person to their worldview. I know atheists who arrived at their positions with the utmost integrity, and some who arrived at their positions out of reaction and hurt. I also know many religious individuals who have not changed at all from fear of moving outside the bounds of the aforementioned imprints.

Secondly, the fact that similarities between my upbringing and this current iteration exist does not imply that the process lacks integrity. Some individuals make a total change in worldview via processes of integrity while others do so out of compromise, concession, and reaction. Total change does not prove that the process was one of integrity. The fact that I fully resigned my theology as a starting point and that numerous foundational principles are gone for good is proof that the process was one of integrity.

Thirdly, there are others, such as G.K. Chesterton, who started out from positions of total contrast, went through similar strange analyses, albeit not mathematical, and ended up with the same conclusion as I: we need a strange GBF. Chesterton was a self-proclaimed atheist by sixteen years of age. His change was clearly one that resulted from an intellectual process with integrity, not from remnants of his upbringing.

In Closing

I am convinced of the GBF's role in the restoration of human kind and of our innate knowledge that such restoration has its price. It is a mathematical necessity. We are broken, so broken. Natural selection is broken. We cannot depend on it to bring us out of the depths of our dysfunction. We need a solution—an infinite one. A proxy will not do. We need God himself to accomplish such a restoration.

Thomas Merton, in *The Seven Storey Mountain*, said, "What is 'grace?' It is God's own life, shared by us."[136] God wants to gift such grace to the world. We complicate things through efforts to accomplish such restoration on our own. God offers us grace simply because it is grace. It is grace that comes in the form of a GBF. Less is more, my friend. We need less religion and more grace. Such an incarnation of grace makes God conceivable, searchable, and tangible.

---

[136] Merton, *The Seven Storey Mountain*, 186.

2.11

Iterations of Truth

Even if we agree that there is an IICP, that the world is broken, and that we need a GBF to restore it, how do we filter through the volumes of available data, hoping to arrive at some semblance of truth to hold on to for our journey? How do we sort through all the religions of the world and their sacred writings, knowing that some insist their texts are the only inspired words of God? I believe an iterative process will be helpful for the task at hand.

In mathematics and engineering, some problems do not have *closed-form solutions*. Closed-form solutions are equations that render a single, definitive answer from the variables inserted into the equation. Plug the numbers in; get the answer out. There are, however, some problems that require iterative equations. In such cases a variable is plugged into an equation that renders an *approximate* value. That answer may be repeatedly plugged back into the same equation to give a more refined answer. Eventually the answer approaches a steady value. Such equations may be referred to as *open-form solutions*.

My first exposure to the iterative process was as a child, though I did not yet know it was labeled as such. I had read that Leonardo Da Vinci was the first known human to have freehandedly drawn a perfect circle. I remember thinking to myself, "I can do that!" So I tried. I tried and tried and tried to no avail. It was clear that the task was beyond my prideful certainty. All of a sudden an idea occurred to me. Though it would not be as authentic as Da Vinci's circle, I decided to draw over one of my previous attempts with another circle, filling in the dips and taking away from the bulges. Each time I drew over the previous circles the composite grew more and more like a true circle. My final version was quite good, at least for the standards of a child. Little did I know that I was participating in an *iterative process*.

Now, many years later, I realize that no one can draw a perfect circle for several reasons. Even Da Vinci's circle, if examined under a microscope, would reveal irregularities in the ink and paper. What is more, a true circle has neither beginning nor end. By using an iterative process we can reach an approximation that will be close to a true circle. An infinite number of iterations will yield a circle without a traceable beginning or end. We, however, must put up with approximations.

Assuming the iterative circle that I drew as a child was a good approximation of a circle, it most certainly had a broad fringe and a much smaller core than Da Vinci's. In the following figure you can see that the iterative process yielded such a broad fringe (Figure 13). This is sometimes a consequence of the iterative process. Yet we need not shy away from the loss of core, for it may be the best approximation at which we can arrive.

Figure 13. Iterations Of Truth

The iterative process is important for establishing reasonable approximations of truth. While I acknowledge that not everyone is comfortable with an *approximation of truth*, I am afraid it is all we have to work with. Even if the GBF *is* the truth, and assuming we know who it is or was, we are still left with iterations of the events and words of the GBF that must be processed to understand.

Agreement & Contradiction

The iterative process implies that there are differences or contradictions, whether minor or major, in our sources of truth. If it were not the case, there would be much less involved in *working out our salvation*, at least in terms of theology.[137] A perfect circle of truth is too convenient and prompts more questions and doubt than diverse accounts with unique perspectives. Because we see things *incompletely* we must iterate to resolve truth. In the following illustration we see such iterations of truth. Where the circles cross each other agreement is found. Where they diverge (one bulging out and another dipping to the interior) disagreement and contradiction exists (Figure 14). Each circle, as well as the composite, is both incomplete and inconsistent.

Iterative witnesses do not yield perfectly matching accounts. Given our human nature, there will be variations in all accounts. The accounts may overlap, yet ebb and flow with differences. This is troublesome to many who need perfect truth. However, Gödelian principles demand that it be otherwise. For instance, look at the synoptic gospels and the book of John, the first four books of the New Testament. They do not match perfectly. Matthew seems to need many Old Testament references to validate his writings. Mark reminds me of the old Dragnet TV series where Sergeant Joe Friday frequently said, "Just the facts, ma'am." Luke, the scientist, made sure all of his sources and references were in order. John was the hippy: *Can't you feel the love?*

---

[137] Philippians 2:12.

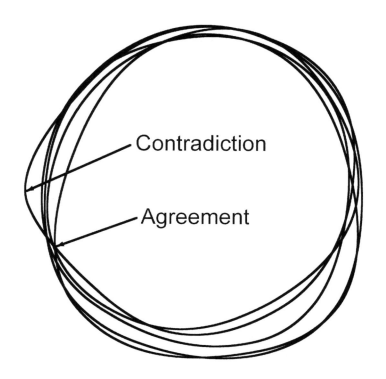

Figure 14. Iterations Of Truth

Differences, and even contradictions, do not take away from the validity of the four previously mentioned texts. Lee Strobel says in his commentaries on the four gospels in *The Case for Christ: A Journalist's Personal Investigation of the Evidence for Jesus*, "There is enough of a discrepancy to show that there could have been no previous concert among them; and at the same time such substantial agreement as to show that they all were independent narrators of the same great transaction."[138] Frankly, I would be more suspicious of the accounts if there were no differences or originality. The individuality of the events gives witness to freethinking observers, each providing their perspective on what was important to them. Composite interpretations are more accurate than any one interpretation by itself.

---

[138] Lee Strobel, *The Case for Christ: A Journalist's Personal Investigation of the Evidence for Jesus* (Grand Rapids: Zondervan, 1998), 48.

Multiplicity of Sources

Multiplicity of sources as a phrase carries a couple of connotations. For Biblical scholars it refers to the number and extensiveness of ancient manuscripts that corroborate the content of the books included in the Canon, or what is called the Bible. Lee Strobel, who had numerous interviews with scholars regarding multiplicity of sources, records in *The Case for Christ*, "In all, there are about 24,000 manuscripts in existence. There is no body of ancient literature in the world which enjoys such a wealth of good textual attestation as the New Testament."[139] This *multiplicity of sources* is an overwhelming and unprecedented number of iterations.

However, *multiplicity of sources* has come to mean more to me than the iterations of Biblical manuscripts alone. While this may be disconcerting for those espousing *sola scriptura*, or Biblical scripture alone, I encourage you to consider it carefully. I believe it is arrogant, and *scripturally* unfounded, for humans to draw detailed lines between what is and what is not scripture. How can any of us prescribe what God has or has not communicated through diverse peoples throughout history, people who faithfully passed down these concepts either through the written word or oral tradition? It is unfathomable to think that the IICP would not communicate thus. The question is: how do we handle or reconcile such diverse lines of communication?

One approach is to focus on the core of the iterations. The two previous illustrations were intended to show perspectives that are broader than one's preferred source(s) alone, whether the Bible, the Koran, The Book of Mormon, or the writings of Buddhists, Hindus, Native Americans, etc. These figures were intended to include *all* of these iterations. Such iterations of truth have a significant center of mass within the overlapping iterations. Granted, some of the iterations wander far from the core, but they still contribute to the core. There is great strength with such a center of mass. I must point out that the 60-plus books in the Bible authored by 40-plus writers, compared to single-author writings, shift the center of mass significantly. For this reason, I rely on these witnesses more

---

[139] Ibid., 63.

extensively throughout this book. Though I quote single author sacred writings, I have a higher degree of confidence in iterative sources.

Jesus acknowledged this core, summing the *entire* law and prophets in two commandments: "'Love the Lord your God with all your heart and with all your soul and with all your strength and with all your mind,' and, 'Love your neighbor as yourself.'"[140] Can a simpler core be derived for the way we are to live?

Iterative Theology

Through the millennia most theologies have mutated, some being abandoned, others evolving as new understandings have emerged. Some of these changes have been responses to pressure from society and government. Others have sprung from special revelations experienced by influential persons. The common denominator in all of them is change. Change comes to all theologies; it is as sure as the sun rises. One could claim to hold a theology that is as solid as a rock, quoting references that are 500 or even 2,000 years old, but even 2,000 years is quite young and represents change.

Right out of high school, I attended a small Bible institute for the sole purpose of intense Biblical and theological study. I came from a moderate to liberal setting. In order to attend, I had to cut my hair, give up my rock music, and be in the dorm by 9:00 PM each night. The theology and practices were quite conservative. I remember questioning some of the legalistic principles that were held to so rigidly. In spite of such questioning, my experience was delightful, allowing me to develop a broader understanding of other theologies and establish friends for life.

What intrigues me now is that 40 years later the theology and practices held by that institute are more liberal. Why the change? Is the adjustment good or bad? Either way, it happens to all of us, from the staunch conservative to the loosest liberal. Why? Are we so weak as to perpetually give in to the forces that prompt change? I think not. Adaptation and accommodation are necessary functions in our lives and theologies.

Our journey involves an iterative path. The iterative path is more than a part of the journey—it is the journey. It is a path aimed at greater and greater

---

[140] Luke 10:27.

understanding of the IICP. Obviously we will never arrive at complete understanding, for that would imply infinitude on our part. However, we must continuously move in that direction lest we grow static and die. This dynamic and expanding path is traversed by individuals and by generations over millennia (Figure 15). We must not be so misled as to believe ourselves faster or further ahead than other people. Location on the iterative path is not the goal. I could point fingers at the aforementioned conservative institute I attended, saying, "See, you finally came around," but doing so only condemns the position I held as an incoming freshman, which is now part of my past iterations. Such bantering is futile. The point is that we are iterating and expanding our understanding.

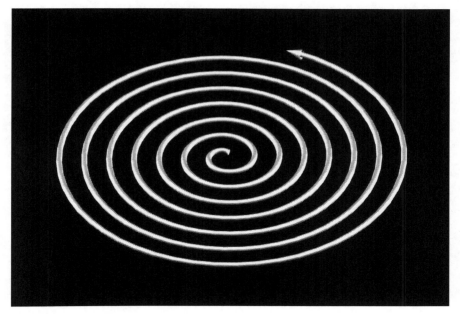

Figure 15. Iterative Theology

By embracing iterative theology I am not implying that the *special revelations* we have been given are insufficient. Rather, our static analyses of these revelations are insufficient; they are insufficient precisely because they are static. We tend to stake our ground and deceive ourselves into believing that we have arrived at our destination. Such theology has arrived at a static point (Figure 16). The paths between static points may be seen as reformations, leading to subsequent static points.

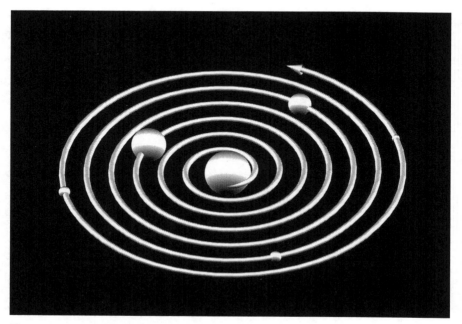

Figure 16. Iterative Theology With Static Points

Does God Iterate?

The question must be asked: "Does God iterate?" John Cobb, a preeminent scholar on process theology, has said, "To be an actual entity, God cannot only act on the world. God must also be acted on. That is, while the occasions of the world feel God, God also feels them . . . Meanwhile God incorporates all that happens in the world into God's own life."[141] Though I do not endorse an evolving God, I do believe God is affected by us. Unlike non-interventionists, I believe God iterates with respect to our needs and prayers. However, with respect to himself, God *is* the eternal and infinite iteration. For finite beings, iteration implies refinement.

---

[141] Jr. John B. Cobb, "Process Theology," http://processandfaith.org/writings/article/process-theology.

For an infinite being, an infinite iteration is a state of being. For God to identify himself as "I Am that I Am" is indicative of an infinite iterative existence.[142] God *is* the ultimate iteration.

In Closing

Albert Einstein once said, "Life is like riding a bicycle. If you want to stay up, you have to keep moving." We must keep iterating our theologies to stay upright. Stanley Hauerwas, in his book *With the Grain of the Universe*, said, "Just as you cannot tell any story 'all at once,' the story that is the story of God requires many tellings. Each telling remains the same story of the same God, but differently told."[143] It is our nature and call to iterate this story. And though God and we may be iterating in opposite directions (God toward finitude and we toward infinitude), we iterate nonetheless.

---

[142] Exodus 3:14; KJV.
[143] Stanley Hauerwas, *With the Grain of the Universe* (Grand Rapids: Brazos Press, 2002), 181.

2.12

Strange Loops: Type I

Iterations are loops. One of the wonderful things about *strange loops* is that there is no beginning or end. "Which came first?" becomes an irrelevant question. A strange loop is equivalent to an infinite number of beginnings and ends, overlapping to form a continuous circle. In the words of Douglas Hofstadter in *I Am a Strange Loop*, "In short, a strange loop is a paradoxical level–crossing feedback loop."[144] It is a loop that influences itself, providing its own input. Elsewhere Hofstadter says, "What else is a loop but a way of representing an endless process in a finite way?"[145] It sounds like the previous descriptions of the IICP.

I separate strange loops into two types. Type I is the self-referential loop, symbolized by a circle. Type II is a flat two-dimensional self-referential loop with a single twist, representing a perpetually negating loop, best symbolized by the *Mobius strip*.[146] The latter type will be the focus of the next chapter. For now we will focus on Type I, the self-referential loops with no beginning or end.

Self-Reference

Philosophy and logic typically avoid and/or reject self-reference. Criticizing the use of self-reference, Hilary Lawson says in *Closure*, "It is a flaw that I shall maintain cannot be obviated and which can be briefly expressed: a complete and true account of the universe is not possible because if it is complete it will be self-

---

[144] Hofstadter, *I Am a Strange Loop*, 102.
[145] *Gödel, Escher, Bach: An Eternal Golden Braid*, 15.
[146] The Type I and Type II designations are not established in the literature. They were developed herein simply to differentiate between the two types. Some, such as Hofstadter, simply refer to both as strange loops.

referential, and if it is self-referential it cannot also be true."[147] As opposed to Hofstadter, Lawson has strong objections to all self-referential thoughts and processes. On the other hand, Kurt Gödel made it clear that self-referential logic is not only impossible to avoid, but that it is a strength, rather than a weakness.[148] Strangely, as we shall see, all such arguments employed to refute self-referential arguments are in and of themselves self-referential.

For instance, if my own logic, which is indeed fed by my perception of what is and is not true evidence, decides that anything contradictory to that perception lies outside the realm of the logical, then what lies outside defines what lies within and what lies within defines what lies without. The argument against self-referential arguments not only uses a self-referential argument, but also relies on it for its very existence. Test yourself by asking yourself, "How do I know that I think?" If you answer that question, then you just used self-referential logic. You just used yourself to answer yourself. The argument against self-reference uses self-reference to prove its own falsehood. Self-referential logic is ultimately unavoidable and is an essential part of the fabric of our strange universe. We are self-referential beings in a self-referential cosmos brought into existence by a self-referential IICP.

Strange Loops in Nature

Nature is full of cyclic processes. Walking is one such loop. The phases of walking, from heel strike, to mid-stance, to toe-off, to mid-swing, and to the next heel strike are repeated to reach the desired destination. Each phase feeds off of the previous phase in momentum and direction. Obviously one has to begin walking to enter the loop. Some of the research I have been a part of has shown that walking is initiated by letting go: turning off the foot extensor muscles and falling into forward motion. This is followed by the first foot-off, flowing into swing and beginning the loop.

The water cycle is another such strange loop. One cannot trace the starting point of its cycle. Is it to be found in evaporation? In precipitation? There is no

---

[147] Lawson, *Closure: A Story of Everything*, xxix.
[148] Hofstadter, *Gödel, Escher, Bach: An Eternal Golden Braid*, 5.

beginning or end. It flows endlessly. Variations occur, leaving some regions in drought, but globally, the loop continues. Obviously, we rely on strange loops like this to survive.

One religious text says, "What has been will be again, what has been done will be done again; there is nothing new under the sun. Is there anything of which one can say, 'Look! This is something new'? It was here already, long ago; it was here before our time."[149] We may think we are ingenious, but time will show that while our presentations may vary, the underlying principles have been around forever.

The Ultimate Strange Loop

It is precisely because humans are strange loops that I am convinced that our causality, the IICP, is a strange loop. Remember, we can have no properties that the IICP does not have. In the interaction between God and Moses as recorded in the book of Exodus, Moses inquired of the name of the voice he heard. God replied, "I Am that I Am."[150] I believe God was declaring purpose in his name, "I am so that I would be the one that is so that I would be the one that is so that I would be the one that is . . ." Perhaps God could just as easily have said to Moses, "Tell them that the *infinite strange loop* sent you."

M.C. Escher expressed this concept in his 1948 *Drawing Hands* sketch. It is a powerful illustration of purpose (Figure 17). God is the reason God *is*. It is self-explanatory; it is self-referential. Scripture says, "I am the first and I am the last."[151] He is the ultimate complete strange loop. It is most logical that God *is* the proof of his self–existence. God is the reason God is the reason God is the reason . . . Much like Escher's sketch, the IICP gives himself permission to be.

---

149 Ecclesiastes 1:9-10.
150 Exodus 3:14, KJV.
151 Isaiah 44:6.

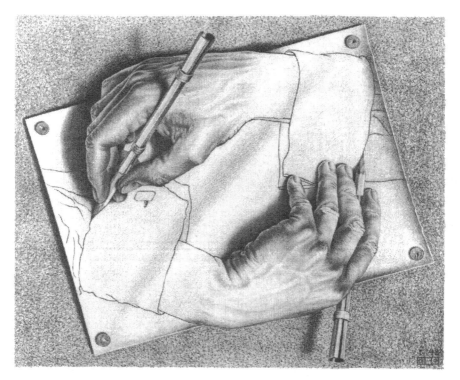

Figure 17. M.C. Escher's "Drawing Hands" Copyright 2014 The M.C. Escher Company - The Netherlands. All rights reserved.

The Self-Love Loop

Does God love himself? The loop would not be complete if there were not an infinite love of self. This is precisely what enables God to be infinitely selfless. One cannot be whole and selfless without true self-love: not arrogance, not selfishness, but secure self-love that frees one from pursuing fulfillment outside themselves. God is totally pleased with himself, totally contented to be who he is. This is true love. It is a freed love. This love is free to give without bounds. Divine self-love makes God complete.

The Mirror Loop

The *Golden Rule* tells us to do unto others as we would have them do unto us. It extends beyond relationships with other human beings to our ultimate relationship with God. God said through a prophet in scripture, "Those who honor me I will honor, but those who despise me will be disdained."[152] We live in a cosmos of reflections that loop back on themselves over and over, just like two mirrors facing each other. This can be both an advantage and a disadvantage. Our perspectives on God's characteristics are a reflection of our own characteristics. If we are faithful people, we will view God as faithful. If we are deceitful people, we will view God as deceitful.[153]

A strange version of the Golden Rule is as follows: *You cannot do to others what you do not do to yourself.* The implications are profound, especially with issues of hatred, cheating, stealing, etc. You cannot cheat anyone more than you cheat yourself. You cannot steal from anyone more than you steal from yourself. You cannot deceive anyone more than you deceive yourself. The same is true for positive actions as well. You cannot love anyone more than you love yourself. You cannot help anyone more than you help yourself. You cannot sacrifice for anyone more than you sacrifice for yourself. As you do to others, you ultimately do to yourself. Such are the mirror loops.

Our relationship with God is a mirror. Theologians get caught in debates concerning predestination vs. freewill, yet miss the strange loop scripture itself proclaims: "Come near to God and he will come near to you."[154] It is a dance in the mirror. My wife and I are married, not because I chose her, nor because she chose me. We are married because we chose each other. So it is with a relationship with God. As you move toward the mirror of God, God will move toward you. In the *Choosing Circle* illustration notice that both God and I are choosing each other because we are chosen (Figure 18).

---

[152] 1 Samuel 2:30.
[153] 2 Samuel 22:26-28.
[154] James 4:8.

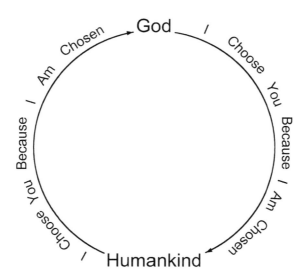

Figure 18. Choosing Circle

The Belief-Obedience Loop

Scripture tells us that if we do the will of God we will know him.[155] Dietrich Bonhoeffer said in *The Cost of Discipleship*, "Only he who believes is obedient, and only he who is obedient believes."[156] In a similar tone, Hans Denck, one of the early leaders of southern German Anabaptism once said, "No one can know Christ truly except he follow him daily; and no one can follow Christ daily except he know him truly."[157] Both Bonhoeffer and Denck understood the strange relationship between knowing and acting on that knowledge. Never will it be one without the other.

The Grace Loop

Grace is one of the strangest loops. It is grace because it is accepted. It is accepted because it is grace. It is through grace that we become aware of our need for grace. Grace opens the receptors to grace. Likewise, we cannot extend grace nor help anyone see their own need for grace until we are completely convinced of

---

[155] John 7:17.
[156] Dietrich Bonhoeffer, *The Cost of Discipleship* (New York: Touchstone / Simon & Schuster, 1995), 63.
[157] Edgework, "Finding God Abroad," http://www.edgework.ca/weeklyedgework94.html.

how much we need grace. Notice the present tense: how much we need grace, rather than *needed* grace. It is through grace that we recognize grace in others. The more grace flows through you to others, the more grace flows into your own life. Conversely, if we withhold grace from someone, we also withhold it from ourselves.

The Graciousness-Faithfulness Loop

One of God's own strange loops is found in the relationship between his faithfulness and his graciousness. God is graciously faithful and faithfully gracious. We can rest in his graciousness and faithfulness. Even if we live with an incomplete understanding of this strange duo, each is consistent with God's infinitude. In grace God extends his faithfulness to us, though it may not come to us on our terms. In faithfulness, God extends his grace to us without end.

God's faithfulness simply is. It is not given to us because we are faithful to him. The latter is a widespread misunderstanding. God is faithful to us because he is faithful to us. It cannot be our faithfulness that his faithfulness hinges upon, because our faithfulness is infinitely less than his. We are totally dependent on God's faithfulness. All we can do is latch onto God's strange loop.

The Repentance-Forgiveness Loop

I grew up believing that repentance was a prerequisite to forgiveness. Some, such as Brennan Manning, have proposed that repentance is a response to forgiveness.[158] While this is a refreshing perspective, I am inclined to believe they exist on a loop. One happens simultaneously with the other. Once again, it is a dance where the twilight of forgiveness coincides with the dawn of repentance. Furthermore, forgiving and being forgiven also exist on a strange loop. The *Lord's Prayer* says, "Forgive us our sins as we forgive those who sin against us."[159] The two happen at the same time.

---

[158] Manning, *The Ragamuffin Gospel.*
[159] Matthew 6:12 NLV.

The Prayer Loop

Prayer is perhaps the single most troubling concept for individuals who are struggling with belief in God. Some theorists, such as Marcus Borg, are convinced that God is a total non-interventionist due to the apparent fact that some prayers are answered while others are not. Such a stance is an all-or-none position.

I acknowledge that it is very tempting to offer simplified answers to the complicated questions surrounding prayer, and I do not wish to skim over the difficulties it presents. However, whether they are answered to our liking or not, I must ask, whose purpose is at the focus of our prayers? We live in a time when the *gospel of prosperity* is prevalent and the purpose of prayer is self-consumption. It is easy to put our purposes, our *will*, at the center. Many of us, including me, get sidetracked on a side loop of my prayer, my answer, and my will. Even if we decide to put God's purpose and will at the center of such prayers, they are clouded by our brokenness. Acknowledging that we have gotten off of God's prayer loop and onto our own will move us in the right direction.

The Futility Loop

Just as good qualities, such as self-love and grace, are on strange loops, so are negative qualities. Scripture says, "They followed worthless idols and became worthless themselves."[160] We perpetuate sin, evil, and worthless pursuits when we seek restoration through them. We become what we pursue. If we hate someone, our behavior toward them will become hateful. If we behave hatefully toward someone our hatred of them will grow. Evil perpetuates evil. Sin perpetuates sin. Futility perpetuates futility.

Jesus said, "For all who draw the sword will die by the sword."[161] This was not necessarily a statement delineating right from wrong, but an acknowledgement of the strange loop. Death begets death: it is its own cause and effect.

Another futile pair is arrogance and ignorance. They walk hand in hand. Ignorance fuels arrogance, convincing one that they own the truth. Arrogance

---

[160] Jeremiah 2:5.
[161] Matthew 26:52.

masks the truth, deceiving one into even greater ignorance. Even stranger is the tendency to be ignorant of our ignorance. I am still working on getting off this loop.

In Closing

I struggled for the first three years of college finding direction concerning vocation and associated studies. Ultimately, I realized that there was no particular vocation that I wanted to pursue. I realized that not only was I unsure what to do with my life, but that I did not want anything. I felt so inadequate. I was void of want, void of a drive. Then it dawned on me that I did want something after all. I wanted want. I wanted to want something. This was enough to start on the journey searching for want. It was enough to get me out of my numbness and on to seeking purpose.

If you find yourself on a downward spiral, falling into purposelessness, lacking motivation to turn around, one hope remains: God's infinite loop of grace and faithfulness is sufficient to lift each and every one of us up out of the futile loops we so easily fall into. King David once prayed and sang, "I waited patiently for the Lord; he turned to me and heard my cry. He lifted me out of the slimy pit, out of the mud and mire; he set my feet on a rock and gave me a firm place to stand. He put a new song in my mouth, a hymn of praise to our God. Many will see and fear the Lord and put their trust in him."[162] This is my prayer for each of us: that we may give up our futile loops and trust in God's loop.

---

[162] Psalm 40:1-3.

2.13

Strange Loops: Type II

The second type of strange loops has all the self-referential characteristics of Type I, but with an unexpected twist. Literally. First of all, Type II loops have an extra dimension. Instead of being 1-dimensional lines that curve back on themselves in a 2-dimensional plane, they are flat 2-dimensional strips that curve back on themselves in 3-dimensional space. These two-dimensional loops also have a single twist, which results in a single-sided 2-dimensional loop. This loop is called a *Mobius strip*. Discovered by August Ferdinand Mobius in 1858, the Mobius strip has conjured many a curious question and puzzlement. Mobius was a mathematician, physicist, and astronomer who had great interest in one-sided surfaces. The concept is counterintuitive to most of us, but not to a mathematician such as Mobius who specialized in geometrical anomalies. (Figure 19)

The Mobius strip is an infinite series of point-counterpoints, never to be on the same side, yet a part of the same loop. This antagonism is the essence of Type II loops. You think you are on one side, only to find out you are actually on the other! This antagonistic tension is not too different from the neurological processes that result in intelligence. Douglas Hofstadter, who specializes in artificial intelligence research, has said, "Strange Loops involving rules that change themselves . . . are at the core of intelligence."[163] Type II loops are such rule-changing entities.

---

[163] Hofstadter, *Gödel, Escher, Bach: An Eternal Golden Braid*, 27.

Figure 19. Oak Mobius Strip

Gödel's incompleteness theorem is consistent with Type II loops. (I do hope you caught the play on words there!) On one side of the loop you find *consistency and incompleteness* and on its adjacent side you find *completeness and inconsistency* (Figure 20). We will never find completeness and consistency on the same side of the loop! It may be that completeness and inconsistency move in a counter direction to incompleteness and consistency. In so doing completeness meets consistency, if only for a fleeting moment on the "far side" of the strip. Whether they meet or not, each becomes the other via a single trip around the loop.

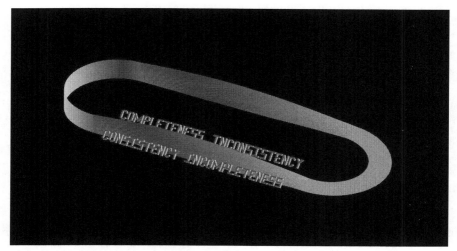

Figure 20. Gödel's Theorem: Strange Loop Type II

Inverse Dynamics

The phrase *inverse dynamics*, as used in bioengineering, describes the process whereby one progressively calculates internal forces in link-models, such as our lower extremities. Engineers start at the bottom with the foot on a force platform, where initial data is known, and work upward, or inversely to the ankle, then to the knee, and then to the hip. I use the phrase herein with a different connotation. Mathematically, *inverse* means dividing one, or unity, by a numerical value. For instance, if I want to calculate the inverse of 2, I divide 1 by 2 and the quotient, or answer, is 0.5. Conversely, if I want to calculate the inverse of 0.5, I divide 1 by 0.5 and the answer is 2. It is proper to say that 0.5 and 2 are inverses of each other. As one of the pair gets larger, the other gets smaller, and vice versa. For instance, 2,000 and 0.0005 are also inverses of each other. While some mathematicians prefer to define the inverse of zero as undefined, you have probably already noticed that herein I define it as infinity and vice versa. Zero and infinity are inverses of each other.

Adjacent sides on the Mobius strip are inverses of each other. Traversing the Mobius strip one revolution is dynamic because it requires movement. Combining the two concepts we derive the phrase *inverse dynamics.*

Strange loops Type II demonstrate inverse dynamics. They are upside down and inside out. This nature is again reminiscent of Kurt Gödel's incompleteness theorem, presenting itself in the form of consistent contradictions. The *Law of Non-Contradiction*, a golden standard in logic, declares that *A* and *Non-A* cannot be one and the same: they cannot be equivalent. Strange loops Type II turn this principle on its side. Some contradictory principles reside on the same Mobius strip precisely because they are inverses of each other. While we will develop this more fully in Phase 3, I must here point out that this law in some cases would be better defined as the *Law of Complementary Contradictions* (Figure 21). While in these cases *A* and *Non-A* may be inverses of each other, they reside on the same side of this strange one-sided strip. We will return to the Law of Non-Contradiction in Phase 3.

Figure 21. A & Non-A: Strange Loop Type II

The Beatitudes

Many great teachers in history have used inverse dynamics in their teachings. Jesus of Nazareth was no exception. He told his followers that to live one must die, to be first one must be last, and to be the greatest one must become the least. These inverse dynamics teachings are in keeping with the strangeness of the cosmos. They proclaim an upside down kingdom of God. In his most famous sermon, the *Sermon on the Mount*, Jesus proclaimed a series of such inverse principles known as the Beatitudes:

> Blessed are the poor in spirit, for theirs is the kingdom of heaven.
>
> Blessed are those who mourn, for they will be comforted.
>
> Blessed are the meek, for they will inherit the earth.
>
> Blessed are those who hunger and thirst for righteousness, for they will be filled.
>
> Blessed are the merciful, for they will be shown mercy.
>
> Blessed are the pure in heart, for they will see God.
>
> Blessed are the peacemakers, for they will be called children of God.
>
> Blessed are those who are persecuted because of righteousness, for theirs is the kingdom of heaven.[164]

Contrary to popular opinion, the kingdom of God is not for the spiritual superiors, the religious right, the fabulous fundamentalists, or the extreme evangelicals. It is for the inverse individuals: those who know they are nothing of their own making.[165]

---

[164] Matthew 5:3-10.
[165] 1 Corinthians 4:9ff.

Loving Enemies

These strange teachings of Jesus included a most difficult command: "Love your enemies and pray for those who persecute you."[166] This command is a difficult saying, especially in an age of rampant violence and terrorism. While one can ponder the eternal significance of obeying such a command, it is helpful to consider the temporal effects of hatred and revenge. The Dalai Lama says in his book *The Art of Happiness: A Handbook for Living*, "If we take revenge upon one's enemy, then it creates a kind of vicious cycle. If you retaliate, the other person is not going to accept that—he or she is going to retaliate against you, and then you will do the same, so it will go on." Such responses are often perpetuated across generations. Everyone suffers.[167] We must address hatred in an inverse fashion.

Dietrich Bonhoeffer, who knew firsthand what it was to be persecuted and put to death in a Nazi concentration camp during World War II, said in *The Cost Of Discipleship*, "The only way to overcome evil is to let it run itself into a standstill because it does not find the resistance it is looking for."[168] We are called to love enemies and do good to those who persecute or insult us in order to stop propagation. Only the inverse of hatred will stop hatred.

I am overwhelmed at the parallels between these teachings and the teachings of the Native Americans. The following prayer, as recorded in *The Gospel of the Redman: A Way of Life*, is overwhelming: "O Great Spirit of my fathers, this is my prayer. Help me to feel Thine urge and Thy message. Help me to be just even to those who hate me; and at all times help me to be kind. If mine enemy is weak and faltering, help me to the good thought that I forgive him. If he surrender, move me to help him as a weak and needy brother."[169] They taught and practiced the inverse of hatred.

Such love does not happen instantaneously. C.S. Lewis in *Mere Christianity* asserts that if we behave as though we love someone, even if we do not presently feel it, we will come to love them.[170] Love comes with practice. It is not an

---

[166] Matthew 5:44.
[167] His Holiness The Dalai Lama, *The Art of Happiness: A Handbook for Living* (New York: Riverhead Books, 1998), 177-78.
[168] Bonhoeffer, *The Cost of Discipleship*, 141.
[169] Seton, *The Gospel of the Redman: A Way of Life*, 19-20.
[170] Lewis, *Mere Christianity*, 131.

instantaneous gift. It is not defined by what we *do not do* in revenge, but by what we proactively do in love.

I have to wonder what would have happened following the destruction of the Twin Towers on 9/11 if the United States of America had demonstrated a genuine desire to understand the extreme hatred. What if we had responded with love and kindness by going to regions that needed hospitals and schools, helping to build infrastructure instead of tearing down? I do not pretend to know what would have been best, but I must ask the question.

Becoming Childlike

Children are innocent and pure. They naturally have no prejudices and are not close-minded, but are hungry to learn and absorb. Children are naturally open-minded.[171] If our childlike character is not nurtured it dies.[172] In cultures around the world, there is a heavy focus on growing up, so much so that the beauty of our childlike nature is quickly lost. Dallas Willard says in *The Divine Conspiracy*, "Interestingly, 'growing up' is largely a matter of learning to hide our spirit behind our face, eyes, and language so that we can evade and manage others to achieve what we want and avoid what we fear. By contrast, the child's face is a constant epiphany because it doesn't yet know how to do this. It cannot manage its face. This is also true of adults in moments of great feeling—which is one reason why feeling is both greatly treasured and greatly feared."[173]

Jesus revered and promoted childlike qualities. On one occasion during his ministry, Jesus' disciples came to him inquiring as to which of them would be the greatest in the kingdom of God. Jesus called a little child to him and said, "Truly I tell you, unless you change and become like little children, you will never enter the kingdom of heaven. Therefore, whoever takes the lowly position of this child is the greatest in the kingdom of heaven."[174] The irony is that in Jesus' day children were not important and not favored. The child symbolized the poor, the oppressed, the

---

[171] Manning, *The Ragamuffin Gospel*, 64.
[172] Ibid., 55.
[173] Dallas Willard, *The Divine Conspiracy* (New York: HarperCollins Publishers, 1997), 76.
[174] Mathew 18-1-4.

down-and-out, the least of these.[175] This is the upside-down nature of the kingdom of God: it is for those on the *far side* of the Mobius strip.

Wisdom & Ignorance

Wisdom and ignorance are another strange duo. When one is convinced of possessing one, they actually possess the other. They, too, reside on the Mobius. True wisdom is found in knowing how little one understands. One who has an appreciation for the vastness of the unknown is most wise. If we reach the point where we have nothing to learn from anyone, we have finally arrived at the place of greatest ignorance. To understand, one must become convinced that they cannot fully understand. It is strange that when we stop being know-it-alls, true learning begins to happen. One is misled to pursue all the areas in their life and personality wherein they are correct. The best pursuit is to seek the areas wherein one is wrong or misled. The least ignorant people in the world are the ones who are truly aware of how ignorant they are. Strange indeed!

Self-Fulfillment

Seeking self-fulfillment is futile, for the more we seek to fulfill ourselves, the emptier we become. The more we empty ourselves, the more full we become and the more direction we find. This is the way of it. C.S. Lewis said in *The Weight of Glory*, "By ceasing for a moment to consider my own wants I had begun to learn better what I really wanted."[176] By focusing on others one ultimately seeks their own good. By focusing only on one's self, ultimately everything will be lost. The Type II loop cries out, "Love your neighbor. Serve others." In so doing, you will ultimately care for yourself.

Pain & Suffering

In this section, I do not attempt to provide a complete or consistent assessment of pain and suffering in this world, nor am I trivializing them. Rather, I simply wish to point out the strange nature of pain and suffering. In the upside-down or inside-

---

[175] Manning, *The Ragamuffin Gospel*, 55.
[176] C.S. Lewis, "The Weight of Glory," *Theology / SPCK Publishing* 1941, 7.

out domain of God, suffering and pain can sometimes be strange gifts. Dr. Paul Brand explored the purpose and value of pain. I had just become familiar with his work, having read one of his manuscripts as part of my Master's thesis, when, much to my surprise, he showed up at church one Sunday morning in Seattle to give a special message. He told us of his years growing up in India as the son of missionaries, surrounded by people living in hardship and pain. Years later, after becoming a physician and returning to India, he took to researching leprosy. He was curious as to why leprosy caused such devastation, resulting in the loss of fingers, hands, and feet. Why did the disease lead to such disfigurement? One day he noticed a group of people cooking potatoes on sticks around a fire. One person's potato fell off their stick and into the fire. The individual turned and called to someone who had leprosy and asked for help. This individual came over, reached into the fire, and retrieved the potato. It was then that he discovered that the disfigurement so common in these patients was not due directly to leprosy but to the loss of pain sensation caused by the leprosy. These patients had lost the gift of pain.

This strange gift is one we so quickly run from. In *The Seven Storey Mountain* Thomas Merton argued that the more we attempt to escape suffering, the greater it becomes.[177] We become our own worst enemy by bringing on the very thing we attempt to escape. We become enveloped by what we fear. We may even become what we fear.

Suffering can serve to reinforce one's purpose. It tends to turn our focus steadily toward the essential and simplest components of life. It strengthens both joy and anger. For those with steadfast conviction and purpose, suffering sheds the temporal and the physical for the eternal and spiritual. It is the gateway between the two realms. The Type II loop ensures that pain will come round to joy eventually, even though it may not be until the next domain, but *joy will come*, for joy is on the flip side of the loop.

---

[177] Merton, *The Seven Storey Mountain*, 91.

Other Strange Pairs on the Loop

Tolerance-Intolerance is another strange pair that resides on the Type II loop. Tolerance advocates are not very tolerant of those who are intolerant of certain issues. Some intolerance groups are totally intolerant of anyone who rejects their intolerance. Few of us can tolerate those who proclaim stances against our tolerances or intolerances. Yet, both reside on the loop.

Religious-Nonreligious is another pair. Staunch atheists who aggressively refute the validity of religion can be quite religious in their aggression. Religious people can be oblivious to the compartmentalized nonreligious elements that lie outside their legalistic constraints. Most of us exhibit some of each.

Illogical Truths

"A man may love a paradox without either losing his wit or his honesty."[178] It is in paradoxes that we find the real essence of the cosmos. Parker Palmer in his book *Let Your Life Speak* asserts that our journeys are full of paradoxes.[179] He goes on to say that paradoxes are "at the heart of reality."[180] Paradoxes permeate our existence.

God chooses to relate to us in paradox when he places himself in our shoes by taking the form of the GBF (the God-become-flesh). Why would we expect to live in a paradox-free world if paradox is the essence of the IICP? I leave this topic with a quote from G.K. Chesterton from his book *Orthodoxy*. "Now, this is exactly the claim which I have since come to propound for Christianity. Not merely that it deduces logical truths, but that when it suddenly becomes illogical, it has found, so to speak, an illogical truth."[181]

God's DNA

It is here that I permit myself to digress into an imaginative interpretation of the nature of God. As I contemplate his attributes I cannot help but see the parallels with DNA. If we are made in the likeness of the infinite driver, the IICP,

---

[178] Ralph Waldo Emerson, 1841.
[179] Palmer, *Let Your Life Speak*, 70.
[180] Ibid., 99.
[181] Chesterton, *Orthodoxy*, 119.

would not God also have DNA, at least symbolically? If so, what would its structure be like? I know this assumes God has a physical nature, but imagine, the double helix strand of nucleic acids that Crick, Watson, & Wilkins discovered, but as a Type II strange loop (Figure 22). Aside from its creative wandering, the illustration communicates self-reference, essence, point-counterpoint, and completeness. I find great delight in pondering such a strange loop in the IICP.

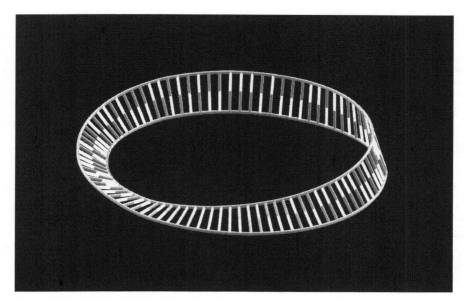

Figure 22. God's DNA: Strange Loop Type II

I cannot help but wonder what God will look like once we are finally privileged to see a representation of him. Might it be that we will come face to face with a child? It would be so in keeping with the nature of the cosmos to meet a small, rather than large, young, rather than old, simple, rather than complex, *Ancient of Days*. Selah!

In Closing

According to Type II strange loops, there must be opposing views of God. Gödel demonstrated as much in his incompleteness theorem. This is not to say that there are not incorrect views of God, but some correct views will be opposing. Yet we continue to fight over which contradictory view is the right view. To be a part of God's domain one must accept its strange nature and the call to live in the inverse. It is a call to turn inside out and upside down. If we claw our way to the top in this world we will find that we have arrived at the bottom in the kingdom of God. The converse is clear. Yet some of us are stuck on one side of the Mobius strip, because we don't move forward. Perhaps we are afraid to experience the other side. I encourage you to move, to breathe, and to live in the inverse dynamics of God. It is on the other side that we not only find the other nature of God, but the other nature of ourselves. It is there that we become less, and in turn become more. We are not only defined by what we are, but also by what we are not.

2.14

Figure and Ground

It is a common phenomenon to describe what is by what is not. When someone is pleased with a just completed project, they may say, "Not bad!" If someone is in a difficult circumstance and chooses to see the bright side of it, they may say, "It could be worse." One can describe a glass as half empty rather than half full. These are all examples of *figure and ground*. In each case figure is what is and ground is what is not. On this page the letters are what *is*, figure, and the white background is what *is not*, ground. Figure and ground have also been described, respectively, as "positive space" and "negative space."[182] Artists use both. Sculptors remove the ground to reveal the figure. Painters may lay down ground before painting the figures. Photographers may choose to highlight either figure or ground. In some cases much of the subject is not present but is inferred from what little is present. Such is the case in the following portrait (Figure 23).

Both figure and ground are necessary to completely portray any given entity. It is quite impossible to have one without the other. We need to know what is not as much as what is. Even once a sculpture is completed we still see what is not there, even if subconsciously. In courts of law it is required that witnesses describe both positive space and negative space. They are asked to swear that they will, "tell the truth, the whole truth, and nothing but the truth." They are accountable for both figure and ground, declaring both what they saw and what they did not see: whom they saw and whom they did not see.

---

[182] Hofstadter, *Gödel, Escher, Bach: An Eternal Golden Braid*, 67.

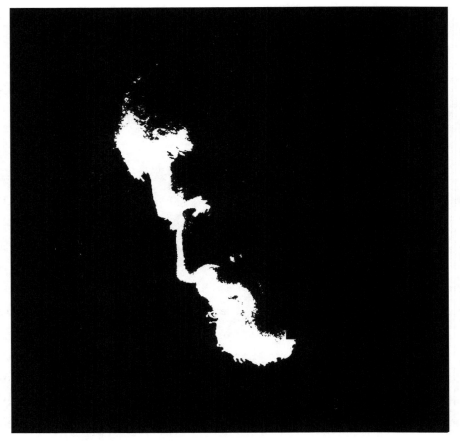

Figure 23. Figure & Ground Self-Portrait

Is & Is Not

Figure and ground are foundations in theology. God is described both by what God is and by what he is not. Though he does not use the terms figure and ground, A.W. Tozer described figure and ground theology in his book *The Knowledge Of The Holy*. "Since our intellectual knowledge of God is so small and obscure, we can sometimes gain considerable advantage in our struggle to understand what God is like by the simple expedient of thinking what He is not like. So far in this examination of the attributes of God we have been driven to the free use of negatives. We have seen that God had no origins, that He had no beginning, that He requires no helpers, that He suffers no change, and that in His essential being there are no limitations."[183] In scripture God is described as "slow to anger and rich in love and compassion."[184] In figure and ground terms, God *is not* quick to anger and *is* abounding in compassion.

The famous *love passage* in scripture describes love as much by what it is not as by what it is. "Love is patient, love is kind. It does not envy, it does not boast, it is not proud. It does not dishonor others, it is not self-seeking, it is not easily angered, it keeps no record of wrongs. Love does not delight in evil but rejoices with the truth. It always protects, always trusts, always hopes, always perseveres. Love never fails."[185] Hate can also be described by what it is not: it is not-love. Love is not-hate.

Darkness & Light

Light is a strange phenomenon: perhaps the strangest in the cosmos. Many a philosopher and physicist has pondered its nature. It remains mysterious. Sure, it can be described as a wave of electromagnetic radiation or a particle known as a photon, but its essence mystifies scientists nonetheless. Darkness is even stranger than light: it is the absence of light. It is the ground, so to speak, giving way to the figure of light. Darkness cannot overcome light; light overcomes darkness. It is inconceivable to think of the opposite of a flashlight, a "flashdark" that could be turned on to put everyone in the dark. Darkness is simply the absence of light.

Jesus of Nazareth said, "Anyone who claims to be in the light but hates a brother or sister is still in the darkness. Anyone who loves their brother and sister lives in the light, and there is nothing in them to make them stumble. But anyone who hates a brother or sister is in the darkness and walks around in the darkness. They do not know where they are going, because the darkness has blinded them."[186] Love is light. The absence of love is darkness.

---

[183] A.W. Tozer, *The Knowledge of the Holy: The Attributes of God: Their Meaning in the Christian Life* (New York: Harper & Row Pubisher, Inc., 1961), 61-62.
[184] Exodus 34:6.
[185] 1 Corinthians 13:4-8.
[186] 1 John 2:9-11.

Good & Evil

Good and evil are figure and ground to most of us. For some they may be ground and figure. Then again, for some they do not exist at all. I, for one, believe the two exist and that good is figure. Scripture says, "Anyone who does what is good is from God. Anyone who does what is evil has not seen God."[187] In other words, anyone who does good has seen *The Figure* and anyone who does evil has not. Those who do evil ironically describe the figure by what they are not!

For Me or Against Me

In an extraordinary encounter, Jesus of Nazareth's disciples came to him complaining that they found some strange men doing the same kind of good that Jesus had been doing. They wanted to know if they should stop these do-gooders. Jesus responded with figure and ground: "For no one who does a miracle in my name can in the next moment say anything bad about me, for whoever is not against us is for us."[188] This saying is strangely inclusive. However, it is also strangely exclusive. Elsewhere Jesus said the converse: "Whoever is not with me is against me, and whoever does not gather with me scatters."[189] If I am one who claims to be for him, yet do things that work against him, then I am not "not against" him, and therefore I am not for him. There is no middle ground. The summation is that we are either for or against; we are either figure or ground. Belief in God cannot be separated from doing good on God's behalf. Both disbelief and acting in not-good ways are ground. Believing and doing good are inseparable and are indeed figure: the figure of God.

The Golden Rule

Earlier, I briefly discussed the *Golden Rule* and Jesus' apparent affirmation of Confucius' words. Confucius said, "Do not do to others what you do not want them to do to you." Jesus said, "Do to others what you would have them do to you."[190] I argued that Jesus was here affirming Confucius as a source of truth: scripture. I

---

[187] 3 John 11-12.
[188] Mark 9:39-40.
[189] Matthew 12:30.
[190] Matthew 7:12; Luke 6:31.

hope it makes more sense now in the light of figure and ground. Though Confucius described the ground and Jesus described the figure, both are necessary to complete the picture.

The Non-Existence Theorem

I have heard people say, "There is no meaning to the universe." Also said, "There is no God." How is it that these individuals have come to define the ground without the figure? How can one describe what is not without something that is? As I pointed out via an earlier quote by C.S. Lewis, if there were no meaning to the universe, we would not know what meaning was in order to identify its absence. Paraphrasing Lewis' thought, if there were no figure, we would not know how to identify the ground surrounding its void.

In Closing

Scripture tells us that God does not despise a "broken and contrite heart."[191] What an amazing figure and ground statement! God loves a humble spirit. The sacrifices pleasing to God are defined not only by what is, but also by what is not. Figure and ground help us understand more of God and the people that God has called us to be. Elsewhere scripture sums it up with three simple figures: "He has shown you, O mortal, what is good. And what does the Lord require of you? To act justly and to love mercy and to walk humbly with your God."[192] These are the figures to seek. It is a call to move away from the ground of injustice, mercilessness, and pride. It is a call to move toward the IICP: the ultimate figure.

---

[191] Psalm 51:17.
[192] Micah 6:8.

2.15

This I Believe

I contemplated waiting until Phase 5 to reveal my convictions on the identity of the GBF, the God-become-flesh, but there are too many references in the upcoming Phases to mask my conviction. I do not speak arrogantly about my belief in the GBF, for it is a personal belief, and one of faith, not an absolute, as some would attest. More importantly, the principles described in the rest of this book are applicable regardless of whether or not you believe as I do. The upcoming principles are applicable to issues of faith and theology precisely because they are applicable to science and mathematics. They are applicable regardless of your religious persuasion. So, whether or not you believe what I am about to describe herein, read on.

I believe the GBF was Jesus of Nazareth. Not in a religious manner or for a select group of people, but in an encompassing manner. I believe God became flesh for all people, for all religions, for all time. But how can this be, since Jesus is a *Christian* figure? This is a misnomer. As I have clarified previously, Christianity is a religion no different from the rest: it too denies and defies the infinitude of God by declaring an exclusive set of answers. The GBF was not about ushering in a new religion. He did not come for Christianity or for would-be Christians; he came for the world. He came to set us free from our religious constraints.

Probability

Scripture says that the GBF came to fulfill the Law and the Prophets.[193] I believe this is a reference to his mission to fulfill all the symbolisms of religious efforts to

---

[193] Matthew 7:12.

move closer to God. In the Old Testament, which includes Judaic laws and prophetic writings, there are over 300 prophetic references to the GBF that Jesus fulfilled. Some scholars register complaints at this claim, pointing out that many of these prophecies are general in nature (which I tend to agree with) and could be applied to numerous messianic types. What about specific prophecies such as the town he would be born in, the type of death he would encounter, etc.? As Fritz Ridenour records in his book *So What's The Difference*, "Computations using the science of probability on just 8 of these prophecies show the chance that someone could have fulfilled all 8 prophecies is 10^{17} power, or 1 in 100 quadrillion."[194] (For those not familiar with scientific notation, 10^{17} is a 1 with 17 zeros after it.) These odds are staggering.

Taking it a step further: 48 of the 300+ messianic prophecies are fairly specific, though not as specific as the 8 that Ridenour refers to. By my calculations, the probability of 48 of these prophecies being fulfilled by one individual is approximately 1 in 10^{157}. Physicists today estimate that the total number of atoms in the entire universe is approximately 10^{100}. In other words, if you were sent on a mission to find one specific atom in the entire universe (not one type of atom; one specific atom), your odds of finding it would be one thousand billion billion billion billion billion billion times more likely than one person fulfilling 48 specific messianic prophecies.

To assume that we can concoct our own GBF as we see fit is mathematically preposterous. We can't even get out of Dodge (our solar system, let alone our galaxy) to search the entire universe for a single specific atom. What makes us believe that any GBF of our choosing will do?

Some scholars complain that Jesus and/or his followers could have manipulated the circumstances in order to fulfill many of these prophecies. Some of the more general prophecies could conceivably be manipulated to fit. As Lee Strobel points out in *The Case for Christ: A Journalist's Personal Investigation of the Evidence for Jesus*, "Jesus had no control over the thirty pieces of silver used to betray him. He could not arrange for his ancestry, or his birthplace, or his method

---

[194] Fritz Ridenour, *So What's the Difference* (Ventura: Regal Books, 2001), 28.

of execution, or that soldiers would gamble for his clothing, or that his legs would remain unbroken on the cross."[195]

There is no other historical figure who matches the criteria for the GBF like the person of Jesus of Nazareth. The degree to which he fulfilled the prophecies concerning his coming, his life, his mission, and his death is staggering. What is more, the aforementioned analyses were calculated on Judaic prophecies alone. The mystics who came from the Far East to celebrate the birth of Jesus were watching the astrological signs that their religious traditions foretold as declarations of the coming of the GBF. This I believe.

Divinity Claims

While some may question whether or not Jesus thought he was divine, the scriptural evidences of his claim to be the GBF, God-in-the-flesh, are too numerous to ignore. Let us look at a few of them. The book of Matthew records a discussion between Jesus and the religious leaders: "While the Pharisees were gathered together, Jesus asked them, 'What do you think about the Messiah? Whose son is he?' 'The son of David,' they replied. He said to them, 'How is it then that David, speaking by the Spirit, calls him 'Lord'? For he says, 'The LORD said to my Lord: 'Sit at my right hand until I put your enemies under your feet.' If then David calls him 'Lord,' how can he be his son?' No one could say a word in reply, and from that day on no one dared to ask him any more questions." [196] Jesus was referring to Psalm 110:1 where David is clearly quoting God, the LORD. The circular nature of the GBF was problematic for the Pharisees. The Messiah was to come after David, a descendant of his, yet existed before him? How can this be, except that he was God himself?

Jesus frequently referred to himself as the *Son of Man*. Lee Strobel explains, Jesus' use of the phrase "Son of Man" does not primarily refer to his humanity. Instead it is a direct reference to Daniel 7:13-14. In this text Daniel's vision includes one who was like "a son of man," who was given authority and glory and

---

[195] Strobel, *The Case for Christ: A Journalist's Personal Investigation of the Evidence for Jesus*, 184-85.
[196] Matthew 22:41-46.

power that could be ascribed only to a deity.[197] The use of this phrase offended the religious leaders, substantiating its reference to deity.

Jesus frequently forgave sins. This is something that only God can do. Humans can forgive sins committed against each other, but not sins committed against God. Once when Jesus forgave the sins of a lame man, the Jews immediately proclaimed the act as blasphemous: "Who can forgive sins but God alone?"[198] Jesus was not concerned with such accusations, but proceeded to declare his divinity.

Ironically, it is more difficult for some to grasp the humanness of Jesus than his divine nature. Eugene Peterson said in *Leap Over a Wall: Earthly Spirituality for Everyday Christians*, "Through the Christian centuries, we've had a harder time taking seriously the human elements of the story than the divine. It's been easier to believe that Jesus was God than that Jesus was human. For millennia, all over planet Earth, we've had gods aplenty. We're used to them. Divinity and the supernatural are old hat to us. But humanity is a mystery."[199] Jesus was fully God and fully human. That is the uniqueness of the GBF.

A Divine Implant

Perhaps the most problematic, and most divine, aspect of Jesus' life on earth is the claim that he had no earthly father, but was conceived miraculously by a virgin. This was foretold by the prophet Isaiah: "Therefore the Lord himself will give you a sign: The virgin will conceive and give birth to a son, and will call him Immanuel."[200] In the account of the life of Jesus as recorded by Luke, the Greek physician, it is told that an angel came to Mary and proclaimed that she would conceive. The conversation between Mary and the angel is quite revealing: ""How will this be," Mary asked the angel, "since I am a virgin?" The angel answered, "The Holy Spirit will come on you, and the power of the Most High will overshadow you. So the holy one to be born will be called the Son of God."[201]

I was quite surprised as I read the Koran to find that it too claims that Jesus' conception was miraculous: "Remember when the angel said, 'O Mary! Verily God

---

[197] Strobel, *The Case for Christ: A Journalist's Personal Investigation of the Evidence for Jesus*, 30.
[198] Mark 2:1-12.
[199] Peterson, *Leap over a Wall: Earthly Spirituality for Everyday Christians*, 7.
[200] Isaiah 7:14.
[201] Luke 1:34-35.

announceth to thee the word from Him: His name shall be, Messiah Jesus the son of Mary, illustrious in this world, and in the next, and one of those who have near access to God; And he shall speak to men alike when in the cradle and when grown up; And he shall be one of the just.' She (Mary) said, 'How, O my Lord! Shall I have a son, when man hath not touched me?' He said, 'Thus: God will create what He will; When He decreeth a thing, He only saith, 'Be,' and it is.'"[202] Even though Jesus is not believed to be divine in Islam, the virgin conception is clearly recorded.

I argue that such a virgin conception is not only an act of God, but also one that boldly proclaims the entrance of God, by God, into our domain. Such was the mission of the GBF. God became flesh to set the world aright: to restore and balance all of creation once again.

Son of God

A theological issue that is problematic for Muslims, Jews, and other monotheists, including myself, is the reference to Jesus being the "Son of God." As I alluded to earlier, I will address this issue more fully in Phase 3, but for now must address the word used in the original manuscripts that is translated as *Son*. The Greek for *Son* (huios) can be immediate, remote, or figuratively a son. Given the problematic mathematical issue with an offspring of God, I believe it is figurative, especially considering the cultural use of *son*, which typically referred to deity.[203] As Lee Strobel points out, "The King James Version translates John 3:16 using the words "his only begotten Son." But in fact, that's not what the word in Greek means. It really means "unique one."[204] There were few ways to describe both the humanity and divinity of the GBF. *Son* was a natural link between the two, describing the GBF as best as that culture could.

Jesus' Mission and Purpose

Scripture says we were *bought* back by God[205] and that we are being *brought* to God[206]. Both of these involve crossing an infinitely wide chasm that only the GBF

---

[202] The Koran as translated by Rodwell, *The Koran*, III:40-42.
[203] Daniel 7:13-14.
[204] Strobel, *The Case for Christ: A Journalist's Personal Investigation of the Evidence for Jesus*, 161.
[205] The Koran IX:112.

can cross. Nowhere are the GBF's mission and purpose stated more clearly than in Isaiah 53.

> Who has believed our message and to whom has the arm of the LORD been revealed? He grew up before him like a tender shoot, and like a root out of dry ground. He had no beauty or majesty to attract us to him, nothing in his appearance that we should desire him. He was despised and rejected by mankind, a man of suffering, and familiar with pain. Like one from whom people hide their faces he was despised, and we held him in low esteem. Surely he took up our pain and bore our suffering, yet we considered him punished by God, stricken by him, and afflicted. But he was pierced for our transgressions, he was crushed for our iniquities; the punishment that brought us peace was on him, and by his wounds we are healed. We all, like sheep, have gone astray, each of us has turned to our own way; and the LORD has laid on him the iniquity of us all. He was oppressed and afflicted, yet he did not open his mouth; he was led like a lamb to the slaughter, and as a sheep before its shearers is silent, so he did not open his mouth. By oppression and judgment he was taken away. Yet who of his generation protested? For he was cut off from the land of the living; for the transgression of my people he was punished. He was assigned a grave with the wicked, and with the rich in his death, though he had done no violence, nor was any deceit in his mouth. Yet it was the LORD's will to crush him and cause him to suffer, and though the LORD makes his life an offering for sin, he will see his offspring and prolong his days, and the will of the LORD will prosper in his hand. After he has suffered, he will see the light of life and be satisfied; by his knowledge my righteous servant will justify many, and he will bear their iniquities. Therefore I will give him a portion among the great, and he will divide the spoils with the strong, because he

---

[206] 1 Peter 3:18.

poured out his life unto death, and was numbered with the transgressors. For he bore the sin of many, and made intercession for the transgressors.[207]

This passage describes an eternal intention to set the world right. The GBF offered himself willingly out of love.[208] The Isaiah passage reaffirms this selfless love.[209] This I believe.

Timing of the GBF's Coming

I have asked the question numerous times, "If Jesus was the GBF, why did God wait so long to come?" One possibility is that the GBF's coming is not time dependent. This is a dimensional issue to be discussed in Phase 3. Having said that, we must still reckon with texts such as, "But when the set time had fully come, God sent his Son, born of a woman, born under the law, to redeem those under the law, that we might receive adoption to sonship."[210] What constitutes the *right time*?

There are many types and symbols imbedded within the Old Testament texts that point to the coming and the timing of the GBF. The most mysterious of all to me is the symbolism of the *Year of Jubilee*. In the Old Testament book of Leviticus, God told the people to give the land rest every seven years, planning ahead and saving up food for the sabbatical year. He also told them to observe yet another special year after every seven sabbatical years: the year of Jubilee. In this 50th year debts were forgiven and land was restored to its original tribal ownership. It was a time of forgiveness and great celebration.[211]

Some scholars have placed the timing of Jesus' announcement of his ministry, found in Luke chapter 4, precisely on a sabbatical year, and specifically in a Jubilee year.[212] The significance of this can be seen in Jesus' pronouncement that he was sent by the Spirit of the Sovereign Lord to bring the ultimate Jubilee. In Luke chapter 4, Jesus is in the synagogue in Nazareth on the Sabbath reading from the

---

[207] Isaiah 53:1-12.
[208] Philippians 2:6-8.
[209] Isaiah 53:4-5.
[210] Galatians 4:4-5.
[211] Leviticus 25.
[212] Ben Ollenburger, *A Mind Patient and Untamed: Assessing John Howard Yoder's Contributions to Theology* (Telford: Cascadia Publishing House, 2004).

scroll of Isaiah, informing the people that *he* is the one who will bring hope, freedom, healing, and forgiveness. The announcement was so clear that many of the people were offended and wanted to kill him right then and there. He revealed that he was the GBF.

Are there other reasons for the chosen time of the coming of the GBF? In an online article, Dr. John Oakes says that Jesus came ". . . at a time when written language existed. At a time of a sustained period of relative peace. At a time when one very large world power allowed for rapid spread of the teaching. At a time when one or at most two languages were used over vast stretches of territory where a lot of people lived."[213] These conditions were crucial for the spreading of the news of the coming and the mission of the GBF.

But what about all the people who lived and died before the GBF came? How are they to be treated? First of all, as we will see more fully in Phase 3, time limits people, not God. In the light of God's domain, which is not constrained in time, all that matters is that the GBF comes.

The Strangeness of Jesus

Jesus was strange. This is particularly why so many people struggle to accept him. He is not the orderly, logical, religious person so many people expect in a messiah. It is precisely the strangeness of Jesus that sets him apart from other would-be messiahs.

We have already discussed the Beatitudes with regards to strange and inverse loops. Jesus lived and taught on the strange loop. To live, one must die. To be the greatest, one must become the least. To keep anything, one must give it away. John Howard Yoder, an Anabaptist theologian, asserted that those ". . . who bear crosses are working with the grain of the universe."[214] Yoder identified the strange loop Jesus' life represented *and* that it was consistent with the strangeness of the universe. This is why so many intellectuals, such as GK Chesterton, CS Lewis, Karl Barth, John Howard Yoder, and Stanley Hauerwas, have come to embrace his life and teachings. It is his strangeness that draws them. Douglas Hofstadter, though

---

[213] John Oakes, "Why Did God Wait to Send Jesus," http://www.evidenceforchristianity.org/index.php?option=com_custom_content&task=view&id=4786.
[214] Hauerwas, *With the Grain of the Universe*, 6.

not a theist, has shown us how strange the universe is (through the eyes of Gödel, Escher, and Bach). Jesus lived, taught, and died with the strange grain of the universe.

For the Weak and Dying

Jesus came to save the weak and the sick, not the strong and indulgent. He did not come for the self-sufficient, the righteous, and the prominent. He hung out with the prostitutes, the alcoholics, the sexually divergent, the thieves, and the murderers. He hung out with everyone who knew they were not good enough for God, yet needed him. This Jesus of Nazareth crossed religious boundaries that most of his followers found, and still find, hard to cross. He attributed the *greatest faith* to a pagan Roman Centurion.[215] It was the pompous, religious, arrogant individuals he condemned.

When we accept the strangeness of the GBF, we accept the strange mission and purpose of the incarnation and the GBF's subsequent death. His death emphatically declares God's intention to move out of the world's limelight and into a place where weakness conquers strength. Through him the weak and dying will live, while the strong and indulgent will die. So it is with the strangeness of God and the cosmos.

The Death and Resurrection of Jesus

Some theologians question the death of Jesus. While it is not my purpose to provide a full treatment of this issue, I must say briefly that the iterations (or witnesses), both inside and outside of scripture, are too numerous to ignore. One can surmise that Jesus fled into another country, or that the Roman soldiers were not efficient in executing Jesus; however, neither is supported by the evidence, rather only by predispositions to disbelief. I believe the evidences: Jesus was executed on a cross.

The resurrection is another story altogether. The most significant and overwhelming evidences of all are found in the changed lives that occurred as a result of the resurrection. As Fritz Ridenour points out in his book *So What's the*

[215] Matthew 8:10.

Difference, "None of the 'standard' explanations can account for the total change that occurred in Jesus' followers after they found the empty tomb. And as for his post-resurrection appearances—to as many as 500 people at a time (see 1 Corinthians 15:6)—they were far more than just a spiritual presence or apparition."[216] Diarmuid O'Murchu in *Quantum Theology* recognizes that,

> The historical facts of the Christian resurrection narrative are a subject of intense debate among biblical scholars and theologians. Basically, we do not know when, where, or how Jesus was buried, nor have we any concrete, historical facts or artifacts to verify his miraculous rising from the dead. What we do have is the life-witness of a group of disenchanted followers, so transformed by the experience (whatever that was) that they give their very lives for their Christian convictions, and, second, a Christian culture of two thousand years numbering today 1.5 billion people spread throughout the earth. It is hard to imagine that the totality of Christian culture, as we have known it to date, is based on a grand delusion.[217]

With so many of Jesus' followers put to death, it is incomprehensible that they went to their deaths on the basis of false or unsubstantiated claims. They believed.

Fundamentally, the question of the resurrection of Jesus boils down to whether or not one believes in miracles. I believe in the resurrection for two significant reasons. First, there are too many iterations, or witnesses, to ignore. Secondly, the main objection from *mystical materialists* is simply that it cannot be so. These mystical materialists, as G.K. Chesterton put it, want to dabble in the mystical, but are held back by materialistic limits.[218] I reject such limited objections. I believe Jesus was raised from the dead: a feat quite plausible for the IICP. But why go to such extremes? Why raise Jesus from the dead, when there are already so many other evidences of the IICP's infinitude? We will address this more fully in Phase 3.

---

[216] Ridenour, *So What's the Difference*, 21.
[217] O'Murchu, *Quantum Theology: Spiritual Implications of the New Physics*, 176-77.
[218] Chesterton, *Orthodoxy*.

In Closing

Jesus did not come as the GBF so that one religion could provide all the answers for all the other religions. It is more simple: he is the truth. It is about God coming as one person, a counter-religious person, providing a God solution. I wish we all could wrap our heads around that. It is not about Christians bringing their religion to the world: it is about God bringing his solution to the world in spite of religious traditions!

We humans work so diligently to disprove what we do not want to be true. As Karl Barth said, "The objective fact is that Jesus Christ has come and that He has spoken His word and done His work. That exists, quite independently of whether we men believe it or not."[219] This Immanuel, this *God-with-us*, performed an infinite act, entering our domain to save lost sheep. This reality is Jesus: the GBF. It is in the essence of the life of Jesus that we find meaning and direction in the strange character of the cosmos. Jesus not only matches the strangeness of the cosmos, but *is* the strangeness of the cosmos. In him we exist and move. This I believe.

[219] Barth, *Dogmatics in Outline*, 132.

Phase 3

Dimensional Perspectives

3.00

The Narrative

Previously, the two mountainous climbs had been among deciduous trees, mostly maples and oaks. On this northwestern range, however, the leafless silhouettes were dwindling. In their place, conifers were appearing in increasing height and density the further up the mountain he climbed. The little snow that remained was rapidly melting, filling the nearby streams with milky water. Signs of spring labored to push through the ground cover. Fresh, cool air filled his lungs with each intake of breath.

At the ridge, Fritz stopped to view the countless mountains undulating in waves ahead of him. They were very alive, yet frozen in time. He stood, dwelling on the naïve objective that had dictated his reactions and impatience at the start of his journey. Over the months, he had softened considerably.

Why not slow down and enjoy the moment? A bit surprised at himself for harboring such a spontaneous thought, he set his knapsack down and began to look about for firewood. The crackle of the cones and needles under his feet was warm and welcoming. He would use them for kindling and bedding.

The sky grew dark and yielded a display of stars unlike any he had ever seen. He lay back on his bed of needles and pulled his arms inside his woolen vest. The starlight was unhampered by the flickering flames. Placing another piece of wood on the fire, he marveled at the setting and at the peace he felt. *There is so much beyond this small rock we call home,* he thought as he gazed at a densely packed night sky and let his mind slide into quiet sleep.

Morning came quickly. The air was cold and the fire was gone. He roused himself with a few shivers and ate the bread and dried fruit Fremd had sent with him. He would warm himself with the hike to come rather than rekindle the fire.

The timber made it difficult to see how far down the mountainside he had gone. Rounding a lengthy switchback, he saw the split in the path. One fork headed northwest and the other proceeded northeast. Remembering Fremd's gentle words, he smiled as he took the northeast fork and continued the descent.

The steep trail gradually leveled out, leading Fritz into a pasture with grazing sheep. A boy sat perched on a boulder, staff in hand, watching the sheep. "Good day!" Fritz said, startling the boy.

"Good day, sir!" the boy replied.

"I was told this path would take me directly to Dimen Castle. How far is it from here?"

"Why it is right there, sir!" said the boy, pointing toward the opposite end of the long meadow.

"I see nothing," said Fritz.

"I didn't say you could see it, sir. I simply said it is there."

Fritz paused and began to replay the strangeness of Isnot. His insistence that things illogical were always illogical had been softened by the humbling inverse lessons from Fremd. The strangeness of Isnot, however, was very visible. Either this little shepherd was playing games with him or the limits of strangeness were being pushed even further.

"What do I have to do to see it?" Fritz asked, knowing the answer was likely to be as convoluted as any he had received yet.

"Take the path to the end of the meadow, turn left and you will see it," explained the boy. Somewhat exasperated, yet open to the possibility of another strange surprise, Fritz left the boy to tend his sheep and continued the path through the meadow.

The serene alpine view that Fritz had admired was disturbed as he looked up to the left, and noticed that one of the mountainsides was scorched. Green timbers were replaced with charred stumps. Snapped off at their bases, logs lay on their sides, as though prostrate before a king. *How could such a disaster have happened? How was it put out before it consumed the rest of the mountain and the lowland?*

Looking ahead once again, he could see that the path ended abruptly in front of a boulder. Still, no castle was in sight. *I can't believe I let that boy . . .* His thoughts reverted to Fremd's words, "It will lead you directly to Dimen Castle." He knew Fremd to be trustworthy; strange, but trustworthy.

Fritz had little option but to continue forward until he could touch the surface of the boulder, worn smooth by glaciers, wind and rain. With his right hand still rubbing the rock, he turned his head to the left. His heart leapt from his chest as he realized the castle wall was only yards away. Convinced he was hallucinating, he turned around and headed back down the meadow path. After a few yards, he turned about. He scanned the landscape carefully, but there was no structure to behold. He repeated his approach, turning left occasionally to test his sanity. *No castle. No castle.* As he approached the boulder, he turned to the left once more. *Castle! How can this be?*

From the distant end of the meadow, he heard the boy yell, "Do you see it now?" Too nervous to respond, he walked toward the castle wall. It towered above the lowly meadow. Gazing up, he tried to estimate its height. He could barely reach the top of the first layer of the stone foundation.

Hoping to find an entrance, he walked along the castle's wall. No entrance existed. He approached the corner of the wall and turned left, intending to search the adjacent wall. However, much to his dismay, the wall completely disappeared. Perplexed, he wandered back to the boulder and sat down, resting his head against the hard, smooth rock.

"Why do you sit there, young man?" Looking to the right, Fritz saw a man escorting the shepherd boy to the castle wall.

"I tried to find an entrance through the castle wall, but with no success. I am tired and hungry, so here I sit," Fritz said gruffly.

"Ah, a newcomer!" said the man as he and the boy passed by the boulder.

Fritz turned away, facing the meadow's end once more.

Suddenly, all was silent. Turning toward the wall again, Fritz realized the man and the boy were gone. *Gone!* He shook his head, blinked his eyes, and began to think they had not been real. Had he been hallucinating? Either way, it was not a good ending to what had been a wonderful trip over the mountain. Fremd hadn't told him it would be so difficult to get into the castle.

"Well, are you coming or not?" Fritz turned to see the man standing next to the castle wall beckoning him with his hand.

"Where did you go? Where did you come from? How did you do that? Are you real?" Fritz sputtered in confusion.

"Yes, I am quite real," said the man in a kind tone. "Come. I will show you how to get through the castle wall."

Fritz picked up his things, and walked toward the man. "Turn away from the wall to the right. Take twelve side steps to the left, then turn left again. Do you understand?"

"I am not sure," replied Fritz.

"Here, take my hand, and do exactly what I do." The man took Fritz's hand and stood next to the wall. Facing down the length of the wall he said, "Here we go. Twelve steps to the left!" In a flash, Fritz was not sure where he was. It was not light. Neither was it dark. Matter and space swirled around him like an ethereal dream. "Now turn left."

Fritz turned to see the interior of the castle wall. Turning back to his guide he asked, "What just happened?"

The man chuckled and said, "Welcome to Dimen Castle."

"How did we just come through a solid stone wall?"

"Are you hungry? Come, we will talk over dinner." The man led Fritz down a path through an area that resembled a park more than what he expected the interior of a castle to look like. The wall they had passed through was not a part of the castle structure as such, but rather a surrounding guardian. The stone path wound through aged fruit trees and flower beds just beginning to show signs of spring.

The path opened into a courtyard in front of the castle. Curving stairs climbed upward to a landing in front of a pair of tall, bronze-plated doors. The sides of the castle were supported with buttresses whose bases almost reached the exterior walls. Stained glass windows filled the spaces between the buttresses. Fritz had hoped the castle would be a glorious sight, but what his eyes beheld far surpassed his wildest expectations.

"Come on, dinner is waiting," urged the man. They quickly climbed the stairs. Just as their feet hit the landing the bronze doors opened.

"Welcome to Dimen Castle," echoed a voice through a foyer where rays of colored light, shining through a stained glass dome above, bounced off the floor and onto the walls. "Dinner is ready and waiting," said the noble looking man who greeted the two of them.

Fritz, numb by the strange events and the unknown hosts who led him to dinner, walked in silence. They left the foyer via a hallway lined with tapestry. Distant voices, muffled by the fabric on the walls, could be heard but not understood. Turning into a doorway off of the hallway, they entered a dining room. One lengthy table filled the center of the room. Candles, lining the center of the table, were lit and flickering. Standing around the table were twenty or more people waiting patiently for their meal.

"Friends, our new guest has arrived. I think it is time for some introductions," said the noble who led the two into the dining room. Turning to Fritz, he exclaimed, "I am Ganz."

Fritz, still nervous and confused, replied, "I am Fritz, Fritz Streuner."

The man who had shown Fritz through the wall said, "Fritz, I am Sorge. Over there is my wife, and here is my son, whom you met in the meadow."

Ganz invited everyone to take their places. "You sit next to me, Fritz," said Ganz. Picking up a glass of wine, Ganz lifted it into the air and said, "To Lord Zeitlos, our kind and generous host!"

"Here, here!" They all replied in unison.

Sitting down, the conversation began. "What do you think of Dimen Castle thus far, Fritz?" Ganz asked cheerfully.

"It is beautiful. It is also quite a mystery. I have many questions."

"There will be time for those. Here comes the food."

The servers brought dishes with various entrees. They did not ask who wanted which entree; they simply set them down in front of each guest. A plate of broiled fish was placed in front of Fritz. Fritz, however, was not paying much attention to the dish in front of him. Instead, he was focused on the other guests with their dishes. Much to his astonishment, the other guests were rotating their plates a quarter turn, inspecting the entree, and then turning their plates again.

He glanced at Ganz's plate and gasped. What had been broiled fish, like his, was now a grilled sirloin steak. Looking around, he observed many new entrees. Some had become smoked ham, and others, skewered shrimp. With each turn, the entrée changed to something new. Some guests, apparently deciding to settle for a previous selection, rotated their plates backwards to find an entrée they had passed.

Without asking, Fritz began rotating his plate. Finally settling on lobster tail, he timidly began to eat. There were too many questions to know where to begin. "Enjoying your meal, Fritz?" said Ganz with a mouth full of steak.

"Yes, sir."

"Now, what were those questions you had?"

Fritz, not sure where to start, blurted out, "The castle wall; how is it that I could see it when next to it, but not from anywhere else? And the entry through the wall? Explain that!"

Ganz set down his fork and said, "Dimen Castle shares only two of the three spatial dimensions common to the rest of the world. It can only be seen when viewed from a perspective that looks directly into the plane of those two dimensions. As to the entry through the wall, the only way to get through such a wall is to face a direction parallel to the wall, causing the wall to disappear, then move sideways into its third dimension."

"Why sideways?"

"Did you try simply walking into the wall, Fritz? It is pretty hard. You have to face a direction in which it does not exist, and then move through it."

Staring down at his plate, Fritz continued the questions, "You referred to Lord Zeitlos as a host. Why is everyone here a guest? Doesn't anyone in this room live here? And where is Lord Zeitlos?"

"You sure have a lot of questions!" Ganz chuckled. "Not everyone here is a guest. Sorge and his family are the caretakers of the castle. The rest of us are guests. Some, including me, have been here numerous times and know what to expect when visiting. As to Lord Zeitlos, he is currently away on a trip and is not expected back for quite some time. I am sorry you missed him."

Fritz's thoughts went back to Allesa's assurance that he would meet Lord Zeitlos. She probably did not know he was traveling at present. He couldn't hold that against her. She had given him too many words of advice that had proven true to doubt her now.

"One more question, Ganz."

"Oh, trust me," interrupted Ganz, "there will be many more!"

"Probably so," replied Fritz. "What kind of plates are these?"

"Aren't they delightful? They are dimensional plates. Here in Dimen Castle, as you will continue to find out, many different and contrasting things are actually one and the same thing. Even some contradictory things are one."

"What do you mean contradictory things?"

"For instance, small things can be large and large things can be small. Just by rotating the object or yourself! Allow me to illustrate." He motioned for Fritz to stand. "Look around you and take in the view. Now, hang your head down, facing the floor, and turn one complete circle to the left."

When Fritz raised his head he gasped at the sight. The room and its contents, including the people, were twice their original size! Without giving it a thought he quickly hung his head and turned completely around to the right. "How can this be? This is illogical. No such changes take place in my home country."

"Well, you are not in your home country!" laughed Ganz. Continuing, he said, "Look, these things are unheard of even just outside the castle walls. This unique ability to have multiple and differing appearances depending on one's perspective is found only inside the walls of Dimen Castle."

"Oh," Ganz interrupted himself, "here comes dessert!" The servers placed empty plates in front of each guest.

"There is nothing on the plates," said Fritz.

"Oh, I failed to mention that the options for dessert include nothing!" Again, each guest began to rotate his or her plate to choose a desert. Fritz settled on a new favorite: humble pie.

At the close of dinner, Ganz said, "Come, I will show you to your room. We will explore the castle tomorrow."

As they left the dining room, Fritz was surprised to find that the hallway was no longer covered with tapestry. Instead, it was lined with portraits. Some of them looked aged with cracks in the varnish. Others appeared to be more recent renderings. Pointing to some of the older ones, Fritz asked, "Are these former lords of the castle?"

"Oh, no," Ganz replied with a deep voice, "They are all of Lord Zeitlos."

"But, they don't look at all like the same person!"

"Remember," said Ganz, "Here in Dimen Castle, many dissimilar things may actually be one and the same." Fritz crinkled his brow. At the end of the hallway he paused, staring at the last portrait. It looked hauntingly familiar.

"What is it, Fritz?"

"Oh, it's probably nothing," replied Fritz.

In the morning, Fritz wandered about the castle while waiting for the call to breakfast. He experimented with the perspective phenomenon. Statues changed. Images in the stained glass windows mutated. He smiled at the changes, but he understood little.

After breakfast, Ganz took Fritz on a tour. They saw magnificent libraries, music parlors, and scores of sculptures. The tour ended in front of a strange, iridescent door. Fritz moved from side to side, observing its radiant colors. "What is behind this door?"

"This," Ganz said softly, "This is the inner sanctuary of Dimen Castle. It is unlike anything you have ever beheld. However, not all who approach it can enter."

"Who can enter?"

Pointing to an inscription above the door, Ganz read, "Only Humble Learned May Enter Here."

"That probably doesn't include me," sighed Fritz.

At that moment, the door opened. "Oh, but it does, Fritz. Come."

The passage through the doorway was much like the passage through the castle wall, but more radiant. Once through, Fritz stood staring in silence. Before him was a miniature of the surrounding mountains and Dimen Castle; but, it was not simply a model. Looking closely and carefully, Fritz could see the sheep grazing in the meadow. They were alive and moving. He could hear them calling. People in and around the miniature castle could be seen walking and heard talking. "Look, but do not touch," Ganz said emphatically.

The room smelled of smoke. Fritz could see the mountainside scarred by fire. Looking around the room, he saw more signs of fire. The ceiling was charred. Smoke damage muted the color of the stained glass windows. "What happened?"

"A traveler, much like you, lost control of a campfire on the mountainside during a very dry time of year. The mountain was quickly engulfed in flames. A few families lived on that mountainside. They lost everything except their lives."

Fritz broke into a cold sweat. If not for the dampness of the forest floor, his campfire could have caused a similar storm of damage. "How did the people get out?"

There was a long, still pause before Ganz began to speak, "Lord Zeitlos ran with all his might up the main entrance, down the corridors, and into this sanctuary. Throwing off his robe, he reached down into the fire, picked up each of the stranded lives, and set them down inside the castle walls. Knowing that the fire would soon reach the castle itself, he suffocated it with his arm.

From the vantage point of the people in the castle courtyards, a large arm descended from the sky and squelched the fire. Cries, from the sky above, shook the castle walls. In spite of the pain, Lord Zeitlos continued until the fire was extinguished.

As Lord Zeitlos came out of the inner sanctuary, he fainted from the pain. Sorge arrived at the sanctuary door just in time to catch him. He carried Lord Zeitlos to his room and tended to his wounds. His arm took years to heal. The scars, as I can attest, remain and are most profound."

"Which arm?" Fritz interrupted.

"It was his right arm. Why do you ask?"

Fritz sat down on a chest next to one of the sanctuary walls. His furrowed face gradually turned into a smile. "I knew I had seen that face before!"

"What face?"

"The last portrait in the hallway leading from the dining room. It was him!"

"Who?"

"The Elder who gave me directions to Listen Inn and to Isnot. It was him! Lord Zeitlos! Allesa knew I would meet him. She probably knew I already had."

Ganz, now puzzled, looked inquisitively at Fritz. Fritz continued, "I do not smile at the sacrificing pain and scars, Ganz. I smile because I *have* met Lord Zeitlos. That was a crucial part of my mission. I wanted to see the castle, and then meet him. Little did I know that I would meet him, and then see the castle. What a kind and wise man! He so graciously gave me what I needed. And humble! He did not proclaim his name. He did not draw attention to his scars. He kindly answered my questions and gave me advice."

Leaving the inner sanctuary, Fritz decided to go outside for a breath of fresh air. He exited the bronze doors and stood in silence on the landing. His eyes grew wide as he surveyed the area surrounding the courtyard. The barren fruit trees that he had walked by when he first entered Dimen Castle were green and laden with fruit. The flower beds that had shown signs of the coming spring were now full of blooming plants, many now past their prime.

He sensed the presence of the two who surrounded him at that moment, Ganz on his right, and Sorge on his left. "This," said Sorge, "is the last surprise of Dimen Castle."

"I don't get it. I have been here for only a day."

"Within the walls of Dimen Castle, one day is like two hundred and forty to the outside world," said Ganz.

"You see," continued Sorge, "the plants share the soil with the outside world. They know their time."

Ganz handed Fritz his knapsack, and said, "If you are hoping to make it home before the first snowfall, you'd better get going. I stocked your sack with food for the journey." Fritz, overwhelmed with the concept of such a time discrepancy, wasn't sure if he was disappointed or not. He did, in fact, want to make it home before the first snowfall, but that was last winter!

"After you go through the wall, pick up the southeast trail behind the boulder. You will have to cross two significant mountains, a northeast range and a southeast range," directed Ganz. "I suggest you stop between the two of them at

Fract Village. It is not difficult to find and will be a restful break. Ask for Teile, he will take care of you and give you directions from there."

Fritz turned and hugged Sorge, and then Ganz. "Thank you. Thank you, both."

"Safe and pleasant travels to you, Fritz!" they both exclaimed.

"Don't forget, look to the left, and twelve steps to the right!" said Sorge.

Fritz picked a ripe apple as he walked past the trees toward the castle wall. What more could he have dreamt? His mission was fulfilled. In addition, his small view of the world had been profoundly stretched. *And, oh, the many wonderful new friends!* Most of all, an internal softening had taken place, a softening that left a very strange peace, an ever increasing peace.

"OK, here we go," he said to himself, as he turned to the left and began his journey back through the wall. He landed on one leg outside the castle wall, and looking around, confirmed that summer was over. Fritz glanced back at the castle wall, and softly spoke, "Perhaps, I will see you again." Picking up the southeast trail behind the boulder, he headed toward the mountain.

3.01

Strings and Things

Phase 3 uses broad brushstrokes to paint a picture of the dimensional nature of the cosmos, our resistance to utilizing extra dimensions, dimensional theology, and very peculiar implications of our dimensional existence.

Chapters 3.01 through 3.07 explore the dimensional nature of the cosmos. I must tell you in advance that chapters 3.01, 3.03, and 3.06 are perhaps the most challenging chapters in the entire book. If you find them difficult to grasp, just know that I do, too! Do not let that stop you from continuing the journey, because the wandering will get easier and more enjoyable once you get through them. They comprise an important backdrop for the rest of the book.

Chapters 3.08 through 3.09 reveal some of the outcomes of our innate resistance to extra dimensions. It is difficult to deal with things we cannot see.

Chapters 3.10 through 3.15 explore the implications that these extra dimensions have on our beliefs. In particular, we will find that our view of God is significantly limited by our dimensional constraints.

Lastly, chapters 3.16 through 3.19 investigate several peculiar implications that are natural outcomes from such dimensional thinking.

So, hang in there, and bon voyage!

Strings and Things

Strings and Things is intended to be a brief discourse on the history of physics and its current theories. It is not intended to be academic or exhaustive. It is only an introduction to a discipline of study that has radically changed my perspectives on God and the cosmos. I highly recommend two books for you by Brian Greene:

The Elegant Universe: Superstrings, Hidden Dimensions, and the Quest for the Ultimate Theory[220] and *The Fabric of the Cosmos: Space, Time, and the Texture of Reality*.[221] Brian Greene does a remarkable job of translating current theories in physics into common, everyday language. I will refer to both extensively throughout this chapter. If you prefer, both books have been put into series by NOVA and are available at your library or on the Internet. They are delightful to watch.

The Atom

The Greeks were the first to propose the existence of the atom as the smallest indivisible building block of all matter. This belief lasted until 1897 when J.J. Thomson suggested a new model based on the electrical properties of the atom and the discovery of the electron. His model resembled a watermelon with electrons interspersed throughout the atom as seeds are in a watermelon. An experiment in 1911 fired alpha particles (consisting of two protons and two neutrons) at a thin metal foil. Most of the alpha particles passed right through the foil as though it were empty space. Because of this apparent emptiness, Ernest Rutherford proposed a planetary model of the atom, with electrons orbiting the nucleus as planets orbit the sun.

In 1913 the Danish physicist Niels Bohr proposed yet another model of the atom due to the observation that atoms absorb and emit only specific frequencies of light. In this model, which became known as the Bohr model, electrons can exist only in specific orbits around the nucleus. As they change orbits, photons of light of specific frequencies are either absorbed or emitted. Electrons never exist between these orbits.

For quite some time protons, neutrons, and electrons were thought to be elementary particles: fundamental constituents of the atom that are indivisible. In 1945, however, experiments at high-energy particle accelerators, such as the Stanford Linear Accelerator, and now Fermilab and CERN (The European Organization for Nuclear Research), revealed that protons and neutrons are made

---

[220] Brian Greene, *The Elegant Universe: Superstrings, Hidden Dimensions, and the Quest for the Ultimate Theory* (New York: W.W. Norton & Company, 2003).
[221] *The Fabric of the Cosmos: Space, Time, and the Texture of Reality*.

up of other sub-subatomic constituents. Though these sub-subatomic particles are unstable and have very short half-lives, more than 300 such new particles have been catalogued. The basic ingredients of these particles are quarks. There are six unique quarks, each with different spins and charges.[222] We will come back to these new *elementary particles* again, but for now we sidestep to a discussion on gravity. There is ultimately a connection!

Gravity

Sir Isaac Newton, in the late 1600's, proposed an invisible force that holds planets in their orbits around their star. He called it gravity. This force acts instantaneously on each planet and emanates from the central star. In a moment of genius, he made an astounding connection between this invisible force and the force that causes an apple to fall to the ground. He used what Einstein would later call the *equivalence principle* to identify the two types of motion as *acceleration*. Planets orbiting their star are accelerating towards that star due to the force of gravity at a rate that is equivalent to their trajectory away from the star due to their horizontal speed. The result is an orbit. The falling apple was also accelerating toward its central mass (the Earth).

This invisible force called gravity was troublesome to some scientists due to its invisible nature, but Newton's explanation became the standard for many years. The calculations Newton made based on this instantaneous force called gravity were accurate enough to eventually put humankind on the Moon. These formulas were good enough for most. Most, that is, except for Albert Einstein.

Relativity

Albert Einstein was obsessed with light. He wanted to know the substance of light and understand its behavior. This obsession eventually led to his formulation of the special theory of relativity. In special relativity nothing travels faster than the speed of light. What is more, light in a vacuum never travels at any speed other than the constant speed of 3.00×10^8 m/s (that is, 300,000,000 meters per second). Regardless of the speed of the observer, light is always observed traveling at that

---

[222] Raymond Serway & Jerry Faughn, *Physics* (Austin: Holt, Rinehart and Winston, 2006).

constant speed. The ramifications on time, distance, and velocity were astounding. Thanks to special relativity we understand that watches and measuring tapes traveling at different speeds will not agree.[223] Einstein realized that the constancy of the speed of light pronounced doom on some of Newton's principles.[224]

Newton's theory of gravity relied on instantaneous responses from masses, such as the planets, if a change occurred in the gravitational field surrounding them. For instance, if the Sun were to suddenly disappear, all the planets would instantaneously launch off into space in various directions. Einstein realized that such instantaneous responses would be faster than the speed of light, which, according to special relativity, is impossible. Nothing, not even gravity, can travel or communicate faster than the speed of light. Light is the ultimate speed limit. That being the case, then what is gravity?

Einstein resolved the issue by introducing general relativity. Therein space and time are not only influenced by motion, but also by the presence of matter and energy, which warp space and time.[225] According to general relativity, space and time have substance; they are the fabric of the cosmos. The presence of matter, or mass, warps this space-time fabric. Einstein believed the gravity that held the earth in orbit around the sun was not some "mysterious instantaneous action of the sun." Instead, it was due to the warped space-time fabric around the sun's enormous mass.[226] The planets travel the easiest and shortest path of motion through the space warped by the sun. Gravity *is* warped space.

Another realization that came out of Einstein's wanderings was that not only do masses warp space, but accelerating and rotating masses warp space, too. Such objects drag space along with them. What is more, such accelerated motion not only warps space: it also warps time![227] Moving masses send ripples through the fabric of space-time. As it turns out, these ripples travel at exactly the speed of light.

---

[223] Greene, *The Elegant Universe: Superstrings, Hidden Dimensions, and the Quest for the Ultimate Theory,* 25.
[224] Ibid., 33.
[225] Ibid., 6.
[226] Ibid., 69-70.
[227] Ibid., 65-66.

Although Newton ultimately got it wrong, he was correct in that there is something absolute. Though space is not absolute and time is not absolute, "absolute space-time does exist."[228] Einstein took Newton's intuitive interpretation of the cosmos and refined it with both the special and general theories of relativity.

How is it possible that light can remain constant regardless of the speed of the observer? Even if the observer is moving away from the source of light at 99% of the speed of light, the light will still be measured at a constant 300,000,000 m/s. The key is in the fabric of space-time: space and time are affected by the observer's speed. Space and time continuously adjust so that the observed speed of light is always constant, no matter how fast one travels.[229] As time changes with increased velocity, distance also changes so that the resulting speed of light is still 300,000,000 m/s.

Einstein proclaimed one more astounding conclusion from his theories of relativity: we are moving through space-time at exactly the speed of light. Space-time has three dimensions of space and one of time, and it is our combined speed through all four dimensions that is constant. If our speed through space is zero, then our speed through time is at the speed of light. The faster we move through space, the slower we move through time, so that our combined speed is always at the speed of light.[230] The slower one travels through time, the less time passes. Technically, time passes more slowly for someone who is running than someone who is still, though the difference is extremely small. If we were able to travel through space close to the speed of light, time would practically stand still. On that timeless note, we return to the atom.

Quantum Mechanics

It was thought for many years that the atom, with its elementary particles, was a very orderly and predictable entity. In 1927, however, Werner Heisenberg showed the world a very different picture of the atom. He found that the more precisely one attempts to measure the location of an orbiting electron around its nucleus, the less precisely one is able to measure its momentum. The more

---

[228] *The Fabric of the Cosmos: Space, Time, and the Texture of Reality*, 59.
[229] Ibid., 47.
[230] Ibid., 49.

precisely one attempts to measure its momentum, the less precisely one is able to measure its location.[231] This new picture of the atom was a bit disturbing to some, including Albert Einstein. It was a model of the atom that was formulated on probability and chance.

This new approach to atomic physics became known as quantum mechanics. Quantum mechanics introduced randomness into science. As Stephen Hawking says in *A Brief History of Time*, "Einstein objected to this very strongly, despite the important role he had played in the development of these ideas. Einstein was awarded the Nobel Prize for his contributions to quantum theory. Nevertheless, Einstein never accepted that the universe was governed by chance; his feelings were summed up in his famous statement 'God does not play dice.'"[232] In spite of the objections, quantum mechanics was growing not only in popularity, but also in its ability to make accurate predictions of atomic and subatomic behaviors.

Contrast, if you will, general relativity and quantum mechanics. The former provides very smooth and predictable analyses of the motion of large objects in space. The latter paints a contrasting picture of randomness, chance, and probability. The smooth space-time that general relativity describes is very violent at the quantum level.[233] How can both be accurate pictures of the universe? How can we be governed by predictable macro theories and unpredictable micro theories at the same time? Are these slices of larger dimensional entities?

Unification

We have Albert Einstein to thank for launching the first unified field theory in his attempt to unite gravity with electromagnetism.[234] Einstein theorized through general relativity that warped space-time was responsible for gravity. He also knew that this warped space-time interacted with light. The two were intertwined. Others also theorized that light, or electromagnetic radiation, is intertwined with

---

[231] *The Elegant Universe: Superstrings, Hidden Dimensions, and the Quest for the Ultimate Theory*, 113-14.
[232] Stephen Hawking, *A Brief History of Time* (New York: Bantam Books, 1996), 58.
[233] Greene, *The Elegant Universe: Superstrings, Hidden Dimensions, and the Quest for the Ultimate Theory*, 129.
[234] Ibid., 15.

gravity in that both are "associated with ripples in the fabric of space."[235] The pursuit of a unified theory of the forces of gravity and electromagnetism was on.

In addition to gravity and electromagnetism, there are two other forces present in nature: the strong and the weak forces. The strong force is the force that holds the nucleus of the atom together. This force is significant in that it holds the protons of the nucleus, which have positive charges and normally repel each other, in close proximity to each other along with neutrons in the nucleus. The weak force is the force responsible for radioactive decay of nuclear particles.

It is theorized that each of these forces is communicated, or transmitted, via a messenger particle: gravity via the graviton, electromagnetism via the photon, the strong force via gluons, and the weak force via weak gauge bosons.[236] The strongest of these forces is the strong force. The electromagnetic force has less than 0.01 of the strength of the strong force, the weak force is approximately 0.00001 times weaker, and the gravitational force is about 10^{-35} times weaker.[237] In spite of these extreme differences, physicists began to postulate that these four forces were related. Why not? Einstein related gravity with electromagnetism. Electromagnetism was related to quantum mechanics through the process of photons being absorbed or emitted from the atom during quantum shifts in electron orbits. Why should they not all be related at some root level? Hence the pursuit of a unified theory of everything: the grandest of all theories.

Black Holes

The loop back and forth between the micro world of atoms and the macro world of stars and galaxies is no coincidental loop. The two, as it turns out are inextricably linked. The common denominator, as many physicists now believe, is a very strange entity called a black hole.

During World War I a young German physicist by the name of Karl Schwarzschild, whose job was to calculate armed trajectories, performed some amazing calculations on stars in his spare time. He discovered that if the mass of a star, in proportion to its radius, is concentrated in a small enough volume, the

---

[235] Ibid., 197.
[236] *The Fabric of the Cosmos: Space, Time, and the Texture of Reality*, 255-56.
[237] *The Elegant Universe: Superstrings, Hidden Dimensions, and the Quest for the Ultimate Theory*, 175.

"space-time warp is so radical that anything, including light, which gets too close to the star will be unable to escape its gravitational grip."[238] They were initially called dark stars. Later, John Wheeler coined the phrase "black hole."[239] Schwarzschild launched a field of study that captivated many physicists for decades.

The connection between massive black holes and the tiny world of quantum mechanics begins with general relativity insisting that all the matter in a black hole is squeezed into a miniscule point at its center. The center is both incredibly massive and tiny. It exists on both sides of the great divide: "We need to use general relativity because the large mass creates a substantial gravitational field, and we also need to use quantum mechanics because all the mass is squeezed to a tiny size." Unfortunately, the equations do not work well together, breaking down due to discontinuities. No one knows for sure what happens at the center of a black hole.[240] Black holes bring general relativity and quantum mechanics face to face, but mathematically a profound conundrum is formed.

Any object that approaches too close to the *point of no return*, what is known as the *event horizon* of a black hole, is doomed. Not even light can escape once inside this boundary. Gravity is enormous and sucks in any such entity, crushing it into nothingness. However, if a person were able to travel to and hover just outside the event horizon of a black hole for about a year, then return to home planet earth, they would find that approximately 10,000 years would have lapsed since their initial departure from earth.[241] Such is the extreme nature of a black hole and its event horizon.

Black holes are quite similar to atomic elementary particles. Scientists have discovered that there are three properties that define a subatomic particle: mass, force charge, and spin. Mass is a simple measure with magnitude. Force charge has both magnitude and electric charge, which is either positive or negative. Spin is primarily a directional measure. Black holes have similar defining traits. It is precisely these similarities that have brought physicists to speculate that, "black

---

[238] Ibid., 78-79.
[239] Ibid., 78-79.
[240] Greene, *The Fabric of the Cosmos: Space, Time, and the Texture of Reality*, 337.
[241] *The Elegant Universe: Superstrings, Hidden Dimensions, and the Quest for the Ultimate Theory*, 80.

holes might actually be gigantic elementary particles."[242] Some have gone so far as to use Einstein's equations of relativity to propose that such gigantic elementary particles are gateways to other universes, suggesting that where time and space of our universe come to an end in a black hole, they may have just begun in another universe.[243]

The presence of black holes in our universe may actually tear holes in the fabric of space-time. Such tears may be portals to another universe. These portals, or *wormholes*, would actually create space that had not previously existed. Removing such a wormhole would actually cause the space it occupied to vanish.[244] No one knows for certain if such wormholes exist, but mathematically they appear to be a possibility.

Tying it Together with Strings

We have talked about very large entities, such as stars and universes, and the theories of relativity that govern them. We have also looked at the very small elementary particles in the quantum world, a world of chaotic and random movement that is quite contrary to the predictable macro world of general relativity. For scientists, the two have been nearly impossible to reconcile philosophically and mathematically. How could one universe contain such dichotomous features?

Both of these macro and micro worlds involve four primary forces that appear to be the basic forces responsible for holding all things together and governing the behavior of the universe: gravity, electromagnetism, the weak force, and the strong force. Einstein began the unification process of reconciling gravity with electromagnetism. Others worked steadfastly to understand the other forces and whether or not they were ultimately related to one another.

One such person was Gabriele Veneziano, who in 1968 was working at understanding the strong nuclear force, using data from high-energy particle collisions from atom smashers around the world. He discovered a two-hundred-year-old equation by the mathematician Leonhard Euler, which seemed to match

---

[242] Ibid., 321.
[243] Ibid., 343-44.
[244] *The Fabric of the Cosmos: Space, Time, and the Texture of Reality*, 461.

the particle data with amazing precision.[245] The most bizarre thing about the equation was that it very precisely described the behavior of subatomic particles, yet no one knew why, especially since Euler had intended the equation to simply model the *vibrations of strings under tension.*

This unanticipated connection led physicists to postulate that if the strong force between two particles was due to an elastic strand connecting them, then Euler's equation might mathematically describe the strong force.[246] These tiny elastic strands of energy were christened *strings,* and *string theory* was born.

These strands, strangely modeled by Euler's equation, became a mathematical obsession of many physicists. The strings are believed to have no thickness, only length, being one-dimensional entities. These strings are so small that they are no more than points to the most advanced atom smashers.[247] So why is there so much intrigue? What is the beauty of these strings?

Imagine the notes produced by a violin. Each note is produced by a string of a certain length and a given tension. So it is in string theory; different vibrational patterns in strings give rise to different masses and force charges. These particle properties are determined by the string's pattern of vibration.[248] Instead of producing notes, such as those a violin makes, these vibrational patterns result in the fundamental elementary particles and their associated forces. The vibrational energy of these strings determines their mass! Einstein showed us through his infamous $E = mc^2$ equation that mass and energy are related. Now string theory was beginning to tie it all together. All the strings in the universe comprise a "cosmic symphony."[249] In this case, it is more than analogous to a symphony: it is the symphony!

More Dimensions of Space

In the mid-1800's James Clerk Maxwell, a Scottish theoretical physicist, published four simple equations that govern electromagnetism, or light. In the early 1900's Theodor Kaluza, a German mathematician and physicist, theorized

---

[245] Ibid., 339.
[246] Ibid., 340.
[247] Ibid., 345.
[248] *The Elegant Universe: Superstrings, Hidden Dimensions, and the Quest for the Ultimate Theory,* 143-44.
[249] Ibid., 146.

that there might be at least one more spatial dimension beyond the three common spatial dimensions for which Einstein had derived his field equations. By permitting an extra dimension Kaluza derived a new set of equations. He discovered that three of the new equations matched Einstein's original field equations. He also realized that the extra equations matched Maxwell's equations for electromagnetism.[250] Not only did this substantiate the underlying symmetry between general relativity (gravity) and electromagnetism (light), but it also opened the door to more spatial dimensions.

As string theory progressed, other spatial dimensions became apparent. It became clear that more than three spatial dimensions must exist for so many types of vibrating strings to exist. In fact, it was determined that nine spatial dimensions would have to exist in order for the mathematical models to sufficiently explain the existence of all these particles. A universe with three or five or even eight dimensions is insufficient to explain their existence. "But with nine space dimensions, the constraint on the number of vibrational patterns is satisfied perfectly."[251] The number of vibrational patterns permitted by nine dimensions of space is sufficient to permit the existence of electrons, which are comprised of strings, and protons and neutrons, which are comprised of quarks, which in turn are comprised of strings.[252]

Five Models

As is usually the case, a snag appeared in the process. Quite independently of each other, five different mathematical models were developed throughout the international physics community to explain strings and the elementary particles they comprised. The irony was that all five worked; they each made verifiable predictions. Yet they were irreconcilable with each other. How can there be five completely different mathematical models that each adequately explain the existence of all subatomic particles, yet do not *agree* with each other?

---

[250] Ibid., 196-97.
[251] *The Fabric of the Cosmos: Space, Time, and the Texture of Reality*, 370-71.
[252] *The Elegant Universe: Superstrings, Hidden Dimensions, and the Quest for the Ultimate Theory*, 14.

Ed Whitten

These irreconcilable differences caused some physicists to question the validity of string theory. Some abandoned it altogether, returning to other arenas in physics. How can a theory intended to provide unity, the ultimate story of everything, have five differing presentations with such apparent dichotomies? This was the case until Ed Whitten, professor of mathematical physics at the Institute for Advanced Study in Princeton, stepped in and quietly resolved the conflict.

In the mid-1990's, Witten gave surprising and convincing evidence that the five current string theories, which relied on nine spatial dimensions, actually missed one spatial dimension. String theory, he argued, actually requires ten spatial dimensions and one time dimension, for a total of eleven dimensions![253] This was earth shaking: we live in an eleven dimensional universe. Whitten's new mathematical theory became known as M-theory. It does indeed seem to more adequately describe the fabric of the cosmos than the five lower dimensional string theories.

Brian Greene likens Whitten's resolution (of the five string theories into one) to a single cellist performing on stage with five mirrors behind her, providing five unique two-dimensional reflections of a single three-dimensional musician. Each reflection is accurate but does not necessarily correspond with the other four views. By adding another dimension, the discontinuities are resolved.

Remaining Issues

Not all questions were immediately resolved by M-theory. There is disagreement on the nature of the eleven dimensions. Some physicists believe ten of the eleven dimensions are spatial dimensions and one is a dimension of time. Others have proposed that nine of them are spatial dimensions and two of them are dimensions of time.

Another, and fairly disturbing, issue to physicists is, "Where are these extra dimensions?" If they are real, then why can we not see them? This latter question has prompted some theorists to conclude that they cannot be seen because they

---

[253] Ibid., 203-04.

are extremely small, curled up dimensions, best described by a complicated shape called the *Calabi-Yau space* (Figure 24). Our three dimensional space could theoretically be filled with these micro-sized Calabi-Yau spaces.

Figure 24. Calabi Yau Space by Lunch. Wikimedia.

Personally, I think we fret too much over making such extra dimensions *comfortable* in size in order to comprehend their invisibility. It may be that they are no different in size, but that we cannot see them for other reasons! We will address some of these reasons in chapters to come.

Have We Reached The Deepest Level?

The Greeks proposed that the atom was the smallest indivisible building block of all matter. This theory gave way to numerous models throughout the centuries, eventually arriving at M-theory today. But is M-theory it? Are strings the final, indivisible building blocks of all matter and forces? Brian Greene astutely acknowledges that whenever we dig deeper into the universe, we discover yet another layer in a never-ending "cosmic onion."[254]

The most astounding outcome of string theory, and its subsequent M-theory, is the process used to resolve five otherwise irreconcilable string theories. By being willing to add yet another dimension, these five verifiable mathematical models were merged into one unified theory. Perhaps unity *is* a possibility and not simply an overstated assumption. What if such a process was applied to theology? What would be the outcome if such divergent belief systems were subjected to a higher dimensional analysis? I have said on numerous occasions that physicists and theologians are each backing themselves up in order to take a broader look, to the point that they may actually back into each other and find common ground. For now, however, put string theory on the back burner and let us take a look at a puzzling confirmation of our strange eleven-dimensional universe.

---

[254] Ibid., 142.

3.02

Vincent

One morning in February of 2006 I woke with the chorus of *Vincent*, by Don McLean, rolling through my head . . .

> Now I think I know what you tried to say to me,
> How you suffered for your sanity,
> How you tried to set them free.
> They would not listen,
> They're not listening still.
> Perhaps they never will . . . [255]

Such a phenomenon is not unusual for me. I frequently have songs playing in my head. When they do, I do not just think about the song, the actual recording of the song plays in my head. I hear the artist's voice and the orchestration. Even the pitch is usually spot-on. I don't try to hear to such a song, it just plays. Usually it is a song that I have heard recently. What was unusual about this encounter was that I had not heard this song for a very, very long time. It caught me off guard at the start, knowing that it is typically a recent listening that spurs such a playing. I quickly passed it off.

I got ready for work and took off for a very busy day. The song continued to play throughout the day. Usually songs like this will play for longer periods of time if I am tired or stressed, so I tried to let go of it and proceed with my work.

---

[255] Don McLean, *Vincent. Reprinted by Permission of Hal Leonard Corporation.,* 1971.

I was a bit perplexed the following day as the song continued to play. I again tried to ignore it, assuming that I was more tired than I realized. By the end of the first week of this chorus playing nonstop during every waking moment, I grew a bit frantic. I have had songs play for several days, but never for a whole week. I spent a few moments evaluating the stresses in my life, hoping that acknowledging them would help. I tried to move on.

At the end of the third week I was ready to pull my hair out. Do not misunderstand me, I love Don McLean's song, but this was overkill. In an act of desperation, I pulled up the lyrics to *Vincent* on the Internet. I thought, "Perhaps there is a message in the text that is intended for me." I read through the lyrics a number of times hoping beyond hope to see a message. It did not happen. There was nothing. I do not mean to say that the lyrics are worthless, for they are rich with meaning and sentiment. What I mean to say is that nothing extraordinary jumped out at me. I closed the browser, and once again decided to move on.

Looking back on this experience, I marvel at how thickheaded I was. It is amazing that even after having the chorus play in my head for so long, I did not catch on sooner. How much sooner? Well, the song played on until the early part of June. For more than 3 months it played. You may wonder how I lasted so long. Finally, desperation threw me into a search for a solution. I am not proud of this encounter, especially since I am the one that preaches, "Listen!" How could it have taken me more than three months to get the message? But it did.

I sat in my office with the door closed. "What am I missing? What am I not seeing?" All of a sudden it hit me: it is not about the song. It is about the subject of the song. For those unfamiliar with *Vincent*, the song starts with, "Starry, starry night . . ." I thought, "Is that it? Is it about the painting?" With urgency I found a copy of Van Gogh's *The Starry Night* online. I expanded the picture to full-screen, and stared at it with an open mind (Figure 25).

Figure 25. The Starry Night by Vincent van Gogh. Public Domain.

All of a sudden visual popcorn began to pop. My face broadened with a smile. Piece by piece I began to see hidden treasures in a work created by a troubled yet prophetically visionary man. In May of 1889 Van Gogh committed himself to the hospital at Saint Paul-de-Mausole, a former monastery in Saint-Remy. While there, he painted numerous paintings, including *The Starry Night*, which he completed in June of that year.[256] Buried in the painting were numerous details that I have not been able to find in any critique or exposé on this piece of art.

The very first thing that struck me was that there are eleven stars in the sky. Eleven. I believe Vincent had an understanding of the eleven-dimensional nature of the cosmos. In addition, he carefully portrayed each of the eleven stars with unique size and character. Looking at the character of the night sky around the

---

[256] Wikipedia, "Vincent Van Gogh," http://en.wikipedia.org/wiki/Vincent_van_Gogh.

stars one can also see that he portrayed the *fabric* of space-time flowing around the celestial bodies. This was 16 years before Einstein introduced the revolutionary concept of the *fabric of space-time* in his theories of relativity, and 100 years before well-developed string theory proposed a universe of eleven dimensions!

The stars appear to be separated into two groups: seven above the large swirl, and four below the swirl. What is more, the stars below the swirl are portrayed in such a way that places them in front of the swirl and the stars above the swirl are behind it. Two of the lower stars overlap the swirl in front of it, validating the perspective. This was no accident. Van Gogh was an expert at portraying depth. What did he intentionally hope to portray? To answer that question, one must assess the role of the swirl itself.

I believe the swirl is a boundary, separating two distinct domains: the domain containing four stars close to Saint-Remy and the domain with seven stars beyond Saint-Remy. The swirl is a dimensional boundary, separating four-dimensional space-time from seven dimensions beyond it. Van Gogh painted *The Starry Night* long before physicists introduced such revolutionary ideas as the *fabric of space-time* and *extra dimensions*. For this reason, I call Van Gogh a prophet.

The swirl also calls into question Van Gogh's perspective. Why does the swirl lap downward in front of the snowcapped mountains and into Saint-Remy, yet move behind the lower four stars? The swirl is both behind space-time and in it! It crosses the boundary that it represents. Think about water draining out of a tub. A swirl or vortex of fluid is formed at the exit. Van Gogh was portraying this *exit*. The swirl is not simply a formation of clouds, or an astronomical arrangement of galaxies: it is a pathway, a vortex leaving four-dimensional space-time for a destination beyond. Why? Why a whirlwind leaving Saint-Remy?

It was at that moment that I saw an abstract self-portrait of van Gogh himself. My eyes grew large as I realized that Van Gogh, among others, was inside the whirlwind! If one looks closely at the upper mid-portion of the whirlwind, spiraling down and into the painting, buried within a transparent water-like stream, is Van Gogh himself. His reddish hair and yellowish skin trail behind the rest of his body, clothed in the blue denim so typical of Van Gogh's attire.

Van Gogh saw the whirlwind by which he would leave this domain. He saw what the prophet Elijah saw and experienced: a wormhole to life beyond his heavy and depressed existence.[257] Contrary to interpretations that simply describe Van Gogh as wanting to escape the endless and depressing black night, *The Starry Night* was a painting of hope.[258] Looking through a window from a room in the asylum, he saw a window into an existence free from pain. He probably saw stars and planets coming at him at the speed of light as he entered the whirlwind. The message Van Gogh portrayed in this masterpiece could not have been communicated in a daylight painting. In spite of Van Gogh's depression and the nighttime setting, the painting is a light-filled encounter. Van Gogh once said, "For my part I know nothing with certainty, but the sight of the stars makes me dream." It was not about depressing darkness, but about accelerating heavenly lights! It was an epiphany reached during his dark years. It was a ray of hope. For Van Gogh, death became a transition of dimensions to so much more beyond.

Van Gogh was a genius. He was a depressed genius, but a genius nonetheless. He, as have other prophets, gradually became less and less connected with four-dimensional space-time, as he moved deeper and deeper into higher dimensions. Was he misunderstood? Yes. Was he misinformed? No. He saw clearly what was to come, not only for himself, but also for everyone else.

I am forever indebted to van Gogh for *The Starry Night*. But I must ask, "Who or what nagged at me through Don McLean's song until I got the message?" Was it the voice of God? Was it the prompting of van Gogh himself? I do not know for sure, but I will hypothesize in a later Phase who might have been responsible for the incessant music. I am convinced it was an intervention.

A most phenomenal thing happened once I saw the imbedded messages in Van Gogh's painting: the chorus that had been playing in my head for three and a half months suddenly stopped. I did not have to exercise some extraordinary self-discipline to prevent my mind from playing it anymore. It just stopped. I had seen what I was supposed to see. I heard what I had been asked to hear. I had finally paid attention and listened. You can only imagine the joy and excitement that filled

---

[257] 2 Kings 2:11.
[258] Biography, "Analysis of Vincent Van Gogh's the Starry Night," http://lifeofvangogh.com/analysis-starry-night.html.

my bones. To have music that played nonstop for so long suddenly come to a halt left me numb, peaceful, and smiling. You could say it was, "The day the music died."[259]

---

[259] Don McLean, *American Pie. Reprinted by Permission of Hal Leonard Corporation.*, 1971.

3.03

Intuitive Wanderings

Admittedly the Vincent encounter was strange, not to mention dimensional, and it spawned more intuitive wanderings than I anticipated. Einstein trusted such intuition. He once said, "The supreme task of the physicist is to arrive at those universal elementary laws from which the cosmos can be built up by pure deduction. There is no logical path to these laws; only intuition, resting on sympathetic understanding of experience, can reach them."[260]

I was once hesitant to voice my opinions on topics pertaining to current theories in physics, due primarily to my less-than-adequate mathematical skills, which are necessary to substantiate such opinions. I hesitate no longer. The physics community itself is leaning more and more towards what appears to be a philosophical approach to a unified theory of everything, backed by mathematical models that in some cases are manipulated to avoid the singularities and infinities that physicists dread. Granted, if theoretical models produce predictions that can be verified by experimental data, then the mathematics are validated. If not, then other philosophical approaches, such as mine, are just as founded, provided that simplicity and equivalence principles substantiate them. So, until my gut intuitions are proven false by experimental data, I will not hesitate to proclaim them. Furthermore, my non-sophisticated mathematical approach does make predictions that can be carried out experimentally, and hopefully with validating results.

This chapter looks more closely into the claims that theoretical physicists purport, embellishing them with my own intuitive wanderings. I give myself much

---

[260] Albert Einstein, 1918.

freedom in speculating on possible organizational structures of extra dimensions, on reasons why special relativity is true (though Einstein may have deemed these reasons unconventional), on the nature of black holes, and on what lies beyond this tiny universe.

Unity

I do not believe all diversity necessarily converges to unity. However, the fact that five dichotomous string theories merged into one beautiful composite, once adequate dimensional analyses were permitted, leads me to believe there is such a unifying connection between all four forces in the universe. This unity resides outside our limited four-dimensional space-time confines. We may find evidences of it within this realm, but even if we do not establish a complete unifying connection here and now, I believe such a unified force and a theory of everything exist. My intuition, as Einstein would have put it, says so.

Extra Dimensions

I am sure you have already caught on to the fact that I believe our universe is comprised of more than four dimensions. I must admit that my Vincent experience was profoundly influential. If it were the only piece of evidence pointing to such a universe, I would not be inclined to such a strong belief. However, given the mathematical evidences from the physics community and other surprising sources, (including logical wanderings yet to be revealed), the signs are overwhelming: we live in a complex universe that is much greater than what we see. The irony is that scientists appear to be more convinced than many theologians of extra invisible dimensions that hold our visible universe together.

It will be no surprise to you that I will draw many *spiritual* parallels to this dimensional existence. This Phase will clarify why I hesitate to even use the word *spiritual*. I have abandoned many of the dualistic views I once held, views that compartmentalized the physical realm from the spiritual realm. All realms have become physical to me. *Spiritual* to me includes all things that exist in the dimensions that are to us invisible. Where I may leave a physicist or two behind is in my belief that more than strings exist in such dimensions.

Light and Extra Dimensions

Albert Einstein unveiled several mysterious properties of light. Serendipitously, perhaps, he opened the door to higher dimensions through the theory of special relativity. The strange nature of light gives evidence to these dimensions.

I believe the constancy of the speed of light is evidence that it is essentially rooted in another dimension. For illustrative purposes, imagine living on a two dimensional plane, such as a sheet of paper. Also envision someone from outside that domain shining a light onto that paper. No matter how fast one moves about on that sheet of paper, the light hits them at the same speed because it comes at them perpendicularly, or from a third dimension. This does not preclude light from moving about within the plane of the sheet of paper, but illustrates that it is rooted in an additional dimension.

Likewise, if we envision light being rooted in a dimension beyond our three dimensions of space, it will always present itself as coming at us with a constant perpendicular speed. In the following figure (Figure 26) the frontal plane, represented by the vertical axis and the axis angled slightly downward and horizontal, represents our three-dimensional space. An observer moving at a speed of v_o can vary their speed from nothing to a very high speed within that plane (symbolized by the arc), but light, which is rooted in the dimension that moves "into the page" in the direction of the v_l axis, and symbolized by the dashed lines, is always perpendicular and constant in nature. The dashed lines are not meant to illustrate direction in three-dimensional space, only speed. I believe the constancy of the speed of light clearly indicates that its roots are in a higher dimension. Where Einstein and I might converge is that this extra dimension may be tied to the dimension of time. Nevertheless, such a phenomenon points to an extra-dimensional component of light that is perpendicular to all three spatial dimensions.

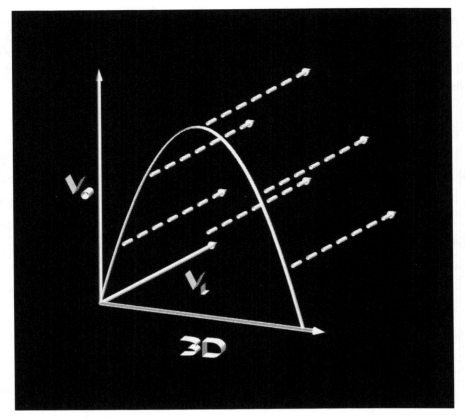

Figure 26. Special Relativity

Light has yet another peculiar feature that reveals its higher dimensional origin. Light has what is called a wave-particle duality. Depending on the experimental setup, light can be demonstrated to be a massless particle known as a photon that behaves as such, and whose force is measurable by particle detectors. On the other hand, if a double slit experiment is set up with a single source of light passing through two close and very narrow slits, light behaves as waves that interfere with each other, creating an interference pattern on a screen on the far side of the slits. Can light be both a particle and a wave? Evidence demonstrates that it is both.

This does not make sense within the simple confines of four-dimensional space-time. However, if more dimensions are permitted to be a part of the explanation, such dichotomous features are to be expected. The following illustration (Figure 27) demonstrates that a particle is detected if such an experiment is so constructed with a particle detector. In this case the experimental design actually *collapses* the higher dimensional particle component of light into four-dimensional space-time. Hence a particle is observed.

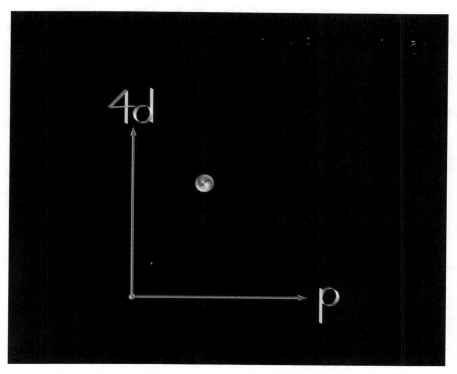

Figure 27. de Broglie Principle: 2D View of 4D Space-Time vs Particle

However, if the double-slit experiment is carried out, the result is to *collapse* the higher dimensional wave component of light into four-dimensional space-time. Hence a wave is observed (Figure 28).

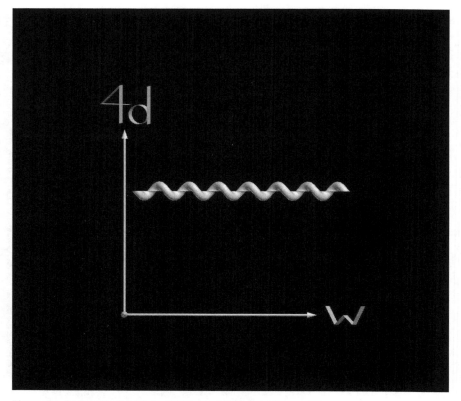

Figure 28. de Broglie Principle: 2D View of 4D Space-Time vs Wave

It should not surprise you that light may have at least two more dimensional components beyond our four-dimensional domain (Figure 29). The most significant point to be made is not how many extra-dimensional features light does or does not have, but that these features verify extra dimensions beyond the ones we normally see and measure in four-dimensional space-time.

Louis de Broglie, the eminent French physicist, carried this principle much further. He hypothesized that the wave-particle duality applies to both light and matter. Einstein had brought matter and energy together with his $E = mc^2$ equation. Plank and Einstein together associated energy with wave frequency.

Therefore, matter would also have wave-like properties.[261] His theory has been confirmed in experiments with double slits involving single electrons. In such experiments a single electron aimed at double slits resulted in an interference pattern on the screen on the far side of the double slits. How could a single electron cause an interference pattern? It would have had to pass through both slits in order to do so! Some hypothesize that each electron "traverses every possible trajectory simultaneously" in its journey.[262] The higher dimensional nature of our universe becomes even more mysterious.

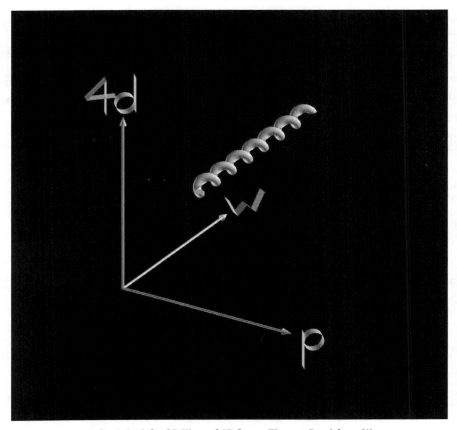

Figure 29. de Broglie Principle: 3D View of 4D Space-Time vs Particle vs Wave

---

[261] Greene, *The Elegant Universe: Superstrings, Hidden Dimensions, and the Quest for the Ultimate Theory*, 103-04.
[262] Ibid., 110.

Eleven Dimensions

There are very pragmatic evidences for more than our four dimensions of space-time, but eleven? Aside from the mathematical reasons physicists use to justify an eleven-dimensional universe, there are a number of other contributing sources that affirm such a claim. These sources are unconventional for a physicist, but not for an intellectual mystic.

Before I had read much on current theoretical physics, I pondered the form and organization of *spiritual* dimensions. It made sense to me that there might be three additional dimensions of space, dimensions with *heavenly* entities moving about, but I had never before considered an additional dimension of time. I had often heard theologians talk about the *timelessness* of heaven, or whatever spiritual realm one believes in. It made sense that such a place would be without time if it were eternal. The concept that bothered me was that timelessness implies changelessness or frozenness. Scripture mentions differences in time, but does not talk about the absence of time. Hence, I became convinced that, in whatever form it may be, there must be at least one dimension of time in the next domain. That means *heaven* could be a four-dimensional place as well.

As I pondered the IICP and the misled belief that someday we will "see God in all his fullness" (remember the argument: we would have to be infinite in order to see infinitude in its fullness), I realized that there would have to be some spatial domain beyond a heavenly domain in which this infinitude dwells. Assuming it had *at least* three dimensions for the IICP, or some representation of it, to move within, I arbitrarily settled on at least these three dimensions beyond heaven.

Without realizing it I had postulated *at least* eleven dimensions: the four we reside in, heaven's four, and three for a representation of a timeless IICP. Now you can imagine the incredible rush that flowed through my body when a friend first filled me in on the eleven dimensions of M-theory.

Once I was aware of the eleven-dimensional concept, my senses were keenly looking for other clues leading to such a dimensional conclusion. One came from an ancient Norse myth. You will recall from Phase 1 that I do not take mythology lightly: it is rooted in real human experience. Here is the myth as told by Todd Reimer.

In the beginning there was no earth or heaven, no sand nor sea nor cooling waves. There was only Ginnungagap, a great void. In the North there was Nilfheim, and from Nilfheim's spring flowed eleven rivers, known as Elivagar. As the rivers flowed south, they cooled and hardened into ice . . . Where the heat from the South met the coolness in the North the ice was thawed and it began to drip and by the might that sent the heat, life appeared in the drops of the running fluid and this fluid formed into the likeness of a man. He was given the name Ymir.[263]

What a fabulous story! I was elated to discover these eleven rivers converging to create the cosmos.

Other texts also support an eleven-dimensional existence. The Koran, referring to creation, says, "He it is who created for you all that is on earth, then proceeded to the heaven, and into seven heavens did He fashion it: and He knoweth all things."[264] It appears from this text that there are seven dimensions beyond the four of space-time. In a Biblical text, one that is not quite so explicit, we find, "From the throne came flashes of lightning, rumblings and peals of thunder. In front of the throne, seven lamps were blazing. These are the seven spirits of God."[265] Whether by means of myth, scripture, deduction, or mathematical necessity, there appear to be seven dimensions beyond the four we call home.

While some physicists may think that eleven dimensions are only mathematical entities necessary to neatly formulate string theory, I am inclined to view these dimensions as more than mathematical necessities. I am convinced of their reality and their role in our universe's existence.

Inverted Dimensions

One of the characteristics of these extra dimensions that troubles many a physicist is that they are apparently *invisible*. If they are real, why can we not see

---

263 Todd Reimer, "The Creation: Norse Mythology," http://todd.reimer.com/norse/story.html.
264 The Koran as translated by Rodwell, *The Koran*, II:27.
265 Revelation 4:5.

or detect them? To get around this anomaly, some physicists believe they are quite small and curled up in the microscopic Calabi-Yau spaces (as illustrated in Chapter 3.01). There they provide the dimensional support necessary to account for strings and their subsequent forces and particles, but remain too small to see and detect. Do they need to be so small to justify their invisibility?

Remember the Mobius strip from Phase 2? I reintroduce it here for illustrative purposes (Figure 30). Imagine if you will, that the flat surface of the strip represents a single extra dimension and that the strip is infinitely thin. Also, because of our dimensional confines, imagine that we are limited to a view that is directly above the strip. The right end would be clearly visible to such an observer, being flat and plainly seen. However, the left end is on its edge and since the strip is infinitely thin, it would be invisible to the observer. The right end is how I envision our three dimensions of space: flat, perpendicular to our observation, and visible. The left end, however, is what I refer to as inverted: flat, parallel to our observation, and invisible. Note that it is not invisible because it is tiny and curled up into an elaborate shape. It is invisible because it is inverted.

Figure 30. Mobius Strip

While it is difficult to imagine the surface of a Mobius strip representing a single dimension, the analogy still holds. Technically the right end of the strip is two-dimensional and the left end is one-dimensional to an observer limited in perspective. The result is the same: the inversion hides one of the two dimensions. I believe the same is true with extra dimensions. They are invisible because of their inversion, not because they are miniscule.

Dimensional Organization

Illustrations are needed to envision such dimensions and the domains they define. Some of these terms need to be defined.

The term *domain* refers to a local set of dimensions and their dimensional boundaries. For instance, I live in a house that is a part of a neighborhood. My house is my domain. The neighborhood is my house's domain. My city is my neighborhood's domain, and so on. Each domain contains smaller domains, yet is contained by a larger domain. In the case of dimensions, *large* and *small* do not refer to size, but to dimensions that contain a domain or that are contained by a domain.

For notational purposes, I will refer to the number of dimensions in a particular domain as 2d, 3d, 4d, and so on, with a lower case *d*. On the other hand, 4-D, with a hyphenated capital *D*, refers to a specific domain, such as our four-dimensional space-time.

The 0-D domain is comprised of a single point. In 1-D, two points can be connected to form a line. From one end of the line, however, it looks like a 0d point. In 2-D, two lines can be connected to form a plane. From the edge of the plane it looks like a 1d line. In 3-D two planes can be connected to form a cube, or 3d space. From the side of the cube it looks like a 2d plane. The same continues on into higher dimensions. Note that a 1d domain can contain an infinite number of 0d domains, and a 4d domain can contain an infinite number of 3d domains, etc. (It may help to think in terms of how many points exist on a line and how many lines exist on a plane, etc.)

Our eleven dimensions are broken down into at least two groups, as far as we can tell: the visible and the invisible (I lump time into the visible group for now).

But are we sure that the seven invisible dimensions are not also organized into other domains? What if our 4d domain is contained by another 4d domain, that is in turn contained by a 3d domain? In the following illustration (Figure 31) each domain is illustrated with three spatial dimensions, portrayed as arrows. Two of the domains have a sphere at the origin simply to illustrate a dimension of time. The upper-right domain, labeled 4d", could be our four-dimensional space-time. We may be contained by another 4d domain, labeled 4d', which is also contained by a 3d domain. Notice that to the visible dimensions in 4d' the entirety of 4d" is but a point, and probably an invisible point. Likewise, 4d' is but a point in 3d.

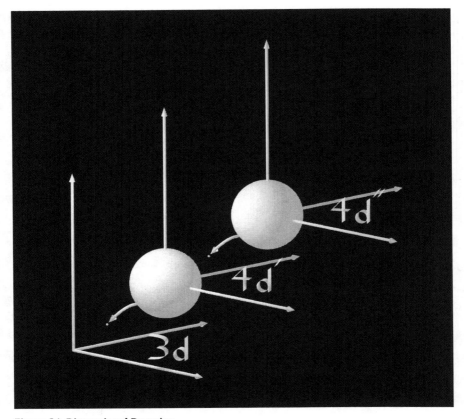

Figure 31. Dimensional Domains

While this dimensional organization is appealing, it assumes, for the moment, that there are no smaller dimensional domains contained within our 4-D domain (illustrated as 4d" above). I think there most likely are, given the whole realm of quantum mechanics.

String theory asserts that seven other dimensions are actively involved in holding our four-dimensional universe together. What if we are sharing some of these dimensions with another domain? It would be a bit like a dimensional support network.

If we define the domain that contains our universe as an *integral domain* and any universe that is contained by ours as a *derivative domain*, we may actually be sharing dimensions with both our integral and derivative domains! If one of our 7 extra dimensions is an extra dimension of time, as some physicists theorize, it is possible that 3 of our extra invisible (or inverted) dimensions may come from our integral and 3 from our derivative. What is more, we may be sharing our visible (non-inverted) dimensions with them! I think a word illustration may be helpful here.

I work for a hospital that is governed by an overarching organization that runs 21 such hospitals. Within our hospital there are diverse departments, each with staff that fill diverse responsibilities. There are communications (shared dimensions) that happen between the overarching organization and our administration. Likewise, there are communications that happen between our administration and each department. Using the terminology I described in the previous paragraph, the overarching organization is an integral domain to our hospital. Each department is a derivative domain in our hospital. The communications are like shared dimensions. Not only does the administration share communications with the departments, the departments also communicate outcomes with the administration. The communications go both directions. It just so happens that not all communications (or dimensions) are visible to each domain.

Let's try a graphical illustration. In the following illustration (Figure 32) each domain has three visible dimensions (arrows) and two dimensions of time (symbolized by the torus surrounding its origin). The Mobius strips illustrate 3 visible dimensions from each of the adjacent domains being shared as invisible dimensions with the center domain. The center domain has 3 visible spatial dimensions, two dimensions of time, and 6 inverted, or invisible spatial dimensions. Our invisible dimensions are visible dimensions in our integral and in our derivative! But, wait, that's not all!

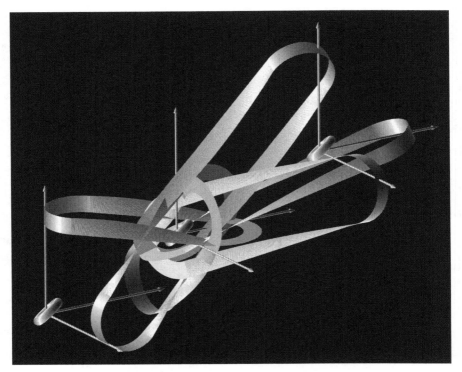

Figure 32. Incoming Inverted Dimensions from Adjacent Universes

Our visible spatial dimensions might be shared as well. In the following illustration (Figure 33) the center domain's visible spatial dimensions are shared with its integral and its derivative as inverted dimensions to them. Such illustrations prompt several discussions. First of all, we may be misled to think of our domain as a standalone universe. Perhaps it is but one of many such domains, or multiverses. Physicists have postulated parallel universes in M-Theory. With the model described above, I am more inclined to think in terms of *interwoven* universes: dimensionally interwoven.

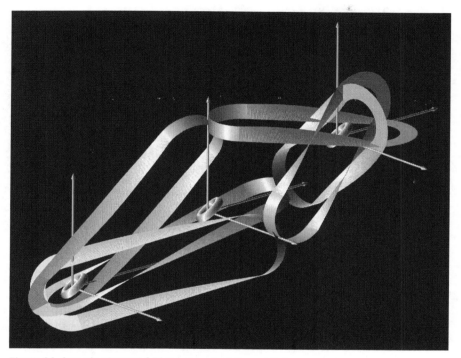

Figure 33. Outgoing Inverted Dimensions to Adjacent Universes

Remember the chaotic realm of quantum mechanics? Though the quantum world is invisible to us, it has been experimentally validated. It is a random world of probabilities, but may be comprised of the orderly spatial dimensions in our integral and in our derivative universes, inverted and supporting our quantum world. In other words, our quantum *emptiness*, so to speak, may be their fullness, and vice versa.

Putting it all together, we may exist in a chain of multiverses (Figure 34), each contributing to its adjacent universe by sharing inverted dimensions. Remembering the Calabi-Yau space, we now see that it may be comprised of 3 dimensions from our integral and 3 from our derivative.

Figure 34. Intersecting Multiverses

We Are Not Alone

We are not alone; we share dimensions; we coexist in a network of supporting spatial domains that are quite physical. It may be a stretch for some, but I believe one particular scriptural passage is a direct reference to such multiple domains that are "in heaven and on earth and under the earth."[266] Whether the writer would have thought in terms of multiverses remains unknown, but this I believe: even though some think there is no room for a heaven in the cosmos, there are without a doubt invisible forces and domains at play that, according to M-Theory, are responsible not only for holding the universes together, but perhaps also responsible for the birthing of these universes.

[266] Philippians 2:10b.

3.04

Boundaries

As a child I wondered, "If I were able to get to the edge of the universe, what would be on the other side?" Others have pondered such questions. Stephen Hawking asked a similar question and the outcome was to endorse the *no boundary condition* of our universe.[267] His belief implies that our universe is essentially eternal: not with respect to our four dimensions of space-time, but with respect to higher dimensions. While this seems to contradict his claim that the universe had a beginning and will have an end[268], in reality it does not. He believes our universe did have a beginning in 4-D, but has always existed in higher dimensions.

Hawking delineates between what we think of as real time and imaginary time, which is an additional dimension of time. If this other dimension of time is perpendicular to real time, it is reasonable to imagine everything existing forever in that dimension, even though it briefly enters then leaves real time. Real time (the dimension of time that is bound to past, present, and future) was birthed in the big bang, leaving imaginary time behind, or at least out of reach. Hawking believes that if and when the universe vanishes, the real dimension of time will vanish as well and imaginary time will continue as it always has. I think Hawking is spot on. We will come back to *time* in a subsequent chapter.

Do the dimensions of space have boundaries? Some imagine space-time as a torus (a giant donut-like shape), circling back on itself both in space and time. In this case, if one travels forever in a given direction, they eventually arrive back at

---

[267] Gevin Giorbran, "Stephen Hawking and the Time Has No Boundary Proposal," http://everythingforever.com/hawking.htm.
[268] Hawking, *A Brief History of Time*, 44.

the same place they started, perhaps even at the same place in time, depending on the speed of the journey. Whether space-time is shaped like a torus or not, I am inclined to envision our universe as contained by 4-D space-time, not defined by it. In the following illustration (Figure 35) our universe is depicted as a stand-alone entity, spinning in 4-D. There may be other such universes in this domain. Perhaps the *boundaries* are vague, with trailing edges at the most remote parts of the universe. This illustration also implies a center wherein may lie the black hole that birthed the universe. Whether or not there are ultimately boundaries to 4-D is another issue. Given that I believe 4-D is contained by 8-D, there may be boundaries in a dimensional rather than a conventional sense.

Figure 35. Spiral Universe

Where Are We?

Where is 4-D in relation to other dimensional domains such as 0-D? In dimensional terms it may seem obvious that since we reside in 4–D, 0–D is only four dimensions away. I do not believe this is so. Remember, our choice to refer to our dimensional domain as 4-D is arbitrary, not knowing what integral domains exist *above* it and what derivative domains exist *below* it. For all we know, there may be thousands of dimensional domains *above* and *below* ours before ultimately arriving at 0–D. These dimensions could include subatomic, and sub–sub–sub–sub–sub–subatomic dimensions that have not even been theoretically touched on in physics. We do not know how far away 0–D is in dimensional terms. We may reside somewhere in the middle of the chain of universes as described in the previous chapter. Our adjacent derivative and integral universes may ultimately *be* our boundaries.

Where Is Infinity?

Do you understand now where the third type of infinity resides?[269] It can be quite close, yet infinitely far away. How can this be? This type of infinity can be just one dimension away from any given domain. For those of us who reside in 4-D, any location in 8-D is infinitely out of grasp, even if it is infinitely close! This, my friend, is how it is possible for an infinite God to reside so close to us: even in us. These boundaries are no hindrance to the IICP.

Where Are The Strings?

As I implied earlier, some of our strings may originate in integral dimensions above us, and some in derivative dimensions below. Intuitively, I imagine the strong force coming to us from our integral, being a force that holds nuclei together. I also imagine the weak force coming to us from a derivative, permitting the constituents of the nuclei of our atoms to radioactively break apart. Perhaps the most important point to be made here is that our *strings* do not exist in 4-D. They reside in other domains, exerting influence on 4-D, but expressing themselves here. They may also be more orderly in their domain than the randomness that is expressed in 4-D! It would seem that adjacent dimensional domains hold us together.

---

[269] The first type was described as infinitely large. The second was described as infinitely small. The third was described as close, but dimensionally inaccessible.

Certainty vs. Uncertainty

As I see it, quantum mechanics is essentially a study of the macro particles of the integral and derivative domains that surround our domain. Heisenberg's uncertainty principle is a dimensional principle. I believe all things are both certain and uncertain. On a macro level in any given dimensional domain, certainty is experienced. At the micro level, however, uncertainty is experienced.

For uncertainty to shift to certainty (quantum mechanics shifting to general relativity) there must be a complete paradigm shift. Therein the random and relative motions of subatomic particles become just as stable and predictable as the universe we call home. It is quite possible that strings are much more orderly and less uncertain than the atomic particles they comprise. The void within an atom may be no different than the vastness of space-time at our macro level. Our *emptiness*, so to speak, may be fullness to either our integral or our derivative. Our *fullness* may be emptiness to our integral and derivative domains. In this case, the distinction between certainty and uncertainty is found in the boundaries.

Degrees Of Freedom

Within our dimensions of space-time we have what are referred to as *degrees of freedom*. There are three possible translations (through our x, y, and z axes) that we can *move* through in space, three possible rotations (about our x, y, z axes) that we can *spin* about in space, and zero degrees of freedom translating in time. Hence we have six degrees of freedom (DOF). Ironically, these degrees of freedom are restrictions, or boundaries. We are not free to move about in time.

However, 8-D entities may not have the same dimensional restrictions. They may be free to move about in 6 dimensions of space *and* in 2 dimensions of time. If that is the case, they may have 14 DOF (6 translations, 6 rotations, and 2 translations in time).[270] Can you imagine having such freedom? We would be immortal, being free to go forward or back in time and experience any given scene again and again. Imagine saying to someone with whom you are visiting, "Pardon

---

[270] Think of translations as moving forward or back, sideways, up or down. Rotations are spinning like a dancer on their feet, spinning forward or back like a diver off a spring board, and waddling from side to side while walking.

me for a second," then move into the other dimension of time, taking a long vacation, returning refreshed, and asking, "Where were we?"

I do not believe such imaginative wanderings are foolishness. I believe in such 8-D entities. Some call them angels. By whatever name they are called, they are quite physical in their domain and in ours. Scripture tells us that these entities are free to physically roam about both domains.[271] Perhaps we have encountered more of them than we realize.

We occasionally have glimpses past our boundaries into 8-D. I believe the *Vincent* encounter was one such glimpse. I am fully convinced that there is more to our existence than meets the eye. There is much, much more beyond our meager 4-D boundaries.

---

[271] Hebrews 13:2.

3.05

In the Beginning

Where did this universe come from? Has it always existed? Will it continue to exist forever? These are questions theologians, philosophers, and scientists have pondered for millennia. Along with these fundamental questions is another: *can we know the answers to any of them?* Some believe we can with a significant degree of certainty.

Some physicists believe that the universe had a beginning and will likely have an end. Stephen Hawking in his book *A Brief History of Time* says, "Roger Penrose and I showed that Einstein's general theory of relativity implied that the universe must have a beginning and, possibly, an end." [272] In addition to Einstein's contribution to the topic, observational data shows us that the universe is expanding. If so there must have been a point in time when everything was much closer together, ultimately at a single point from which everything sprang. Others believe that a cycle of beginnings and ends has gone on perpetually. How could such a universe be birthed? Unless one believes in *something from nothing*, it had to come from somewhere. [273]

Black Holes

If you recall, the mathematical wanderings of Karl Schwarzschild predicted the existence of black holes long before any evidences of their existence were observed. The enormous mass of black holes, along with their invisibility, confirms their ability to pull in anything, including light itself, once inside the black hole's

---

[272] Hawking, *A Brief History of Time*, 44.
[273] For the record, I do believe in ex nihilo creation from a four-dimensional perspective. However, from a higher dimensional perspective there may be more to the story, as we will see.

event horizon. The following illustration (Figure 36) is an artistic representation of the event horizon, and is meant only to emphasize the enormous force with which such a black hole vacuums everything within its event horizon into an infinitesimally small point. I suppose the illustration would be more accurate if the picture were in the negative, given that everything inside the event horizon would be invisible to an outside observer. Nevertheless, such a massive entity poses possible scenarios for the creation of the universe.

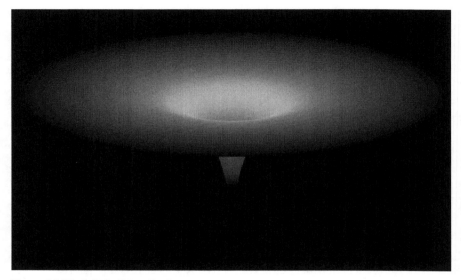

Figure 36. Black Hole Event Horizon

It has been theorized that the mass within a black hole is focused in an extremely small point, a point that some think may be infinitely small. It is literally a mathematical point, or *singularity*. In a mathematical sense, a black hole occupies no space at all, yet is enormous in mass.[274] Perhaps the big bang was an explosion of such a black hole, bursting forth the entire contents of the universe. (I find it quite ironic that theoretical physicists postulate that an entire universe may be packed inside such a singularity, yet avoid singularities in the derived

---

[274] Greene, *The Fabric of the Cosmos: Space, Time, and the Texture of Reality*, 337.

mathematical formulas that attempt to explain the existence of everything.) Did our entire universe emerge from such a singularity?

From a perspective within our dimensional domain, everything *did* come from nothing: from zero. From an expanded dimensional perspective, it may not have been so. What if black holes are simply points at which matter has fallen out of our dimensional domain, leaving an immense gravitational trail or hole behind? The mass entering a black hole may simply have entered another domain. Perhaps our entire universe simply fell out of another dimensional domain through the portal of a black hole at the big bang. I imagine there have been many such big bangs in derivative domains, as matter from our universe falls out via black holes. Our universe may give birth to other universes as matter leaves, entering such derivative domains (Figure 37).

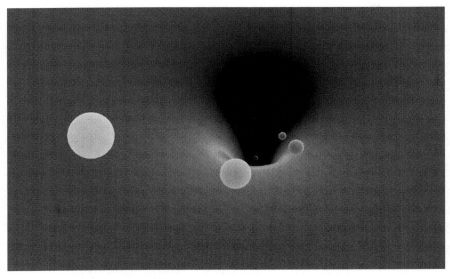

Figure 37. Stars Falling Out of Space Via a Black Hole

Dimensionally, *infinity* may have turned a singularity inside out at the big bang. That which was zero in our domain was substance in our integral. Whether one believes this process has repeated itself cyclically, or that our iteration is the first and only such creation, the process may be the same. Even if our universe has existed forever, perpetually cycling through a big bang and an eventual collapse, it does not change the mathematical necessity of an IICP.

Echoes

A young high school physics student once came to me following a discussion on current string theory and said, "Mr. A, I think strings are echoes." Quite intrigued I responded, "What do you mean?" He replied, "Echoes of God's voice." I was taken aback at the insight this young man offered. Scripture indicates that everything that is came to be via the spoken word: God's voice. The creation account in Genesis portrays God *speaking* space, light, and matter into existence. The book of John calls the GBF the *Word*, or *Logos*.[275] John says, "In the beginning was the Word, and the Word was with God, and the Word was God. He was with God in the beginning. Through him all things were made; without him nothing was made that has been made."[276] This voice brought everything into existence.

The mystic side of me loves to imagine God's voice resounding in echoes that are the strings of our universe. Remember, it was the physics community that first introduced the concept of our universe being one big symphony of strings! The intellectual side of me fully embraces Einstein's equation: $E = mc^2$. Einstein knew that matter and energy are interchangeable. I find it quite exhilarating to envision energy coming out of God's mouth and coalescing into matter. The IICP spoke into a portal, a black hole, and our universe was born. I believe his voice continues to birth other universes.

---

[275] Strong's Greek Lexicon describes Logos as the Divine Expression, the cause.
[276] John 1:1-5.

3.06

Time Flies

Einstein once said, "For we convinced physicists, the distinction between past, present, and future is only an illusion, however persistent."[277] Events simply are. They forever occupy a specific place in space-time.[278] Yet, why the illusion? What physicists, such as Einstein, refer to as an illusion of time, I think of as a *confinement in time*. Why else would it be such a persistent illusion? I do not dispute the possibility that the future already is just as the past or present are, but I question the illusion concept. We are confined to the present. For the most part.

Is there another dimension of time that intersects our domain? I believe something in us senses that there is such a dimension of time. As children we sensed it. Even as adults we sense it, albeit with a dim perception. Whether by means of a lengthy dream that took only seconds to occur in our current dimension of time, or the lostness in thought during a daily commute, we have an innate sense of another dimension of time. This dimension may be orthogonal (at a right angle) to our familiar vector of time, providing an avenue to pass time in one vector of time while not in the other. Scripture claims that with God a thousand years are like a day and a day like a thousand years.[279] It would seem that God is free to move about in these dimensions of time.[280] This may be what eternity is: freedom to move about in time rather than the absence of time.

---

[277] Greene, *The Fabric of the Cosmos: Space, Time, and the Texture of Reality*, 139.
[278] Ibid.
[279] Psalm 90:4; 2 Peter 3:8.
[280] Recognizing that this is a hotly debated topic, more will come in support of this assertion.

The Beginning and End of Time

As pointed out earlier, physicists believe that our dimension of time began at the big bang and will end if the universe collapses. Some theologians also believe time will end. There are references in Biblical scripture to the beginning of time but no apparent references to the end of time.[281] There are references to the "time of the new order," and the "end times," but none directly pointing to the ending of time itself.[282] In fact, there are passages that indicate a continuation of time.[283] If time ended, we would have no measure of experience or change. I am more inclined to believe we will have unconstrained freedom to move about in multiple dimensions of time. We may get our DOF (degrees of freedom) back![284]

Perceived Time

One of the mysteries of life is that time seems to flow consistently with chronological instruments such as clocks. However, our perception of time can be quite irregular. When I was a boy a day lasted forever! Summer vacation was an eternity. Now as a man, a day is as fleeting as a second. What is the difference? Is time truly warped by experience and age? Are we so sure that it is as steady as the clocks claim it to be? Is real time truly more real than *perceived* time? Could it be that perceived time is *real*, and is a function of the length of an interval within one's frame of reference?[285]

When I was a five-year-old child, a single day was a much larger percentage of my entire lifetime than it is now (0.05% then as opposed to 0.005% now.) This differential is real and impacts my perception of time. The beginning of a given interval of time seems to move more slowly than it does toward the end of the interval. In the following illustration (Figure 38) multiple intervals of time are graphed on top of each other. The entirety of the graph may illustrate one's

---

[281] 2 Tim 1:9, Titus 1:2.
[282] Hebrews 9:10, 1 Peter 1:5, 1:20, Jude 1:18.
[283] Isa 9:7, 59:21.
[284] Knowing how I argued early on that a literal 6-day creation was not plausible, I will now shoot my argument in the foot. If in fact there were multiple degrees of freedom in time before the great rebellion, Adam quite possibly could have taken an excursion in a different dimension of time to name all the animals! In fact, it is quite possible that God took 6 days to create all things in one dimension of time and millions of years to accomplish each evolutionary step in another dimension. This is not the first time and will not be the last time I argue against some of my own developing ideas. That's process!
[285] As has been duly pointed out to me, I tend to ask a lot of rhetorical questions. These, however, do serve distinct purposes and will hopefully be helpful.

lifetime, while each subset illustrates major blocks of time within that lifetime. Each of the subsets has sub-subsets. For instance, the first subset could represent the first five years of my life. Within that period there were individual years, each with significant events. The second subset could represent high school years, and so on. Perceived time moves more rapidly toward the end of any given interval, regardless of the length of the interval.

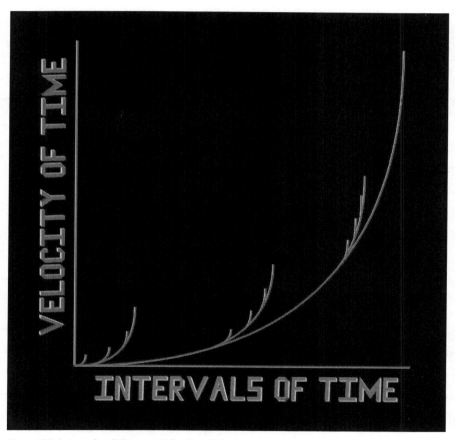

Figure 38. Intervals of Time vs. Velocity of Time

Variations in Time

There are a couple of assumptions the physics community holds regarding real time that I would like to address. The first assumption is that time has always been constant, always having the same rate of passage or velocity, so to speak. Secondly, excluding exceptions from relativity, time is a uniform field everywhere in the universe. I question both assumptions. Our microscopic region and brief time in this universe give us no assurance whatsoever that the *constancy* of the time we observe now and here always has been the case throughout the history of our universe. While any point in time may be fixed in 4-D space-time, it is an assumption to claim the amount of time that passes throughout 4-D is uniform. To put it differently, it is an assumption to claim that adjacent points in space-time experience the same real time intervals. Just as there is topography in space, so there may be in time. In the following illustration (Figure 39) the horizontal axes along with the sphere represent the three dimensions of space and the vertical axis is time. Notice the topography of time. This illustration does not imply time is flowing in an irregular fashion, but that it has variations from one point to another in 4-D space-time. We know from Einstein's theories of relativity that time can be impacted by both gravity and speed—that time changes in a fashion to guarantee the constancy of the speed of light. There may, however, be other influences on time besides gravity and speed. It may be possible that there are local time fluctuations without any known cause.

Imagine an abnormal amount of time passing through a given region. On a small scale, quantum mechanical processes may speed up. On a large scale, a day would appear longer. The movement of the stars and the sun would appear to have slowed down.[286] A most significant change would be in the observed gravitational acceleration. Falling objects would appear to take longer to hit the ground. In reality, gravity, which is mass dependent, would not vary, but the observed time for objects to fall would be greater, causing gravity to appear to have decreased. All the while, the velocity of light would remain constant.

---

[286] There are Biblical accounts where the Sun appeared to stand still (e.g. Joshua 10:13).

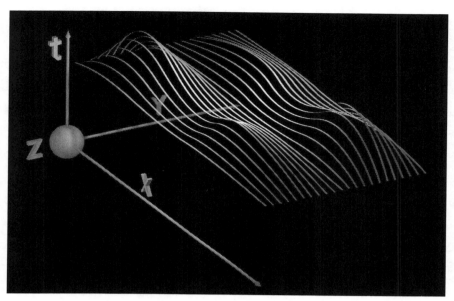

Figure 39. The Surface of Time

I imagine that at the big bang the turbulence of time would have been like an exponential storm, with hurricanes of time. There may have been intense turbulence for most of the life of the universe. But all this, of course, implies that time flows. Does it? Einstein was certain that time does not flow. In fact, he postulated we are moving through the dimension of time at the speed of light. It may be that we are moving through irregular time terrains.

Does Time Flow?

I do agree with Einstein that time is inextricably linked to our three space dimensions. However, I believe the dimension of time may be a conduit for time variations, just as the spatial dimensions are conduits for objects to exist in and move through. Time may not be simply a rigid uniform dimension we pass through. Einstein postulated that we are moving through the dimension of time at the speed of light. This is not very different than time moving through us, or flowing. I think it is an Einsteinian assumption that time is uniform throughout the universe. I don't think we can be so sure.

Density of Time

If time does not flow, following Einstein's reasoning, but we allow for variations in time at different locations in space-time, then we may speak in terms of topography of time. Such variations would not be due to our velocity through time, but variations in time itself, even if we maintain a constant velocity. More precisely, we may refer to these as variations in the *density* of time.

Just as there are electric, magnetic, and gravitational fields, I believe there may also be a time field, with an associated messenger particle and particle density. Just as electromagnetism is communicated via the photon (its messenger particle), and, as is postulated, gravity is communicated via the graviton (its messenger particle), I believe that time is *communicated* via a messenger particle: the chronon.[287] While these particles may not be observed directly, as will most likely be the case with gravitons, indirect evidences may prove their existence. Is there a viable experiment to validate the existence of such a particle? I believe there is and we will return to such an experimental proposal shortly. For now, however, we must look at the interplay between electromagnetism, gravity, and time.

The g-c-t Particle

One of the peculiar attributes of the chronon is that it is directly impacted by gravity. Einstein demonstrated this via general relativity: mass warps space-time. So mass affects change on chronons. How? Perhaps the graviton and the chronon are one and the same particle but with differing manifestations. How could the same particle present itself differently?

String theory, as you recall, is viable because there are eleven dimensions to our universe. Just as we can rotate in space, changing our appearance to a two dimensional camera, perhaps such a particle rotates through extra dimensions, changing its manifestation in 4-D. Perhaps the presence of mass, or gravity, rotates the chronons in its vicinity, changing their manifestation to the graviton messenger particle, thereby decreasing the chronon density. Such a rotation may involve strings colliding and transferring waveforms and energy. Perhaps one

---

[287] Physicists typically refer to the chronon as a discrete measure of time. I herein refer to it as a particle that communicates a discrete amount of time.

string causes sympathetic wave energy in another, much like a stringed instrument does.[288] Regardless of the mechanism, less time passes by in a gravitational field caused by a mass of significant proportion.

The story does not end there. Einstein's general relativity brought gravity and electromagnetism together as well. Maxwell's four simple equations governing electromagnetism, if you recall, were discovered by Kaluza to perfectly match Einstein's spatial field equations, if just one more than our three spatial dimensions is permitted to exist. Gravity and electromagnetism are inextricably intertwined. This *entwinement* is not a new concept. Physicists frequently refer to such particle entwinement in other dimensions. It may be that this entwinement includes *all* messenger particles.

Where does this leave us? Perhaps the messenger particle that communicates gravity is, on a different dimensional level, one and the same as the messenger particle that communicates light! Summing it all up, the graviton, the photon, and the chronon may be one and the same particle at a higher dimensional level. Obviously the three messenger particles are manifested as different particles in our limited 4-D domain, but behind the dimensional curtain they may be one and the same. Just as mass may rotate chronons into gravitons, it may also be that electromagnetism rotates chronons into photons, thereby slowing time down. My intuition tells me that this higher dimensional messenger particle in its natural or low energy state is manifested as a chronon unless acted upon by mass or electromagnetism.

From here on I will refer to the higher dimensional counterpart of the graviton, photon, and chronon as the g-c-t particle. In the following illustration (Figure 40) is an artistic representation of three g-c-t particles, one casting a shadow onto 4-D as a graviton (g), one as a photon (c), and one as a chronon (t).[289] The three torus rings surrounding each g-c-t particle symbolize the 6 extra spatial dimensions (Calabi-Yau space) beyond our 3 spatial dimensions.

---

[288] This theory is an intuitive wandering of mine and has not been proven mathematically or tested experimentally, though an experimental verification is forth coming. I do not claim that this is an original idea, for there may be others currently thinking along similar lines. However, it is a principle I encountered during one of my contemplative sessions.

[289] The variables g, c, and t are commonly used variables for gravity, light, and time.

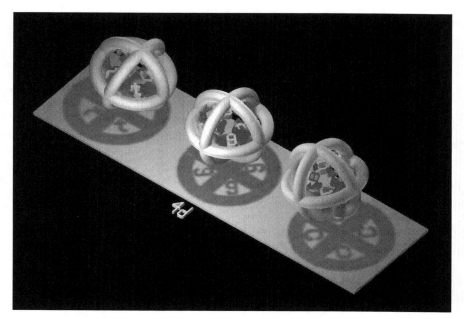

Figure 40. The g-c-t Particle

Properties of the g-c-t Particle

Just as Einstein postulated that gravity is communicated at the speed of light and that we are moving through the dimension of time at the same speed, we can conclude that the g-c-t particle travels at the speed of light. I am sure this would be troublesome to Einstein, given that he was convinced time does not flow. It may be, however, that chronons flow *through* the dimension of time, even though that dimensional conduit does not flow. Conversely, it may be just as Einstein thought, but with the proviso that the time field we are moving through has variations in its density.

We know that atomic processes are intertwined with the emission of and absorption of photons. When an electron drops to a lower state of energy it emits a photon of a given frequency; when it rises to a higher state of energy it absorbs a photon of a given frequency. This being the case, it may be that the chronon is affected by atomic changes. Conversely, the chronon may affect atomic processes.

Black Holes and the g-c-t Particle

As we have previously discussed, theoretical physics asserts the existence of black holes, masses so great and so dense that space-time is warped to the extent that everything within the black hole's event horizon, including light itself, is sucked in and held captive. Time itself would stand still. But is this all that happens? Light is simply held and time just stops? I think not. It is more likely that every photon and every chronon that enters the event horizon is rotated into gravitons. Perhaps it is true that light cannot escape, but also a possibility that it exists no more, having been rotated into gravitons. Black holes may in essence create pockets of timelessness in our universe.

An Experimental Proposal

As I alluded to earlier, I believe there is a way to indirectly observe and measure the density of the chronons that permeate 4-D. To understand it more fully we need to go back to 1971 and an experiment performed by Joseph Hafele and Richard Keating. Einstein's theories of relativity predict a dilation of time as one accelerates through space-time and around massive objects. To test these theories, Hafele and Keating flew cesium-beam atomic clocks around the world. When compared with identical clocks left on the ground, they discovered that less time had passed on the moving clocks. The difference was small but consistent with Einstein's discoveries.[290] Time dilation is a real phenomenon.

If chronons are a real entity, three synchronized cesium-beam atomic clocks could be used to assess their average density. To establish a baseline of time, one of the clocks would remain on the ground, just as in the Hafele and Keating experiment. A second clock would be positioned above the atmosphere in such an orbit so as to remain on the light side of the Earth. The third clock would be positioned in a similar orbit on the dark side of the earth and shielded with lead to minimize cosmic photon exposure to the clock. The average density of photons on the light side of Earth would be measured and the average photon density within the shielded clock on the dark side would be measured (most likely close to zero).

---

[290] Greene, *The Fabric of the Cosmos: Space, Time, and the Texture of Reality*, 50.

After a set period of time the recorded times in each clock would be compared to each other and to the ground clock.

If the two clocks record different times, we are on the way to validating the chronon theory. Why? Any kinematic and kinetic effects on the orbiting clocks (the effects of motion through a gravitational field) would be negated since the two clocks would have identical kinematic and kinetic orbits. The only possible source of a time differential would be directly related to the difference in the photon densities. But how can the density of chronons be assessed?

The theory predicts that the clock on the light side of the Earth would record less time passage, assuming the increased density of photons is responsible for the decreased density of chronons. The average density of the chronons could be expressed by the following equation:

(Equation 3) $\rho\chi = (\rho\gamma_{\text{light side}} - \rho\gamma_{\text{dark side}})\, \Delta t_{\text{dark side}} / (\Delta t_{\text{dark side}} - \Delta t_{\text{light side}})$

Herein $\rho\chi$ represents the density of chronons, $\rho\gamma_{\text{light side}}$ represents the density of photons on the light side of the Earth, $\rho\gamma_{\text{dark side}}$ represents the shielded density of photons on the dark side of the Earth, $\Delta t_{\text{dark side}}$ represents the time passage on the dark side of the Earth, and $\Delta t_{\text{light side}}$ represents the time passage on the light side of the Earth.

While the previous equation (Equation 3) may be gibberish to some readers, the point is that such an experiment is plausible and the outcome would settle the question once and for all: "Is there topography, or variation in time at different locations in 4-D, independent of motion and gravitational fields?" I look forward to the day when such an experiment is carried out. The wonderful thing about scientific research is that whether the answer to a hypothesis is *yes* or *no*, there is an answer. *That* is good research.

Mr. Buckethead and Time Dilation

If you recall, Einstein postulated that we are moving through 4-D at the speed of light. Granted, the vast portion of our speed is through the dimension of time and very little through space. As our speed increases through our three dimensions of space, our speed through time decreases. This explanation of time dilation is fully accepted in the physics community and the results of the Hafele and Keating experiment are consistent with it. While this may be the case, what if the previously described chronon experiment demonstrates that chronons do exist? How could such a theory mesh with Einstein's reasons for time dilation?

I remember experiencing a peculiar problem in a fluid dynamics class in graduate school. The question regarded a theoretical person with a flat head running through the rain. We were to solve for the amount of rain experienced by the flat head as the speed of the theoretical person increased. Much to our astonishment, as the speed of the person increased, the amount of rain experienced on the top of the flat head decreased. If the person's speed had reached c, the speed of light, the flat head would have experienced no rain.

Imagine, if you will, a Mr. Buckethead, running through space, always perpendicularly to the dimension of time and the direction of oncoming chronons (Figure 41). As his velocity increases, his bucket absorbs fewer and fewer chronons, and he experiences less and less passage of time. If his speed were to increase to the speed of light, no time would pass at all. This analogy is quite consistent with Einstein's explanation for time dilation.

Past, Present, & Future

Besides our intuitive sense of past, present, and future, how can we tell the difference scientifically if they are all simply locations in 4-D space-time? One explanation has to do with what is called the thermodynamic arrow. The second law of thermodynamics tells us that the universe is constantly undergoing increased disorder, or increased *entropy*. While local exceptions have been theorized, such as at the center of black holes, the law is true everywhere else in our day-to-day experiences. Even if I work my heart out bringing more order to my room, I have expended, or lost, energy due to the exertion. In the end the total amount of entropy has increased. Entropy, or the thermodynamic arrow, always points to the future. (By the way, if entropy decreases inside black holes, they may point to the past!)

Figure 41. Mr. Buckethead and Chronons

Does such a thermodynamic arrow exist in 8-D? Probably not, if we are free to roam about both dimensions of time. A thermodynamic arrow implies a physiological constraint and mortality. I am inclined to believe in immortality in 8-D and therefore no such arrow. We may be free to roam the past, present, or future at any *time*. In a sense, the separation into past, present, and future may be quite nonsensical in 8-D.

Einstein realized that if quantum mechanics are taken at face value, some events separated by very large distances would have to be instantaneously linked.

This seemed ludicrous to Einstein.[291] However, experimental results indicate that such quantum mechanical predictions are indeed correct.

Numerous experiments have been carried out demonstrating that past, present, and future are quite different in the quantum world. In one such experiment a single electron was projected at a double slit filter with a detection screen behind the filter. Now, one may be able to imagine how numerous electrons passing through both slits could form a diffraction pattern on the screen, but amazingly the single electron created the same diffraction pattern as though it passed through both slits and interfered with itself. How is this possible? Some physicists explain that "both potential histories," or *possibilities*, of the single electron contribute to the interference pattern.[292] It appears that the quantum world really does exist in a time-independent state.

Closing Wanderings

Why do I question so many commonly believed theories and assumptions? In the case of chronons, and more specifically time topography, I simply leave room for the possibility that time may not be so uniform throughout the universe. I agree that a point in time is simply a location in 4-D, but question whether or not that location necessarily experienced the same density of time as every other location. We will come back to topics on time later on. For now we need to look into a few more peculiar topics, adding to our tool sacks, so to speak. A few chapters from now these peculiar concepts (or tools) will coalesce to form dimensional expansions of the God concept and its implications.

---

[291] Ibid., 11.
[292] Ibid., 179.

3.07

The Real Projective Plane

We have already discussed the Calabi-Yau shape, one with peculiar twists and turns, folding back on itself, and passing through itself, in an attempt to draw what six dimensions would look like if limited to three. Of course the drawing was two-dimensional, but we are accustomed to representing three dimensions in two. This type of depiction is known as a real projective plane. The real projective plane is basically a higher dimensional entity with only one two-dimensional surface projected into three dimensions that is "closed and non-orientable."[293] *It cannot be represented in three dimensions without crossing over or intersecting itself.* This is seen in the convoluted shape of the Calabi-Yau space (Figure 42).

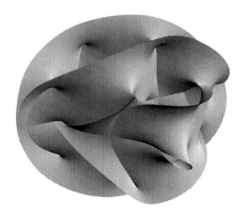

Figure 42. Calabi Yau Space by Lunch. Wikimedia.

[293] The Center For Geometry, "The Projective Plane," University of Minnesota, http://www.geom.uiuc.edu/zoo/toptype/pplane/.

We have already discussed another real projective plane shape: the Mobius strip. If you look at it closely you will see that it has only one two-dimensional surface (Figure 43). What is more, it has only one edge. Traversing the Mobius strip by two full revolutions brings one back to the starting point. What if the Mobius strip were extended to more dimensions? This leads us to Felix Klein.

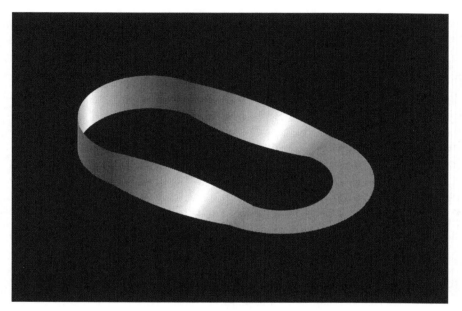

Figure 43. Mobius Strip

The Klein Bottle

Felix Klein was born on April 25, 1849, in Prussia. One could say he was destined to mathematical greatness solely on the peculiarity of his birth date. The month, day, and year are each the square of a prime number (2^2, 5^2, and 43^2).[294] Klein imagined sewing two Mobius strips together to create a single sided entity with no boundary. The inside surface is its outside surface. It is, as are the other

---

[294] J.J. O'Connor, "Klein Bottle," http://www.gap-system.org/~history/Biographies/Klein.html.

real projective plane shapes, a closed non-orientable surface.[295] It cannot be represented in three-dimensional space without intersecting itself (Figure 44). As you follow the surface around the *Klein bottle*, you will see that there is only one surface.

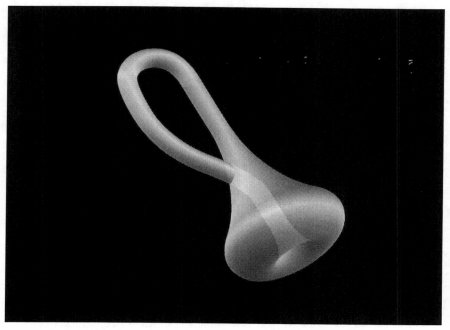

Figure 44. Klein Bottle: One With One Surface

Strangely, if one were to link two Klein bottles together in a continuous loop, the real projective plane character vanishes, for we end up with a two-sided entity (Figure 45). Surf the surfaces and see.

---

[295] Ibid.

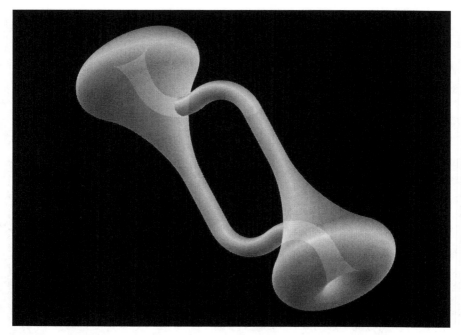

Figure 45. Klein Bottles: Two With Two Surfaces

However, when three Klein bottles are linked together in a continuous loop, the real projective plane character returns, resulting in a one-sided entity once again (Figure 46). When an odd number of Klein bottles are linked together the real projective plane character is maintained, but lost if an even number of bottles are linked together.

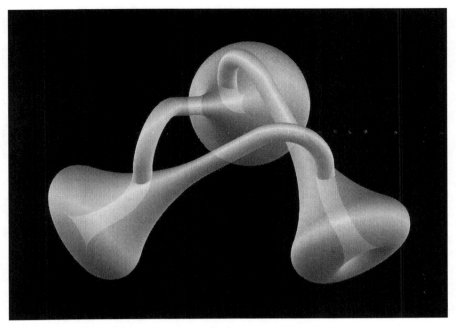

Figure 46. Klein Bottles: Three With One Surface

One of the most confounding things about the Klein bottle is that what we see in the illustration is in reality a two-dimensional rendering of a three-dimensional rendering of an even higher-dimensional surface. If we could *see* in five or six dimensions, the Klein bottle would not intersect itself. How can this be? Let us look at a less complex example for illustrative purposes. In the following two-dimensional illustration the two lines cross each other (Figure 47). If they exist in the same two-dimensional plane, they have no choice but to intersect each other.

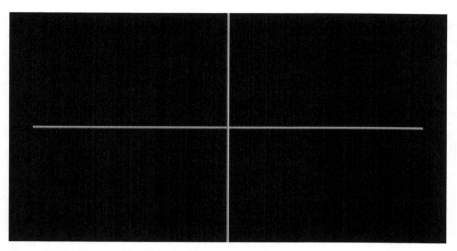

Figure 47. Non-Intersecting Lines in 2D

I can demonstrate, however, that the two lines can exist in the same plane, but with the help of a third dimension, do not intersect each other. How? See for yourself (Figure 48). So it is with the real projective plane and the Klein bottles.

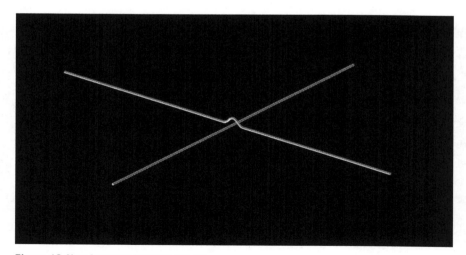

Figure 48. Non-Intersecting Lines in 3D

Real Projective Plane Theology

We find a peculiar passage of scripture in the New Testament that says, "For from him and through him and to him are all things."[296] This passage is referring to the IICP and is a wonderful word picture of the Klein bottle (Figure 49). Soak it in.

Figure 49. Klein Bottle: From God Through God to God

---

[296] Romans 11:36a, NRSV.

The three Klein bottles in the figure titled *Klein Bottles: Three With One Surface* also have theological significances. For those who are inclined to believe in the Trinity, the illustration is quite illuminating: there are three bottles with only one surface. A more significant parallel is found between the three Klein bottles and Jesus' words regarding the IICP, the GBF, and us: "Before long, the world will not see me anymore, but you will see me. Because I live, you also will live. On that day you will realize that I am in the Father, and you are in me, and I am in you."[297] If one follows this logic by visualizing the three Klein bottles, the GBF is in the IICP, we are in the GBF, hence we are in the IICP and the IICP is in us. That is a very strange and amazing concept. What is illogical in this 4-D realm is quite logical in 8-D.

In Closing

In Phase 2 we talked about the inverse dynamics of the kingdom of God. The Mobius strip was used to illustrate this principle. The inverse dynamic principles of the IICP are *real projective plane theology* principles in practice. In other words, the Klein bottle is simply an extension or expanded version of the Mobius and its inverse dynamics. Even in higher dimensions we come round to Jesus' teaching that the least is the greatest!

The greatest challenge we have is to create real projective plane images and/or concepts from the higher dimensional slices we have to work with. The process is tedious and difficult, yet I believe it is what we must perform in order to understand and work within the framework of our existence. Our task is to work at transforming these lower dimensional perspectives, dimensions that are necessarily incomplete and inconsistent, into higher dimensional entities. This is the nature of the cosmos.

---

[297] John 14:19-20.

3.08

Dimensional Transformations

Resistance to believing in and working with the extra dimensional nature of the cosmos is strong, and for good reasons. Sometimes it is difficult to work with the dimensions we can see, let alone ones we cannot see. Inconsistency and incompleteness prevail. Our views of truth are necessarily incomplete. Kurt Gödel proved this in his incompleteness theorem. This incompleteness results in warped or distorted views, especially if one holds to the assumption that these views are complete. In his poem, *The Blind Men and the Elephant*, based on an ancient legend, John Godfrey Saxe (1816-1887) portrayed the problem of limited perspectives quite effectively. I include it in its entirety, for it describes the problem of dimensional limitations better than I could ever hope to.

It was six men of Indostan
To learning much inclined,
Who went to see the Elephant
(Though all of them were blind),
That each by observation
Might satisfy his mind.

The *First* approach'd the Elephant,
And happening to fall
Against his broad and sturdy side,
At once began to bawl:
"God bless me! but the Elephant
Is very like a wall!"

The *Second*, feeling of the tusk,
Cried, -"Ho! what have we here
So very round and smooth and sharp?
To me 'tis mighty clear

This wonder of an Elephant
Is very like a spear!"

The *Third* approached the animal,
And happening to take
The squirming trunk within his hands,
Thus boldly up and spake:
"I see," quoth he, "the Elephant
Is very like a snake!"

The *Fourth* reached out his eager hand,
And felt about the knee.
"What most this wondrous beast is like
Is mighty plain," quoth he,
"'Tis clear enough the Elephant
Is very like a tree!"

The *Fifth*, who chanced to touch the ear,
Said: "E'en the blindest man
Can tell what this resembles most;
Deny the fact who can,
This marvel of an Elephant
Is very like a fan!"

The *Sixth* no sooner had begun
About the beast to grope,
Then, seizing on the swinging tail
That fell within his scope,
"I see," quoth he, "the Elephant
Is very like a rope!"

And so these men of Indostan
Disputed loud and long,
Each in his own opinion
Exceeding stiff and strong,
Though each was partly in the right,
And all were in the wrong!

MORAL:
So oft in theologic wars,
The disputants, I ween,
Rail on in utter ignorance
Of what each other mean,
And prate about an Elephant
Not one of them has seen!

In the case of the blind men, each was missing the dimension(s) of sight. We, too, are missing such dimensions, though I argue more than two, and prate about a God not one of us has seen. Albert Einstein once said, "You cannot solve a problem at the same level at which it was created." We must move beyond the domain in which the problem exists in order to solve it. We must move to at *least* one additional dimension beyond the dilemma.

To help illustrate what Einstein meant, let us look at an example of the reverse. Einstein described this dimensional problem by rediscovering the world called *Flatland*, created in the 1884 novel by Edwin Abbott. In Flatland, space is limited to two flat dimensions. That which we normally see in three dimensions takes on a new and limited character. For instance, imagine a bouncing ball in Flatland. A miniscule circle would appear in one spot, gradually growing in diameter, then decrease, only to reappear elsewhere on the two-dimensional plane. Such is the limited perspective in Flatland. A bouncing ball becomes an appearing and disappearing pulsating disc.

While it is difficult to extend such an illustration into a four-dimensional domain, it is helpful nonetheless to illustrate that what we see in our three-dimensional spatial domain may be a very limited view of what is actually a four or five-dimensional entity. Though we are often so certain of what we see in our limited views, we need added perspectives and subsequent dimensional transformations to gain insight into the higher dimensional entities we wish to adequately observe. Such dimensional transformations assimilate two or more lower dimensional perspectives into a single unified higher dimensional perspective.

Perspectives

A starting point is to increase the number of perspectives. Humans could learn much about this process from owls. Some owls move their heads from side to side to formulate a more accurate 3-D image and to assess distance. The angulation provides clarity to both size and distance. We, too, need multiple perspectives to formulate accurate constructs.

When making solitary observations we may make misled conclusions about both size and distance. In the following illustration (Figure 50) it is clear that the bottom right cube is closest. What is not clear is how large or far away the upper left cube is. When I drew the cubes I intentionally made each dimension in the distant cube three times the size of the closer cube, but drew it far enough away that it appears to be comparable in size. If a second perspective were available, the size difference would become more apparent.

Figure 50. Large vs. Small and Near vs. Far

Projections

Few of us can imagine having to choose which one of our three dimensions of space we would be willing to live with and endorse as the *correct* dimension. Living in one dimension of space, on a line? How ridiculous! It is the same with higher dimensional issues, yet we seem to be content to live with less than adequate dimensional views, often insisting that they are complete, consistent, and correct. These inadequate perspectives are but projections of much larger entities.

I sat in the car one rainy evening, waiting on my kids to come out of swim practice. The streetlight above cast a projection of the rain on the windshield onto the dash below. The *rain* on the dash was very realistic, very 3d in appearance. However, it was odd to see water flowing up my dashboard. So it can be with projections in our domain; they may appear illogical and as such, be rejected. Projections from higher dimensional domains may not be logical. What seems impossible in this domain may well be due to its limited projection.

Imagine looking at plans of a prospective new house with your spouse. What is more, imagine arguing over which house each of you prefers. Not realizing that there are usually several 2d renderings of such a house (front, side, and plan views), you continue to debate. Finally the architect steps in and points out that you both are looking at the same house, but from different perspectives.

So it is with projections of higher dimensional entities. In the following illustration (Figure 51) it is clear that the two parallel arrows within the coordinate system are pointing in the same direction.

Yet someone else, looking at the same entity argues they are pointing in opposite directions (Figure 52). How can both possibly be correct?

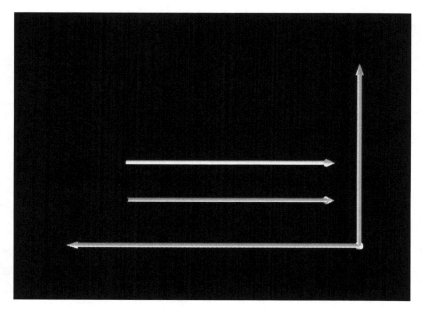

Figure 51. Arrows in the Same Direction?

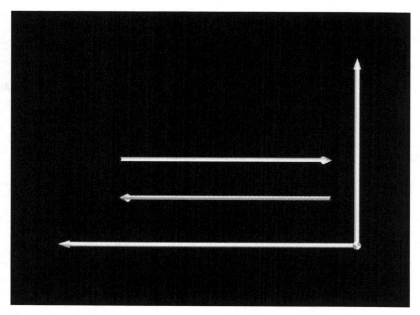

Figure 52. Arrows in the Opposite Direction?

Each observer is looking at a different 2d projection of a 3d image (Figure 53). The observer who sees the arrows pointing in the same direction is viewing a projection from the far side of the coordinate system. The observer who sees the arrows pointing in opposite directions is viewing a projection from the right side of the coordinate system.

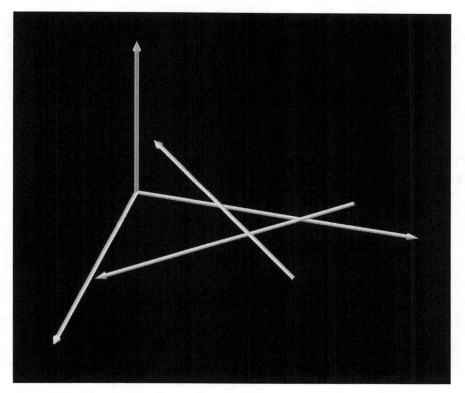

Figure 53. A Higher Dimensional View of the Arrows

Not only can direction be affected, but length can as well. In the following figure (Figure 54) path B is clearly the shortest path between the two points.

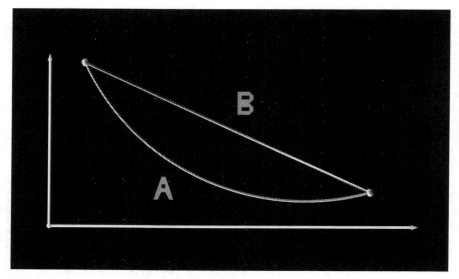

Figure 54. The Shortest Path from Point to Point

But once again, when viewed from a higher dimensional perspective, it is clear we are mistaken (Figure 55).

Multiple Projections

Often there are more than two divergent views that result from missing dimensions. Such a collection of views may represent positions from within theology, politics, philosophy, and even science. What is more, each may have very solid evidence that their position is the correct one. It is not uncommon for one group to argue that a circle best encloses the proper worldview, while another group argues for the rightness of a square, and yet another sect for the stability of a triangle. How can they all be right? In the following illustration (Figure 56) you can see shadows of one central entity on each of the three planes.

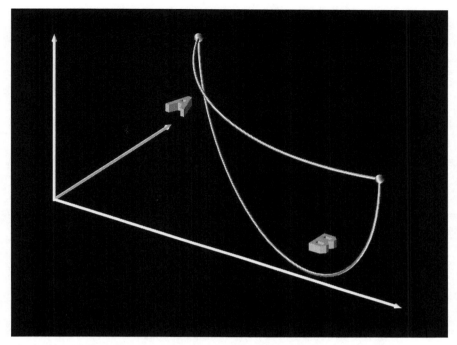

Figure 55. A Higher Dimensional View of the Shortest Path from Point to Point

Dimensional Transformations

One day while talking about views being projections of a larger dimensional entity, my son, who was very young at the time, asked, "Then how can we figure out what we are really looking at?" What a profound question! There are some innate skills that most of us are born with that may be of assistance in this process.

We humans (and other animals too) are equipped with one-dimensional rods and cones in our eyes. These are assimilated into two two-dimensional images. From these images our brains extrapolate a single three-dimensional view. We innately extrapolate higher dimensional views. This process is *dimensional transformation*. We innately perform transformations from 1 to 2 dimensions and 2 to 3 dimensions. If you think about it, we also do four-dimensional transformations as well. When we monitor changes in 3d images over time, we perform 4d transformations. In everyday terms, when we combine our five senses to identify objects, we perform dimensional transformations.

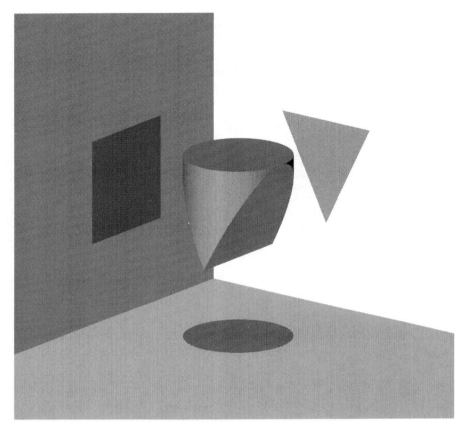

Figure 56. Three Divergent Views

Many professions perform dimensional transformations. Medicine uses numerous 2d image slices to create 3d images via CT and MRI scans. Architecture, mathematics, engineering, and chemistry solve 3d problems from numerous 1d and 2d images. Hospitals use motion analysis systems to create 3d models of motion pathologies. As we saw in the *Strings and Things* chapter, physicists used 11 dimensions to resolve 5 string theories into one M-Theory.

As you can see, we utilize dimensional transformations in many arenas in life. Why not in theology? Why is it that we, in one breath, want to believe God is bigger than our world, but in the next breath avoid performing dimensional transformations on divergent views? I hope it is very clear by now that if God is of a dimensional realm beyond our own, then we *must* have divergent perspectives. If we do not, then the God we have created in our heads is but a limited shadow. We cannot espouse an infinite God *and* a dichotomy-free idol.

Mapping

Mapping is a very different process than performing dimensional transformations. In a sense it is the reverse, but performed in such a way that lays out multiple higher dimensional views into a single lower-dimensional representation. Often these *maps* have fold lines so that the observer can see how to reconstruct the original shape. In the following illustration a cube is *unwrapped*, so to speak, into a flat 2d map (Figure 57). Obviously there are multiple ways to unfold a cube. This is but one way.

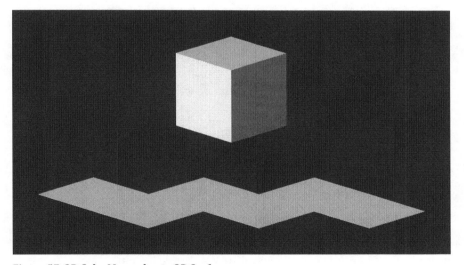

Figure 57. 3D Cube Mapped onto 2D Surface

The goal is to make it obvious what the map represents. In the second illustration, a pyramid is unwrapped into a 2d map (Figure 58).

Figure 58. 3D Pyramid Mapped onto 2D Surface

Some maps do an adequate job of representing the higher dimensional entity, so long as one is willing to put up with slightly skewed images. In the following case (Figure 59) each piece of the map of the sphere loses some of its curvature as it is forced onto the flat map. Nevertheless the observer is usually adept at noting that the original entity was a sphere. In this case we put up with aberrations, knowing the intent.

Figure 59. 3D Sphere Mapped onto 2D Surface

Maps are very useful after dimensional transformations have been performed. They bring issues back to one's normal domain, yet retain a representation of the higher dimensional entity. Jesus of Nazareth performed both of these: he regularly took religious projections and dimensionally transformed them (in his words, *fulfilled* them) into higher dimensional images, then unwrapped them onto maps (parables) to help people understand the ideas. For instance, Jesus took the religious definitions of *neighbor*, dimensionally transformed them into a much broader entity, and then mapped it onto the parable of the Good Samaritan.[298]

Sometimes we need to perform dimensional transformations and at other times dimensional mapping. Just as we are called to assimilate lower dimensional

[298] Luke 10:25-37.

perspectives into higher dimensional entities to gain understandings beyond our limited surroundings (as Jesus did with the law), so also we are called to map these understandings for others to understand (as Jesus did with parables). In a limited fashion, this book is an attempt to map some of the difficult concepts I have been wrestling with for the past decade or so.

Just for fun, I leave this topic with a mystery map (Figure 60). I hope you are up to the challenge of sleuthing out the original 3d object!

Figure 60. 3D Shape Mapped onto a 2D Surface

Incongruent Mergers

Without a doubt, some attempts to merge discontinuities result in failures. It should be no surprise that not all contradictory images necessarily belong to a single higher dimensional entity. There are, after all, such images that are either false or that belong to a different higher dimensional entity. Such an example is seen in the following illustration (Figure 61). While the square and the circle appear to be candidates for a dimensional transformation, the triangle is too disproportional and does not fit. Likewise the square and the triangle are good candidates, but the circle does not fit. There are plenty of theological mergers that are incongruent, such as good and evil, and omnipotence and insecurity. What about predestination and freewill? As we will see in a subsequent chapter, some apparently incongruent issues, such as predestination and freewill, are time dependent and as such may not necessarily be incongruent mergers within the context of unbounded time.

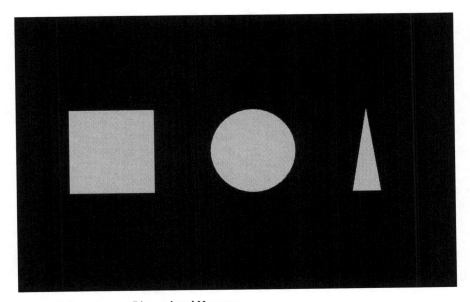

Figure 61. Incongruent Dimensional Mergers

In Closing

One possible distortion that dimensional transformations can produce is relativism. While we all may be called to move out of our comfort zones in the direction of more open-minded perspectives, we obviously cannot merge everything. When dimensional transformations work, they are much greater than the sum of the parts. What is more, the transformed entities do not necessarily need to take the place of the projections that went into their formation. We still need squares, circles, and triangles. They are part of what scripture refers to as diverse gifts. There are, after all, many members to one body.[299] What we need is the recognition that such diverse gifts are just that: projections of one body.

---

[299] Romans 12:4.

3.09

Chaos and Contradictions

Einstein wrestled deeply with randomness as he came face to face with the chaotic behavior that his contemporaries described in quantum mechanics. He insisted, "God does not play dice." Perhaps he was right, but with respect to a higher dimensional domain. Einstein was a higher dimensional thinker, whereas the quantum mechanists of his day were simply describing the atomic quagmire observed in this domain. Is it possible that Einstein and his contemporaries were right, that order and chaos are divergent dimensional representations of the same entity?

Some of what appears to be quite chaotic in 4–D may also be chaotic to an 8–D observer. However, some chaos in 4–D may resolve into order in 8–D, and vice versa. What is the difference and how can we tell? Whenever possible, we must at least attempt to view the circumstances from higher dimensional perspectives. It is through assembling these projections that we discern which is truly chaos and which is truly order.

In the following illustration (Figure 62) the data is clearly chaotic from a frontal perspective. However from an end perspective (Figure 63) not only do the lines appear to be orderly, but have a progression to their peaks.

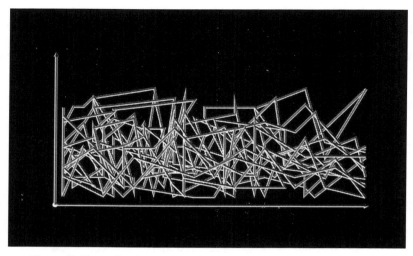

Figure 62. Lines of Order vs. Chaos YZ Plane

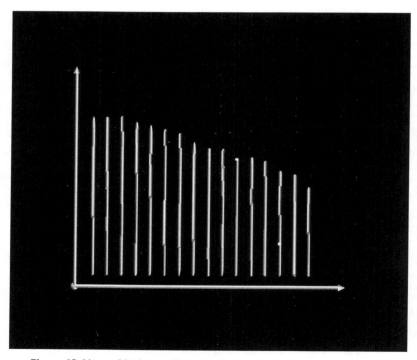

Figure 63. Lines of Order vs. Chaos XZ Plane

If we too quickly reject what we see here and now as chaos, we may eventually be disappointed to find out that we rejected higher dimensional order. The converse is also true. The goal is to seek more projections of the same entity in an effort to discern whether it is an entity of ultimate order or chaos. While it may be helpful to observe the single higher dimensional entity now, it is still somewhat difficult to see through the chaos to find the order (Figure 64). Quantum mechanics is one such example: the chaos that Einstein rejected may ironically be due to his higher dimensional genius. I believe he innately knew that order reigns in higher dimensions (8-D).

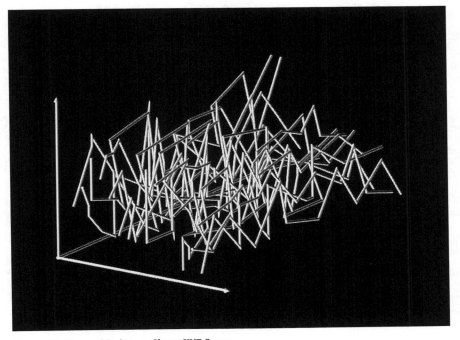

Figure 64. Lines of Order vs. Chaos XYZ Space

Randomness

When the wind blows randomly through the countryside, with unexpected lows and highs, eddies and straight line winds, we are often quick to assume randomness. I am not so sure anymore. The apparent randomness may be the result of underlying order. In the following illustration (Figure 65) we are presented with random data points.

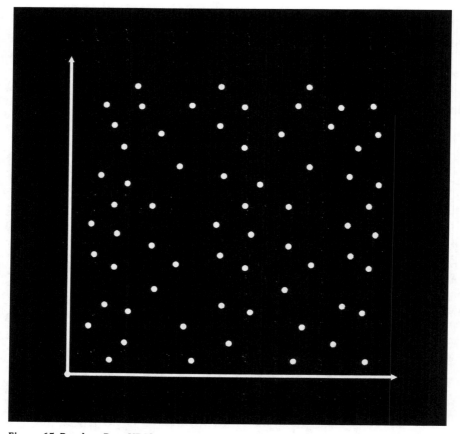

Figure 65. Random Data YZ Plane

It is interesting, however, that even in my attempt to make them appear random, I scattered them uniformly across the frontal plane. I am not even equipped to efficiently describe randomness in an illustration! Nevertheless, from the side perspective we can begin to see that there is shape to the depth of the points (Figure 66).

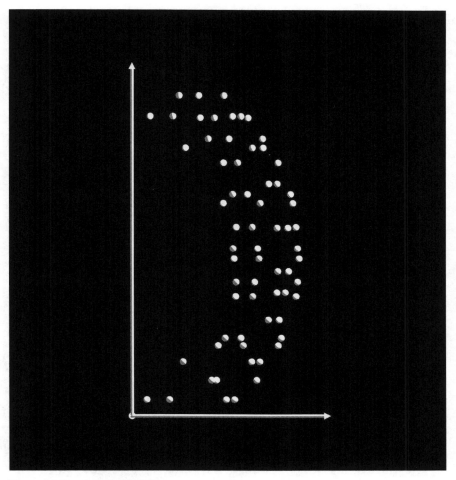

Figure 66. Random Data XZ Plane

The 3d view (Figure 67) brings into clarity the spherical surface upon which each point resides.

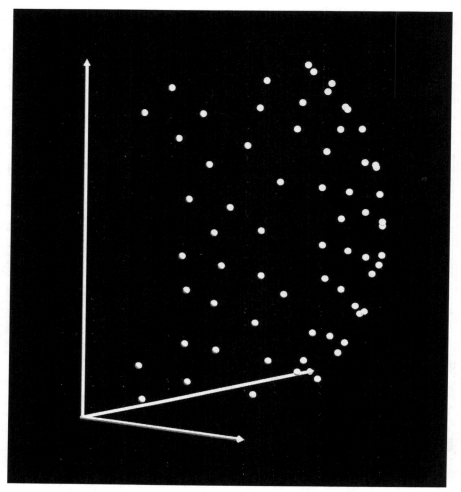

Figure 67. Random Data XYZ Space

I have often pondered the role of apparent randomness and dissonance in some musical scores. One day out of curiosity I took a familiar and very melodic musical score (*Ode to Joy* by Ludwig Van Beethoven) and calculated the *derivative* of the melody. The derivative is a measure of the steepness and direction between two adjacent points, or in this case two adjacent notes. Once I translated this derivative into a musical score, I found that it was a very disjointed piece of music.

It was not pleasing to the ear whatsoever. So it may be with randomness in our domain: it may be music to ears in our integral domain.

When my son was young we struggled to understand why his morning glucose readings varied so much, especially knowing how hard we worked to keep the variables in his life constant. One day, out of desperation, I took three years' worth of morning readings and put them in a spreadsheet and graphed the data. It was an extremely random display of data. There was no apparent rhyme or reason for such noise. Then, in a moment of curiosity, I decided to run the data through a mathematical filter.[300] I did so several times. Much to my amazement the resulting graph was a beautiful sinusoidal wave, with regular peaks and valleys. There was uniformity to the data. I measured the time lapse between adjacent peaks and adjacent valleys in the plotted curve. I was astonished to find that the average time lapse was 28.2 days. From as far back as my college anatomy and physiology classes I recalled that some bodily functions are subject to circadian rhythms (daily) and some to lunar rhythms (monthly). There was music in the randomness of my son's data.

Some theologians, such as Marcus Borg, believe God is a total non-interventionist due to the apparent randomness of answered (or unanswered) prayers. Other people reject the God concept altogether for this reason. Jesus said, "The wind blows wherever it pleases. You hear its sound, but you cannot tell where it comes from or where it is going. So it is with everyone born of the Spirit."[301] The kingdom of God is not of this dimensional domain! However, its higher dimensional orderliness may appear random here and now. If we reject God and/or Godly interventions due to our limited dimensional perspectives, we sadly do so in error.

Abstractness

The ability to see *form* in abstract works of art is also an integrative skill. Picasso was a master at this. Such individuals naturally have the integrative engines necessary to lay such visions down using various media. For those who

---

[300] It is a fancy mathematical process that can smooth the data into a more useful pattern.
[301] John 3:8.

lack appreciation for the *random noise* in a Picasso painting or in a Samuel Barber composition, perhaps their integrating engine has stalled or is nonexistent.

A man once criticized Picasso for his unrealistic art. Picasso asked him: "Can you show me some realistic art?" The man showed him a photograph of his wife. Picasso observed: "So your wife is 2 inches tall, two-dimensional, with no arms and no legs, and no color but only shades of gray."[302] As Picasso noted, the concept of realism is less obvious than we would like to make it.

I am fond of abstract art. It is randomly expressionistic and refreshing. It speaks of the artist's ability to see beyond what we commonly think of as order and realism in this domain. After all, even that which most of us would identify as realistic art, if examined under a microscope, is extremely random. In the latter sense, all art is abstract.

The Law of Non-Contradiction

We have the Greeks to thank for many logical processes and theorems. Aristotle contributed to a theorem that has driven logic for centuries: *A* cannot equal *Non-A*. This is commonly known as the *law of non-contradiction*. I have heard individuals rant on about the infallibility of this principle, exclaiming the non-existence of any contradictions to its claim.

Many of the *laws* that humankind has derived are based on the assumption that the overall governances of things in our existence are limited to 4-D. The law of non-contradiction is one such example: surely A cannot be the same as Non-A. This is quite equivalent to saying that predestination cannot be the same as freewill. It must be one or the other!

If one takes the same approach as Gödel in his dissection of *Principia Mathematica* by Whitehead and Russell, and carefully examines the law of non-contradiction dimensionally, we will find the same incompleteness and inconsistency. Let us look at a very simple example. Let $A = 2$ and $Non-A = 4$. Clearly 2 does not equal 4 and the law of non-contradiction is upheld. Yet if we add a dimension, moving from length to area, we increase our scope and may find that

---

[302] Pablo Picasso, "Picasso Response to Criticism," http://cubism-picasso.blogspot.com/.

A has an area of 2x4=8 and *Non-A* has an area of 4x2=8. Once again the law of non-contradiction comes under question.[303]

In the following illustration (Figure 68) we find an entity casting projections of *A* and *Non-A* on two different planes. In contradiction to the law of non-contradiction, these two images come from the same entity simultaneously.

Figure 68. A and Non-A Shadows

I have intentionally presented illustrations that question such laws to prove a point: we too quickly assume a law of *no exceptions*. Of course there are occasions wherein the law is upheld. It *is* possible for *Non-A* to be something other than *A* in a higher domain (Figure 69). My goal is to nudge each of us, even if just a little bit, outside our limited comfort zones and explore the possibilities.

---

[303] We discussed in Phase 2 how contradictory principles might exist on the same side of a strange loop type II, or Mobius strip. Here we expand the principle dimensionally.

Figure 69. B and Non-A Shadows

Complementary Contradictions

Whenever we encounter valid evidences that are contradictory to each other, it is a fairly good sign that we are dealing with a single entity of a higher dimensional origin. The contradictions are complementary. Often such dimensional transformations are hard to grasp, but many such contradictory sets exist in the cosmos. We have discussed several such sets, including light as a particle vs. a wave, and predestination vs. freewill. What other contradictions plague us and spur divisive beliefs because we so readily dismiss higher dimensional solutions? How many Non-A's have we written off as we cling steadfastly to A's?

In Closing

Sorting through and resolving dimensional contradictions requires diligence. Not all contradictions resolve, but we may not come to know that without at least attempting such dimensional transformations. Some are admittedly more difficult to deal with than others. Some transformation attempts may actually provide intermediate answers that have to be transformed again and again to reach resolution. These problems require an iterative dimensional solution.

3.10

SR, NT, and EU

It is a challenge to develop dimensional theology. Often we must sift through sundry sources of information to discern if we are looking at chaos whose integral origins are chaotic noise or rhythmic order. As I explained in the previous chapter, since this is a dimensional problem, it requires a dimensional solution. For instance, we cannot solve three-dimensional problems without entering 3d (or a higher domain). It is necessary to either literally immerse ourselves in that domain or to use dimensional transformations that utilize multiple 2d perspectives. So it is with truth.

I believe there are three general sources of truth that aid our understanding of God and the cosmos: special revelation (SR), natural theology (NT), and existential understanding (EU). As you have already seen in Phases 1 and 2, my definitions of these are fairly broad and less technical. I argue that each of us relies on all three, regardless of any insistence on a single dominant source. What is more, I believe we need all three to formulate systems of belief that have dimensional integrity.

Special Revelation

Special revelation, for the purpose of this discussion, includes all communications by God to humankind, including the incarnation of the GBF. Yet as miraculous as SR may be, it is not free from the influences of NT and EU. Not only do we need the latter two sources of truth to adequately interpret and apply SR, they also play an intricate role in the formation of SR in the first place. For instance, if current scientific knowledge had been available during the time that the Old Testament books were written, the geocentric view of the earth and sun would not have prevailed. Scientific understanding, as limited as it was, influenced the texts. So, too, it was with texts that third century Biblical authorities felt *at peace* with (being consistent with their experience), thereby permitting EU to confirm what was written, leading to the canonizing of such writings.

I do not think I need to elaborate much further on the importance and relevance of SR in my theology. Hopefully, you have caught on by now that I am a devoted reader of scripture (though my definition of scripture is broader in scope than it once was) and a firm believer in the incarnation of the *Word*, the GBF, working steadfastly at permitting SR to speak into my theology. But I also work diligently at deciphering the influences of NT and EU on the formation of said texts and on my understanding of the texts as I read them.

Natural Theology

Herein the phrase *natural theology* (NT) is used quite broadly. I include not only observations of the natural world which lead to understandings of God, but also scientific processes and data, as well as mathematical and logical approaches to understanding God and the cosmos. As you observed in Phase 2, mathematics and logic have played major roles in the development of the theology I describe. I argued in Phase 1 and 2, and do so here as well, that NT influences every one of us, though some permit it to speak more boldly into their theology than others.

Many great theologians and thinkers have acknowledged the importance of NT. Saint Thomas Aquinas greatly respected the role of science in interpreting scripture. According to G.K. Chesterton, in his biography of Aquinas, "(Aquinas) practically said that if they could really prove their practical discoveries, the traditional interpretation of Scripture must give way before those discoveries."[304] Here we see scientific data given permission to speak into the theology of one who had great respect for scripture, but who was aware of human inadequacies in both writing and interpreting SR. Chesterton went on to say, "St. Thomas was willing to allow the one truth to be approached by two paths, precisely because he was sure

---

[304] Chesterton, *St. Thomas Aquinas / St. Francis of Assisi*, 83.

there was only one truth."[305] Aquinas' position represented balance between SR and NT.

Existential Understanding

Brennan Manning, in his book *The Ragamuffin Gospel*, reports, "Philosopher Jacques Maritain once said that the culmination of knowledge is not conceptual but experiential: I feel God. Such is the promise of the Scriptures: Be still and know (experience) that I am God."[306] Our understanding of God and the cosmos is affected by our experience. Our journeys bear witness to this.

SR contains many examples of Jesus and the early church leaders consciously employing EU. The phrase "It seemed good to the Holy Spirit and to us " is such an example.[307] Elsewhere in one of the Apostle Paul's letters he affirms that *peace* is criteria and evidence for truth.[308] Whether or not they would have admitted to using EU in their processes, it was and is unavoidable. Jesus said, "Peace I leave with you; my peace I give you. I do not give to you as the world gives. Do not let your hearts be troubled and do not be afraid."[309] EU at its best!

Dimensional Iterations

Truth is not handed to us on a silver platter. It is not simply found between the leather bindings of sacred books. God said through the prophet Jeremiah, "You will seek me and find me when you seek me with all your heart."[310] Jesus said, "Seek and you will find."[311] In Phase 2 we discussed the importance of the iterative process in establishing truth, and in particular as a test of what is and is not scripture. Our discussion, however, was aimed at SR alone. Here now we extend the iterative process dimensionally to include NT and EU.

Our call is to process, to permit *ultimate truth* to expand us, to become dimensional thinkers. Blaise Pascal, the seventeenth century philosopher, mathematician, and physicist, was one such dimensional thinker. Though he was

---

305 Ibid., 86.
306 Manning, *The Ragamuffin Gospel*, 46.
307 Acts 15:28.
308 Colossians 3:15.
309 John 14:27.
310 Jeremiah 5:1.
311 Luke 11:9.

tormented by doubts and questions regarding God, he too acknowledged the triune nature of SR, NT, and EU as the path to truth. He argued for a combined implementation of "intellectual, moral, and physical understandings."[312] I see SR, NT, and EU imbedded in this trio.

As deep calls out to deep, so each member of the trio of truths calls to the others.[313] We do not simply need NT and EU to fill in the missing pieces of SR. We need them because SR calls out for their wisdom. Nature calls out for the strange existence of God, yet needs revelation and experience to confirm its voice. Experience finds validation by looking to the cosmos and to the enlightenments of SR. The following illustration (Figure 70) shows the interdependency of SR, NT, and EU. The order of the iterative process in the illustration, flowing from SR to EU to NT and back to SR, is not intentional (at least not consciously!), but simply conveys the joint wisdom they provide, zeroing in on the truths of God.

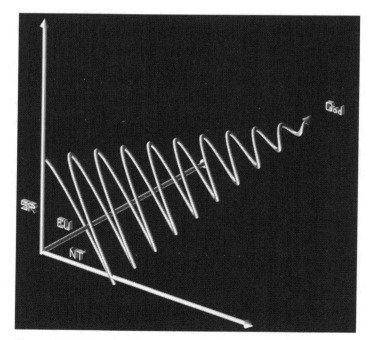

Figure 70. A Dimensional View of Special Revelation, Natural Theology, and Existential Understanding

---

[312] James A. Connor, *Pascal's Wager: The Man Who Played Dice with God* (New York: HarperCollins Publisher, 2006), 180-81.
[313] Psalm 42:7.

In chapter 2.11 I provided an illustration titled *Iterative* Theology that described the iterative process as moving outward in an ever-increasing spiral. That illustration was meant to convey the need to expand our sources of truth, while the illustration here is meant to convey the iterative transformation of lower dimensional truths into a higher dimensional perspective on God. God is not shrinking; rather, we are being refined as we permit divergent, inconsistent, and even chaotic perspectives to meld into unity.

The Starting Point

For some, the debate over SR, NT, and EU centers on the starting point. I believe the starting point is not of primary importance. The greater issue is whether or not one is willing to iterate enough times through the dimensions of truth so as to ultimately obscure the starting point. Then and then only will we move toward a more refined, and perhaps even more consistent, understanding of God.

3.11

Dimensional Attributes of God

In Phase 2 we discussed some of the attributes of the IICP. Most were developed using mathematical and logical processes (NT). One can, of course, find many attributes of God described in scripture (SR). By now you have encountered my *gut intuition* on many God issues (EU). We will now attempt to dimensionally merge some of these characteristics into higher dimensional perspectives.

Infinite unto Himself

Is God infinite unto himself? If God is, then God experiences his own infinitude. If we are content for the moment with the dimensional definition of infinitude, that infinitude is always at least one dimension away, and the conjecture that there are an infinite number of dimensions, then the answer would have to be, "No." God is in all of the infinite dimensions. There are no dimensions outside of God for him to point to his infinitude! If God were infinite to himself, then there would always be a part of himself unreachable to himself. Therefore, he would have a limitation and thereby not be infinite. Infinity is not infinite unto itself. Obviously God knows he is infinite to every derivative domain, but he is not infinite relative to himself. He is not beyond himself.

Having said that, I have immediately placed a restriction on God: he cannot be outside his infinitude to observe it! What is more, neither can he be inside his infinitude to recognize and experience it! How can the two opposite perspectives coexist? This is strange indeed.

Perhaps God's infinitude is not linear, but circular! If he were to move to higher and higher dimensions, perhaps he too ends up back where he started from: *I Am that I Am* for an infinite number of iterations! In the latter case God has been everywhere on the infinite and dimensional loop an infinite number of iterations. I perceive (EU) that when scripture quotes God calling himself the *I Am that I Am* (SR) it is a recognition of all three types of infinity: infinite in magnitude, infinite dimensionally, and infinite in intricacy (NT). Surely, he knows and experiences his infinitude. I do not doubt that God is in awe of himself, not as we frail humans arrogantly view ourselves, but with true and infinite knowledge. That God delights in himself (in his infinitude) is what makes it possible for him to delight in us! I believe God is infinite unto himself. Delightfully so!

Inconceivable and Unsearchable

Some scriptures describe God as inconceivable and unsearchable.[314] One of the Old Testament writers, said, "(God's) way is in the whirlwind and the storm."[315] Only weather radar can track such activity! Not that I doubt scripture, but why bother with such a book as this if all that is true? Dimensional perspectives (NT) greatly aid in understanding such texts (SR). It is clear that I cannot search out God in his ultimate dimensional domain. Such an existence is indeed inconceivable. However, the unsearchable, unprovable, and inconceivable portions of God are those that do not enter our dimensional domain. Where God's and our domains overlap, we can search and understand God. Is scripture wrong? No, it is just too high in its dimensional context.

The Immutability of God

We established in Phase 2 that God is infinite and therefore immutable, or unchangeable. Remember the argument? If God is anything now that he was not at some previous time and place, then he was not infinite then, nor is he now. However, this analysis does not take the dimensional nature of God into consideration. For instance, immutability in three dimensions does not necessitate immutability in two dimensions. Various and changing two-dimensional slices of an unchanging three-dimensional object can be observed in two dimensions.

---

[314] Jeremiah 33:3; Romans 11:33-36.
[315] Nahum 1:3.

To claim that God is the same yesterday, today, and forever is a higher dimensional statement.[316] Even though an immutable n-dimensional object may exist, it is not a guarantee that the associated (n-1)-dimensional representations of that object are immutable. Furthermore there is no guarantee that the numerous (n-1)-dimensional entities will be consistent with each other or free of paradox. An immutable n-dimensional object, passing dynamically through n-1 space, will appear to change.

Process Theology

Process theology is a theology of a growing, changing, improving God. When I first encountered theories on this topic I reacted to them vehemently. For God to be God he must be infinite. An evolving God is not infinite. The IICP is not growing! However, over time as I have proceeded with dimensional analyses, I have come to realize that the bulk of the evidence that such theorists use to develop the evolution of God is dimensionally limited. While evidences exist that God changes, at some dimensional level God ceases to change.

I do not believe in the development or evolution of God. God, being infinite, is not in the process of development. God *is*. God is all change, infinite change. However, God does move in and through lower dimensions, leaving slices behind that contribute to an evolving view of God. Admittedly our lower dimensional perspectives of God have historically been very rigid. If anything needs to be truly processing, it is our narrow perspectives, which need to grow and iterate toward God. Let us not confuse progressive revelations and iterations of understanding of God with an evolving God.

Of all the observed changes of God, the most significant is found in his moving toward the finite. This is the beauty of the incarnation: God iterating toward us. This iterative process includes change that interacts with human prayers. Yes, an infinite God, iterating through infinite changes, includes our prayers as part of his infinite change. God infinitely cares for the smallest detail (the third type of infinity).

---

[316] Hebrews 13:8.

If God is infinite and we are finite, then portions of God will continue to be revealed, now and forever, portions that we have never seen before. This necessitates a form of process. This form, however convincing it may seem, is dimensionally dependent. God, on the other hand, is not.

Unbounded Time

The Psalmist said, "Before the mountains were born or you brought forth the whole world, from everlasting to everlasting you are God."[317] Notice that the verse does not say, "you were God." It emphatically exclaims, "you are God." I believe this reflects God's existence outside the bounds of time. The Psalmist was very dimensional in his perspective. It took millennia for the rest of us to catch up.

God is not bound by time. This does not mean he does not exist in time, but that God is in all time. In Einsteinian terms, he occupies the space-time continuum in its entirety. He is in the past and the future as much as the present. His infinite change loops include our past, present, and future prayers.

The exception to this unbounded nature was expressed in the GBF. In the incarnation God bowed to space-time constraints, giving of himself in a time-limited form, *for all time*. God willingly confined part of himself to our bounds precisely because of his infinitude.

Merging Attributes into One

Scripture paints a beautiful dimensional picture of the attributes of God by declaring how wide, long, high, and deep they are.[318] On one hand it is a limited view, in that it assumes these dimensions can be known, but on the other hand it acknowledges that God's attributes are beyond our meager dimensions. We can attempt to merge God's attributes into a single dimensional perspective, assuming we do not pick and choose which ones to include. To formulate a more accurate dimensional view of God we must include all God has revealed about himself through SR, NT, and EU.

---

[317] Psalm 90:2.
[318] Ephesians 3:16-19.

In the following illustration, a number of God's attributes are merged into a single entity with multiple faces (Figure 71). The illustration is obviously limited by words. We cannot adequately describe God with any human language.

Figure 71. Dimensional Attributes of God: Limited by Words

What is more, we cannot begin to grasp the number of attributes of God, for they, too, are infinite. If one were to take the previous illustration to the limit (the calculus process whereby the number of faces goes to infinity) the result would become very like the entity in the following illustration (Figure 72). God, both complexly and simply, *is*.

Figure 72. Dimensional Attributes of God: Unlimited

3.12

The Arms of God

All of this discussion on the infinitude of God and God's infinite attributes leads to another question: Is God one or three (not to mention more)? While I will indirectly address those religions with many gods, we are going to focus here on those who believe in the *Trinity*.

Many religions have held to a triune God or triune godlike figures. Diarmuid O'Murchu, in his book *Quantum Theology*, explains that in Hinduism there is the triune Vishnu, Shiva, and Shakti; in Buddhism the dharma-kaya, nirmana-kaya, and sambhoga-kaya; in Zoroastrianism the triune Zurvan, Ahriman, and Ormazd; in Egyptian cult Isis, Serapis, and Horus; and the Neoplatonic triune Good, Intelligence, and the World Soul.[319] Though there are uniquenesses to Christian trinitarian theology, it is not alone in its claim that God is *three-in-one*. Does the IICP, the infinite God, truly have differential components, defying our understanding of infinitude?

Challenges to the Trinity

Both the Old Testament and the Koran assert that God is *One*! Mathematically, as I have shown, this must be so. Christians, based on New Testament texts, assert that God is comprised of three separate persons. Yet even in the New Testament texts, only the Father and Son are mentioned as existing in heaven. One exception is 1 John 5:7, but its reference to all three members of the trinity existing in heaven simultaneously was added in later manuscripts, causing some scholars to question

---

[319] O'Murchu, *Quantum Theology: Spiritual Implications of the New Physics*, 88.

its legitimacy. All other scriptural descriptions of heaven do not seem to include the Holy Spirit. Why?

In some Biblical texts the Holy Spirit is referred to as the *Spirit of Christ*.[320] In one text we find that Jesus intercedes for the saints,[321] yet in another we find that it is the Holy Spirit that does the interceding on behalf of the saints.[322] Who intercedes for whom? Why, according to scripture, does the Father know when the ultimate end will come, but not the Son? Do these things not seem peculiar and contradictory to you? They do to me ... unless there is a dimensional issue at play.

A Dimensional Phenomenon

I believe the *Trinity* is a dimensional phenomenon. I demonstrated mathematically in Phase 2 that God must be *One*. If each of the members of the Trinity has qualities that the other two do not, then none of them is infinite, at least not in magnitude. However, what if they are infinite in a dimensional sense? (Remember, there are three types of infinity: magnitude, dimensions, and intricacy.) So what do I mean by the Trinity being a dimensional phenomenon?

Karl Barth once wrote, "He is, in Himself by nature and in eternity, and for us in time, the One in three ways of being."[323] Notice Barth's references to both *time* and *ways of being*. Whether or not Barth meant to communicate the dimensional nature of God, he did so quite aptly. Are these *ways of being* dimensional representations of the same single entity?

Aquarium Maintenance

When I was in my youth I had an aquarium with tropical fish. My first aquarium was a small 5-gallon tank, but it was large enough to handle a school of my favorite fish: *Neon Tetras*. They were beautifully iridescent. I watched them for hours as they swam and darted together under the aquarium light. But, just as my parents warned, it took work to keep a healthy tank of fish. I cleaned the tank, conditioned the water, and changed the filter regularly.

---

[320] Romans 8:9, 1 Peter 1:11.
[321] Hebrews 7:25.
[322] Romans 8:27.
[323] Barth, *Dogmatics in Outline*, 42.

Early on in my aquarium maintenance career I was struck by a peculiar phenomenon. I was certainly not thinking about God, let alone the Trinity, at the time. I was simply cleaning the aquarium. As I knelt down next to the aquarium table and reached up and into the tank to adjust the decorative pieces that were sitting on the bottom, I was struck by the fact that I could not see through the surface of the water. All I could see was the portion of my arm and hand that were in the water. I slowly backed my arm out of the tank until all I could see were five fingers. They danced as though they were independent of each other. I am sure the fish thought they were the five maintenance gods who watched over them, as fish so often do.

Later, in a high school physics class, I learned about the *critical angle* in water and the resulting mirror-like behavior of the surface of water when observed at an angle greater than the critical angle. So it was as I looked through the side of the aquarium toward the surface of the water. I could see nothing beyond its gleaming surface. An entity above that barrier became visible if it actually penetrated the surface of the water, entering the aquarium's domain. So, how many *ways of being* did my arm have, as far as the fish were concerned? Was there one arm? Or was it just a hand? Or, *Arm* forbid, were there five separate entities, each moving in sync with the others, *as though* they were *One*? Chances are there were one or two Neon Tetras that just happened to be in an angular position less than the critical angle while the fingers danced, noticing they were indeed attached, though the rippling water distorted *what* they were attached to. "Ah," they may have said, "The Fingers are indeed One." Little did they know that there was much, much more to me than a unified belief in my five fingers!

Fish Theology

So it is with God and us. Yes, God is surely *One*, but two common errors plague us all: believing that what we see and experience in this domain is all there is to God, and that even if we are so privileged to see beyond our realm, as blurry as the view may be, we fail to grasp how much more there is beyond even that view. God is infinitely dimensional. How could we possibly be so sure we understand it all, except via fish theology?

I have come to both acknowledge and resign my fish theology. Even if there is a literal Trinity of *physical* entities in our integral domain, mathematically in some ultimate dimensional domain there is but one entity. The writer of the book of Job, which is a very dimensional book, says, "Can you fathom the mysteries of God? Can you probe the limits of the Almighty? They are higher than the heavens above—what can you do? They are deeper than the depths below—what can you know? Their measure is longer than the earth and wider than the sea."[324] So much more resides beyond our tiny aquarium and our fish theology.

The Dimensions of God

It is with tremendous risk that I present the following illustration, hoping to shed light on the dimensions of God. My fear is that some may cling to it as the latest fish theology. It is simply meant to enlighten the possibilities. All representations, analogies, and/or illustrations of God fall short of adequately representing the IICP. This must be so if God is infinite. Treat this illustration, if you will, as a dimensional parable that came out of my dimensional and transformational wanderings (Figure 73).

As you can see, there is a person entering a dimensional domain by sticking their head and arms through its boundaries. Let us imagine for the moment that it is God entering 8-D. Therein exist angels and other fanciful creatures that both the Head and the Arms delight in and care for. There are probably some creatures wise and privileged enough to glimpse through the boundaries to understand that it is a single entity that so warmly envelops and cares for them. Inside 8-D there is a derivative domain. Let us think of it as 4-D: our domain. The Right Arm is shown entering this domain.

---

[324] Job 11:7-9.

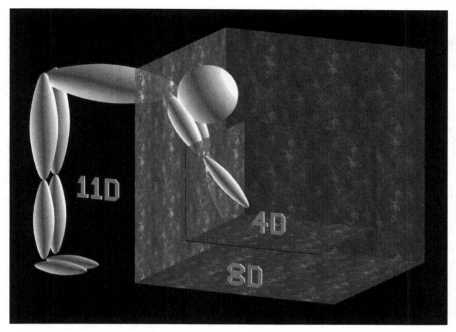

Figure 73. Dimensions of God

I have already developed the arguments for the 4-D, 8-D, and 11-D domains. There are scriptural references to God in all domains (though not necessarily visible),[325] the Head (Father) in 8-D, but not in 4-D,[326] the Right Arm (Son) in 8-D and 4-D,[327] and the inverted presence of the Left Arm (Holy Spirit) in 4-D.[328] By *inverted presence* I mean the Left Arm enters our domain via our invisible, or inverted, dimensions.[329] This causes me to deduce the following: God is an 11-D representation or slice of an infinite dimensional entity. Why? The IICP, being infinite, cannot be bound by any dimensional boundaries. Therefore, any 11-D representation of the IICP is just that: a willful representation of itself in bodily form. This 11-D representation may have pushed its head and arms into 8-D (one of the aquariums it created). Therefore, the Head and Arms are 8-D slices of this

[325] Proverbs 15:3; Jeremiah 23:24; Psalm 139:7-10; Job 11:7-9; 2 Kings 8:27.
[326] 2 Chronicles 2:6; Isaiah 55:9; John 1:18; 1 John 4:12.
[327] John 1:1-14.
[328] Psalm 91:1; Luke 1:35; John 14:16, 26; 16:7; 1 John 2:1; Romans 8:9-11.
[329] I postulated in 3.03 that the 6 extra spatial dimensions that physicists propose are part of the structure of our universe may be inverted and rendered invisible.

11-D God. The Head is both seen and experienced in 8-D. It is not *seen* in 4-D at all, though evidences point to its existence.[330] The 8-D Right Arm entered 4-D as the Arm-Become-Flesh: the GBF. The inverted Left Arm is what we are now left to experience in 4-D. We will come back to this invisible presence in more detail later.

What we have are dimensional slices of a single entity. God is *One*! However, it is possible that even God, in 11-D, is but a dimensional representation of a higher dimensional entity. I tend to think of this infinite and unbounded entity as *Essence*. All dimensions, by definition, have boundaries. Therefore, either Essence has access to an infinite number of dimensions to satisfy its boundless condition, or it has no dimensions, thereby being boundless. Quite honestly, I prefer to think the latter of Essence. Most likely dimensions were invented by Essence for the sake of its creations. Perhaps Essence chose to enter some of these boundaries as a *Being*, who in turn chose to create and enter the boundaries of our integral domain as the Head and the Arms, one of which chose to create and enter yet another derivative domain: ours. What if? Just, what if?

The Trinity

So, does the Trinity exist? I have already shown that God is One, but that does not prohibit God from showing up in our integral domain as three distinct and very real entities. Furthermore, it does not preclude the Arm from showing up in our domain as a distinct and very real entity as well. Mathematically, God is One and is infinite. Dimensionally, the IICP can express itself through diverse and sundry *ways of being*. The absolute infinitude of God remains irreducible by dimensional analyses. It is beyond reduction. It simply is.

The Right Arm of God

I hope the *offspring of God* issue is resolving for you. I believe God has no offspring. I understand why Muhammad reacted to the idea of Jesus being an offspring or child of God. Scriptural references to the Son of God are expressions designed to describe the essence of God himself, fully expressed in the flesh

---

[330] John 1:18.

through the GBF. The GBF's name was Immanuel, meaning *God with us*. The GBF was God himself extending his Arm into our domain. The prophet Isaiah foretold that salvation would come from the "holy arm" of God.[331] The Apostle Paul claimed that the fullness of God was expressed in the GBF.[332] Many have read such texts figuratively; I read them quite literally.

But why extend his arm into our domain? Some of the reasons were expressed in Phase 2, and we will visit more reasons in a later chapter. It seems evident at this point, however, there may have been a bonus reason for such an expression. Perhaps God wanted us to know what he looks like. Perhaps God simply wanted us to recognize his Arm. It was, after all, the handiwork of the Right Arm that brought all things into existence.[333] Many, of course, did not, nor do they still, recognize the creator image of God in the GBF. It is my hope that if you stare deeply and long enough into his eyes you will recognize him.

The Left Arm of God

Jesus said to his disciples near the end of his ministry: "Unless I go away, the Advocate (or Comforter) will not come to you; but if I go, I will send her to you."[334] Why did Jesus have to leave in order for the Holy Spirit to come? My dimensional paraphrase of Jesus' words is, "Physically I cannot cover the whole earth, but if I go, my inverted twin can." He was expressing to the disciples, though they did not understand it at the time, God's desire to be with them *and* the rest of the world always.

I am overwhelmed by the role of God's Spirit. By whatever designation we use (the Spirit of God, the Shadow of the Almighty,[335] the Holy Spirit, the Comforter, etc.), we survive this broken world solely because of the presence of the Left Arm. We are sustained, strengthened, comforted, empowered, envisioned, guided, held steadfast, made tolerable, filled with compassion, given knowledge, and encompassed because of the presence of God's Spirit here and now.

---

[331] Isaiah 41:10.
[332] Colossians 2:9-10.
[333] Jeremiah 32:17; John 1.
[334] John 16:7 (SFA paraphrase) The Greek word paraklētos is indeed masculine. However, elsewhere the original language for Spirit is feminine. We will come back to the gender issue.
[335] Psalm 17:8, 36:7, 57:1, 63:7, 91:1; Isaiah 51:16; Luke 1:35.

Though there is much evil in this world, I doubt we could imagine the increased orders of magnitude of evil that would fill the earth without the overwhelming infiltration of God's presence.

Additionally, scripture tells us that when we open ourselves to transformation, this Spirit not only encompasses us, but also fills us with God's essence. The Left Arm of God lives *in* us! We have her power, her wisdom, her peace, and her comfort.

I leave this brief discussion with one of my all-time favorite passages regarding the role of the Holy Spirit in our lives, and especially on the subject of praying.

> In the same way, the Spirit helps us in our weakness. We do not
> know what we ought to pray for, but the Spirit himself intercedes
> for us through wordless groans. And he who searches our hearts
> knows the mind of the Spirit, because the Spirit intercedes for
> God's people in accordance with the will of God.[336]

I find it very difficult to know how to pray much of the time. Because of the freedom this passage offers, I often find myself praying by simply groaning . . . thanks to the interceding inverted Left Arm of God.

Twin Arms of God

I believe the Arms of God are twins. Not identical, but almost mirror images of each other. They obviously have unique functions. Why not unique genders? Granted, I do not believe God is confined to our gender designations, but who is to say that God cannot or does not render his arms with gender in 8-D? You have already witnessed my reference to the Holy Spirit as feminine. The Greek word *parakletos*, translated *Advocate*, or *Comforter*, in the John 16:7 passage, is indeed a masculine noun. However, in the Old Testament the Hebrew word *ruach*, translated *Spirit* in passages such as Isaiah 61:1, is a feminine noun. Why the discrepancy? It is we humans who have limited God's Spirit to the masculine sense in the Old and New Testament translations. There are cultures around the world,

---

[336] Romans 8:26-27.

including some Asian traditions, which commonly refer to the Holy Spirit as feminine.[337] I delight in thinking of the Holy Spirit in the feminine sense.

These twins have different functions, as do our own arms. Scripture tells us that the Right Arm spoke all things into existence, projecting vibrating strings of matter into the cosmos. It holds the cosmos together still.[338] The Right Arm also became the GBF, the Salvation of God. He bears the scars from that mission.

At creation, the Left Arm calmed the waters of the deep, the waters that were brought into existence by her twin. She filled the earth with her presence before the Great Rebellion. After the rebellion she communicated with humankind only now and again, until the coming of the GBF. Most significantly, she is the one who entered Jesus' tomb via our inverted dimensions to breathe life back into his corpse. She returned to 4-D after the GBF returned to 8-D, filling the earth with her presence, giving life, strength, wisdom, and peace to those who welcome her transforming presence.

Inextricably Attached

God's Head and Arms are inextricably attached. For instance, my arms are in my body and my body is in my arms. Blood and neurological impulses flow continuously through them. Do my arms know what my head is going to tell them to do? No. The only actions that my arms do on their own are involuntary, reflexive movements, responding to the environment and stimuli. Otherwise, they do what my head tells them to do. Jesus said, "Very truly I tell you, the Son can do nothing by himself; he can do only what he sees his Father doing, because whatever the Father does the Son also does."[339] The two are inextricably attached. The GBF was not an independent entity, but was truly God himself in the flesh.

However, a most mysterious event happened moments before Jesus died on the cross. If the GBF and God are truly one, being inextricably attached, and assuming Jesus was the GBF, why did Jesus scream out from the cross, "My God, my God, why have you forsaken me?"[340] How can this be? Some substitutionary

---

[337] Dr. Art McPhee, Asbury Theological Seminary.
[338] Colossians 1:17.
[339] John 5:19.
[340] Mark 15:34.

atonement theologies claim that God was required to turn away from the GBF, since the GBF had to carry the weight of the world's sin in total isolation. I have already expressed concerns over the substitutionary atonement concept in Phase 2 and find this explanation quite unsatisfactory. There must be more to the story.

During my high school years I took a woodworking class. I was quite good at working with my hands. Or so I thought. One day, while chiseling out hinge notches for a box and lid I had made, I foolishly forced the chisel with my right hand. It slipped and sliced right through the base of my left thumb. To make matters worse, I fainted from the trauma. My parents picked me up and took me to the doctor's office. The doctor proceeded to clean the wound and sew it up. I do not remember if an anesthetic was used or not, but it hurt like H . . . I winced my face, gritted my teeth, and looked the other direction.

A few years ago, while pondering the crucifixion scene, I remembered that fateful high school experience. If the GBF and God are truly and inextricably one, then such a cruel and painful death *had* to be felt by the Head, the Father. I believe God experienced every bit of the pain that the GBF did and turned his head in pain. The Head and Arm are, after all, inextricably attached.

An Inverted Attachment

I hope the significance of our inverted dimensions is becoming clearer. Three of the inverted, or invisible, spatial dimensions that we share with our integral domain are the dimensions through which the Left Arm of God moves while interacting with our domain. What is more, it is via these inverted dimensions that the Right Arm of God remained attached to God the whole time he was physically confined to our domain. The GBF was not simply attached in attitude, or "in spirit." In spite of his apparent physical independence, I believe he was physically attached. What the people *saw* was not all there was to him. He was literally attached to God. Again, this is why his name was Immanuel: he was God-with-us, extended into our limited domain.

Subjected to Time

One of the peculiarities of the GBF was his confinement to space-time. God knows no bounds of time. I believe the IICP created time. Yet he willingly extended his arm into space-time. To me this is more miraculous than presenting himself in the flesh. Such a confinement for one who is accustomed to being *in all time*, and in *no-time*, is nothing short of selfless abandonment. Jesus said, "Before Abraham was born, I am."[341] If anyone doubts Jesus' claim to divinity, this text alone says it all. In addition to a claim to divinity, it is an acknowledgement of his confinement to space-time. According to scripture, God's purpose and mission were established before time existed.[342] The GBF *was* before space-time came into existence (it was the arm that built space-time). Yet he willingly subjected himself to the confines of space and time.

One of the fallouts of the Right Arm's confinement to time is that the Head and Left Arm were not confined to time. The mission was truly timeless. The timing of the GBF's coming and his purpose, though experienced here in time, were truly outside the bounds of time: at least outside the bounds of 4-D space-time. His mission was for all time.

Modalism and Other Known Heresies

During the editing process of this book it was brought to my attention that some of the concepts in this chapter come quite close to known heresies, such as modalism. I will address both modalism and the concept of *known heresies*.

Modalism is anti-trinitarian. The Father, Son, and Holy Spirit are simply different *modes* of a single entity that shows up in various ways at different times. This belief was condemned by the Church Fathers as heresy since it denied the existence of three divine Persons.[343] The church's primary counter to this belief is found in the four gospel accounts of the baptism of Jesus.

When John the Baptist baptized Jesus the Holy Spirit descended from heaven in the bodily form of a dove and lit upon Jesus. At the same time a voice came from

---

[341] John 8:58.
[342] 2 Timothy 1:9.
[343] Polkinghorne, *Science and Religion in Quest of Truth*, 128-29.

heaven proclaiming approval of Jesus and his ministry.[344] Since all three persons of the divine Trinity were present at that moment, the belief of a single entity showing up in different modes at different times was ousted. It became a known heresy.

What I have proposed herein is not modalism. It may be similar in some respects, but it is not modalism. I believe there are three divine persons in 8-D. However, as you have seen, I believe there is one divine person in 11-D who enters his 8-D aquarium as three people simultaneously. Admittedly, to some this may be a higher dimensional version of modalism. Will this become yet another known heresy?

I have to admit that whenever I hear someone point a verbal finger at a *known heresy*, I cringe. It is we humans who have drawn such detailed lines, pronouncing judgment on someone else's wanderings. It is not God who is doing the drawing. We are invited by God to inquire, to dream, to ponder, to speculate, to invent, to believe. And yes, even to swim in heretical ideas. It is part of the process we are called to. It is part of our journey. One of the Psalms expresses my sentiment quite aptly,

> One thing have I asked of the Lord, that will I seek after; that I may dwell in the house of the Lord all the days of my life, to behold the beauty of the Lord, and to inquire in his temple.[345]

Even if it is heretical inquiry.

Full Circle

Mathematically, God is *One*. Early on this realization prompted me to move away from belief in the three equal but unique persons of the Godhead. However, I have come to believe that the IICP presents itself dimensionally in sundry ways in its various aquariums, ways that may extend beyond the Trinity. But for the moment, I have come full circle. I believe that when I enter the next domain, I will

---

[344] Matthew 3:16-17; Mark 1:9-11; Luke 3:21-22; John 1:32.
[345] Psalm 27:4, RSV.

see three persons: the Father (Head), the Son (the Right Arm), and the Holy Spirit (the Left Arm). This process brought about another significant change in me. Whereas I once believed the Holy Spirit was an ethereal essence of God, I now believe the Holy Spirit is a real person.

In Closing

I believe the Right Arm of God, the same arm that created space-time, entered this domain with purpose. This God, who resides in dimensions beyond dimensions, lowered himself into our domain intentionally. It was a painful encounter, one perhaps felt by all of heaven. Yet he willingly subjected himself to space-time to accomplish a timeless mission.

3.13

Locked Out

We live in a broken world with broken processes. But we are more than broken. We are lost and far from home.

Somewhere along the line a major paradigm shift took place, leaving us strangely limping along, gnawing away at our existence. We are clearly not what we once were, nor what we could be. Sure, we have made many advances in science, technology, and medicine, but we also have made advances in weaponry that continue to bring devastation on the world. This brokenness is perpetuated by evil and selfish means. We are wandering and homesick, infinitely far from home, yet close enough for memories to persist.

The Genesis story addresses our condition beautifully. Therein we find fragments of the memories of our origins. One of those fragments describes humans as image-bearers of God. Over time our images went to our heads and we decided we could fill the role of God quite adequately. Dimensionally, we thought we saw God in God's entirety and could do his job, handling things quite well on our own. The Great Rebellion ensued and, according to Genesis, we were *locked out* of the Garden of Eden. We are still children of God, but we wander far from our homeland, as lost as sheep in the desert. It is as though we entered the *Twilight Zone* and frantically work either at getting back or at convincing ourselves we *are* home. We innately long for the Garden.

Eden

If not a literal place, Eden was a dimensional existence with different dimensional properties than our current domain. For instance, in Eden there was a special tree called the *Tree of Life*: the ultimate fountain of youth.[346] I believe this tree is an allegorical reference to another dimension of time, perhaps an unbounded dimension of time. Such a dimension would have resulted in immortality, or at least very long life spans. We also understand from the Genesis story that all of humankind was expelled from Eden following the Great Rebellion. This expulsion was from a *place*, perhaps a place with other spatial dimensions. This would seem to be the case, since according to Genesis angels were posted at the entrance of Eden with flaming swords to guard humans from returning.[347]

The Great Rebellion, or *fall*, resulted in a lockout from another dimensional domain. In the dimensional terms we have already defined, I believe we once lived in 8-D, roaming freely about with 14 degrees of freedom. We lost 8 of these degrees of freedom in that fateful expulsion. The doors were shut, and we were locked out.

What We Lost

We lost access to portions of who we once were and regions we once had access to. Humans are still essentially 8-D entities, but are now locked out of 8-D. One of the reasons I am so convinced is that we still seek access. Why would we seek passage to Shangri-La or the Fountain of Youth if they were not part of our past? What did we lose that we seek so steadfastly?

We lost immortality. I believe we had freedom to move about in both space and time. For some, that may be a stretch, but it is a natural conclusion if we did in fact inherit a bounded dimension of time with only a forward arrow. The Genesis story describes mortality ensuing as a side effect of the fall.[348] All one has to do is watch TV for a few hours and observe the number of times that we are told, "You deserve better," or "Look younger instantly." We steadfastly pursue immortality. Allegorically or not, we long for the Garden.

We lost our innocence. Our eyes were opened. We see things now that we did not before and no longer see things we once held as commonplace. Our vision has switched from 8-D to 4-D. We see nakedness, depravity, evil, selfishness, hurt,

---

[346] Genesis 3:24
[347] Ibid.
[348] Genesis 3:19.

loneliness, and we experience pain. We have to work by the sweat of our brows to climb over our competitors to get to the top of what turns out to be a pile of dung. We lost our vision of God, wholeness, selfless love, purity of heart, and unadulterated pleasure. We profoundly seek pleasure, which turns out to be but a shadow of what we once lived in continuously.

What We Did Not Lose

We did not lose our 8-D roots. We did not lose our innate awareness of who we are. For that matter, we did not lose our awareness of our awareness. We know who we are.

We did not lose our image, the image that was created in God's likeness, the part that knows that "I am." We are image bearers still. For all the brokenness that holds us back, God's image in us prevails. We fight it, we attempt to rid ourselves of it, and we run from it. The spark in us that wants to kindle a fire of wholeness is there still. This remnant is the portion of us that remains in 8-D. Some call it our *spirit*. Whatever tag you prefer, it is the portion of us that knows where we come from, and that longs to be reunited with the 4-D portion of us that lost access to the Garden.

A Thermodynamic Shift

As poetic and metaphorical as the Genesis account of the Garden of Eden may be, it prophetically contains great truth. It describes a thermodynamic shift ensuing after the expulsion from the Garden. The couple (Adam and Eve) is told that childbearing will become painful; that the land will begin to produce thorns; that they will have to sweat and fight to survive. What is that? It is a thermodynamic shift; it is an onset of a bounded arrow of time: it is entropy. What they left was the antithesis of that: naturally increasing order. The energy input and unbounded time they were accustomed to living with was replaced with an expenditure of energy and a bounded arrow of time. There was clearly a thermodynamic shift: poetic or not.

It is quite interesting that John Polkinghorne, a highly regarded scientist and theologian, affirms in his book *Science and Religion in Quest of Truth*, that there will be a thermodynamic shift in "the world to come" (the next domain), reversing the tendency toward disorder that exists here and now. He says, "It seems a coherent belief that God can bring this about by endowing 'matter' with such strong self-organizing principles that it will not be subject to the thermodynamic drift to disorder which is the source of mortality in the present age."[349] Though he questions why God did not put such a world in place from the beginning, Polkinghorne affirms that such a shift (though in the opposite direction) is within reason. I believe God did put such a world in place, but that we lost it through the thermodynamic shift toward entropy.

Frankly, I find it more reasonable to endorse such a thermodynamic shift than current theories which describe order spontaneously springing out of chaos without any energy input. As I argued in Phase 2, such a spontaneous increase in order is contrary to the laws of thermodynamics. However, perhaps such overriding thermodynamic principles do not exist in 8-D as such. The natural selection we so quickly endorse is not now what it once was in 8-D. As I indicated in Phase 2, I believe natural selection is broken.

Boundaries of Love

Why would God *kick us out* of 8-D? As I showed in Phase 2, God is not so finite as to respond in uncontrollable anger when his sovereignty is threatened. The IICP is not so limited. Everything he does is motivated by infinite compassion. He has always and will always look out for our best interest, even if it is not presently obvious.

I believe our expulsion was motivated by a love that moved us out of eternal disaster and into a realm where restoration could begin without permanent loss of our image-bearing. Perhaps the restriction will be in place until the whole of the redemption story has taken place for all of creation. Until then, we exist within boundaries of love.

---

[349] Polkinghorne, *Science and Religion in Quest of Truth*, 106.

All Creation Groans

The Apostle Paul wrote, "For the creation waits in eager expectation for the children of God to be revealed. For the creation was subjected to frustration, not by its own choice, but by the will of the one who subjected it, in hope that the creation itself will be liberated from its bondage to decay and brought into the freedom and glory of the children of God. We know that the whole creation has been groaning as in the pains of childbirth right up to the present time."[350]

First of all, Paul's words confirm the thermodynamic shift as *bondage to decay*. Secondly, the passage confirms that the expulsion from 8-D was a subjection aimed at eventual liberation. Thirdly, and most significantly, all of creation groans, waiting patiently for the return to 8-D. What a powerful image! The rocks, rivers, oceans, mountains, and plains, along with all life forms, yearn for home. They too lost access to the Garden. I believe C.S. Lewis and J.R.R. Tolkien were prophetic in their fanciful portrayals of sentient animals longing for home.

Returning Home

All this talk about being far from the Garden, our 8-D home, is one thing. Getting back is quite another. It is here that I must ask a fundamental question: *Would we be aware of such a place, yearn for its time independence, and hope to return to it if it were out of the realm of possibility?* Can we really contemplate anything that either has not or will not exist? If we think we can, we have a fairly exaggerated view of our imagination.

This is not a fanciful fairytale. This *is* our condition, and knowing so is proof enough that a solution exists. In Phase 2 I introduced the need for a GBF based on the infinite chasm between our broken world and God's realm. What I did not clarify therein was the *how* of the GBF's restorative mission. I am not so foolish as to think I have a comprehensive grasp on the fullness of that mission, but of this I am convinced: God became flesh for the sole purpose of bringing us back home. Let us look more closely at the timeless mission that unlocked our domain.

---

350 Romans 8:19-22.

3.14

The Portal

What was the mission of the GBF? According to ancient scripture, it was to give hope to those in despair, to give freedom to those oppressed by this world, to heal the brokenhearted, and to forgive all who are weary of the debt of brokenness.[351] It was a four-fold mission: hope, freedom, healing, and forgiveness. Jesus of Nazareth proclaimed his intent to fulfill this ancient mission.[352] As we discussed in Phase 2, there is a great mass of evidence that he was the GBF and did accomplish this mission.

Jesus proclaimed a *Way* that would bring about the aforementioned four-fold mission. In fact he not only proclaimed the Way, but that he *was* the Way.[353] It is this Way that I now wish to focus on. Jesus made it clear that it was not the latest and greatest way to self-improvement springing from human origins, but that it was the Way made by God.

Dimensional Constraints

We have already discussed the dimensional constraints that we live with. We are in 4-D and behave in sundry ways that we hope, even if subconsciously, will get us back to the Garden. We develop self-improvement techniques, gospels of prosperity, even lies that insist we are OK as we stand. The bottom line, however, is that there are no dimensional bootstraps. We are dealing with a dimensional separation from home and from God, an infinite separation. This separation, I

---

[351] Isaiah 61:1-3.
[352] Luke 4:18-21.
[353] John 14:6.

believe, involves boundaries that were put in place out of infinite love. Only such infinite love can remove them, restoring us in the process.

The Tree of Life

In the previous chapter I introduced the Tree of Life. It was present in the Garden (8-D) but access to it was shut off following the rebellion as we were jettisoned into 4-D.[354] Scripture tells us that it exists in heaven still.[355] The references in both Genesis and Revelation portray this tree as bearing fruit that brings life and healing to its recipients.

This tree is also referenced in Native American scriptures: "Then Deganawidah uprooted the Tree, and under it disclosed a Cavern through which ran a stream of water, passing out of sight into unknown regions under the earth. Into this current he cast the weapons of war, the hatchets and war-clubs, saying, 'We here rid the earth of these things of an Evil Mind.' Then replacing the Tree, he said, 'Shall the Great Peace be established, and hostilities shall no longer be known between the Five Nations, but peace to the United People.'"[356] What was this tree? Is there a connection between the Tree of Life and the Way?

It is intriguing that this Tree is referenced in two particular places in the Biblical texts: at the rebellion, when we lost access to it, and at the climax of the story as we are brought back into 8-D, or heaven. This Tree is described as standing on both sides of a river, out of which flows life-giving water.[357] Notice that the same tree stands on both sides of this river of life.

During Jesus' ministry he had an encounter with a woman at the well in Samaria. Jesus said to the woman, "Everyone who drinks this water will be thirsty again, but whoever drinks the water I give them will never thirst. Indeed, the water I give them will become in them a spring of water welling up to eternal life."[358] The dimensional analyst in me sees more in the story than a literal tree, a river, and an artesian well of life.

---

[354] Genesis 3.
[355] Revelation 22.
[356] Seton, *The Gospel of the Redman: A Way of Life*, 63.
[357] Revelation 22:1.
[358] John 4:13-14.

The Portal

If the Tree was present when we left 8-D and will be present when we return, it seems to be intricately involved in our passage in and out of 8-D. It sounds quite like a way of passage, a portal to and from 8-D. Is it the portal that was closed following the rebellion? In a term the physics community uses, it may be a *wormhole* that penetrates the fabric of space-time, one not unlike the whirlwind that Vincent painted in his starry night landscape, one quite like the tunnels of light that so many near-death experiences report.

The Apostle Peter described the work of grace, or the Way, as bringing us to God.[359] If God is everywhere, why do we need to be brought *to* him? It is clearly a reference to more than being in God's general presence. I believe it is a reference to our journey back to 8-D via the Way, the portal.

Since 8-D was closed to us at the rebellion, how are we to regain access? What great and mighty soldier could penetrate the fabric of space-time to open a portal? It was not to be a warring horse, or a mighty knight, or a legion of brave soldiers that would open the portal. No, just as the prophecies foretold, it would be the smallest, the meekest, the most righteous, and the most worthy servant who could accomplish this feat. The GBF was all of these things, and more. He, the one who proclaimed that it would be the poor, the least, the downtrodden, the humble, and the peacemakers who would inherit the kingdom of God—he it is who would provide a portal. It is just as Jesus proclaimed to the people, "I am the *thura*," or portal.[360]

A Singularity

The portal back to 8-D must penetrate the fabric of space-time. A physicist would declare its impossibility, for only an object moving near the speed of light would have a fighting chance of breaking through. Such an object would require momentum that approaches infinity. On the other hand, if such an object became infinitely small, it could potentially squeeze through the fabric of space-time, not too unlike an object being squeezed into nothingness as it enters a black hole.

---

359 1 Peter 3:18.
360 John 10:9.

The only way out of this broken domain is to die. But when *we* die, we only butt our heads against the next dimensional domain, for we are neither singularities nor infinities. Remember the inverse dynamics we discussed in Phase 2? Here we come upon the reason behind such teaching. Only the inverse of infinity is small enough to push through the bounds of space-time to create such a portal. Ponder it: the GBF entered our domain as a singularity via the maiden Mary, and left as a singularity to open the portal. Following is one of the most poetic and profound scriptural references to this journey.

> In your relationships with one another, have the same mindset as Christ Jesus: Who, being in very nature God, did not consider equality with God something to be used to his own advantage; rather, he made himself nothing by taking the very nature of a servant, being made in human likeness. And being found in appearance as a man, he humbled himself by becoming obedient to death—even death on a cross![361]

This death was the ultimate singularity: *the* Way through the bounds of space-time, *the* portal for all time (Figure 74). The GBF became nothing dimensionally in his mission to restore us. The most poignant concept of all is that he not only opened the portal, but became the portal: he became *the Way*. When Jesus said, "No one comes to the Father except through me," I believe he was saying, "I not only opened the portal: I am the portal."[362] The Right Arm of God *made* the Way and *is* the Way.

[361] Philippians 2:5-8.
[362] John 14:6.

Figure 74. The GBF's Portal

A Dimensional Transformation

One night a secret disciple of Jesus' named Nicodemus came to him. He was a noble man of great reputation and could not afford for the religious leaders to find him with Jesus in the daylight. He asked Jesus about the requirements to be a part of God's kingdom.

> Jesus replied, "Very truly I tell you, no one can see the kingdom of God unless they are born again." "How can someone be born when they are old?" Nicodemus asked. "Surely they cannot enter a second time into their mother's womb to be born!" Jesus answered, "Very truly I tell you, no one can enter the kingdom of God unless they are born of water and the Spirit. Flesh gives birth to flesh, but the Spirit gives birth to spirit. You should not be surprised at my saying, 'You must be born again.' The wind blows wherever it pleases. You hear its sound, but you cannot tell where it comes

from or where it is going. So it is with everyone born of the Spirit."[363]

When Jesus said, "You must be born again," I believe he meant, "If you want to live in God's domain, you must enter his domain." One must go through the portal God has provided, not just any portal of our choosing. His portal. In the words of Erwin Raphael McManus, in his book *An Unstoppable Force*, "Jesus did not tell Nicodemus that he needed to be rebuilt; he told him that he must be reborn."[364] That is transformation.

The portal is very small. One must become a *less* to pass through it, not more (remember the Beatitudes). It is a narrow passage, and only when we realize that we are too large to get through and choose to surrender our greatness, can we become small enough to pass, small enough for such a transformation. The grace and strength of the GBF enables any such size reduction, any such transformation.

When and how does it happen? This is where theological complexities often get in the way. Jesus never described the transformation process as complex; he described it quite simply. While some insist that certain incantations must be uttered and certain rituals performed, Jesus simply said, "I am at your door knocking, Can we please spend time together?" [365] Scripturally, the only requirements for such a dimensional transformation are to want it and ask for it. It is that simple. There is no religious requirement. In fact, one must give up religious requirements to inherit life with God.

For some of us it happens early in life. For others it does not happen until much later. I personally believe it does not happen until after death for some. I am convinced that the only ones who will not experience rebirth and passage through the GBF's portal are those who adamantly do not want it and refuse it. Call me a Universalist or whatever you will, but I believe the words of the writer of the book of James when he said, "Mercy triumphs over judgment."[366] Who will be given

---

[363] John 3:1-8.
[364] Erwin Raphael McManus, *An Unstoppable Force: Daring to Become the Church God Had in Mind* (Loveland: Group, 2001), 211.
[365] SFA paraphrase of Revelation 3:20.
[366] James 2:13b.

passage via the portal? As we will find out a couple of chapters from now, I believe there is much, much more to the story than our limited dogma permits!

Life after Transformation

It may be that our *spirit* enters God's domain at transformation, but what happens in this domain? Some hope for a magical and instantaneous transformation here and now. I wish it were so. It is but the beginning of spiritual wanderings that take place in God's presence. The good news is that these wanderings do not happen alone. Scripture tells us that not only do our spirits enter God's domain, but also that his Spirit enters us in this domain. It is quite like the Klein bottle: we are in God and God is in us. We will touch on most of these issues in chapters and Phases to come. For now let it suffice to say that such a transformation is real: very real. We are talking about real dimensions and a real entry for whoever wants to enter.

For All Space-Time

When and where did the right arm of God enter our domain? Well, if you asked this question of any angelic entity that happened to be standing by when God extended his arm into our domain, they would probably answer, "Yes." It sounds nonsensical, but it is we who are stuck in space and time. The 8-D entities are not so limited in time. God entered space-time: all of it. The *when* of his entry may be important to theologians and historians who are stuck in our domain, but it is not so with God. Sure, scripture says that the GBF opened the portal at "just the right time,"[367] but more importantly, he tore open the fabric of space-time for all space and all time.

Defeating Death

Before Jesus died, he said, "The reason my Father loves me is that I lay down my life—only to take it up again. No one takes it from me, but I lay it down of my own accord. I have authority to lay it down and authority to take it up again."[368]

---

[367] Romans 5:6.
[368] John 10:17-18.

His listeners did not know what he meant by these words. This is why they were so surprised when they saw him three days after his death. They did not expect a resurrection. Resurrection, in fact, was beyond the scope of beliefs at the time— even pagan beliefs. N.T. Wright says, in his book *Surprised by Hope*, "The early Christian belief in resurrection remains emphatically on the map of first-century Judaism rather than paganism." It opened a whole new perspective on history.[369] It was no wonder Jesus' disciples did not understand him when he said that he had authority to take his life back up again. It was a brand new concept! Many believed in an eventual resurrection, but not one in this domain.

There is also one very peculiar event that took place on the morning of the resurrection that further substantiates its claim. This event was also contrary to prevalent culture in the ancient world at the time. N.T. Wright points out that in spite of the fact that "women were not regarded as credible witnesses in the ancient world," they were "in all four gospel stories, front and center, the first witnesses, the first apostles."[370] What an amazing validation! Why would male gospel writers include the women as witnesses and apostles, given their view of women, if what they wrote was not the truth?

But why must there have been a resurrection? Surely God did not need to demonstrate his power by flexing his biceps. Such behavior goes against the strange and humble nature of God. I have come to believe there are at least two reasons for such a grand expression.

Scripture implies that the GBF did not go all the way through the portal, returning home to stay. He went far enough to open it, then came back. Upon meeting Mary in the garden that resurrection morning he asked her not to touch him since he had not yet gone back to the Father.[371] To have gone all the way through the portal may have been a very selfish act. But he did not have his sights on returning to his dimensional domain alone. Once again, he gave up his own desires. I believe he returned to show us the way, to proclaim that the portal was opened. He had done it! To not come back via the resurrection, which was, as we

---

[369] N.T. Wright, *Surprised by Hope: Rethinking Heaven, the Resurrection, and the Mission of the Church* (New York: HarperCollins Publisher, 2008), 51-52.
[370] Ibid., 55.
[371] John 20:17.

saw earlier, a choice, would have been selfish. The resurrection was not a show of power, but a demonstration of unending love. The resurrection was a sacrificial act.

So, do *I* believe that Jesus came back from the dead to show us the way and to demonstrate what we have to look forward to? I most certainly do. I admit that the resurrection cannot be unequivocally proven. N.T. Wright aptly says, "Historical argument alone cannot force anyone to believe that Jesus was raised from the dead, but historical argument is remarkably good at clearing away the undergrowth behind which skepticisms of various sorts have long been hiding."[372] I have come to see through such skepticisms, especially the ones whose roots reside in a deep-seated need for such an event to not be true. I, for one, do not need it to be true, nor do I need it to be not true. The evidences and reasons are sufficient for me to believe.

In Closing

I believe the most overwhelming accomplishment of the GBF was that he broke through the fabric of space-time, opening the portal so that all may pass through. All: past, present, and future. All. The religious efforts and sacrifices of humankind are but knocks on the door of higher dimensions. Only God could, and did, open the portal.

I leave you with a dimensional paraphrase of a most famous passage of scripture: "Because of God's infinite love for our dimensional domain, in excruciating pain he pushed his right arm through the fabric of 4-D space-time, so that anyone may come through the resulting portal to live in unbounded time in 8-D."[373]

---

[372] Wright, *Surprised by Hope: Rethinking Heaven, the Resurrection, and the Mission of the Church*, 64.
[373] SFA paraphrase of John 3:16.

3.15

Dimensional Theology

As described in the chapter on dimensional transformations, our job as dimensional thinkers is to assimilate multiple lower dimensional views into higher dimensional perspectives. The task is extensive and can be quite challenging. There is simply not enough space in this book for an exhaustive treatment of dimensional theology. It merits a book of its own. Therefore, the concepts covered here are but smatterings of the vast number of theological concepts that cry out for dimensional expansion.

Most of us who are familiar with the Old Testament know that it is full of legalistic rules. I have often wondered why God *needed* to make the Old Testament, as well as many other scriptures, so legalistic, especially if the GBF was eventually coming to usher in a new perspective. It was not until part way through this process that it occurred to me that God needs nothing. It was the people who needed such rigidity. People *still* seem to need it, though it accomplishes little to nothing. Together these laws present a very formidable image of God. Yet even in the Old Testament there are signs of dimensional hope.

One of the requirements of Old Testament law was to circumcise all male infants. Circumcision was a definitive sign of who belonged to God and who did not. Yet one of Israel's own prophets said, "'The days are coming,' declares the LORD, 'when I will punish all who are circumcised only in the flesh . . . even the whole house of Israel is uncircumcised in heart.'" [374] This clearly was a foreshadowing of dimensional transformations to come.

---

[374] Jeremiah 9:25-26.

The sacrificial system was very important in ancient religions such as Judaism. The shed blood of animals was required for the covering of sins. Yet King Solomon said, "To do what is right and just is more acceptable to the LORD than sacrifice."[375] The prophet Hosea spoke on behalf of God when he said, "For I desire mercy, not sacrifice, and acknowledgment of God rather than burnt offerings."[376] Jesus himself quoted Hosea to the Pharisees.[377] The prophet Micah exclaimed, "He has shown you, O mortal, what is good. And what does the LORD require of you? To act justly and to love mercy and to walk humbly with your God."[378] These prophets acknowledged the inadequacy and incompleteness of external sacrifices. The humble sacrifice of the heart was the most important act. This was expansion foreshadowed.

The Fulfillment of the Law

The GBF came to expand the law. The law, after all, was but a foreshadowing of the GBF's mission. When Jesus affirmed that his intention was not to abolish the law, but to fulfill it, he ushered in a new dimension, a new understanding, and a new dwelling place for God: our hearts.[379] By bringing fresh perspectives to the law, Jesus dimensionally transformed it into a higher dimensional entity: one full of grace.

By what authority did Jesus usher in such change? As Dietrich Bonhoeffer so eloquently pointed out in his book *The Cost of Discipleship*, only the author of the law could expand the law. "He makes it perfectly clear that he, the Son of God, is the Author and Giver of the law."[380] Only the right arm of God, the arm who wrote the law, could usher in change. The finger that carved the Ten Commandments in stone is the same finger that carved grace and truth in the sand for the woman who had been accused of adultery.[381]

Jesus did not come to expand the law for Judaism. He came to expand it for all of humanity, for all religions. Jesus said, "I have other sheep that are not of this

---

[375] Proverbs 21:3.
[376] Hosea 6:6.
[377] Matthew 9:10-13.
[378] Micah 6:8.
[379] Matthew 5:17-19.
[380] Bonhoeffer, *The Cost of Discipleship*, 126.
[381] John 8:1-11.

sheep pen. I must bring them also. They too will listen to my voice, and there shall be one flock and one shepherd."[382] There is truth in Judaism, but it alone will not save you. There is truth in Islam, but it alone will not save you. There is truth in Christianity, but it alone will not save you. However, all sheep may enter the pen via the portal the GBF has provided.

We, too, must continue the expansion, for we follow in the footsteps of the ultimate expander. The dimensional expansion that was modeled by Jesus was not a *once for all* expansion. He modeled for us what we are to continue to do.

The Physicality of the Mind

Jesus announced the expansion of our reality. According to his teachings, our minds and thoughts are as physical as our bodies. He implied that in 8-D our minds already exist as real physical entities. Many of us believe that what we think is less real than what we do with our 4-D bodies. This is natural because physical symptoms carry more significance in our limited physical realm. Physical sins seem orders of magnitude worse than mental sins. To God, however, mental sins are more significant because he resides in the realm where they take place. Those who insist on the literal posting of the Ten Commandments are missing the point of the GBF's expansion of the law. Such principles are now to be written on our hearts, not posted as the iconic graven images that the Ten Commandments themselves forbid. It is our minds and hearts that matter most.

Specific Examples

Jesus expanded murder: "You have heard that it was said to the people long ago, 'You shall not murder, and anyone who murders will be subject to judgment.' But I tell you that anyone who is angry with a brother or sister will be subject to judgment."[383]

---

[382] John 10:16.
[383] Matthew 5:21.

Jesus expanded adultery: "You have heard that it was said, 'You shall not commit adultery.' But I tell you that anyone who looks at a woman lustfully has already committed adultery with her in his heart."[384]

Jesus expanded justice: "You have heard that it was said, 'Eye for eye, and tooth for tooth.' But I tell you, do not resist an evil person. If anyone slaps you on the right cheek, turn to them the other cheek also. And if anyone wants to sue you and take your shirt, hand over your coat as well. If anyone forces you to go one mile, go with them two miles. Give to the one who asks you, and do not turn away from the one who wants to borrow from you."[385]

Jesus expanded oaths: "Again, you have heard that it was said to the people long ago, 'Do not break your oath, but fulfill to the Lord the vows you have made.' But I tell you, do not swear an oath at all: either by heaven, for it is God's throne; or by the earth, for it is his footstool; or by Jerusalem, for it is the city of the Great King. And do not swear by your head, for you cannot make even one hair white or black. All you need to say is simply 'Yes' or 'No'; anything beyond this comes from the evil one."[386]

Jesus expanded family: "'Who are my mother and my brothers?' he asked. Then he looked at those seated in a circle around him and said, 'Here are my mother and my brothers! Whoever does God's will is my brother and sister and mother.'"[387]

Jesus expanded worship: "Yet a time is coming and has now come when the true worshipers will worship the Father in spirit and truth, for they are the kind of worshipers the Father seeks. God is spirit, and his worshipers must worship in spirit and in truth."[388]

Jesus expanded the Sabbath: In response to the Pharisees rebuking Jesus when they saw his disciples picking grain to eat on the Sabbath, it is recorded, "Then he said to them, 'The Sabbath was made for man, not man for the Sabbath. So the Son of Man is Lord even of the Sabbath.'"[389] Elsewhere he said, "If any of you has a sheep and it falls into a pit on the Sabbath, will you not take hold of it and lift it

---

[384] Matthew 5:27-28.
[385] Matthew 5:38-42.
[386] Matthew 5:33-37.
[387] Mark 3:33-35.
[388] John 4:23-24.
[389] Mark 2:27-28.

out? How much more valuable is a person than a sheep! Therefore it is lawful to do good on the Sabbath."[390]

Expansions Come Hard

Before moving on to more examples of dimensional expansion I acknowledge that expansions are difficult to accept and can take lifetimes to incorporate. Jesus' expansions took everyone out of their comfort zones, as evidenced by a dyed-in-the-wool zealot like Saul, who became known as the Apostle Paul. Jesus expanded the law beyond Paul's cultural and religious comfort zones. Paul clearly struggled with some of these tensions, evidenced not only in his temperament before his conversion, but afterwards as well. The transformation that resulted from his conversion was not instantaneous, but a process that would take the rest of his life. When I read his letters to the various churches in the order in which they were written, I sense a softening throughout his ministry years, moving away from legalism towards a grace-filled message. So it is with us.

Dimensional Triplets

The American activist Ammon Hennacy once said, "Love without courage and wisdom is sentimentality, as with the ordinary church member. Courage without love and wisdom is foolhardiness, as with the ordinary soldier. Wisdom without love and courage is cowardice, as with the ordinary intellectual. But the one who has love, courage, and wisdom moves the world, as with Jesus, Buddha, and Gandhi."[391] This is a profound assessment of lower dimensional characteristics merging into a more effective higher dimensional persona.

Look again at the illustration titled *Three Divergent Views* from the chapter on dimensional transformations (Figure 75). There are many triads in life that fit such a higher dimensional entity as the single solid shape that casts shadows of the circle, triangle, and square. Some of the more difficult ones will come later. For now, staying consistent with Hennacy's quote, scripture also mentions similar triune shadows. The prophet Micah mentioned such a triad: justice, mercy, and

---

[390] Matthew 12:11-12
[391] Ammon Hennacy, *The Book of Ammon* (Salt Lake City: Self Published, 1965), 149.

humility.[392] One by itself misses the mark. The Apostle Paul also mentioned such a triad: faith, hope, and love.[393]

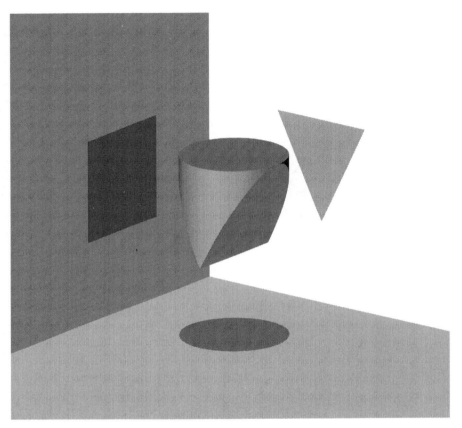

Figure 75. Three Divergent Views

David Augsburger, in his book *Dissident Discipleship*, points out another dimensional triplet when he says, "Authentic spirituality, which I am calling tripolar spirituality to clearly identify it as fully three dimensional, is self transforming, God encountering, and other embracing. It accepts no substitute for

---

[392] Micah 6:8.
[393] 1 Thessalonians 1:1-10.

actual participation."[394] It is not enough for anyone to declare that they have been transformed, and live no differently. Neither is it enough to be transformed and have a warm and affectionate relationship with God, yet ignore or be isolated from our brothers and sisters. Only when the three are merged into a wholesome spirituality will it be authentic: authentic in the higher dimensional sense that Jesus taught and lived.

Dimensional Couplets

Dimensional couplets offer another glimpse of higher dimensional existence. Dimensional couplets (quite like the type II strange loops of Phase 2) appear frequently in scripture and theology. Some of them are more peculiar than others. A.W. Tozer pointed out one such couplet in his book *The Knowledge of the Holy*, "In the inspired Scriptures justice and righteousness are scarcely to be distinguished from each other. The same word in the original becomes in English justice or righteousness, almost, one would suspect, at the whim of the translator."[395] God's justice is righteous and his righteousness is just.

Karl Barth gave us another higher dimensional glimpse when he referred to such a couplet in his book *Dogmatics in Outline*, "The grace of God and the omnipotence of God are identical. We must never understand one without the other."[396] If you recall from Phase 2, God's attributes can be derived from his infinitude. Grace is a natural outcome of infinitude. Omnipotence has no insecurities to get in the way of being infinitely gracious.

John Newton, the 18th century abolitionist and hymn writer, also gave us a glimpse of dimensional thinking when he penned a couplet in the hymn we have come to know as *Amazing Grace*, "T'was Grace that taught my heart to fear. And Grace, my fears relieved." Herein Newton fully understood the strange dimensional character of grace both feeding and relieving fear.

---

[394] David Augsburger, *Dissident Discipleship: A Spirituality of Self-Surrender, Love of God, and Love of Neighbor* (Grand Rapids: Brazos Press, 2006), 26-27.
[395] Tozer, *The Knowledge of the Holy: The Attributes of God: Their Meaning in the Christian Life*, 92.
[396] Barth, *Dogmatics in Outline*, 126.

Scripture has numerous dimensional couplets. It equates believing with doing[397] and faith with works.[398] Dimensionally, one cannot exist without the other. While faith and works may be orthogonal (at a right angle) to each other, the combined dimensional effect is, according to Jesus, a necessity.

A most odd couplet is found in joy and pain.[399] As is the case with other couplets, such as general relativity and quantum mechanics, the natural conclusion is that the two are incompatible. But just as general relativity and quantum mechanics hold the universe together by crossing dimensional boundaries, so it is with joy and pain. In extended spiritual dimensions, together they form a fulfilled entity. These couplets offer important glimpses into the higher dimensional nature of our existence.

Symbolism and Reality

Symbols offer a deep, satisfying experience for people of faith. Sadly, they too easily become rote physical expressions, rather than powerful dimensional experiences.

I was raised in a religious tradition that believed the sacraments were symbols and not reality. When we participated in the Eucharist, or communion, we understood that the bread symbolized the body of Christ and the wine (in our case grape juice) symbolized his blood. By participating in these symbols we were identifying with the infinite love of the GBF. My Catholic friends, however, argued with me vehemently that what we were eating was transformed into the actual body of Christ! They believed that the symbol could become reality under the right conditions. Transubstantiation, as it is referred to, miraculously changes the bread and wine into the literal body and blood of Christ.

For many years I chuckled arrogantly at such ignorance. Communion is just a symbol! Or is it? All this was before I began to understand more about Jesus' teachings regarding our thoughts and words, and came to believe that they are *real* in 8-D. I soon found myself recanting *my* ignorant fundamentalism. Whether the act is communion, baptism, fasting, or praying, I am now convinced that in 8-D

[397] John 6:29.
[398] Matthew 7:25.
[399] John 14:27; Romans 5:3; Roman 8:18-21; James 1:2-4.

they are realities. Perhaps when I fast I actually feed my 8-D body. Some firmly believe the sacraments are realities here in 4-D, and I do not attempt to dispute such beliefs. I simply want to acknowledge my failure to see the higher dimensional significance in such traditions.

Non-Resistance and Pacifism

The most significant expansion of all is Jesus' expansion of love. He expanded love to include our enemies. He said, "You have heard that it was said, 'Love your neighbor and hate your enemy.' But I tell you, love your enemies and pray for those who persecute you, that you may be children of your Father in heaven."[400] Some find reasons to get around these words. Some take them literally.

I grew up in an Anabaptist tradition. The Anabaptists were referred to as the *Radical Reformers* during the Reformation: radical because they took Jesus' words *too* seriously. When Jesus said, "Love your enemies," he meant, "Love your enemies." I took this teaching seriously during my growing up years. It was put to the test numerous times in high school. Some of the students knew of my non-resistant stance and did not hesitate to take it out on me when they felt like it. My head was beaten against the pipes in the bathroom. I was kicked and thrown out of the front door with books and papers flying everywhere, and I was threatened frequently.

On one occasion, I was on the basketball court behind our church, shooting hoops by myself. An acquaintance, who was known to be a mean and angry character, came over to pick a fight with me. I tried to ignore him but he was relentless. Eventually, he landed a punch low in my gut. I buckled over unable to breathe. When I could finally muster a few words, I said, "Billy, you can beat me all you want, you can even kill me, but there are two things you cannot do." He retorted angrily, "WHAT!" Slowly and softly, I said, gasping for air, "You cannot change the fact that God loves you and that I love you." It was as though a bolt of lightning struck Billy. He jumped back, paused, and then said, "Man, you are crazy!" He turned and walked away. I never saw Billy again.

---

[400] Matthew 5:43-45a.

After all the memories, fear, and even bitterness, I still believe that followers of Jesus are called to live like Jesus did. I believe it is the expanded way. Despite already living out part of an expanded view, there was still more for me to learn. Frankly, I was humbly arrogant and judgmental about my beliefs. Now, rather than pronouncing judgment on those who see things differently, I pray for grace for both sides. I pray frequently for military and law enforcement personnel. It is my way of admitting that I am not through wandering and processing. I acknowledge that there are surely other dimensional components I do not see or have not yet integrated. There may be much more to the picture than I typically permit.

Peace and Love

I grew up during the peak of the hippie era. On many occasions I raised my hand with the peace symbol, and said, "Peace, dude." Though popular, such peace and love were lower dimensional entities. They were temporal and dependent on circumstances. The GBF expanded both into higher dimensional entities that are not so circumstantially dependent.

Jesus spoke of an expanded peace when he said, "Peace I leave with you; my peace I give you. I do not give to you as the world gives. Do not let your hearts be troubled and do not be afraid."[401] It is a higher dimensional peace, not the kind the world commonly knows. It is a deep, inner-rooted peace that transcends our dimensional domain: it transcends our circumstances. The prophet Isaiah foretold such peace when he wrote, "You will keep in perfect peace those whose minds are steadfast, because they trust in you."[402] The Apostle Paul also wrote of the strangeness of this dimensional peace, "Do not be anxious about anything, but in every situation, by prayer and petition, with thanksgiving, present your requests to God. And the peace of God, which transcends all understanding, will guard your hearts and your minds in Christ Jesus."[403]

This peace does not exist everywhere in 4-D, though the awareness and longing for it does. There are obviously many people who are not experiencing peace in this domain, people whose lives are filled with worry and violence. Yet for

---

[401] John 14:27.
[402] Isaiah 26:3.
[403] Philippians 4:6-7.

some there is a strange peace that *transcends* this domain. It exists outside our circumstances, untouched by the struggles of this world. Such deep-seated peace is untouchable by 4-D circumstances because it lives in 8-D. There are also those in 4-D who know prosperity, pleasure, and lower-dimensional peace, but who worry themselves to death because there is no 8-D peace.

The same is true of higher dimensional love. Scripture makes amazing claims about this love. First of all, if one does not love with this higher dimensional love, they do not know God, because God *is* love.[404] It is with God's love that we are called to love others. It is a complex and expanded love. *It is the summation, the dimensional transformation, of all religious laws combined.* Again, Paul so aptly says, "Let no debt remain outstanding, except the continuing debt to love one another, for whoever loves others has fulfilled the law. The commandments . . . are summed up in this one command: 'Love your neighbor as yourself.' Love does no harm to a neighbor. Therefore love is the fulfillment of the law."[405] If one were to transform the thousands of religious laws that exist in this domain into one grand expanded collage, it would spell *LOVE*.

Treasures

Scripture tells us to store up treasures in heaven, not on earth.[406] There are at least two reasons for this call. First of all, treasures in this domain fade away. They all rust, decay, or are passed on to someone whose use we will have no control over. Secondly, if we hold onto treasures now, we will lose them later. If we lose them now, we will gain them later. Do not let anyone fool you: not all will be equal in 8-D.[407] Jesus said, "Do not be afraid, little flock, for your Father has been pleased to give you the kingdom. Sell your possessions and give to the poor. Provide purses for yourselves that will not wear out, a treasure in heaven that will never fail, where no thief comes near and no moth destroys. For where your treasure is, there your heart will be also."[408] Sacrificial living here gives rise to an eternal fragrant treasure in 8-D. This sacrificial living takes seriously the call to envelop

---

[404] 1 John 4:8.
[405] Romans 13:8-10.
[406] Luke 12:32-34.
[407] Matthew 5:17-19.
[408] Luke 12:32-34.

the expanded law, the dimensional triplets and couplets of scripture, and expanded living witnessed through loving enemies. These are implications of dimensional theology.

3.16

Backward Causality

Sometimes dimensional theological processing results in peculiar implications. For instance, all of our dimensional wanderings thus far have taken place within the confines of time. We are stuck in time. No, we are lost in time. Time's hold on us runs deep. Many disputes and wars have run their courses because of *time*. We looked at many strange loops in Phase 2, but we did not consider what would happen if we removed our dependency on time from loops such as *predestination vs. freewill*. I must ask, "What would happen to our theology if time was suddenly removed from the equation?"

The Dalai Lama says in his book *The Universe in a Single Atom: The Convergence of Science and Spirituality*, "In the Buddhist philosophical world, the concept of time as relative is not alien." He points out that the Sautrantikas believed in the interdependence of the past, present and the future.[409] Likewise, physicists, including Einstein, have argued that no matter how convincing, the past, present, and future are only illusions. They are simply *places* in four-dimensional space-time. Given this interdependency, is it possible that the future affects the past in the same way that we think of the past affecting the future?

We may be more dependent on the future than we realize. Physicists seem to think so. In fact, experiments have shown it to be true: events in the future do impact events in the past. In the April 2010 issue of *Discover Magazine*, Zeeya Merali reported on theories and experiments that demonstrate this strange phenomenon.

---

[409] Lama, *The Universe in a Single Atom: The Convergence of Science and Spirituality*, 60.

Merali reports that Physicist Jeff Tollaksen's group, from Chapman University, "is looking into the notion that time might flow backward, allowing the future to influence the past."[410] One of the members of Tollaksen's group, a young physicist named Yakir Aharonov, believes we cannot fully understand the way subatomic particles behave at present because some of the influences on these particles do not yet exist.[411] Tollaksen and Aharonov set out to propose an experiment that just might demonstrate this phenomenon. Though their efforts were not met with the results they were hoping for, they did influence others to pursue the same theory.

In 2009, physicist John Howell and his team from the University of Rochester were successful. To adequately describe their experimental design and its outcome is beyond the scope of this book. The bottom line is their experiment validated Tollaksen's theory that the quantum realm has access to the future and the future has access to the past. Physicists are convinced that subatomic particles rely on future and past events to explain their current behavior. It would seem that these particles are not bounded by our dimension of time, but are free to use both the past and future to determine their current behavior.

A Slice in Time

Backward causality may extend beyond the quantum realm. Our future may have more impact on our present than we realize. In a visionary sense, we know this to be true. Visionary leaders see what a given organization can become, know the steps to bring such a vision to fruition, and then take the organization there. One could argue that it is but the past, present, and idea of the future that drive such leadership, but is that all there is to the picture? Are we sure such visionaries are not truly driven by the future?

If you will, imagine a view of one's entire lifetime, unbounded by time. In such a view, the past, present, and future are all in the same picture. In the following illustration (Figure 76) we see a continuous path traversed by one individual over a given period time. In the middle, however, I have cut out a slice in time to demonstrate the present. Without the cutout, the whole of the individual's lifetime

---

410 Zeeya Merali, "Back from the Future," *Discover Magazine* 2010, 39.
411 Ibid., 40.

and path traversed is but a single entity. Using a *worm* as an example, how could stimuli on the head or the tail *not* affect the entirety of the worm? The only reason that such impacts of the past and future are not real to us is that we are overwhelmingly constrained by time.

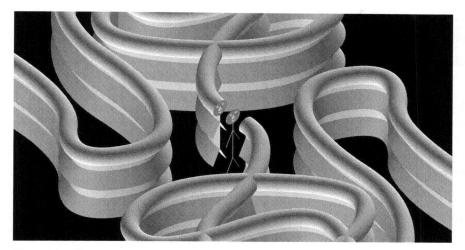

Figure 76. A Slice in Time Moving Forward and Backward

God, and quite likely other higher dimensional entities, sees the whole 4-D picture. It may be quite nonsensical to talk in terms of past, present, and future, except to refer to a location on the worm's anatomy. What we refer to as the *omnipresence* and *omniscience* of God may be reflections of this higher dimensional view. God sees all of time, hovering over the past, present, and future, observing the entire worm. Perhaps these omni-qualities of God are an outflow of God's time-independence rather than God's magnitude.

It was quite by accident, when I drew the previous illustration, that the path of the individual crossed the same location in space-time more than once, though the individual is facing a different direction. I have to wonder if such a looping back in space-time is part of the reason we experience what we commonly refer to as déjà vu? Perhaps one's worm is twisted up in a pretzel with only a few repeated places in space and time. For some, it may be interwoven into a knot of numerous repeated visits to a given location.

I realize that all this rhetoric about the future influencing the past is unfamiliar and even uncomfortable to some, especially since it is not commonly talked about within the context of theology. While it may not be explicitly described in scripture (SR), it is indirectly referenced. In natural theology (NT) and existential understanding (EU), it is explicitly revealed, opening a thought-provoking door for us to wander through.[412]

Backward Causality Theology

Quite a few years ago, I found myself spontaneously praying for an event that had taken place in the past. It took me totally by surprise. I had not thought through backward causality or what I was doing; it just happened. Did my future influence me to pray for the past? Perhaps a higher dimensional portion of me had already read the previous paragraphs and realized that it was OK to pray outside the bounds of time.

In scripture, there are numerous references to unbounded time. Peter had such an unbounded perspective: "But do not forget this one thing, dear friends: With the Lord a day is like a thousand years, and a thousand years are like a day."[413], [414] This could be a literal expression of the time dilation between God's domain and ours. However, I am inclined to think that it has more to do with the directions of time than with literal time differentials. Perhaps Peter was acknowledging that time goes in both directions in God's domain. Why else would he express the ratio in both directions? King Solomon confirmed this by saying, "Whatever is has already been, and what will be has been before."[415] I love the way Eugene Peterson words this text in *The Message*, "Whatever was, is. Whatever will be is. That's how it always is with God."

In a previous chapter we talked about dimensional couplets. I want to take a look here at such a couplet, but from a time-independent perspective. Consider the

---

[412] We will encounter some of these references as we progress through this topic.
[413] 2 Peter 3:8.
[414] Clarke's, Barnes', and Wesley's commentaries agree: the past and future are "present every moment" to God (Wesley's Notes).
[415] Ecclesiastes 3:15a.

relationship between forgiveness and repentance. I was taught that forgiveness was dependent on repentance. Some, including Brennan Manning, proclaim that repentance is an outcome of forgiveness. [416] There is certainly scriptural precedence for the latter.[417] Is there a dimensional relationship we are missing? Perhaps before and after are irrelevant. The two are interwoven in time. Even in our bounded time, we may experience the two in both directions. This concept has been discussed before—the idea of two things happening together—forgiveness and repentance.

The mission of the GBF is one such time independent phenomenon. On one occasion Jesus said, "I have overcome the world."[418] How could this be stated in the past tense when he had not yet fulfilled his mission? From a backward causality perspective, it was already completed. Quite likely, from God's perspective, the GBF's mission started with the final outcome driving the whole plan. The final outcome may have prompted the GBF to descend onto a mountaintop, progress to the tomb, the cross, and ultimately back to the womb, disappearing. Perhaps the GBF had already gone through his un-birth when the prophet Micah wrote about it in the 8th century B.C., "But you, Bethlehem Ephrathah, though you are small among the clans of Judah, out of you will come for me one who will be ruler over Israel, whose origins are from of old, from ancient times."[419] From the perspective of God's domain, Micah was simply remembering the GBF's birth.

If we remove the bounds of time from our theological thinking (*achronostic theology*) we may read scripture differently. For instance, Paul's words regarding the eventual outcome of our actions may be read, "You will sow what you reap."[420] In another place, Paul said, "I press on toward the goal to win the prize for which God has called me heavenward in Christ Jesus."[421] This prize, already in our future, is influencing our present and past.

---

[416] Manning, *The Ragamuffin Gospel*, 74.
[417] John 8:2-11; Luke 5:17-26.
[418] John 16:33b.
[419] Micah 5:2.
[420] Achronostic paraphrase of Galatians 6:7.
[421] Philippians 3:14.

Predestination vs. Freewill

There is a debate, which has resulted in multitudes of factions across the globe and across time, which we must address: predestination vs. freewill. This debate wages still, producing arrogant, even if humbly arrogant, theologies, which wreak havoc on the rest of the world, establishing divisive lines which surely test the patience of God.

I believe that debates over predestination and freewill are stuck in time and, as such, are lower dimensional debates, outcomes of lower dimensional observations and reasoning. I do not deny that the evidences on both sides are real and plentiful, but they are easily manipulated by people living in a domain bound by time.

I am not going to extensively quote passages of scripture in this discussion, for there are many on both sides of the debate.[422] Whenever we encounter valid, but contradictory, evidences, there is usually a higher dimensional entity that our perspectives and reasoning are missing. So it is with predestination and freewill. Each is a 4-D slice of a much bigger dimensional issue. However, before pursuing such a dimensional solution, let us look at some of the lower dimensional weaknesses of each side of the debate.

Freewill acknowledges that God has provided a portal, but the onus is on us to decide whether or not we want to be a part of God's domain. Time is of the essence: forward time, that is. At some point in time the offer will end, the doors to heaven will be closed, and the eternal future will begin. Freewill theologies seem to minimize the sovereignty of God.

On the other hand, predestination places the entire outcome in God's hands. Time matters not; what will be will be. Our choices have little to no impact on our eternal future. A sense of fatalism is one of the potential negative outcomes of such beliefs. Why bother to pray if everything is already decided? Predestination theologies seem to minimize the mercy and foreknowledge of God.

If God knows the future as much as the past and present, then the future is already a reality. The very act of *knowing* solidifies its existence.[423] That being the

---

[422] See Appendices A and B for such references.

[423] It should be noted here that this is one of the rationales for open theism: surely the future, including God's, is not preset, therefore it must not exist as such yet. On the other hand, others, including myself, are open to the future already existing, therefore are not troubled by such foreknowledge. As you will

case, how much of the debate is focused on foreknowledge vs. predestination? The two are difficult to separate. Does knowing the future imply fate? The answer is domain dependent. Both freewill and predestination depend on the domain from which they are observed and described. We will come back to this shortly.

There are passages of scripture that speak of predestination and freewill in the same breath. [424] As I have stated previously, whenever valid contradictory evidences exist, there is likely something of a higher dimensional origin going on.

Arrows of Time

It is my conviction that both predestination and freewill exist and are essential parts of our existence. How can it be? Remember, we are the ones stuck in time. Or should I say, stuck on a forward arrow of time. Both predestination and freewill exist, but with opposite arrows of time. Looking forward to the future, a future that already is, *is* predestination. Looking back into our past, or our *backward causality future*, we influence the future past via freewill. Predestination faces the past future. Freewill faces the future past. Choice is certainly a factor, but it is affected by our future, or should I say our past future.

In the following illustration (Figure 77) we have two arrows of time. The *forward* arrow (there is great irony in identifying it as forward) points to what already *is* in the future. Whether one wants to identify this direction as election, predestination, or fate, it looks at a future that already exists.

On the other hand, the reverse arrow of time is consistent with what physicists have identified as backward causality via an unbounded dimension of time. It brings freewill into a very different light. Our future impacts the choices we make today. What is more, and perhaps even more significant, our future choices are impacting *today*. I am what I am today not only because of the choices I have made in the past and present, but also because of the future choices I have already made. *From a backward causality perspective, it is my past that is called into question, not my future.* Rewording it in backward causality terminology, it is my future past that is up for grabs, not my past future.

---

see, I do not believe that foreknowledge precludes freewill. There will be more discussion on this topic in 3.18.
[424] John 6:35-40; 2 Peter 1:10-11.

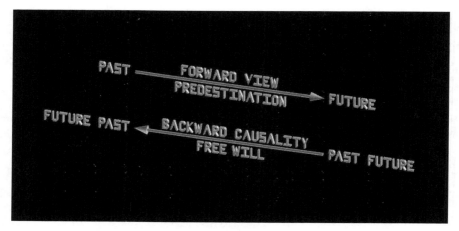

Figure 77. Backward Causality: Freewill and Predestination

A wiggling worm may help to illustrate the point at hand. Imagine such a worm whose head represents the future and whose tail represents the past. The total length of the worm represents its lifespan. The worm's head has just entered a hole that leads into another domain (perhaps underground), but the tail is still outside this new domain, wiggling about with freedom. The future is in the hole, but the past is quite undecided. The head is in the past future. The tail is in the future past. Yet the worm is one, and the past slowly catches up with the future.

This dimensional relationship is held in balance between two arrows of time. God created this balance by virtue of his sovereignty, foreknowledge, and mercy. If one removes the before and after from the discussion entirely, predestination and freewill become irrelevant. We will return to this in a very unusual way in a later chapter.

Since I am an image bearer of the great *I Am*, perhaps I simply *am* in God. My purpose in this life is timeless: it just is.[425] It is the future that already exists and the past that is undecided. No wonder I find myself spontaneously praying for people and events in the future past.

---

[425] Ephesians 2:10.

3.17

Backward Causality Coaching

As we examined predestination and freewill in the previous chapter, we saw that the two may have opposite arrows of time. This is no coincidence, for there is a boundary issue at play. Quantum mechanics has shown us that interactions between our domain and the quantum realm experience a reversal in the arrow of time. What is more, this same phenomenon may be true of interactions between this domain and its integral. To put it more concisely, the arrows of time in our derivative and integral domains may move in opposite directions from time in this domain. Our understanding of the past and the future may indeed be backwards. Let us also look at this issue from a theological standpoint.

In Phase 2 we developed the necessity of the infinitude of God. We expanded this in Phase 3 to reveal that God is beyond the bounds of both space and time. We did not, however, fully explore the implications of this unbounded nature of God. Such an unbounded nature has implications on our domain, especially our past future and our future past. Follow with me very carefully as we progress through the logic.

If God is unbounded by time, then he exists in all time: in the past, present, and future. He does so simultaneously.[426] He does not simply know the future: he *is in* the future. God's future is as real as the present or the past. That being the case, it includes *our* future. And if it includes our future, then it also includes the future us. In other words, by nature of God's boundlessness, we exist in the future with God.

---

[426] I realize that not everyone believes God is unbounded by time. Such positions will be addressed more fully in 3.18.

Though our knowledge of our future existence is diminished by our dimensional constraints, we are already there.

This principle is a function of the forward arrow of time, as illustrated in the previous chapter. We referred to the forward arrow, with the future already in existence, as predestination. We also referred to the reverse arrow, pointing to our future past, as freewill. I specifically made the point that it is the past that is undecided and up for grabs, not the future. This is consistent with quantum mechanical discoveries. What we did not discuss, however, are the implications of this backward and unbounded arrow of time, pointing to the future past.

In the past future, what awareness do we have of our future past? Has it even taken place? According to backward causality, it has yet to be decided. I believe it is possible that our past future self is free to view and influence our future past self. What is more, I believe that there may be a crowd of past future individuals influencing our future past.

A Cloud of Witnesses

A most intriguing passage of scripture exists in the New Testament. The writer of the book of Hebrews expounds on significant people of faith who have gone before us. Then he launches into these words, "Therefore, since we are surrounded by such a great cloud of witnesses, let us throw off everything that hinders and the sin that so easily entangles."[427] Surrounded? Witnesses? Are those who have gone before us watching us? It would appear so, and perhaps they are doing more than simply watching.

I was taught as a young man that these witnesses see us from afar, through a haze, so to speak. They see us, cheer for us, and hope we finish the race well. Each of these interpretations is manmade: none of them are explicitly implied by the text. First of all, the text says *we are surrounded by witnesses*. The word *surrounded* literally means *enclosed* in the original language. Furthermore, the text says nothing about *cheering* us on, though I like the imagery.

The crowd that is referred to in Hebrews 11 includes many notable figures that exhibited profound faith during their lives. But is this crowd limited to these few

---

[427] Hebrews 12:1a.

people? If so, it is not much of a crowd. No, I believe there is quite a crowd watching us. What is more, this crowd is in the past future with the boundless God. That being the case, we are there with them as well. *We are part of the crowd.*

Furthermore, the text does not say these witnesses are viewing our race from a distant window. For all we know, they are right here, next to us, influencing our daily lives. It may be that our past future selves are not just cheerleaders, but coaches too. This may be precisely because the future past is undecided!

Participating in the Sovereignty of God

I believe we are not simply privileged to gaze into the future past from the past future, but privileged to be a part of it. We interject into the future past from the past future. Of this I am convinced. Why?

Let us go back to the encounter I had with Starry Night. Who sang the chorus of *Vincent* to me for those three and a half months? Was it God? Was it Vincent van Gogh himself? Or, was it my backward causality self, in communication with the others, trying desperately to get my attention in order to deliver the message? Obviously, I do not know for sure, but it was someone who, without a doubt, was quite determined to get through.

If my past future self is indeed a part of this process, it is in essence a *backward causality coach (BCC).* Our coaches are participating with God in the process of bringing about the future that already is, while the past that leads up to the future is still being formed through our current participation.

Participation? For most of my life I have assumed that only God (and perhaps an angel or two) influences my life from outside this domain. Why such a limited perspective? Surprisingly, I am not alone in the belief that there is more influence on our lives than only God and the angels. Parker J. Palmer says, in his book *Let Your Life Speak*, "The figure calling to me all those years was, I believe, what Thomas Merton calls 'true self' . . . It is the self planted in us by the God who made us in God's own image—the self that wants nothing more, or less, than for us to be who we were created to be."[428] This *true self* is our coach: our backward causality coach.

---

[428] Palmer, *Let Your Life Speak*, 69.

Scripture tells us, "(God's) divine power has given us everything we need for a godly life through our knowledge of him who called us by his own glory and goodness. Through these he has given us his very great and precious promises, so that through them you may participate in the divine nature, having escaped the corruption in the world caused by evil desires."[429] According to Eugene Peterson, to participate in the divine nature of God is to participate in the sovereignty of God.

> Work derives from and represents the sovereign God, who expresses his sovereignty as a worker; kingwork. Sovereigns work to bring order out of chaos; guard and fight for the sanctity of things and people; deliver victims from injustice and misfortune and wretchedness; grant pardon to the condemned and damned; heal sickness; by their very presence bring dignity and honor to people and land. God's sovereignty isn't abstract—it's a working sovereignty and is expressed in work. All of our work is intended as an extension of and participation in that sovereignty.[430]

Peterson makes clear two points: we are participants in God's sovereignty, and it is expressed here and now in our work.

Interventionism

In both Phase 1 and Phase 2 we discussed non-interventionism. Most significantly, we deduced that if God were a total non-interventionist, as some claim, we would not know it, for if he were not involved in our existence we would not even know of his existence. It is through intervention that we are made aware of God's presence.

Some who endorse total non-interventionism do so based on the apparent inconsistency of God's responses to prayers. The mistake in such a position is that it is a reaction to a false assumption: that answers are entirely dependent on those

---

[429] 2 Peter 1:3-4.
[430] Peterson, *Leap over a Wall: Earthly Spirituality for Everyday Christians*, 31.

praying and on God's will. Perhaps there are additional reasons for *unanswered prayers*.

In the New Testament we find a very peculiar story with a backward causality twist. As Jesus and his disciples walked along one day they came upon a man who had been blind since birth. The disciples asked Jesus, "Rabbi, who sinned, this man or his parents, that he was born blind?" Jesus replied, "Neither this man nor his parents sinned, but this happened so that the works of God might be displayed in him."[431] This passage has a couple of issues that beg our attention.

The disciples seem to be aware that things we do in the future can impact the past. Even if the blindness was a consequence of the blind man's sin, it clearly could not have been sin that was committed by him before his birth. It would have been the consequence of sin committed at some point in his past future. The disciples' question seems to make it clear that backward causality, though not labeled as such, was not a foreign concept to them.

Jesus' response clearly indicates that misfortunes here in this domain may be intentional, so that the "works of God might be displayed." But intentional on the part of whom? It may not always be God who decides to inflict pain on someone's life so that his purposes can be accomplished. There has to be more going on than meets the eye.

There is no doubt in my mind that God can cause good to come out of apparent bad. But is that enough reason to allow bad things to happen? First of all, we exist in a broken world. Good and bad things happen to all of us. It is part of our brokenness. Secondly, perhaps we should not be so quick to believe that we play no part in the *decision* to allow difficult things to happen to us. It may be, my friend, that our future self, our BCC (backward causality coach), sees a much broader picture and the far-reaching positive outcomes of such difficulties, and in turn voices an opinion to God.

Once again, my imagination takes over here. I can just see God coming to my BCC and saying, "So, your future past self is asking to win the lottery. What do you think I should do?" Knowing what good came from not winning the lottery, my

---

[431] John 9:1-3.

BCC replies, "No way, man. He will thank himself one day." To which God replies, "As you will."

I am so quick to blame the answers to prayers, or the lack thereof, on God. Perhaps God, in his infinite graciousness and consideration for me, cares for my future opinion more than the present opinion. After all, my future self, or BCC, has already been through such narrow-mindedness and now sees the broader picture. My BCC, the ultimate me, sees the whole squiggly me (a reference to the *Slice in Time* illustration in the previous chapter), more than the thin temporal slice in time that the current me sees.

A Team Effort

Are we doing this backward causality coaching alone? I think not. As I mentioned earlier, I do not know who sang to me all those months. For all I know it was Van Gogh himself, or my past future self, or God. It could have been a choir. My imagination is quite active on this topic. I imagine God calling a huddle that included Van Gogh, my BCC (backward causality coach), and perhaps Don McLean's BCC, and maybe others, to discuss how they were going to communicate that *Starry Night* is imbedded with many messages.

It is quite likely that this coaching is a team effort, with God standing beside each of us, observing and discussing, perhaps shaping the understanding of the observed scenes. There may literally be two or three witnesses agreeing together as the coaching takes place. The Apostle Paul tells us, "The Spirit of God intercedes for us because we do not know how to pray as we should."[432] God is coaching right alongside our BCC, trusting that we will listen and respond. Our team is working steadfastly on our behalf.

Conscience

I have often wondered what and where my conscience is. To say that it is simply a sub-layer to my complex psychological makeup is unsatisfying to me. There are without a doubt such psychological influences on my conscious and unconscious mental activity, but there has to be more to the story.

---

[432] Romans 8:26.

I have come to believe that the strongest voice in my psyche, my conscience, is my BCC speaking to me. It is the "true self" Thomas Merton spoke of, but it is also the self that exists beyond the present. It is my past future BCC.

What are the implications of such a claim? The first, and most significant, is this: if I have a conscience then I am already there. I am a BCC, participating in the sovereignty of God. Secondly, we apparently have a choice to listen or to not listen to our BCC. The latter does not change the fact that the BCC is there, but it does impact the efficiency with which we listen and respond, *and* the path we take leading to the past future.

Listening to Our BCC

In light of backward causality coaching, what is a *seared conscience*? It may be a misnomer. I believe either it exists or it does not. If it does exist, either we listen to it or we tune it out. It may be better described as an ignored conscience. Notice that these scenarios are independent of any religious efforts on our parts.

A very real tension exists between our coaches and us. A tongue-twisting passage of scripture refers to this tension.

> We know that the law is spiritual; but I am unspiritual, sold as a slave to sin. I do not understand what I do. For what I want to do I do not do, but what I hate I do. And if I do what I do not want to do, I agree that the law is good. As it is, it is no longer I myself who do it, but it is sin living in me. For I know that good itself does not dwell in me, that is, in my sinful nature. For I have the desire to do what is good, but I cannot carry it out. For I do not do the good I want to do, but the evil I do not want to do—this I keep on doing. Now if I do what I do not want to do, it is no longer I who do it, but it is sin living in me that does it.[433]

---

[433] Romans 7:14-20.

What a text! This is the tension between our consciousness in this present domain and our BCC. Even if we are listening to our BCC, we do not always follow through.

In Phase 1 I made a case for active listening. Here we see more specifically whose voices we are beckoned to hear. I believe our past future self wants desperately to be a part of our now-choices. *God, along with our BCC, is hoping for a fruitful past leading to the future.*

The Pretenders

During his *Sermon on the Mount*, Jesus made a very puzzling statement: "Not everyone who says to me, 'Lord, Lord,' will enter the kingdom of heaven, but only the one who does the will of my Father who is in heaven. Many will say to me on that day, 'Lord, Lord, did we not prophesy in your name and in your name drive out demons and in your name perform many miracles?' Then I will tell them plainly, 'I never knew you. Away from me, you evildoers!'"[434] This saying begs our attention for a couple of reasons.

First of all, it is a refutation of universalism. Jesus states clearly that there are some who will not be in the next domain. Evildoers, as he calls them, will be sent away. Whether they face a suspended state, a fiery hell, or annihilation, they are simply not in the next domain. Secondly, and perhaps more troublesome, is the statement, "I never knew you." What does Jesus mean here? Given the infinitude of the GBF, it is not surprising that he knew these people were wolves pretending to be sheep. He obviously knew who they were. Perhaps he is saying something entirely different. I have to wonder if Jesus was talking about their coaches. Perhaps he was saying, "Go away from me. You were never there. Your coaches were never in my domain."

When I was a child I spent much time worrying about heaven and hell, until one day when my father said to me, "Son, if you are worried, it is a good thing. It is a sign that you care." Translated into BCC terminology: if anyone is worried about whether or not they will be in the next domain, they will be. It is most likely a

---

[434] Matthew 7:21-23.

result of their coach trying to get through to them. Ironically, the ones who really have cause for concern are those who simply do not care.

I believe that people who came to Jesus in tears for the broken and weary lives they were leading, were also ones who had coaches trying desperately to get their attention. On the other hand, the staunch religious leaders, who had it all together, had no need to listen to Jesus or their coaches. It is they who have just cause for concern, for their coaches may not be there. They are pretenders.

Evidences and Objections

The only scriptural objection to backward causality coaching that I have been able to find is in one of Paul's letters where it says, "And he who searches our hearts knows the mind of the Spirit, because the Spirit intercedes for God's people in accordance with the will of God."[435] In spite of the reference to the Spirit doing the interceding, it does not rule out the BCC. It may be that God's Spirit hovers over each coach, not only *interceding*, but also coaching the coaches.

Numerous other texts affirm the BCC concept. The prophet Jeremiah quoted God saying, "Before I formed you in the womb I knew you, before you were born I set you apart; I appointed you as a prophet to the nations."[436] Some may object, claiming this is simply a declaration of God's foreknowledge. To that I exclaim, "Precisely!" God's foreknowledge *is* a declaration of what *is*.

Another text says, "For those God foreknew he also predestined to be conformed to the image of his Son, that he might be the firstborn among many brothers and sisters. And those he predestined, he also called; those he called, he also justified; those he justified, he also glorified."[437] Notice that the sequence starts with us being there in the first place.

There is one more occurrence in scripture that is most revealing. When Jesus was put to death by crucifixion he was hung beside two other prisoners. These men were most wicked: they were seasoned murderers and thieves and rebels. They were the scum of the earth. In the final moments of their deaths, however, we find this discourse,

---

[435] Romans 8:27.
[436] Jeremiah 1:5.
[437] Romans 8:29-30.

One of the criminals who hung there hurled insults at him: "Aren't you the Messiah? Save yourself and us!" But the other criminal rebuked him. "Don't you fear God," he said, "since you are under the same sentence? We are punished justly, for we are getting what our deeds deserve. But this man has done nothing wrong." Then he said, "Jesus, remember me when you come into your kingdom." Jesus answered him, "Truly I tell you, today you will be with me in paradise."[438]

It would appear that one had a coach and the other did not. And though the one with a coach spent his life ignoring his BCC voice, in the end he heard it calling, and responded in humble repentance.

All Who Can Stand It

William P. Young, in his novel *The Shack*, portrays a discussion between Mack, the main character, and Jesus: "'Does that mean,' asked Mack, 'that all roads will lead to you?' 'Not at all,' smiled Jesus as he reached for the door handle to the shop. 'Most roads don't lead anywhere. What it does mean is that I will travel any road to find you.'"[439] This is a beautiful portrayal of the discussions we had in Phase 2 describing the need for an infinite solution and the discussion in Phase 3 on the portal that God opened via his right arm. It is God who is looking for us, not we for him.

Contrary to popular opinion, God is not in the business of keeping people out of the next domain. We do a sufficient job of that on our own. No, he works the midnight shift with infinite effort to restore and bring us all home. God did not send the GBF into the world to condemn it, but to restore it.[440] Whoever wants to drink of life and eternal water can come.[441] Anyone.

---

[438] Luke 23:39-43.
[439] William P. Young, *The Shack* (Newbury Park: Windblown Media, 2007), 182.
[440] John 3:17.
[441] Revelation 22:17.

Dallas Willard, in his book *The Divine Conspiracy*, says, "I am thoroughly convinced that God will let everyone into heaven who, in his considered opinion, can stand it."[442] While some may squint and turn away from such a saying, it is precisely because of God's hot pursuit of our restoration that such a saying has merit. Any theological criteria that we devise for who God saves and doesn't save is exactly that: *our* criteria, not God's. I believe that anyone, regardless of his or her earthly religious persuasion, will have the choice, even if after death, to pass through the portal provided by the GBF. The ones who will not experience rebirth via this portal are those who adamantly do not want it and refuse it.

Extraordinary Coaches

There have been extraordinary people with extraordinary coaches that have walked the face of this earth. I am sure you have read about some of them, if not met them. Why are these people so extraordinary? It may be that their coaches speak with more clarity, but it is also apparent that they worked steadfastly at listening and responding to what they heard. One such person was C.S. Lewis.

Lewis sensed and heard a presence many years before his transformation. It took him by surprise again and again. He sensed a strong desire, or as Lewis put it, a *Joy*. In the words of the biographer Devin Brown in *A Life Observed: A Spiritual Biography of C.S. Lewis*, "Lewis defines Joy to mean a special kind of intense longing he felt, beginning in childhood, for something he could not quite put his finger on."[443] In Lewis' words, "Before I knew what I desired, the desire itself was gone, the whole glimpse withdrawn, the world turned commonplace again."[444] Brown goes on to explain, "He described this Joy that surprised him now and again as an unsatisfied desire which was more desirable than any other satisfaction."[445]

What is so intriguing is that Lewis sensed the presence of a desire, even in the midst of disbelief. Who or what was impressing *Joy* upon him? Sure, it could have been God, and probably was so on occasions. But I am also inclined to think it was his backward causality coach, whispering to him on occasion. His past future self

---

[442] Willard, *The Divine Conspiracy*, 302.
[443] Devin Brown, *A Life Observed: A Spiritual Biography of C.S. Lewis* (Grand Rapids: Brazos Press, 2013), 3.
[444] Lewis in ibid.
[445] Ibid.

knew of the vastness of the mission that was to be accomplished and would not let him go. I hate to think of this world without Lewis' contributions, had he not responded to transformation's voice, to his BCC.

So What?

One of my reviewers asked several rhetorical questions pertaining to this whole chapter. You may be asking them as well. *So what? This is intriguing, but why and how does it matter? If the future already exists, why should I be concerned about the present, let alone the future?*

First of all, we *are* participants in the inversion, or the setting aright, of this world here and now: either by slowing it down or by speeding it up through intentional participation. We know that war, pain, suffering, evil, and death will be no more in the past future, and even though we are not privileged to see the transformation in its fullness here and now, our knowledge of its reality drives our actions in this future past. To listen to and respond to our coach's call to participate is to work "with the grain of the universe," rather than against it.[446]

Secondly, scripture makes it clear that not all will be equal in the next domain. God will judge those who enter, giving rewards based on the fruit of their lives here. Many have bought into the myth that no matter when and how one is transformed, even if they get into the next domain by the hair of their chinny-chin-chin, life hereafter will be equal for all. Not so, my friend. Read and see.[447]

Thirdly, and perhaps most importantly, is the peace that the past future provides. I know that I am there. I hear my voice in the midst of the great cloud of witnesses. I find great comfort in this vision.

A Very Strange Loop

Backward causality coaching is perhaps the strangest of strange loops. Once we die we become the coach that is *currently* standing with God, looking back and coaching us now. Is that paradox not consistent with the cosmos! I will one day become the coach that will go back in time to ensure that I will become the coach I

---

[446] Yoder in Hauerwas, *With the Grain of the Universe*, 6.
[447] Matthew 16:27; Luke 6:35; Ephesians 6:8; Colossians 3:24; Hebrews 11:6; 2 John 1:8.

need to be. I will then understand how difficult it is to get through to *the me* in the future past, to get me to listen and participate in the sovereignty of God. Knowing that now, I have a deep, deep desire, or should I say *Joy*, to be faithful in the process.

.

3.18

Open Theism

Not everyone is open to the concept known of backward causality coaching. There are those, including some philosophers, theologians, and scientists, who question the existence of the past future. Of particular relevance at this point are the theologians who believe that not even God knows the future, because it does not yet exist.

From early times philosophers have believed that the "true nature of reality is timeless and that our impression of the flow of time is simply a trick of human psychological perspective."[448] Albert Einstein substantiated this perspective by theorizing the existence of 4-dimensional space-time in his theory of general relativity. Einstein believed that different points in time are simply different locations in this 4-dimensional domain, and that all points in time exist concurrently. Some refer to this view, that all of space and time are one entity, as a *block universe* view of space and time.

Thomas Aquinas essentially believed in a block universe. Though Aquinas believed in free choice, he believed that from God's eternal perspective, all of time exists simultaneously.[449] But not everyone sees it as Aquinas and Einstein did.

John Polkinghorne, a physicist and theologian, says in his book *Science and Religion in Quest of Truth*, "However, many of us refuse to deny the commonsense experience of the passage of time and believe that the universe is an open realm of true becoming, so that the future is not 'already' in existence, so to speak waiting

---

[448] Polkinghorne, *Science and Religion in Quest of Truth*, 62.
[449] Ibid., 64.

for us to arrive."[450] This is *open theism*: the future is open, undecided, and unknown. Even to God.

Polkinghorne develops his open theism by exploring the notion that God, through an act of "kenotic condescension" freely limited himself to time when he brought this temporal creation into existence.[451] God remains in this limited state with respect to our domain. Given that Polkinghorne believes in the eternal nature of God, he proposes a "dipolar view of the divine," in which God has both an eternal essence with respect to his domain and a temporal essence with respect to our domain.[452] Polkinghorne does not see this as an imperfection on God's part, since the future of our domain does not yet exist in order to know it. "God possesses what philosophers call a current omniscience (knowing now all that can be known now) but not an absolute omniscience (knowing all that eventually will be knowable)."[453]

It should be noted here that open theism and process theology are distinctly different. In the former, the future is evolving. In the latter, God is evolving. I am sure you know by now that mathematically I believe both are problematic. However, the issue at hand demands that I respond to open theism and some of its specific issues.

A Response to Polkinghorne

I must start by affirming my deep respect for John Polkinghorne. He is easily the foremost thinker and writer on the convergence of science and religion. I tread fearfully and lightly as I address these issues.

Some physicists do not believe in Einstein's block universe. To them the future simply does not exist. However, I sense that Polkinghorne, being both a physicist and a theologian, knows the discontinuity that such a stance represents with respect to an eternal God. He reconciles the two by claiming that God imposed a self-limitation with respect to our domain. This is clearly a better option than to claim that God is constrained by time, for this would deny God's infinitude.

---

450 Ibid., 62.
451 Ibid., 100.
452 Ibid., 101.
453 Ibid.

However, to assert that God chooses not to know the future implies that the future is still there. *If, on the other hand, no future exists, then no self-limiting action on God's part is required.*

The second issue pertains to quantum mechanics. I was surprised to find that Polkinghorne's *Science and Religion in Quest of Truth* does not address the experimentally verified backward causality nature of the quantum realm. The future not only exists in the quantum realm, but events in the future affect outcomes in the past. How does an open theistic physicist account for this peculiar discontinuity?

Thirdly, Polkinghorne expresses a clear *hope in the future*. He affirms that even though there is much we do not know, there is sufficient evidence that "the eschatological hope of a destiny beyond death is not an incoherent expectation."[454] I couldn't agree more, however, I believe this implies some knowledge of a future. Not a future *to be*, but one that is.

In the next chapter I will delve into more issues, including the question of whether or not we can imagine anything, such as a future, that God has not imagined. Also, there is the very real issue of prophetic encounters: how do we account for futuristic visionary occurrences if the future does not yet exist?

In Closing

To John Polkinghorne's credit, it may well be that the future in *this* domain has not yet happened. Our future may in fact be empty from a 4-D perspective. From an 8-D vantage point, however, the future is now!

---

[454] Ibid., 107-08.

3.19

In-Plane View

You have seen how I can have fun with imaginative wanderings. This chapter is no exception. It is not intended to be even remotely academic. It stems from scientifically unexplainable experiences. I have witnessed and experienced too many prophetic encounters in my life to lightly pass them off as either coincidences or as hallucinations. I have witnessed detailed scars on a total stranger's face that I saw the night before in a dream. As a 21-year old I had an experience clearly beyond my control that I repeatedly dreamed about as a boy. Such encounters are very real. So, here we go.

Who Sees the Future?

Is God the only one who sees the future? In light of previous discussions on the past future, I think not. Occasionally, humans are privileged to see into this past future. In Phase 1 I stated that mythology has its roots in real human experience. It may also have roots in the past future. Most human glimpses into the past future are shadowy, lacking crystal clear definition, resulting in prophetic declarations that are more general than specific. Some, however, are well defined and are presented to listeners with crisp clarity.

Prophetic gifts are much more extensive than Nostradamus-type declarations. What is more, they are more common than one would expect. The presentations of such gifts come in various shapes and sizes, and through diverse mediums and individuals. Along with Isaiah and Daniel, I would include Mozart, Bach, and Beethoven, Mahatma Gandhi, Martin Luther King, Jr., Mother Teresa, and Nelson Mandela, Rembrandt, Picasso, Da Vinci, Michelangelo, Van Gogh, and Escher,

Galileo, Archimedes, Newton, and Einstein, Thoreau, Cummings, and Tolkien, and Pete Seeger, Bob Dylan, and Don McLean, to mention a few. Prophetic gifts are very diverse. There is, however, one common denominator: they all see the past future.

Creativity

I believe creativity is prophetic. While it manifests itself in sundry ways, it starts with a vision. Quite often it is a vision of a finished product. The creator literally hears the composition in his or her head, sees the finished sculpture or painting, understands the scientific principle before investigation even begins, or foresees a community of unity and an end to pain and starvation. These people see what will be. Or, in backward causality terms, what already is in the past future.

It may be more accurate to say that the creative process has more to do with finding a means of getting to the finished product than the formation of the vision. When asked how Michelangelo created the sculpture *David*, he reportedly replied, "I simply removed everything that was not David." Whether the encounter was made up or real, it is quite relevant. The product already *was*. He simply had to find a way to get to it.

I remember reading a comic strip as a boy that portrayed a man with a jet pack on his back, flying through the sky to rescue someone in need. Such an imaginative comic strip was so far-fetched, yet I remember relishing its wonderful impossibility. We all know that such jet packs now exist. They are commonplace. Back then they already existed in the comic strip writer's past future.

This is not figurative rhetoric. The entity that is envisioned literally exists in the past future. The creative challenge is bringing it back in time to the present in a form that others will recognize and benefit from. I believe we humans cannot imagine anything that either has not or will not exist at some point in time and in one form or another.[455] I think of this as the *principle of conceptualization*: if we can conceive or envision anything, then it already exists in the past future. Getting to that envisioned entity is the challenge. Plato probably would have argued that such visions are more real than their material equivalents, and that reality always

---

[455] And yes, this may include unicorns, flying spaghetti monsters, and Greek deities!

precedes conceptualization.[456] Ironically (and prophetically) I believe this *is* the case. Reality does exist before it is envisioned. Whether or not Plato would have thought of it in terms of *past future* realities is of course another issue.

Time Independence

The noted physicist Stephen Hawking, in his book *A Brief History Of Time*, asks, "Why do we remember the past but not the future?"[457] While this question may seem simple and obvious, it is most profound. Most of us do remember only the past. While this may be the case most of the time, there are occasionally remembrances of the future that come our way. Such occurrences are not confined to a forward arrow of time. I believe prophecy is simply remembering what once was in the past future.

Prophetic vision is being able to look up and down the stream of time, and not just at the ripples in front of us. It is time independent. Prophecy is not only the foretelling of what will be, but also the aft-telling of what has been, of things we were not formerly privileged to know.

For instance, King David cried out in one of his songs, "My God, my God, why have you forsaken me?"[458] Jesus utters the exact same words from the cross.[459] Who is quoting whom? Often it is thought that Jesus was quoting David's song. I think not. I think it was David who prophetically remembered Jesus' words on the cross, though he lived about a thousand years before Jesus. David heard the words from the past future.

In-Plane View

Imagine, if you will, that we exist on a four dimensional plane. It should not be too hard to visualize, since we often draw three dimensions of space onto a flat piece of paper. The only difference is that this two-dimensional piece of paper, representing 3d space, also has a time-stamp. Therefore, it represents a slice of 4-D space-time. If one were to view multiple slices very rapidly it would be just like

---

[456] Wikipedia, "Theory of Forms," https://en.wikipedia.org/wiki/Theory_of_Forms.
[457] Hawking, *A Brief History of Time*, 148.
[458] Psalm 22:1a.
[459] Matthew 27:46.

viewing a movie. In the following illustration (Figure 78) you see such slices of four-dimensional space-time separated by intervals of time. Note also the typical arrow of time, and the vertical line marking a current slice of 4-D. At any given location in space and time we are each privileged to observe and know our surroundings on that plane. Such an observation is an in-plane view.

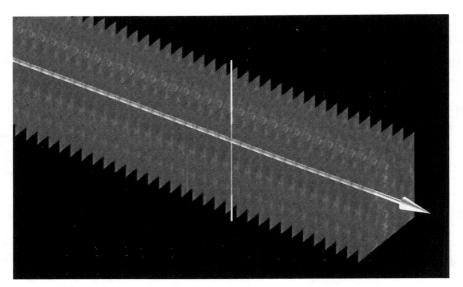

Figure 78. In-Plane View: No Angle

Occasionally some of us have planes that rotate slightly, intersecting with adjacent planes (Figure 79), intersecting both the past and the future. The larger the angle, the further back and forward in time one can see. While this vision may not be crystal clear, it provides glimpses into the past and future.

Some individuals have planes that rotate very sharply, intersecting with planes that go much farther back and forward in time (Figure 80). The prophet Isaiah had a plane that rotated as much as 700 years. Some have had planes that rotate thousands of years.

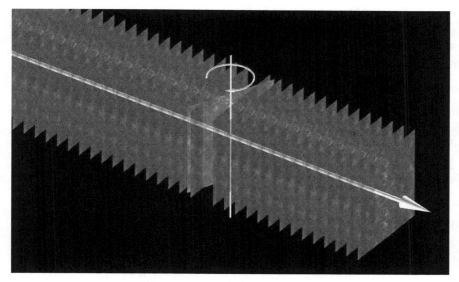

Figure 79. In-Plane View: Slight Angle

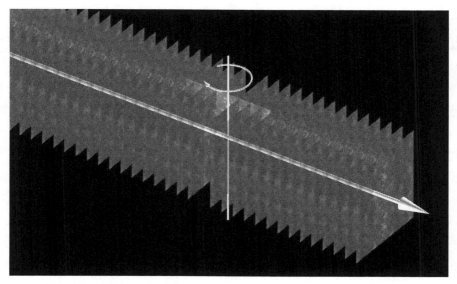

Figure 80. In-Plane View: Right Angle

Do we have the ability to rotate our plane of vision at will? Perhaps. Is it a gift that can be exercised? I believe so, especially in terms of paying attention and listening. Clear visions seem to come in unexpected waves. There are surprising moments of clarity when the vision, even if it is an in-plane view, is also in plain view. I believe our planes rotate at specific moments for specific purposes. Ultimately, I believe both the purpose and the gift come from God. The Left Arm of God is at work communicating with us in ways that defy normalcy. This is why I believe it is a gift.[460]

Dreams

Dreams are peculiar rotations. Science tells us that dreams last only seconds, or at most less than a minute, yet seem to last much longer. While dreaming, our physical boundaries no longer limit us to our normal bounded dimension of time. Some even enter 8-D, being privileged to experience things beyond our dimensional domain, things unimaginable during waking hours. Others simply move about in time.

Some of my own dreams have been fulfilled the very next day. On one such occasion I dreamt I was riding a bicycle across an overpass. Suddenly, a car struck me from behind. I can still see the sky swirling as I tumbled over the car and landed on my back. I was motionless. People gathered around me and asked, "Is he dead?" I rose and walked away from the accident scene. I woke from the dream with my heart racing.

The next evening my wife and I were driving down the interstate, headed for a family gathering. I just happened to glance up, only to see a bicyclist riding across the overpass above. A car came from behind, struck him, sending him tumbling over the car and onto the overpass. Again my heart raced. Later that evening I called the local police department inquiring on the fate of the bicyclist. Amazingly, though bruised, he had gotten up and walked away.

---

[460] For the record, I am not attempting to come up with a means by which to see into the past or future. I am simply attempting to derive a physical explanation (as frail of an explanation as it may be) for what already happens. It *is* happening. A couple of examples are forthcoming. This is but a pragmatic approach to understanding a very complicated phenomenon.

Why such a dream? I am certainly not an expert on dreams and their meanings. However, two things became clear to me through that experience. First of all, not all dreams that I am in are about me. They may be about someone else I am being called to pray for. Secondly, they may be calls to pay attention to upcoming dreams. Either way, such dreams are clear messages that portals into the past future *do* open, and when they do, we are called to pay attention.

Intertwined Rotations

My father is a dreamer. It must run in our genes. In one of his dreams he found himself in a different town praying for a very sick woman, who also happened to be a friend of the family. As he usually did, he told my mother about the dream the next morning. Sometime later both he and my mother were in that very town attending church. The daughter of the sick woman came to them and informed them that her mother was doing better. She also told them that a very peculiar incident had happened a short time previously. She had gone in to check on her mother one morning and her mother told her that my father had been there the night before, praying for her. Of course the daughter told her she had been dreaming. The mother was adamant that he had been there praying for her. My father and mother looked at each other in wonder.

Is it possible that both were in the same intertwined dream? It would seem so. Though I do not know of any other such cases, it may happen more often than we realize. It just may be that our rotated planes intersect with other such rotated planes, resulting in simultaneous in-plane views.

Playing a Role in Fulfillment

I often question my visions of *things to be* if I also play a role in fulfilling them. J.R.R. Tolkien understood this phenomenon. In *The Hobbit* a conversation takes place between Gandalf and Bilbo:

> 'Then the prophecies of the old songs have turned out to be true, after a fashion!' said Bilbo. 'Of course!' said Gandalf. 'And why should not they prove true? Surely you don't disbelieve the

prophecies, because you had a hand in bringing them about yourself? You don't really suppose, do you, that all our adventures and escapes were managed by mere luck, just for your sole benefit? You are a very fine person, Mr. Baggins, and I am very fond of you; but you are only quite a little fellow in a wide world after all!'[461]

Just because we may play a role in the fulfillment of a given prophecy does not negate such a fulfillment, for we, too, are imbedded in such a prophecy.

Can I interfere with God's purpose by interfering with any of God's prophetic declarations? No. He knows when such prophecies are uttered that any attempt on my part to force a fulfillment or to stand in the way will actually be a part of the prophetic utterance and its fulfillment. It is a strange dimensional loop! Our actions are already seen in the past future.

In Closing

I have encountered too many in-plane rotations to ignore. The explanations offered here are meager attempts to put some scientific meat on what are skeletal and quite mystical experiences. I believe the past future exists, that we occasionally get glimpses into its strange nature, and that such visions are gifts of God. Whether they are expressed through creative media such as sculpture, painting, architecture, or the written word, such encounters are very plain views of in-plane rotations.

I leave you with a quote by Robert Orben: "Always remember there are only two kinds of people in this world - the realists and the dreamers. The realists know where they are going. The dreamers have already been there."

---

[461] J.R.R. Tolkien, *The Hobbit* (The Random House Publishing Group, 1996), 305.

Phase 4

Fractal Perspectives

4.00

The Narrative

The morning sun outside of the castle was still low on the horizon in front of Fritz. He smiled as he realized that Ganz and Sorge somehow knew the right moment had come for him to leave the castle.

The cool air was filled with the aroma of conifer resin. Small birds moved quietly through the trees. The meadow was behind him now. The path quickly moved into the wood.

Conifers. Fritz stopped for a moment to look closely at their branches. He had never taken the time to notice their peculiar patterns; repeating patterns; branches within branches; stems within stems; lined with leaves that were comprised of even smaller parts. For some, the smallest visible part was a needle. For others, it was bundles of scale-like tentacles. Regardless of their unique structures, all had one thing in common: parts were connected to parts that were connected to parts that were connected to parts that were connected to a tree trunk. For that matter, the trunks too were connected - to the earth.

His thoughts wandered to his many new friends who also were connected by stems. They were parts, too, so to speak, connected by interwoven journeys. Every one of his new friends had played an important role in his venture and in his growing understanding and peace. He smiled at the familiar patterns his thoughts naturally chased as well, always seeking to understand what life was giving him.

The ascent through the sweet trees was interspersed with the sun's blinding rays filtering through the trees. Fritz turned his eyes toward the ground more than once. The sunlight's autumnal direction gave him assurance that he was on a southeastern trek.

By the time he reached the top of the mountain, the sun was high and the trees had thinned at a bluff. He scanned the mountainside and the valley below and saw a network of streams merging into larger streams, leading into rivers. This pattern was much like within the trees: branches and streams were both interconnected, stemming from a base source, and flowing outward in a repetitive cycle. *Philosophical wanderings!* He chuckled at himself and his mind, and headed down the mountainside.

One of the streams he had observed from the peak was now running along the right side of the path. Fritz set down his pack and knelt next to the stream's edge. Cupping his hands, he took a drink of the clear, cold water. Opening his sack, he pulled out the apple he had picked on the way out of Dimen Castle. Without realizing it, he started rotating it. He caught himself with a laugh. *I guess I'm not in Dimen Castle anymore.* He bit into the crisp apple. *Hmm, I wonder what it would be now if I had rotated it before passing through the wall.*

Fritz gathered his things and continued his descent. As he glanced to the left, he saw another stream heading his direction; soon, it would merge with the one he was following. The new stream also had a path on its left. He should have seen the dilemma coming. The path he was on ended abruptly where the two streams merged. The path that had been on the left of the other stream continued on the left of the merged streams. To continue the descent, he would have to cross the stream.

Stepping from stone to stone, he managed to cross the stream without soaking his boots and continued on the path. As he walked, he recalled the view of merging waterways from the mountain's peak. He stopped in his tracks as it occurred to him that he would have to cross numerous merging waterways before arriving at Fract Village. No doubt, they would be progressively wider and deeper, and perhaps, even treacherous. Fritz shook his head as he muttered, "Ganz didn't say it would be easy or dry! He simply said it would not be difficult to find!"

Teile was waiting at the village's edge when a wet and cold Fritz arrived. "So," said he, "You took a bath, did you?"

Fritz smiled, as best he could, and asked, "Are you Teile?"

"Yes, I am Teile. Welcome to Fract Village. Perhaps, it would be best if we got you some dry clothes and hot tea."

At the village center, there was one large building. In many ways, it resembled the buildings on the outskirts of the village. It was larger, but very similar. As they approached its entry, Fritz stopped to look at the exterior wall constructed of bricks. The construction, in and of itself, was not so unusual. The bricks, however, were unusual. They were miniatures of the building they comprised! Looking even more closely, Fritz could see that they, too, were made of bricks that were miniatures of the bricks that formed the central building. "Come along, Fritz. I don't want you getting ill in those wet clothes," called Teile over his shoulder.

They followed a long narrow hallway into a seven-sided foyer. Each of the seven walls had an opening to a hallway. The walls, hallways, and ceilings were lined with mirrors. The sight was disorienting. Teile chuckled at the confused Fritz and said, "It takes getting used to. Isn't it amazing how one, let alone two, can be many?" Pointing down one of the hallways, he continued, "Your room is down that hallway, first door on the left. There are dry clothes on the bed. Leave your wet belongings outside the door. We will take care of them."

As Fritz looked around, he could see thousands upon thousands of images reflected off the walls. Some grew smaller and more distant as his eyes roamed the walls. "Which hallway do I follow?"

"Actually, any of them will do. Meet me back here, and we will have tea."

The hot tea was a welcomed tonic. After a few sips, Fritz noticed the cup he held. "How does it hold tea?" asked Fritz as he examined its structure. The cup, quite like the building they were in, was constructed of smaller cups that were constructed of smaller cups that were constructed of smaller cups . . . There were many apparent holes!

"Perhaps, this will help," offered Teile, "Think about the smallest cup that comprises the cups that comprise, well, eventually this cup. If it is, indeed, the smallest cup, then it should be able to hold tea. Right?"

"I suppose so."

"Well, then, if it holds tea, then the cup it helps to comprise will hold tea by virtue of the smaller cups within it that do, in fact, hold tea!"

"OK," replied Fritz, trying to keep up with the thought pattern.

"Well, if you carry that logic to its fullest extent, you have a cup of tea! No guarantee that it's hot, however," laughed Teile. "Individual things in Fract Village are actually many. They are made of parts quite like the part they make."

"Why?" asked Fritz.

"Why? You ask why?" questioned Teile. "My friend, you have many lessons to learn, not only about Fract Village, but about life."

"I am listening," replied Fritz calmly.

"Well, then I see you have learned at least one. All of life is made of parts that are made of parts, and so on, and so forth. Even outside Fract Village, life is so," Teile continued.

"I have never seen such things outside Fract Village," retorted Fritz.

"Oh, but you have, you have. For instance, each tiny experience you have had on your journey this far has contributed to a larger experience, perhaps a leg of your journey. Each leg of your journey contributes to a larger experience, such as the whole journey itself. But, it does not stop there. Each journey contributes to a larger voyage, perhaps that of a lifetime. Do not think that this journey is it! The sole journey of a lifetime? No, it is but a part of a larger journey that is, in turn, but a part of another.

"Even parts that appear not to be connected may, in fact, be intertwined. The challenge is, my friend, to not assume that the life you hold, or a journey you take, is an isolated entity. It may, in fact, be but a part of a much larger entity that is part of a larger entity, and so on.

"The reverse is also true. For instance, think of the parts that make up your very own body! You are made of parts that are made of parts that are made of parts that are made of parts. While not all parts explicitly resemble each other, as they do here in Fract Village, they do, in fact, have many similarities. Do not close yourself off to the repeated mysteries that lie outside your walls or to the ones that lie within." Having said that, Teile excused himself to check on dinner.

Fritz sat in silent contemplation, occasionally glancing at the reflections on the walls. He had been given much to ponder. He could see and understand some of the parallels, like the patterns in the trees and streams, but many were too vague to grasp. Perhaps, his narrow ambitions had obscured a larger picture.

Teile returned pushing a cart with plates, utensils, and several entrees, "Dinner is served!" They gathered around a small table with two chairs next to one of the seven walls. The dinner plates were, well, consistent with the rest of Fract Village, as were the entrees.

"We have Repetitious Roast, Iterative Beets, Successive Salad and, my favorite, Apple, Apple, Apple, Apple, Apple, Apple Pie."

"I am not even going to ask," said Fritz.

"Good, let's eat."

Dinner was quite good and filling, and filling, and filling, and . . .

"I know just what you need now, Fritz. You need a good storytelling! It is a tradition of ours that each evening following dinner, the residents of Fract Village gather at the village square for storytelling. This evening, it will be the infamous Glatten, the smoothest storyteller ever heard." Not wanting to offend his host, Fritz pushed off his sleepiness and accepted the invitation.

Teile introduced Fritz to some of his friends as they took a seat toward the back of the crowd, "And now, fellow Fract Villagers, the infamous, the incessant, the ever-repeating Glatten!" The applause was ear-piercing.

"Shhh! He's starting!" whispered through the crowd.

Glatten's strong, soft voice began, "Once upon a time, there lived a glorious storyteller in the land of Fable. He gathered around himself all those who longed for such a gift and would become his apprentice storytellers. He told them of a storyteller who once told a story of an old man giving a lecture on storytelling. It was quite an interesting story. He spoke of the day when storytelling was a rare gift possessed only by those known as storytellers. Furthermore, any given storyteller was not, officially, known as a storyteller unless they knew who the storyteller was who taught the storyteller who taught the storyteller who taught the would-be-official storyteller to tell stories. Once it was determined that such a would-be storyteller was, indeed, an official storyteller, they were given permission to stand in the town square and tell the following story . . .

"Once upon a time, there lived a glorious storyteller in the land of Fable. He gathered around himself all those who longed for such a gift and would become his apprentice storytellers. He told them of a storyteller who once told a story of an old man giving a lecture on storytelling. It was quite an interesting story. He spoke of the day when storytelling was a rare gift possessed only by those known as storytellers. Furthermore, any given storyteller was not, officially, known as a storyteller unless they knew who the storyteller was who taught the storyteller who taught the storyteller who taught the would-be-official storyteller to tell stories. Once it was determined that such a would-be storyteller was, indeed, an official storyteller, they were given permission to stand in the town square and tell the following story . . .

By this time, Fritz could hardly keep his eyes open. "Perhaps, you are too tired for such storytelling," Teile said, considerately.

"Yes," replied Fritz, "I think I better get some rest for tomorrow's journey." At that, he said good night, and quietly left the square.

Upon entering the mirrored foyer, he realized he couldn't tell which of the seven hallways led to his room. Remembering that Teile had said, "Actually, any of them will do," Fritz made a random choice of a hallway, and entered the first door on the left. He found his clothes, boots, and knapsack, clean and dry, all neatly stacked at the foot of the bed. His knapsack had been restocked with food for the next day's journey.

During the night, Fritz's dreams were very strange. The longest and most unsettling was a dream about a dream about a dream about . . . Fritz lost count of how deeply the dream was imbedded. He woke several times trying to clear his mind of the repetition. By morning, he had managed to get only a few hours of sleep uninterrupted by dreams of dreams.

Fritz finished dressing, threw his knapsack over his shoulder, and left the room. Standing in the center of the foyer, he pondered the seven hallways. Given that it did not matter which hallway he chose coming in, it probably did not matter which he chose going out.

Sure enough! He exited the building right where he had first entered with Teile. Looking around, he wondered if Teile would show up to give him directions out of the village and over the next mountain.

"Are you looking for Teile?" A chorus of small voices came from behind him. He turned around to see seven identical boys. "Follow me, and I will take you to him," they said. At that, all seven boys left in seven different directions.

"Wait, which of you do I follow?"

"Me!" They all exclaimed.

From behind Fritz, came a familiar voice, "Good morning, Fritz." Teile smiled at the practical joke the septuplets were trying to pull on Fritz, "They often take advantage of their village's reputation to pull pranks on visitors. Come, let us have breakfast."

While sharing boiled eggs, toast, and tea, Teile began to explain to Fritz how to get over the next mountain. "I will lead you to the south edge of the village; from there, head south toward the mountain. You will come to forks in the path three times. Any choice will lead you up the mountain to the pass, for they all converge near the top. However, if you do not want to get soaked again, you must stay with the rightmost path. It will provide you with the only continuous path that does not cross water. Once you get to the pass, you will be able to see Seekers Bridge. Now hear this very clearly, for you may lose your life if you do not:

"The path descending the mountain is quite steep. For that reason, it is very important that you watch, carefully, at all times. As you approach the bridge, the path will take a slight turn to the right. At that precise point, you must stop and look, carefully, to the left. There is a little-known path, very narrow, and often obscured by brush. You must find it, and take it. Do not proceed down the path to the right. Many a life has done so, never to return."

"What is so dangerous about the main path?" asked Fritz.

"It is known for treacherous rock slides. The path is loose, and even the slightest disturbance can cause a rock slide that will, certainly, take you with it down into Satisfaction Gorge."

"I will watch for it."

"Fritz, do not be so casual about it. It is very deceiving. It looks like the path leads directly to the bridge. Be on careful watch."

At the edge of the village, Teile gave one final warning, "Please be careful. Please be careful. Please be careful. Satisfaction Gorge is full of skeletons."

"Thank you, Teile. I deeply appreciate your hospitality and concern."

"Farewell, friend," said Teile, and with that parting benediction, Fritz turned and headed south.

4.01

The Nature of Fractals

Fractals are all around us. They are in us. We are in them. Nature is ordered by fractals. They are complex geometric patterns that exhibit self-similarity, patterns which repeat over and over with ever-decreasing size and ever-increasing detail. Fractals are the essence of the cosmos.

Fractals are present in governments, businesses, economics, societies, ecology, science, anatomy, and mathematics. Some are visible in nature, such as the progression from forests to trees to limbs to branches to twigs to leaves to veins to compounds, etc. Others are subtle, such as societal structures containing relationships that contain relationships that contain relationships. The strangest point to be made is this: there is nothing in existence that is not a part of *the fractal*.

Examples in Nature

One example from nature is found in orbits. From an electron spinning and orbiting the nucleus of an atom, to the moon spinning and orbiting around our planet, our planet spinning and orbiting around the Sun, the Sun spinning through our galaxy, our galaxy spinning around a sector of the universe, to the universe itself spinning within 4-D space-time: everything spins. The orbit theme permeates the cosmos.

Looking at biological examples, fractals are present in the structure of seashells, with each species spirally repeating unique shapes over many years of growth. Cross-sectional cuts through seashells reveal amazing uniform and intricate loops of ever-increasing detail.

Plants are fractal. Below ground, they spread out their root systems in repeated divisions, multiplying their roots, resulting in miles and miles of rootlets and root hairs within very small volumes of soil. Above ground, they continue the fractal patterns from woody structures to leaves and leaflets. Two plants in particular stand out to me when I think of fractals: ferns and cedars (Figure 81). There are at least 4 *orders* of the fundamental repeated pattern visible in this illustration of a cedar branch.

Figure 81. Fractal Cedar

From waterways to animal vascular systems, from ancestral trees to literal trees, from seed patterns in sunflowers to reproductive patterns in rabbits, from seconds to millennia, fractals are expressed throughout the cosmos. A most fanciful example is found in Romanesco Broccoli (Figure 82).

Figure 82. Romanesco Broccoli by Owen Burkholder

Recursive Processes

Fractals result from *recursive* processes, ones that are self-referential and iterative. Through recursive processes an entity defines itself in terms of itself, specifically through smaller and smaller versions of itself.[462] Notice in the previous illustration that the overall cone-like shape of the Romanesco Broccoli is recursively repeated in smaller cones, which are in turn repeated recursively in smaller and smaller similar shapes. Each tiny cone is a recursive representation of the overall broccoli shape. This process is distinctly different from circular processes that only refine the circle. Of primary importance is that smaller and smaller portions of an entity are recursively self-similar to the overall entity.

In 1202 Leonardo of Pisa, otherwise known as Fibonacci, discovered a sequence of numbers based on a recursive mathematical process.[463] Fibonacci

---

[462] Hofstadter, *Gödel, Escher, Bach: An Eternal Golden Braid*, 127.
[463] Ibid., 135.

started with 0 and 1, defining each subsequent number in the sequence as the sum of the previous two numbers. The result was 0, 1, 1, 2, 3, 5, 8, 13, 21, 34, 55, 89, 144, 233 . . . Numerous fractals in nature follow the Fibonacci series: leaf arrangements on plants, seeds in a sunflower, pinecones, the spirals in a Nautilus shell, and rabbit reproductive patterns. For instance, sunflowers use these numbers because they facilitate packing as many seeds as possible into one flower, starting from the center of the flower and moving outward.

One way to demonstrate the recursive process is to hold a mirror up to a mirror. The resulting image seems to *go on forever*, though it is tough to get into the center of the reflections to get a center-stage view. What is more, light is lost with each reflection, causing each subsequent reflection to grow dimmer.

Many years back, before I was aware of fractals and recursive processes, I wondered what would happen if I aimed a video camera (with a live feed) at the video monitor. Much to my wonder (and much to the demise of my time) many fanciful recursive images resulted (Figure 83).

Figure 83. Recursive Video

The Third Type of Infinity

In Phase 2 we discussed the first type of infinity: magnitude. This type of infinity is typified in the IICP, who by its magnitude brought all things into existence. In Phase 3 we discussed dimensional infinitude. This type can be quite close and is not magnitude dependent, but is always at least one dimension away and therefore inaccessible. Here, as I alluded to in these earlier Phases, we examine the third type of infinity: *intricacy*. Fractals, if *taken to the limit* mathematically and geometrically, result in intricacy that goes on forever. Furthermore, fractals also exemplify the first type of infinity because their borders and/or surface areas grow to become infinitely large in magnitude. Very small fractals can have infinite details and infinite surface areas. Fractals strangely exhibit both magnitude and intricacy in their mysterious and beautiful expressions.

The Father of Fractals

In my opinion there are two *fathers* of fractals. The first is the IICP, who expressed the fractal nature of his essence throughout the cosmos.[464] The second father, in earthly and mathematical terms, is Benoit Mandelbrot. Mandelbrot was a visionary in the truest sense, ignoring the criticisms and rejections of old school mathematicians, steadfastly pursuing the world of fractals.

---

[464] That God is fractal may be disturbing to some readers. If so, I encourage you to think on the pre-existing attribute criterion we discussed in Chapter 2.04. If God expresses fractal attributes throughout the cosmos, surely he is expressing his own fractal nature.

4.02

Mandelbrot

Early on in my inquiry into fractals I *stumbled* onto the work of Benoit Mandelbrot.[465] At that point I did not even realize that Mandelbrot coined the word *fractal*. Benoit was a Polish-born French and American mathematician whose gifts and interests led him beyond typical mathematical interests, exploring the highly unusual world of self-similarity. He specialized in the mathematics of geometric shapes that have rough edges.[466] To many, Mandelbrot became the *father of fractals*. His pioneering work spawned many practical and artistic uses of the fractal mathematics we are about to explore.

The Mandelbrot Set

Before we can adequately get into a discussion on Mandelbrot's discovery we must first take a look at an illustration of what became know as the Mandelbrot set (Figure 84).

When I first laid eyes on this geometric shape I found myself in awe and disbelief. Supposedly this intricate shape had always existed, and was waiting for someone to uncover it. That someone was Benoit Mandelbrot. I say *supposedly* because I did not believe its origin was as simple as what was being described in the literature I was reading at the time. The equation that Mandelbrot derived, and which defines the *Mandelbrot Set*, is,

$$(\text{Equation 4}) \qquad z_{n+1} = z_n^2 + c$$

---

[465] It is, of course, not possible to enter the world of fractals without encountering Mandelbrot!
[466] NOVA, "Hunting the Hidden Dimension," in *NOVA* (PBS, 2011).

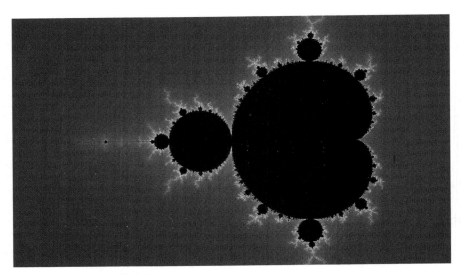

Figure 84. The Mandelbrot Set

In order to explain Equation 4 we must briefly discuss imaginary numbers and the imaginary plane. Even the name sounds fairytale-like. Nevertheless I knew from my mathematics and engineering days that imaginary numbers are used to solve very real everyday problems, especially in engineering. Imaginary numbers come from equations that contain the square root of a negative number. If you recall from high school mathematics, the square root of a number is the number that when multiplied by itself produces the original number. For instance 2 is the square root of 4 and 3 is the square root of 9. But what number, when multiplied by itself, results in a negative number? I was taught that any number multiplied by itself results in a positive number. How can such an entity exist? Well, many engineering problems and their derived equations are very real, yet require us to deal with the square roots of negative numbers.

To get around the problem we simplify such a number by *factoring out* the square root of -1 from the rest of the number, dealing with it separately. The square root of -1, symbolized by the expression $\sqrt{-1}$, is also symbolized by the letter *i*. This number *(i)* is technically undefined, or incalculable. However, we do know how it behaves. For instance, we know that when *i* is multiplied by itself the result is -1. Hence, even though it is undefined, we can use it to solve equations simply by knowing how it behaves.

The next step is to define the imaginary plane. This plane of numbers has real numbers on the horizontal axis, (such as -3, -2, -1, 0, 1, 2, 3) and imaginary numbers on the vertical axis (such as -3i, -2i, -1i, 0i, 1i, 2i, 3i). In the latter sequence, 3i, for example, is equivalent to 3 multiplied by i, or 3 multiplied by the square root of -1. For the mathematically inclined reader, it can be expressed as $3\sqrt{-1}$, or $\sqrt{-9}$. Lost yet? Hang in there! Perhaps the following illustration will help (Figure 85).

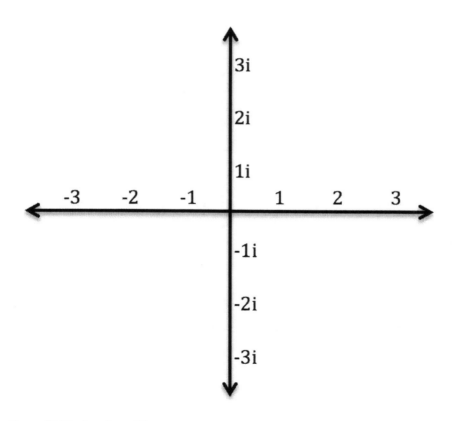

Figure 85. The Imaginary Plane

Every location on this plane of numbers has an address, or a set of coordinates, that defines its location, and is referred to as a *complex number* (Figure 86). For instance, the location described by 1 on the horizontal axis and 2i on the vertical axis would be expressed as the complex number (1+2i). Another complex number is (-2-1i). These complex numbers (or coordinates) are symbolized by the letter *z*.

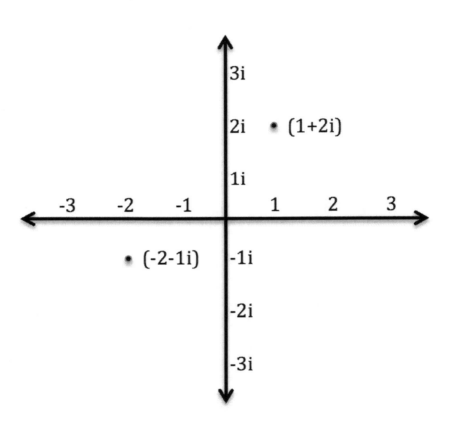

Figure 86. The Imaginary Plane with Complex Numbers

Now back to Mandelbrot's equation. Equation 4 takes a given complex number (z), or address on the imaginary plane, and multiplies it by itself, then adds the original complex number (symbolized by the letter *c*) to the result. This new complex number is again multiplied by itself, again adding the original complex number to the new result. This process is repeated many times. What Mandelbrot discovered is that any given complex number, or address on the imaginary plane, will do one of two things: either it will bounce around the imaginary plane, yet stay within a short distance of the origin (where the two coordinate lines cross each other), regardless of the number of iterations, or it will grow larger and larger, moving further and further away from the origin. Mandelbrot used computer graphics, which were very primitive at the time, to plot the results. Much to his surprise and delight the base Mandelbrot shape resulted (see the previous *Mandelbrot Set* illustration). As a note, all of the interior black regions of the Mandelbrot set are the set of coordinates that never escaped their proximity to the origin.[467] The coordinates outside this black region escaped their proximity to the origin.[468]

Disbelief

I had already come to understand and endorse self-referential and iterative processes, but this one threw me for a loop! Literally. I did not believe such an elaborate shape could possibly come from such a simple equation (Equation 4). There had to be some magic wand waving involved, or at least fancy graphic arts applied, to come up with such an elaborate geometrical design. In other words, *I could not believe what was outside my comfort zone and experience.*

Do you see the irony in this? There I was, working on a book that confronts disbelief in things that reside outside our comfort zones and/or realms of experience, rejecting the possibility that the Mandelbrot shape was so simply created!

Well, you guessed it: I had to prove it for myself. I sat down and wrote a simple computer program to test this simple equation. It just couldn't be true! The image that resulted from my program was very disappointing and disturbing (Figure 87). I thought to myself, "I knew it! Someone took this basic shape and dressed it up graphically to look more ornate and orderly than what that simple equation could

---

[467] During the repeated calculations the result did not get larger and larger, but stayed small and close to the origin.
[468] During the repeated calculations the result grew larger and larger, moving farther away from the origin.

produce!" When will we (I) ever learn? The most profound lesson that came out of this whole experience had not to do with Mandelbrot's equation, but with my profound arrogance and ignorance.

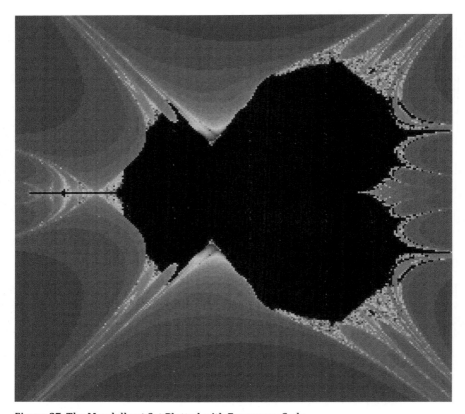

Figure 87. The Mandelbrot Set Plotted with Erroneous Code

As I sat staring at the *proof* that the article I had read was falsified, I began to marvel at the fact that my program rendered as much as it did, though the image was quite frightening! Could it be that I, *even I*, made a mistake? God forbid! Nevertheless, I went back into my program code and examined it. Lo and behold, I had mistakenly overwritten the original coordinates with each iterative step the code passed through. I fixed the problem, and my ignorant smirk left my face. It was true: the Mandelbrot set was real, simply real. What a lesson!

Surfing the Mandelbrot Set

With today's computer technology one can *surf* the Mandelbrot set very quickly and easily. By surfing I mean zooming in on given regions of the set, discovering greater and greater detail as one explores the fringe of the set. Given the capabilities of most computers, the Mandelbrot set image can be enlarged to approximately 1.5 times the size of our solar system, obviously with a very small portion of it on the computer monitor. Super computers can explore even more deeply.

Four thoughts have occurred to me from surfing the Mandelbrot set. First of all, the intricate detail of the set lies at the *fringes* of the set. The interior and the exterior are nondescript or void. Secondly, because the set can be expanded to at least 1.5 times our solar system, one can truly go where no one has gone before, exploring regions never before viewed by human eyes. Thirdly, numerous shapes appear within the set that strangely resemble common shapes present throughout the cosmos (one example is included below and many more in chapter 4.12). Lastly, regardless of how far into the set one zooms, images similar to the original base shape appear again and again and again. The Mandelbrot set is a fantastic example of a self-referential iterative process, yielding ever-increasing detail, with repeated self-similar representations of its primary shape.

In Closing

In 2009 an image of a whirlpool galaxy was broadcast back to earth from the Hubble spacecraft (Figure 88).

During one of my Mandelbrot set *surfing* sessions I discovered a region that was strikingly similar (Figure 89). The similarities between the two images caused me to ask several questions. What other patterns within the cosmos are modeled within the Mandelbrot set? Some theoreticians, including Benoit Mandelbrot himself, have discovered connections between the Mandelbrot set and economics, chaos theory, art, nature, theoretical physics, and more.

Figure 88. Whirlpool Galaxy from Hubble

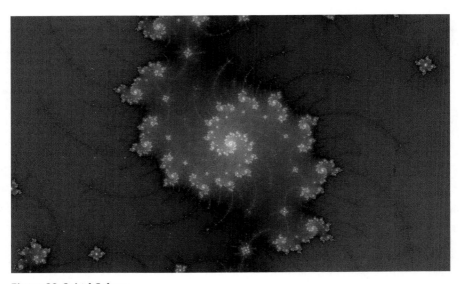

Figure 89. Spiral Galaxy

Several things stand out regarding the Mandelbrot set. First of all the base shape repeats itself throughout the entire set. Secondly, all regions of the set appear to be connected to the base shape. Thirdly, there is apparently no end to the detail.[469] Let us continue our exploration of these intriguing attributes and more!

---

[469] The Mandelbrot set is only one of numerous mathematical fractal models. There are, of course, many non-mathematical fractal models present throughout nature. The mathematical models are attempts to model the fractals in nature. We will focus primarily on the Mandelbrot set.

.

4.03

The Fractiverse

Are there other planets out there with life forms on them? First of all, I think it is quite arrogant of us to think we are *it*, the only such planet with life forms, in the only such galaxy, in the only such universe! Fractally, I believe there must be other such worlds. For those inclined to look into scripture (SR), there are innuendos of such worlds.[470] The fractal evidences that surround us (NT) seem to indicate that we are not alone. The fact that we humans have launched searches for life-sustaining planets and launched communicative objects into space is sufficient existential evidence (EU) that such life forms exist. Remember the *principle of conceptualization*: if we can conceive of or creatively envision anything, then it already exists in the past future and/or in the future past!

The world of fractals, especially the Mandelbrot set, screams, "Multiplicity!" From strings to planets to solar systems to galaxies, our universe is self-similar: it is fractal. Why would it stop with very small strings (surfing into the micro) or a very large universe (surfing outward into the macro)? While I acknowledge that the Mandelbrot set has a base set, outside of which no other fractal images exist on the imaginary plane, it is presumptuous for any of us to think that our universe is the base set! For all we know, we are a miniscule complex number on the set, seen only at a magnification of 10^{100} (that is a 1 with 100 zeros following it)!

From atoms to universes, the fractal nature of the cosmos tells us that we are not alone. Physicists have estimated that there are approximately 10^{100} atoms in our universe. This may also be the number of universes in our derivative dimensional domains. But wait, if we are but one of 10^{100} derivative universes in

---

[470] Matthew 18:12-14; Ephesians 4:8-10.

our integral domain, then there may be a total of 10^{200} universes all together. That is, at least within a miniscule sector of 8D!

This is no mere fanciful and imaginative wandering. In his book *The Fabric of the Cosmos*, physicist Brian Greene asserts that whatever conditions were necessary for a "spatial nugget" to inflate into our universe were most likely present for many other universes to also sprout. Others may still be sprouting.[471] There is a scientific consensus, even though it is next to impossible to prove, that only a narrow perspective believes that our universe is the only one of its kind in existence. Lee Smolin of Penn State University has suggested that, "every black hole is the seed for a new universe," each having their own big bang. However such events would be invisible to us, hidden by their black hole's event horizon.[472] I find great delight in such scientific wanderings!

The Fractiverse

Physicists have proposed that the cosmos may contain many universes. They refer to such a multitude of universes as the *multiverse*. The Mandelbrot set makes it easier to visualize such a multiverse. Even if our universe were as much as one one-hundredth of the size of the base, we would still be but a fraction of the entirety of such universes in the cosmos. But the word *multiverse* does not adequately communicate the branching and self-similarity of the fractal. I am more inclined to refer to a *fractiverse*. Building on the dimensional interconnectedness of integral and derivative universes, as developed in Phase 3, I offer the following illustration to symbolize such a fractiverse (Figure 90). Notice that the fractiverse is strange, dimensional, and fractal: the triune nature of the cosmos.

---

[471] Greene, *The Fabric of the Cosmos: Space, Time, and the Texture of Reality*, 320.
[472] *The Elegant Universe: Superstrings, Hidden Dimensions, and the Quest for the Ultimate Theory*, 369.

Figure 90. Fractiverse

Regardless of our order of magnitude on the fractal, all sub-universes in the fractiverse are connected to the base, or what I refer to as the 0th order. Our universe may be a 2nd order or a 100th order derivative, but is connected to the 0th order base nonetheless. In the following illustration we see numerous universes interconnected within the web of the fractiverse (Figure 91). This image, by the way, is from the Mandelbrot set. I love the way it serendipitously implies that sub-universes emanate from the light. Herein we can imagine the universes sharing extra dimensions, both supporting and being supported by adjacent universes.

Figure 91. Interwoven Universes

I do not believe in parallel universes as such. Such a designation implies separation or even isolation. I believe the fractiverse is intertwined and interdependent. Our invisible, or empty, dimensions are visible and quite full to both our integral and derivative universes, and vice versa. As we discussed in Phase 3, we are occasionally privileged to see into these dimensions, this fractiverse, sharing slices of the past future and the future past.

A Fractiverse Loop

We witnessed in Phase 2 the strangeness of our existence. The loop is a great illustration of this strangeness. But what if this strange loop is dimensional *and* repeated fractally throughout the cosmos? Furthermore, what if someone, while zooming in on the fractal, went so far as to end up back at the starting point? That would be the ultimate strange-dimensional-fractal (SDF) loop (Figure 92).

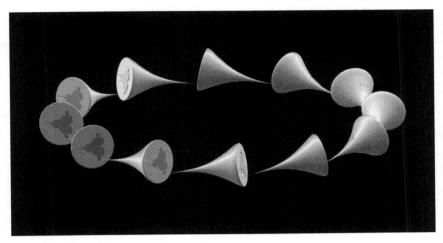

Figure 92. A Mandelbrot Loop Type I

The imaginative, artistic, and wandering side of me has to go further. What if our universe is in an SDF loop, one that intersects with other such loops to form a chain of fractiverses (Figure 93)? Where would such a chain exist? The existential artist in me imagines such a chain ornately hanging around the neck of the IICP. Selah!

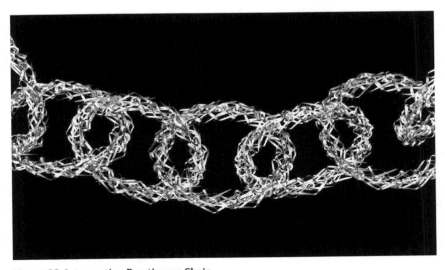

Figure 93. Intersecting Fractiverse Chain

As fun and inconsistent as such imaginative wanderings are, there are profound conclusions to be drawn from our fractal existence. First of all, the detail on the fringe is ever increasing and ever self-similar. Secondly, it is arrived at through, and only through, self-referential iterative processes, not unlike the self-description of the IICP.

> The I Am that…

Thirdly, the base shape repeats itself ad infinitum throughout the fractal. Fourthly, and as we will see in the next chapter, every part of the fractal is connected.

4.04

No Islands

From all appearances there seem to be islands on this planet of ours. Yet, even islands are grounded to the same bedrock as the continents. What is more, our earth, according to Albert Einstein is attached to the rest of the universe. He demonstrated through general relativity that mass, no matter how small or large, warps space-time. The entire universe feels the presence of even the smallest mass.

From the realms of quantum mechanics, to general relativity, to theology, it seems that all things are connected. Reggie McNeal says in his book *The Present Future: Six Tough Questions for the Church*, "The science of quantum physics also contributes to this new way of thinking. The quantum universe is not a universe of things but a universe of relationships . . . The quantum vision of the universe is more interested in the whole, in how things interrelate. Its fundamental unit is not even single, but plural."[473] Diarmuid O'Murchu concurs in *Quantum Theology: Spiritual Implications of the New Physics*, "In the quantum worldview, nothing makes sense in isolation; basically, there are no boundaries, and influences can emerge from several sources, many probably unknown to the human mind at this stage of our species evolution."[474] There are no islands.

Local Connectivity on the Mandelbrot Set

It has been conjectured that all points on the Mandelbrot set are connected. It certainly appears to be the case, as one surfs the Mandelbrot set. But is it true

---

[473] Reggie McNeal, *The Present Future: Six Tough Questions for the Church* (San Francisco: Jossey-Bass, 2003), 57.
[474] O'Murchu, *Quantum Theology: Spiritual Implications of the New Physics*, 32.

mathematically? In one online article we read, "The celebrated work of Jean-Christophe Yoccoz established local connectivity of the Mandelbrot set at all finitely–renormalizable parameters; that is, roughly speaking those which are contained only in finitely many small Mandelbrot copies. Since then, local connectivity has been proved at many other points of M (the Mandelbrot set), but the full conjecture is still open."[475], [476] It seems quite unlikely that anyone will prove otherwise.

Universal Connectivity

I believe the entire universe is fractal. What is more, I believe every point in the universe is connected, not only internally to itself, but also externally to every other universe in the fractiverse. There is no isolation in the fractal. When I refer to *the fractal*, I do indeed imply but one fractal. Everything, including all life forms, all planets, all galaxies, and all universes, is connected to the fractal. Even space and time, the very fabric of the cosmos, are thus connected.

John Donne (1572-1631) once wrote,

> All mankind is of one author, and is one volume; when one man dies, one chapter is not torn out of the book, but translated into a better language; and every chapter must be so translated . . . As therefore the bell that rings to a sermon, calls not upon the preacher only, but upon the congregation to come: so this bell calls us all: but how much more me, and who am brought so near the door by this sickness . . . No man is an island, entire of itself . . . any man's death diminishes me, because I am involved in mankind; and therefore never send to know for whom the bell tolls; it tolls for thee.[477]

---

[475] Wikipedia, "Local Connectivity and Mandelbrot," http://en.wikipedia.org/wiki/Mandelbrot_set.
[476] There are indeed many scholarly papers on this topic, most of which go over my head mathematically. However, if you are interested in them simply search for "local connectivity" and "Mandelbrot" on the web.
[477] John Donne, *Devotions Upon Emergent Occasions* (1624), Meditation 17.

This innate awareness of the interdependency of all things is clearly demonstrated in the fractal. None of us can do anything that is not felt by the fractal. Furthermore, none of us can become anything without the fractal. I find tremendous humor in listening to those who claim to be self-made individuals, whether entrepreneurs or isolationists. Show me a millionaire whose wealth did not come from someone else and/or ultimately the earth. Ironically, there would be no millionaires if it were not for the non-millionaires. Even a politician who claims to have climbed to the top on their own ignores those whom they climbed over to get there. No, we are all a part of the fractal. We are connected.

We Need Each Other

When I read the news, I weep at the brokenness so prevalent in the fractal. The news seems to be all about *us* against *them*, our economy versus theirs, our dominance and their subservience, our rights juxtaposed to theirs. There is great irony in such stances, for they are rooted in the belief that we are detached from the fractal. Perhaps, in a sickening sense, we are. The world is, after all, broken.

An individual or group who thinks of their existence as distinctly unique and separate from the rest of the world does not grasp the fractal nature of the universe, let alone the nature of God. Some may come close to functioning as separate and sustainable entities, but still breathe the same air, drink the same water, spin on the same planet, and warp the same space-time. In the following illustration we see a small piece of the Mandelbrot set that appears to exist in isolation, yet it too is attached to the rest of the fractal, even if by miniscule hairs (Figure 94).

We need each other. We need community. Community needs a global village. Nations need nations. Salvation, whether spiritual or political, is fruitless in isolation. Even in a spiritual sense scripture makes it clear that salvation is not just about individuals; it is about larger bodies of people, about humanity, about all of creation. The Apostle Paul wrote, "We know that the whole creation has been groaning as in the pains of childbirth right up to the present time. Not only so, but we ourselves, who have the firstfruits of the Spirit, groan inwardly as we wait

eagerly for our adoption to sonship, the redemption of our bodies."[478] Even our
bodies need salvation.

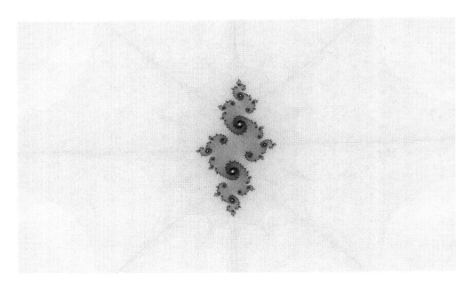

Figure 94. Alone But Attached

One of the problems we deal with today is that religious peoples have come to
believe that only *people* need salvation, all the while exploiting the rest of creation
to meet selfish whims. Creation needs salvation and healing from the damage that
saved people have wrought. We, including all of creation, need salvation and each
other. Creation, too, is an *image bearer of God*.

A Dysfunctional Fractal

Being self-serving runs against the grain of the universe. It runs against the
grain of the fractal. Yet even the dysfunctional parts of the fractal are still parts of
the fractal. We all feel the effects. We all feel the pain. We all suffer. And yes, when
possible, we all rejoice together as well. Though many of us will die without seeing

---

[478] Romans 8:22-23.

complete fractal resolution, still we see it from afar, in the past future. As such, we live in hope.[479]

Remember the strange nature of ignorance: you never know when you have it. Fractally, we cannot identify and heal our ignorance without community. We need others to speak into our lives, to diagnose our ignorance. Strangely, this dysfunctional ignorance is both a result of the broken fractal and a contributor to the brokenness of the fractal. Perhaps we need to move beyond our isolated perspectives to permit the fractal to be a part of healing the fractal.

Ubuntu

Anthropologists have observed that various cultures around the world are keenly aware of the connectedness between all things. Diarmuid O'Murchu reports in *Quantum Theology*, "In prehistoric societies, and in many parts of today's world (especially Africa, Latin America, and Asia), the individual's value and worth are esteemed relative to the person's role within, and contribution to, the common good, vividly expressed in the Bantu proverb *ubuntu umuntu ngabantu*, meaning: 'I am because we are.'"[480] Parker J. Palmer says in his book *Let Your Life Speak*, "Inner work can be helped along in community. Indeed, doing inner work together is a vital counterpoint to doing it alone. Left to our own devices, we may delude ourselves in ways that others can help us correct."[481] Furthermore, Desmond Tutu exclaims in *No Future without Forgiveness*, "We are individually only what we are by our connectedness to the whole of humanity. This is ubuntu."[482] Ubuntu!

In a sense, ubuntu is a rephrasing of the Golden Rule: As you do to others, you do to yourself. To be a flourishing global community we must live knowing we are part of the fractal. As John B. Cobb said regarding process theology, "Although the community is constitutive of personal being, it is equally true that personal being is constitutive of community. People are neither isolated individuals nor mere

---

[479] Though it is beyond the scope of this book to develop, scripture is full of eschatological promises, visions of ultimate resolution. Search and you will find.
[480] O'Murchu, *Quantum Theology: Spiritual Implications of the New Physics*, 91.
[481] Palmer, *Let Your Life Speak*, 92.
[482] Desmond Tutu, *No Future without Forgiveness* (New York: Doubleday, 1997), 31.

parts of a greater whole. They are persons-in-community." [483] The two are inseparable.

David Augsburger says in *Dissident Discipleship*, "But in the Christian scriptures, the highest word, the most virtuous form of love, is not agape, but koinonia, the mutual, reciprocal, committed, and celebrative love of intimate relationship, authentic community, and responsive fellowship."[484] Community is a higher level of love than individual love. Strangely, community is the goal and the means to the goal. Parker J. Palmer says, "Community doesn't just create abundance— community is abundance."[485] Community, or *koinonia*, is indeed fractal at every possible level.

A Tribute to Paul

We all warp the space around us. We affect change. My brother-in-law, Paul, who now knows in full what I only hope to know in part, brought about positive fractal change. During his life he gave us many words of wisdom. On one occasion, having pondered the significant influence my wife had on his son, and the wonderful influence he had on my daughter, Paul said with deep gratitude, "It takes a family to raise a family." It doesn't get more profound than that. We are connected: we are the fractal. Thank you, Paul.

---

[483] John B. Cobb, *Process Theology*, www.religion-online.org.
[484] Augsburger, *Dissident Discipleship: A Spirituality of Self-Surrender, Love of God, and Love of Neighbor*, 69.
[485] Palmer, *Let Your Life Speak*, 108.

4.05

Progressive Resolution

If one looks back over history, studying the diverse discoveries humans have made, it becomes clear that all such advancements involved process. None of our knowledge or technology came to us all at once. It came progressively through process. This is part and parcel of the fractal nature of the cosmos: it is a domain built on progressive resolution.[486] To understand this more fully, we need to review Mandelbrot's equation,

$$(\text{Equation 5}) \qquad z_{n+1} = z_n^2 + c$$

If you recall, in Mandelbrot's set z is an address on the imaginary plane that is squared (multiplied by itself) then added to the original address. But of course creating the Mandelbrot image was not as simple as performing this calculation once and stopping there. The sequence had to be repeated numerous times to see whether the address would forever stay near the origin or move farther and farther away with each iteration. In the Mandelbrot image, a color (or in the case of black and white images, a shade of grey) was assigned to each address based on its behavior. The addresses that stayed close were assigned the color black. All of the remaining addresses (the ones that moved away) were assigned various shades of grey depending on how quickly they moved away. The result brought the Mandelbrot set image to life.

But how many iterations are necessary to create the Mandelbrot image? Well, it depends on two things: the width of view (how far one wants to zoom into or out

---

[486] In some respects, it may also be called progressive revelation.

of the fractal) and the degree of resolution one desires to achieve. If one wants to view the overall Mandelbrot image, then, as you can see in the following illustration, anywhere from 1 to 100 iterations will suffice, depending on how much resolution you wish to achieve at the fringes (Figure 95). Obviously, 1 iteration (the top left image) yielded no resolution at all. But as we progress to 10 iterations (top right image) a silhouette begins to appear. Gradually, as we move through 20, 30, 50, and eventually 100 iterations, more and more definition forms. There is little enough change from 50 to 100 iterations for me to conclude that 100 iterations are sufficient to develop an adequate view of the overall image.

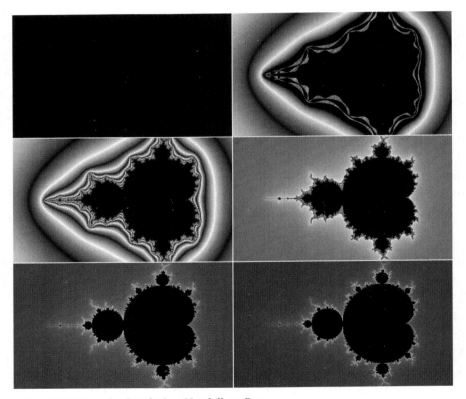

Figure 95. Progressive Resolution: Mandelbrot Base

In mathematical terms, some of the addresses in the less refined images did not experience enough iterations to escape the bounds of the Mandelbrot set. Hence they were included in the black region.

Let us now zoom into the Mandelbrot set, into the first deep valley just left of center, zooming to the point of making the original image 7,000,000 times larger. As you can see in the following illustration, a similar pattern emerges, but not with a mere 100 iterations (Figure 96). (I am not sure why, but this landscape reminded me of *The Lord of the Rings*, so I named it thus.) The first image (top left) resulted after 500 iterations. Obviously 500 iterations gave us nothing. The rest of the images resulted from 1,000, 1,500, 2,000, 10,000, and 50,000 iterations. It is clear to me, looking carefully at the last image, that no less than 50,000 iterations will suffice to adequately view this miniscule landscape on the Mandelbrot set. By the way, it takes 50,000 iterations for every pixel in the image!

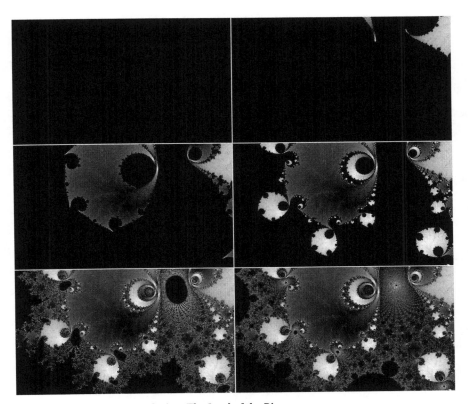

Figure 96. Progressive Resolution: The Lord of the Rings

If one wants to go deeper into the fractal, many more iterations are required for clarity and detail. Obviously it is a function of how deep one wants to go and how much resolution is sufficient to be content with the view at hand.

Cosmic Resolution

I hope you see the significance without saying much more. I am spellbound, dumbfounded, discombobulated, overwhelmed, shocked, appalled, disgusted, along with a few other expletives, to think that I spent 50 years of my life believing that I had iterated enough times to understand God and the cosmos clearly. And, assuming you have bought into the fractal nature of the cosmos thus far, I hope you are just as appalled as I am at other sub-fractal entities, such as nations, communities, political groups, religions, denominations, etc., for assuming the same. We will be nowhere near the level of resolution we could be, and need to be, if we permit ourselves to slide into Satisfaction Gorge.

We are nowhere close enough to an adequate resolution to be pointing crooked little fingers at each other's beliefs. Even if we include multiple generations, numerous reformations, academic advances, and personal enlightenments, we are still nowhere close to a resolution that permits us to "prate about an elephant" none of us has seen.[487]

Progressive Theology

So does this mean we know little to nothing? No. But it does mean that we must be cognizant that what we hold dear is only the result of a finite number of iterations. Real theology is not static, but undergoes continuous refinement. You know by now that I do not believe in *process theology*, wherein God progresses or evolves, for God is infinite. However, I do believe in the progression of humankind, wherein we progress in our understanding of God. This can only happen, though, as we continue to iterate.

---

[487] John Godfrey Saxe, "The Blind Men and the Elephant," http://www.wordfocus.com/word-act-blindmen.html.

It is one thing to think we have arrived at a defined edge of the fractal (complete theology), another to know that we have not, but believe we cannot go on (agnostic theology), yet another to purpose to keep moving on, continuously seeking refinement at deeper and deeper levels of the fractal (progressive theology). Perhaps the latter would be more appropriately called *fractal theology*. We must continuously process, be ever about refining, refocusing, and increasing the depth of our understanding. Hence the need to progressively iterate between SR, NT, and EU!

Fuzzy Boundaries

If we, as I developed in Phase 2, have no characteristics that the IICP does not have, then God, too, is fractal. God, however, *is* infinite iterations. One quality of an infinitely iterated fractal is infinite detail. This is a reflection of infinite intricacy (the third type of infinity). It is also an admission that none of us will ever get close to an absolute resolution on God.

Rob Bell says in his book *Velvet Elvis*, "Truth always leads to more . . . truth. Because truth is insight into God and God is infinite and God has no boundaries or edges. So truth always has layers and depth and texture."[488] What a profound understanding of the fractal nature of God and the cosmos! Because the edge of the fractal is ever increasing in detail, it is *fuzzy*. Regardless of the depth of our zoom, fuzziness prevails. Sure, some of our previous fuzzy knowledge refined into deeper and deeper fuzziness as it was iterated, but it is fuzziness nonetheless.

One source of the fuzziness comes from the fractal nature of language. Language is fractal. Each word in a sentence is in a sense redefined by the string of words surrounding it. Each word in this string is redefined by another substring, and the fractal pattern continues (Figure 97).[489] There is no clean, precise edge to language. Just as in Gödel's theorem, extension and precision in language are mutually exclusive. We cannot have both consistency and completeness. This is also the case with the iterations of sacred writings.

---

[488] Rob Bell, *Velvet Elvis: Repainting the Christian Faith* (Grand Rapids: Zondervan, 2005), 33.
[489] This illustration is intended to be more artistic than realistic, since the text is so small. The primary point is that each word has a definition that contains words that have definitions, that contain words that have definitions, and so on, and so on.

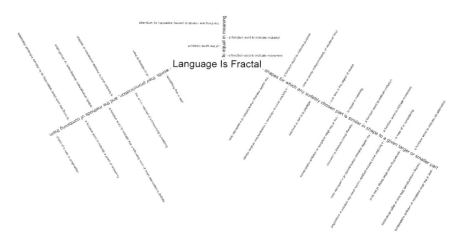

Figure 97. Language Is Fractal

These fuzzy boundaries are not curses; they are blessings. They are the nature of God. Such fuzziness facilitates diversity, intricacy, and beauty. Vern Poythress says in his book *Symphonic Theology*, "The existence of such fuzzy boundaries also means that we must be willing to admit that other people can, if they wish, draw the boundary at a different point."[490] This book is one such drawing of fuzzy boundaries, which will, with more and more iterations, be redrawn again and again. Only as we draw, redraw, and continue to redraw, seeking higher and higher resolution, will we travel deeper into the fuzzy boundaries.

Have you ever stood on a beach and wondered if the tide was coming in or going out? Watching only the fuzzy boundaries can be misleading. You may observe numerous waves in succession that come farther and farther up the beach, yet the tide is going out. The overall movement may be outward bound. The boundaries, however, may be fuzzy or contradictory. The overall resolution may not even happen in *my time frame*. I may die being totally convinced that the tide is coming in, yet it is not. Will life on earth go on forever? Fuzzy boundaries. Is climate change real? Fuzzy boundaries. Is the GBF coming back? Fuzzy boundaries.

---

[490] Poythress, *Symphonic Theology*, 65.

Is this book true? I would like to think this iteration is at least headed in the direction of the tide. Yet, this iteration too is subject to fuzzy boundaries.

All this is not to say that boundaries do not exist. They do indeed. The point is, however, that our perceptions of the boundaries are functions of the depths to which we are willing to go to bring about resolutions that are functionally satisfactory for our current wanderings.

Recursive Processing

Our existence is full of cycles. From seconds, to minutes, to hours, to days, to years, and on to lifetimes and eras; from orbiting planets to electrons; from the growth of cells, to organs, systems, and life forms: cycles prevail recursively. Cycles exist within cycles within cycles. Small steps add up to larger steps that add up to even larger steps. Every process, whether biological, industrial, literary, philosophical, or theological is a result of recursive processing. Each recursive process is important.

Each cyclical iteration we work through in life is comprised of sub-cyclical iterations, each of which is also comprised of sub-sub-cyclical iterations. On and on it goes (Figure 98).

No cycle we are a part of is too large or too small. None is too significant. None is insignificant. Fractally, each and every iterative process is crucial to the wellbeing of the fractal. Whether I apply a specific nut to a given bolt in an assembly line or write a line of code in a module for a software product or give aid to one single person in need, each and every recursive action is crucial to the sustenance of the fractal.[491] There are no unimportant sectors on the fractal. Nothing is too small to matter to God or to the rest of the cosmos. This is the way of the fractal.

---

[491] As is the case with our broken world, there are also broken fractal processes that perpetuate the brokenness.

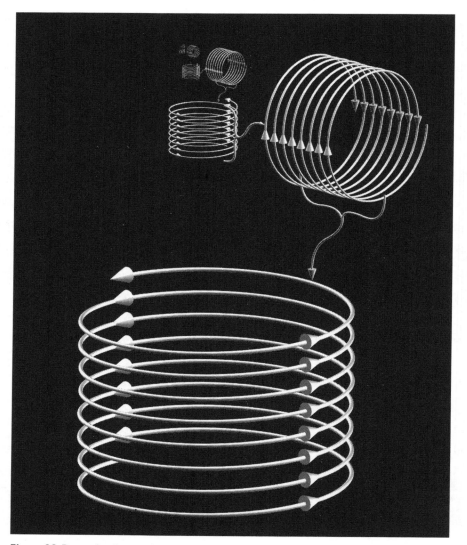

Figure 98. Recursive Processing

Be Perfect as I Am Perfect

When does one arrive at the edge of the fractal? Never. Mathematically, using limits equations, one discovers that the fractal has an infinite edge. The process is forever. There is infinite detail and zero resolution. There are no endpoints. Elmer Jantzi, a favorite professor of mine at Rosedale Bible College, once said, "The deeper one looks into man's creations, the more disorder one finds. The deeper one looks into God's creations, the more order one finds." While you definitely do not want to examine my creations too closely (including this book) for risk of running into imperfections and error, you only stand to observe infinitely more intricate detail in examining God's creations. So it is with the fractal.

Strangely, in scripture God is quoted as saying, "Be holy, because I am holy."[492] One text, quoting Jesus, uses *perfect* in place of holy.[493] How can finite beings such as we ever achieve perfection or holiness? Perhaps God was simply saying, "Live in me." However, this scripture may be a direct outcome of the fractal nature of God and the cosmos. To paraphrase this text in fractal terms, "Iterate because I iterate." God is the infinite iterator. We must seek more detail because God is the detail.

I leave you with a fractal quote by G.K. Chesterton from his book *Orthodoxy*,

> The real trouble with this world of ours is not that it is an unreasonable world, nor even that it is a reasonable one. The commonest kind of trouble is that it is nearly reasonable, but not quite. Life is not an illogicality; yet it is a trap for logicians. It looks just a little more mathematical and regular than it is; its exactitude is obvious, but its inexactitude is hidden; its wildness lies in wait.[494]

Lies in wait of what? Progressive resolution.

---

[492] Leviticus 11:44-45; 1 Peter 1:16.
[493] Matthew 5:48.
[494] Chesterton, *Orthodoxy*, 117.

.

4.06

Fractal Theology

We have already inadvertently touched on some theological issues that are impacted by *the fractal* and its principles. Here we will look more specifically at a number of issues that are directly, and I believe significantly, illuminated by such principles. A few issues are important enough that I will dedicate several chapters to them.

Transformation

An amazing passage of scripture is found in the letter written by the Apostle Paul to the church at Rome. Paul said,

> But the gift is not like the trespass. For if the many died by the trespass of the one man, how much more did God's grace and the gift that came by the grace of the one man, Jesus Christ, overflow to the many! Nor can the gift of God be compared with the result of one man's sin: The judgment followed one sin and brought condemnation, but the gift followed many trespasses and brought justification. For if, by the trespass of the one man, death reigned through that one man, how much more will those who receive God's abundant provision of grace and of the gift of righteousness reign in life through the one man, Jesus Christ![495]

---

[495] Romans 5:15-17.

In today's terminology Paul is describing the *trickle-down* effect of the fractal. Whether everyone on this planet chose to be a part of the Great Rebellion or not, all were impacted by the choices of those who rebelled. Everyone was impacted by the thermodynamic shift toward entropy. Everyone was impacted by the decision to *go it alone. Everyone* experienced the lockout. And not only those present at the Great Rebellion, but also those who would walk the face of this planet after the rebellion.

Likewise, the gift of the GBF and the opened portal is fractally available for all people and for all time. God extended his fractal arm into our domain to open a portal to a restored state, one not with blurred edges, but with infinite intricacy for us to surf forever and ever. Sharing this gift meant subjecting himself to another fractal principle: becoming less to become more.

Karl Menger, who, interestingly, was the son of Carl Menger (the economist whom I quoted in Phase 2 on the topic of cause and effect) was a mathematical theorist. One of his developments was the *Menger sponge*, a fractal curve or shape that illustrates the principle at hand (Figure 99).

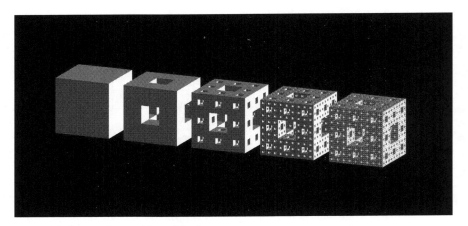

Figure 99. Menger Sponge Fractal Series

This fractal image results from punching three center cuboid portions out of the overall cube, from face to face, through the entirety of the cube. Following this first iteration, or first order sponge, the process is repeated for each of the 20 sub-cubes that resulted from the first iteration. This second order sponge has 400 sub-sub-cubes. For our purposes, the process was repeated through the fourth order, resulting in 160,000 sub-sub-sub-sub cubes (Figure 100). Notice, however, that the *sub-cube* description is a bit misleading since this fractal is truly one continuous shape with one volume and one surface area.

Figure 100. Menger Sponge Fractal: Four Iterations

Using the calculus terminology that I employed in Phase 2, what would happen if we were to take this process *to the limit* with an infinite number of iterations? The result would be a single shape, or fractal, with zero volume and infinite surface area. We probably could not see such an entity. It would be so empty as to be invisible.

Dr. Duk Lee, a professor of mathematics at Asbury University, said in an issue of *Ambassador Magazine*, "Fractal geometry demonstrates that infinity and emptiness are not far from each other."[496] Because all matter in the universe is reducibly complex (can be continuously broken down into smaller and smaller components), it too has a volume of zero and an infinite surface area. Here again, we see infinity and nothingness nested side by side, thereby accounting for all that exists in the cosmos.

The GBF was remarkably similar. He became nothing to open the portal: an infinite task. Our transformation is to be no less: we are called to die inwardly so that we may live outwardly; to die to self and this broken world to live in and for a restored fractal.

Who is this transformation for? Is it for individuals alone? No, fractal principles say otherwise. The expression of transformation is also fractal: it is for families, communities, nations, global villages, and so on. It is for the entire fractal: all creation waits eagerly for the restoration of the fractal.[497]

The Tree of Life

A tree is a beautiful example of the fractal. Its trunk branches progressively into smaller and smaller entities, culminating at the source of its life: leaves. The *Tree of Life*, as referenced in the Genesis and Revelation accounts, symbolizes fractal life. Before the fractal blur, this tree was available to us, offering a myriad of possibilities for us to live into. There was latitude on this tree, latitude to move about its branches (surf, if you will), exploring the vastness and intricacy of our domain. There were global villages, nations, communities, families, and individuals, free to associate, care, and love, bearing fruit continuously.

I often hear people expressing their worries about whether they are in or out of God's will concerning the minutia of life. Such worries are nonsensical on the Tree of Life. Any branch we are on *is* the will of God, for it is God's Tree. And even though we lost unlimited access to it, transformation brings us home to live on the

---

[496] Duk Lee, "In Pursuit of a Formula for Beauty," *Ambassador Magazine* 2012.
[497] Romans 8:18-25.

Tree once again. We do not yet freely roam its intricacy, but by squinting through the haze, we know we will one day surf again.

God Is the Base

One very peculiar attribute of the Mandelbrot set is that there is one base. We can zoom out further and further, only to end up in nothingness. There is but one base, or 0th order to the fractal. I do not know on what order of the fractal we reside. We could be at the 100th order for all I know. Regardless of our order, there is but one base.

Yet, small versions of the base's shape are repeated ad infinitum throughout the fractal. Who are they? The answer is simple: *we* are the smaller versions scattered throughout the fractal. We are the ones who were created in God's image. We will come back to this idea more fully later. For now let it suffice to say that this is why God looks out for the wellbeing of each one of us. God, the fractal base, looks out for each and every infinitely detailed part of the fractal *and* the whole fractal.

Evil

The origin and nature of evil are also fractal. In fractal terms, evil comes from assuming a *base* posture, rather than a *component* posture. When we exalt ourselves to anything other than components of the fractal, we take on the role of evil. Evil also results from assuming a posture that is *any* order of magnitude higher than the one we are in. Brokenness results from assuming a posture lower than the one we are in. Rightness, on the other hand, is found in knowing our order of magnitude, accepting it, and working with the base to fulfill our purpose.[498]

If there is a base to God's fractal, is there also an evil base? Many do not believe in an ultimate evil persona. The scriptural stories of Lucifer, or Satan, a beautiful angel who was the first to assume a base posture, are categorized as myths. The fractal, however, boldly says otherwise. Not only is mythology rooted in truth, but

---

[498] Romans 12:3.

the fractal nature of the cosmos itself implies there is an evil base. Mathematically, it is not an infinite base, but one that blindly pretends to be so.

Sadly, this evil base propagates its evil through broken fractal means. For instance, those who hate others are taught to hate by the ultimate hate. Never forget, the one who teaches you to love does so by loving you. The fractal implications on evil and hatred are staggering: the one who teaches you to hate also hates you. Those who worship evil, worship what hates them. This may be the ultimate fractal deception! Evil seeks to destroy the fractal.

Sin

Sin, too, is fractal. However, recalling the discussion on the nature of sin from earlier Phases, sin is rooted in our efforts to bring about restoration of the fractal *on our terms*. This can be done at many levels, from personal levels all the way up to national levels. Fractally, regardless of the level of sin, one attribute of sin plagues us all: its effects propagate fractally.

A very peculiar passage of scripture is found in the Old Testament. Therein God said to Israel, "Keeping mercy for thousands, forgiving iniquity and transgression and sin, and that will by no means clear the guilty; visiting the iniquity of the fathers upon the children, and upon the children's children, unto the third and to the fourth generation." [499] I believe this passage is *descriptive* rather than *prescriptive*. God was giving the people a heads-up warning of the trickle-down fractal nature of sin. It takes generations and generations to get away from the ramifications of any sin. Sin trickles down the fractal, wreaking havoc on the innocent in its way. Thankfully, the story does not end on that note.

Love

Thankfully, love too is fractal. But, it is more than that. It resides much closer to the base than all other fractal principles. In fact, it *is* the base. [500] In scripture we find Jesus discussing the Law with the Pharisees and Sadducees:

---

[499] Exodus 34:7 KJV.
[500] 1 John 4:8.

One of them, an expert in the law, tested him (Jesus) with this question: "Teacher, which is the greatest commandment in the Law?" Jesus replied: "Love the Lord your God with all your heart and with all your soul and with all your mind. This is the first and greatest commandment. And the second is like it: Love your neighbor as yourself. All the Law and the Prophets hang on these two commandments."[501]

Jesus was declaring that love *is* the trunk of the fractal. All other commandments are derivatives, or branches, of love. *If any of us keeps all of the derivative commandments but has not love, we do live on God's fractal.*

These two greatest commandments are bi-directional. We are called to love God, the base, in one direction, and in the other direction to love our neighbors: all of the fractal. Of course, there were those around Jesus who questioned exactly who our neighbors are. Remember the map, or parable of the Good Samaritan, the one Jesus translated for the people, expanding the definition of neighbor? No one is outside the scope of the love with which we are called to love. And, yes, that includes cultures, religions, and nations. Love permeates the fractal, from the trunk to the tiniest twig. Jesus said, "They will know you are part of the fractal if you love one another."[502]

Prayer

When his disciples asked Jesus to teach them to pray, he said, "When you pray, say: 'Father, hallowed be your name, your kingdom come. Give us each day our daily bread. Forgive us our sins, for we also forgive everyone who sins against us. And lead us not into temptation.'"[503] Notice that he started with the base, moved on to the base's domain, then on to branches. Also, notice that forgiveness flows throughout the fractal.

---

[501] Matthew 22:34-40.
[502] SFA paraphrase of John 13:35.
[503] Luke 11:2-4.

We were once enemies of God. Yet, God loved us while we were still enemies.[504] So it must be with those around us on the fractal. This includes those who may still be enemies of God and/or of us. How else will they see the unselfish love of God? If we do not love them, our love is not fractal, nor do we love God. God calls us to love with his love, the base love, a love that permeates the whole tree. We, too, are branches in need of love. We are branches called to extend this love, *even to branches not yet transformed.*

Bearing Crosses

The Apostle Paul said, "And we boast in the hope of the glory of God. Not only so, but we also glory in our sufferings, because we know that suffering produces perseverance; perseverance, character; and character, hope." [505] Fractally, suffering that results from bearing crosses ultimately results in hope! It is strange, but it is so. Those who preach gospels of prosperity without sacrificial living miss the mark and miss out on the unique hope that such suffering nurtures. In the words of the Anabaptist theologian, John Howard Yoder,

> It is that people who bear crosses are working with the grain of the universe. One does not come to that belief by reducing social processes to mechanical and statistical models, nor by winning some of one's battles for the control of one's own corner of the fallen world. One comes to it by sharing in the life of those who sing about the Resurrection of the slain Lamb."[506]

To not walk the same path as the GBF, the path of suffering-become-hope, is to lose out on the fractal nature of his gift.[507]

---

[504] Romans 5:8.
[505] Romans 5:2b-4.
[506] Yoder in Hauerwas, *With the Grain of the Universe*, 6.
[507] Philippians 3:7-11.

Servanthood

To be served, we must serve. Jesus led by example: he served his disciples. He washed their feet. He fed them. He led them to the cross. He showed them the Way. Even he could not be served without serving.

Fractal Worth

I hope it is quite clear that God cares for every part of the fractal. Each of us is crucial to the purpose and life of the Tree. There are no useless or worthless sectors in the fractal. Each of us is infinitely important to God. We are part of something much, much bigger than ourselves.

Those whose lives have been transformed throughout all time (past, present and future) are referred to in scripture as the *body of God's right arm.*[508] If one were to zoom in on (surf, so to speak) God's arm, we would find the people of God. This model gives us purpose and identity: purpose to represent God fractally and identity because each of us resembles God. No wonder the *body* analogy is used throughout scripture. Fractally, we are a part of God's flesh. Are we a healthy resemblance? No. Are we any resemblance at all? By God's grace: yes.

Imaginary Theology

Let us, for a moment, go back to the Mandelbrot set. This fantastic set would not have become visible in such an elaborate, infinitely detailed, and exquisite display if it were not for numbers that are not defined, or, quite frankly, that do not exist. That's right: imaginary numbers (the square roots of a negative numbers) do not exist! Sure, we know how they behave, but we cannot calculate their values. They are imaginary.

What if we permitted our theology to form such infinitely intricate designs by using imaginary elements? Imaginary theology?

We know that predestination and freewill cannot both be correct. Such a combination is imaginary. We most certainly know that God is either One or Triune, but not both. Such a combination is imaginary. We know that God is either

---

[508] 1 Corinthians 12:27.

beyond the bounds of death or that he subjected himself to death to open a portal, but not both. Such a combination is imaginary.

But...

Imagine.

Just imagine.

.

4.07

Fractal Fulfillments

Textual criticism has caused some Biblical readers to doubt the accuracy and legitimacy of certain Biblical writers. One of my college professors hurled criticisms at Matthew because he *abusively proof-texted scripture to prove his points*. In other words, he found isolated verses that substantiated the proof at hand, even if these verses were *out of context*.

I believe *higher criticism* makes two gross and erroneous assumptions. First, that each and every text (particularly Old Testament texts) has one and only one context and application. Secondly, that we, the later and more educated critics, know better than those who walked and talked with Jesus. Jesus frequently used isolated scriptural texts to prove *his* points.

On one occasion, after Jesus' resurrection, he joined two disciples on the road to Emmaus, walking and talking with them about the recent events. He helped them understand everything that had taken place, by using scripture. "And beginning with Moses and all the Prophets, he explained to them what was said in all the Scriptures concerning himself."[509] He, no doubt, would have been accused of proof-texting his way through these scriptures. (Ironically he may have used the original intended meanings of such texts instead of the latest and greatest academic textual critiques!)

But how and why are there multiple fulfillments to any given prophecy? When a prophet, or seer, witnesses an entity (past, present, or future), it is a *shape on the fractal*. All shapes on the fractal will have similar repeated shapes throughout the

---

[509] Luke 24:27.

fractal, and at all levels. And though each repeated occurrence has unique variations to its shape and edges, the entity is repeated nonetheless.

Fractal Prophecies

In the book of Hosea the writer says, "When Israel was a child, I loved him, and out of Egypt I called my son. But the more they were called, the more they went away from me."[510] This is clearly a reference to the nation of Israel being called out of captivity in Egypt. Yet we find in the book of Matthew, "So he (Joseph) got up, took the child and his mother during the night and left for Egypt, where he stayed until the death of Herod. And so was fulfilled what the Lord had said through the prophet: 'Out of Egypt I called my son.'"[511] Matthew clearly quoted Hosea. Was he in error? Which is it: a reference to the nation of Israel or to Jesus? Strangely (and fractally) the answer is, "Yes."

Another example pertains to the Old Testament observance of the Year of Jubilee. If you recall, Jubilee was a celebratory year that was to be observed every 50 years, wherein all sins and debts were forgiven and land was returned to its tribal origin. Isaiah wrote about this year of Jubilee: "The Spirit of the Sovereign Lord is on me, because the Lord has anointed me to proclaim good news to the poor. He has sent me to bind up the brokenhearted, to proclaim freedom for the captives and release from darkness for the prisoners, to proclaim the year of the Lord's favor . . ."[512] This was an explicit reference to the year of Jubilee, or the *year of the Lord's favor*.

However, Luke records a very peculiar event in the life of Jesus, at the beginning of his ministry. One Sabbath Jesus went into the synagogue in Nazareth, asked for the scroll of Isaiah and read the previously quoted passage. When he sat down the eyes of everyone were fixed on him. Then he said, "Today this scripture is fulfilled in your hearing."[513] Jesus fractally ushered in yet another Jubilee: one that would reach beyond financial debt and land loss, to touch the poor, the blind, the imprisoned, and the oppressed. He *announced a fractal Jubilee.*

---

[510] Hosea 11:1-2a.
[511] Matthew 2:14-15.
[512] Isaiah 61:1-2a.
[513] Luke 4:21.

The Beast

One of my college professors taught us that *Satan*, or the *Beast*, is not a person but a symbol of *institutional evil*. Was he correct? He may be both right and wrong. Satan may be a human institution, as my professor espouses. His mistake, however, may be in not understanding the fractal nature of the universe. If there is an institutional *persona*, then there is also a real base persona, albeit a finite persona. The institutionalized Beast is very real, and perhaps more so than even my professor realizes. But it exists because the base persona gives rise or birth to smaller personas. And, yes, the institutionalized Beast is smaller than the base.

It does not stop there. Fractally, any time I deny God, I am a representation of the Beast. The New Testament writer John warned us of the fractal nature of this Beast, or the Antichrist when he wrote, "Dear children, this is the last hour; and as you have heard that the antichrist is coming, even now many antichrists have come."[514] There are and will be many.

The Coming of the Lord Draweth Nigh

On the front glass pane of the old grandfather clock I inherited from my father, who inherited it from his father, is a sticker that reads, "The Coming of the Lord Draweth Nigh." This text was imprinted over the image of an old steam locomotive train, implying that the Lord's return was imminent. It has been there for many years, for I remember looking up at it as a child. In spite of the fact that I gradually became skeptical of one grandiose return of the Lord (leaning instead toward a symbolic return via our individual deaths) still, I did not have the heart to remove the sticker: Grandpa put it there. However, given my growing understanding of the fractal nature of the cosmos, I now question my skepticism. Perhaps the coming of the Lord *is* drawing nigh.

---

[514] 1 John 2:18a.

4.08

Slices of Slices of God

What are the fractal implications of the *slices of God*? It is precisely because there are slices of God that there are also slices of slices of God. All creation is comprised of slices of slices of slices of God. Just as pieces of art contain the signature of the artist, so the signature of God permeates all creation. We are slices of slices of God by being image bearers.[515]

According to scripture, not only were we created in God's image, but we were also created to be *image bearers*. Scripture refers to the GBF as an *exact representation* of God.[516] We are fellow image bearers with the GBF.[517] We resemble the GBF, who is the right arm of the base. Even though this broken domain of ours distorts our images, or reflections of God, they reflect God nonetheless.

It is quite difficult, from where we stand on the fractal, to view the base. This is yet another beautiful outcome of the GBF: he provided a "window to divinity" and a "mirror of our humanity."[518] Through the GBF we can see both directions from our location on the fractal.

Since we are image bearers of God, do we comprise God? Do our slices add up to the slices that add up to God? Mathematically, no. There is a distinct difference between being an expression of God and being God. We are a part of God, but are not God. We do not comprise God, as some would have us believe, for the sum of the parts does not infinity make.

---

[515] John 15:5, 8.
[516] Hebrews 1:3.
[517] Romans 8:16-17.
[518] Augsburger, *Dissident Discipleship: A Spirituality of Self-Surrender, Love of God, and Love of Neighbor*, 203.

Part of God's Glory

As image bearers we participate in God's glory. The prophet Isaiah told us that the earth is full of God's glory.[519] All of creation *is* God's glory. *We* are God's glory. The Apostle Paul reaffirmed this concept when he said, "Do you not know that your bodies are temples of the Holy Spirit, who is in you, whom you have received from God? You are not your own; you were bought at a price. Therefore honor God with your bodies."[520] Just as God's glory filled the temple in the Old Testament, so our bodies are filled with God's glory now. We participate in the divine nature of God when we *live into his likeness.*

Live As He Lived

John, a New Testament writer, wrote,

> We know that we have come to know him if we keep his commands. Whoever says, "I know him," but does not do what he commands is a liar, and the truth is not in that person. But if anyone obeys his word, love for God is truly made complete in them. This is how we know we are in him: Whoever claims to live in him must live as Jesus did.[521]

This is how we *participate in the divine nature!*[522] We participate in it by following the GBF, by being imitators of God.

To follow the GBF we must live as he lived. The GBF claimed to be the light of the world.[523] He also asserted that we, too, are the light of the world.[524] David Augsburger says in his book *Dissident Discipleship*, "We are co-buried, co-united, co-crucified; we have co-died and now we co-live, co-inherit, and co-suffer as we are co-glorified and co-formed into the Son-of-God image to become sisters and

---

[519] Isaiah 6:3.
[520] 1 Corinthians 6:19-20.
[521] 1 John 2:3-6.
[522] 2 Peter 1:4.
[523] John 8:12.
[524] Matthew 5:14.

brothers with Christ."[525] Fractally, we are to shine as he shined, live as he lived, and yes, die as he died, thereby inheriting as he inherited.

This is why we are called to servanthood. Erwin Raphael McManus says in his book *An Unstoppable Force*, "There is something mystical about servanthood because God is a servant. When we serve others, we more fully reflect the image of God, and our hearts begin to resonate with the heart of God. We may never be more like God than when we're serving from a purely selfless motivation."[526] Well said.

Suffer As He Suffered

Looking back at Phase 3 and the analogy of God extending his right arm into our domain to open a restorative portal, we find another fractal implication. The arms of the arm of God were pierced. Those whose lives have been transformed by the arms of the arm of God are themselves arms: arms of the arms of the arm of God. As such, we, too, are subject to piercing and suffering.

Remember, God felt every bit of the pain and agony that the GBF felt. He, the base, was not exempt from piercing and suffering. It was, after all, his very arm that was pierced. Alfred North Whitehead wrote, "God, too, participates in the suffering of his creatures." He is "the fellow-sufferer who understands."[527] Strangely, it is not only that we must suffer as God suffered, but also that *God suffered precisely because we suffer*.

The Resurrection

The fractal model does not stop with suffering. The Apostle Paul wrote, "And if the Spirit of him who raised Jesus from the dead is living in you, he who raised Christ from the dead will also give life to your mortal bodies because of his Spirit who lives in you."[528] The implication is that just as Jesus was raised from the dead, so the transformed will be resurrected.

---

[525] Augsburger, *Dissident Discipleship: A Spirituality of Self-Surrender, Love of God, and Love of Neighbor*, 38.
[526] McManus, *An Unstoppable Force: Daring to Become the Church God Had in Mind*, 175-76.
[527] Whitehead in Cobb, *God and the World*, 97.
[528] Romans 8:11.

N.T. Wright expounds on the necessity of human resurrection, given the model set before us by Jesus. He proclaims that what God did for Jesus in his resurrection is a model of what he will do for the whole cosmos.[529] His resurrection was and is fractal! What is more, Wright affirms that not only does Jesus' resurrection model our future, but it is also the means by which it will be possible.[530]

Resurrection is indeed fractal. It is and will be the start of a new order, a new world. Jesus's resurrection is the "prototype of what God is now going to accomplish in the rest of the world."[531] The transformed are a part of this new order, this restored fractal slice of the base fractal. We are slices of slices of God.

---

[529] Wright, *Surprised by Hope: Rethinking Heaven, the Resurrection, and the Mission of the Church*, 91.
[530] Ibid., 149.
[531] Ibid., 238.

4.09

Conduit

We have all encountered versions of Christianity, or religion in general, that focus on individual salvation. You know the type: it is all about me. It is all about my forgiveness, my transformation, my destiny, and my eternal reward. It is all about my ticket to heaven rather than damnation to Hell. It is a theology of buckets. These buckets accumulate forgiveness, grace, blessings, honor, and love. They store up and hold tightly to the treasures of heaven *that I have been given*.

I do not know how else to say it, my friend, but there are no buckets on the fractal. You will not find them on the Mandelbrot set. You will not find them in scripture. You will not find them in the cosmos. They do not exist. Surfing any fractal does not lead to endpoints with a storehouse of goods. Rather, surfing leads to more detail that leads to more detail that leads to . . .

There are no buckets on the fractal; there is only conduit. Scripture tells us (as did Benoit Mandelbrot!) that being a part of the fractal means propagating the fractal. Jesus said, "I am the vine; you are the branches. If you remain in me and I in you, you will bear much fruit . . ."[532] What comes before us must come after us. It must pass through us! We must be conduit to be alive on the fractal. Let me put it more bluntly: *we cannot receive anything that does not flow through us to the rest of the fractal.*

Various analogies in scripture substantiate this principle. The tree analogy is perhaps the best. Branches will not survive if they do not receive sap from the trunk. But unless the sap also flows through the branches to the rest of the tree, not only will the tree fail to produce fruit, but that branch, too, will die. No wonder

---

[532] John 15:5.

Jesus talked about cutting off branches that do not bear fruit, or should I say, that do not let the sap flow.

Jesus said, "From everyone who has been given much, much will be demanded; and from the one who has been entrusted with much, much more will be asked."[533] In other words, "A large sap flow *in* must equal a large sap flow *out.*"

Let me word it more concisely and bluntly. To be forgiven, we must forgive. We can receive forgiveness *only* as it flows through us to those around us. There are no forgiveness-accumulating buckets.

To receive grace, it must flow through us to others. We can receive grace *only* as it flows through us. There are no grace-accumulating buckets.

If we judge others, we will receive the same *sap.* We will receive judgment as it flows through us. There are no buckets before us to stop the flow on to us.

There are no buckets on the fractal: only conduit.

Dynamic Forgiveness

As such, forgiveness is not static. It cannot be held. It is like a dynamic current. Either we are a part of the forgiveness fractal or we are not (Figure 101). David Augsburger says in Dissident Discipleship, "The prayer our Lord prayed from the cross[534] confirms that he lived as though—as well as taught that—forgiving and being forgiven are inextricably interwoven."[535] This applies to the whole fractal!

Nations will be forgiven only as they forgive other nations. Religions will be forgiven only as they forgive other religions. Races will be forgiven only as they forgive other races. Remember the Lord's Prayer: "And forgive us our debts, as we also have forgiven our debtors."[536] It happens simultaneously. If only the citizens of the world would endorse such forgiveness.

---

[533] Luke 12:48.
[534] Luke 23:34,
[535] Augsburger, *Dissident Discipleship: A Spirituality of Self-Surrender, Love of God, and Love of Neighbor,* 18.
[536] Matthew 6:12.

Figure 101. Fractal Forgiveness

Jesus' Words vs. the Fractal

I hope it has become perfectly clear by now: *I do not believe in the fractal because of Jesus's words. I believe in Jesus's words because of the fractal.* His words are entirely consistent with the strange, dimensional, and fractal cosmos we find ourselves in. These words are, after all, the very strings that brought this fractal cosmos into existence. Let these words flow through you. You are the conduit, for you are part of the fractal.[537]

---

[537] John 15:5.

4.10

Surfing the Mandelbrot Set

I considered including these illustrations in an appendix, but decided instead to place them here as an intermission in the text. They reveal many common, everyday images that are imbedded in the Mandelbrot set. They also speak to the enjoyable nature of surfing the fractal. I had as much fun naming them as discovering them. Enjoy!

Black Mandel on Lace

Figure 102. Black Mandel on Lace

Cell Division

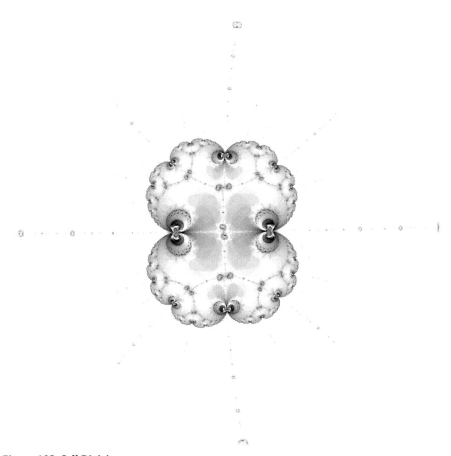

Figure 103. Cell Division

Double Conch

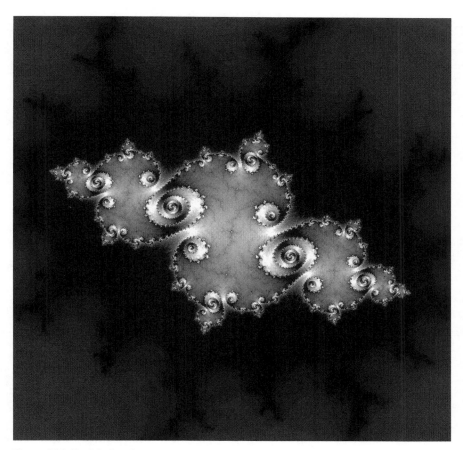

Figure 104. Double Conch

Double Inner Sanctuary

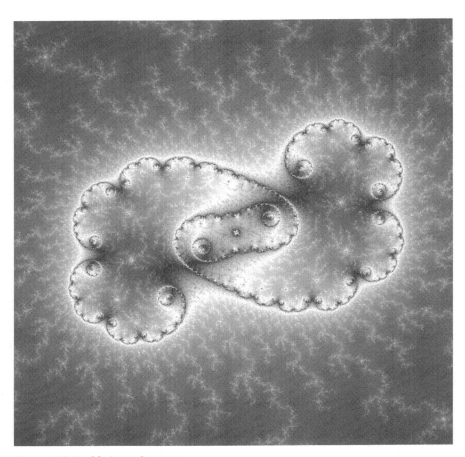

Figure 105. Double Inner Sanctuary

Double Spiral with Center Piece

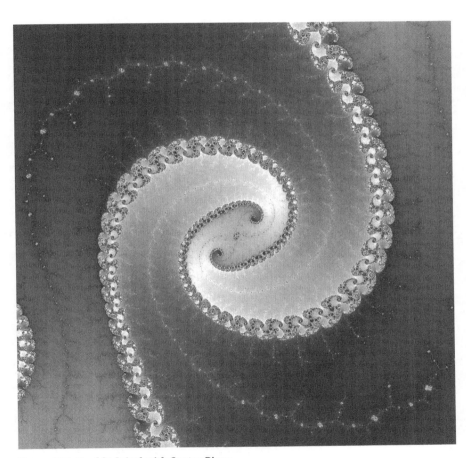

Figure 106. Double Spiral with Center Piece

East Indian Mandelbrot

Figure 107. East Indian Mandelbrot

Eternal Thunderbird Stairway

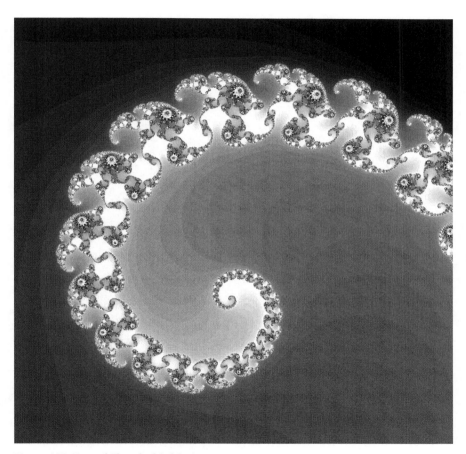

Figure 108. Eternal Thunderbird Stairway

Field of Rosette from the Mandelbrot Set

Figure 109. Field of Rosette from the Mandelbrot Set

Figure and Ground: Seahorses and Dolphins

Figure 110. Figure and Ground: Seahorses and Dolphins

Fish Rug: After M.C. Escher

Figure 111. Fish Rug: After M.C. Escher

Jewelry Swirl

Figure 112. Jewelry Swirl

Linked Beauty

Figure 113. Linked Beauty

Mandelbrot in a Sphere

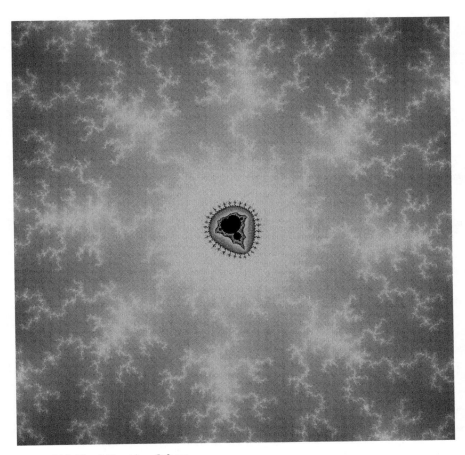

Figure 114. Mandelbrot in a Sphere

Mandelbrot Thunderbird

Figure 115. Mandelbrot Thunderbird

Medieval Mandelbrot

Figure 116. Medieval Mandelbrot

Oriental Mandelbrot

Figure 117. Oriental Mandelbrot

Spiral of Lights

Figure 118. Spiral of Lights

Renaissance Spiral

Figure 119. Renaissance Spiral

Seven Graceful Lines

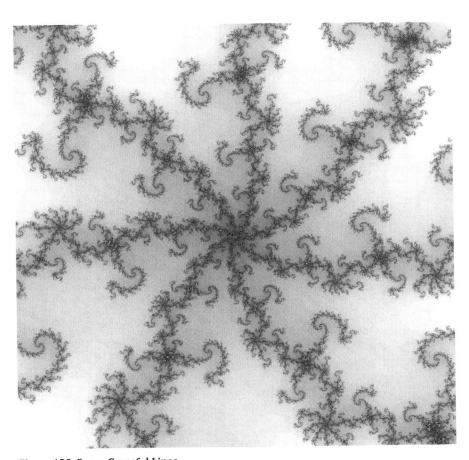

Figure 120. Seven Graceful Lines

Swirls of Swirls

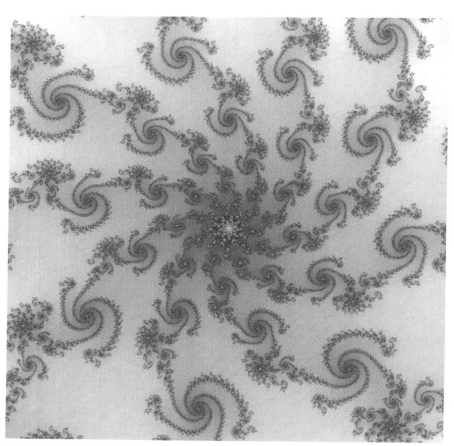

Figure 121. Swirls of Swirls

Woolly Mammoths

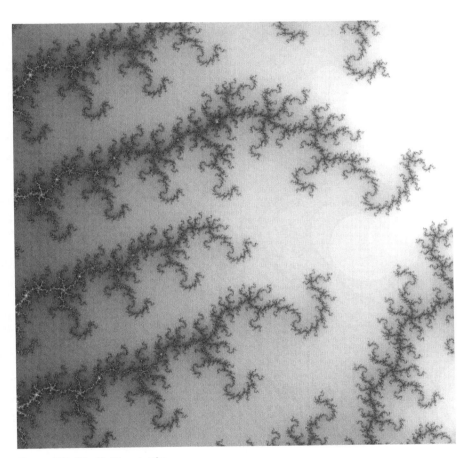

Figure 122. Woolly Mammoths

Phase 5

Conclusionary Perspectives

5.00

The Narrative

The air was cold. Wind descended the mountainside causing Fritz to squint and pull his scarf close to his neck. The conifers had all but disappeared, giving way to grand oaks. Dry leaves barely clung to the branches. The wind moved freely through the trees, unlike within the sheltering conifers, but reminiscent of home.

The trek was slow. Fritz was tired from little sleep the night before. The thick air hampered his gait. His knapsack seemed heavier than usual. Perhaps a stop at the peak would refresh him before a cautious descent.

The sun was nowhere to be seen. Clouds, heavily laden with moisture, rolled across the sky; yet, the wood was a beautiful sight. Leaves partially covered the ground, and tree silhouettes outlined a very appealing path. The path was wide enough to be unmistakable, and smooth enough to walk without worry of stumbling.

The forks were just as Teile had said. Staying with the right-most fork each time, Fritz continued up the mountain without fording a waterway. His confidence in Teile's words grew, but so did his concern with the warnings.

Fritz set his knapsack down to take in the view from the mountaintop. The climb had taken him much longer than he had hoped. He took little time to eat what had been so kindly packed for him. Rest would have to wait. If the descent was truly as treacherous as Teile had warned, he would need to make up time where he could. There would be time for rest at home.

Just beyond the ridge, Fritz looked down at the gorge and could see the bridge that crossed its expanse. It was not at all what he had expected. It was a rope bridge. Even at such a distance, he could see that the wind moved through the gorge with force, tossing the bridge from side to side. Fear overcame his previous thoughts of comfort and home. He hadn't taken Teile seriously enough.

The northerly wind that had hindered his ascent now aided his descent. Even though it was bitter to his face, his knees thanked its support. His surefootedness was replaced with tentative steps amid loose rocks. Picking up a broken branch, he fashioned a walking stick for stability.

Going slowly, he began to consider the time of day. Even with an obscured sun, he knew it had to be getting on into the afternoon. His energy was torn between focusing on the difficult path and the warnings Teile had offered repeatedly.

He reached forward with his stick to catch himself when he tripped on a rock. The commotion sent a couple of rocks tumbling down the incline. Wondering if he had passed the cut-off he had been warned to carefully watch for, his heart sank; yet, there had been no turn to the right. He gathered his thoughts and continued downward.

The bend in the path was more subtle than he had expected. He was sure it was the turn Teile had warned of after careful examination. There had been a glimpse of the bridge not long before. Scanning to the left, he saw no obvious path given the undergrowth amid the trees. Moving to the edge of the rocky trail, he looked for signs of previous travelers.

His thoughts drifted to Allesa's call to listen, Fremd's embrace of the strange, Ganz's comfort in a timeless castle, and Teile's repeated words. *What would they do at this moment?*

He scanned left, then right. Scanning left again, he stopped suddenly. Behind the undergrowth, and amid the trees, stood a deer. As quickly, and as quietly, as the deer had entered the wood before him, it took off through the autumn leaves, down and away.

Stepping through the brush and into the wood, he found an area of compact leaves where deer had been resting. Looking beyond, he saw a narrow path apparently worn by deer. He was not unfamiliar with the habits of deer. They make their own paths when necessary, but often use manmade paths to avoid scrapes with branches and undergrowth. Perhaps it was a path worth exploring. At least it was away from loose rock.

Ducking his head a few times to avoid low branches, he continued down the trail. It was narrow indeed. Occasionally scraping tree trunks as he went, he continued down and away from the main path.

The trail led him out onto a rocky ledge, right in front of the bridge. The deer trail turned and continued on along the gorge's edge. He smiled as he remembered Teile's concerned expression. The smile soon gave way to the sight before him. He faced a swaying rope bridge, undulating with wind-driven waves. Looking down . . .

Suffice it to say, he quickly chose not to look down. He had faced numerous perplexing situations on his journey, but this was not perplexing. It was frightening. The only consoling factor in what he saw was that the ropes and slats were fairly new. They appeared strong and able to withstand the wind's torment. With that little bit of encouragement, he took a step onto the bridge.

Having left his walking stick behind, he gripped both ropes as tightly as possible. In spite of wanting to avoid looking down, he had to at least glance to avoid the spaces between the slats. On he went.

A dozen paces into the crossing, he lost his grip with one hand as the wind snapped at the ropes. Instinctively, he dropped low, avoiding being hurled over the rope's edge. Shaking profusely as he held his low posture, he considered returning; but in looking back, he realized that it would be as treacherous to return as it would be to keep going. Keeping his low profile and an even tighter grip, he continued.

Fritz collapsed on the opposite rocky ledge. He had crossed Seekers Bridge and had denied Satisfaction Gorge. Weak with tremors, he huddled among the rocks and rested his head.

Sleep came without warning. Fritz woke to a sky that had grown dark. Quickly slipping his arms through the straps of his knapsack, he turned to look for the trail. Climbing up from the rocky ledge, he discovered that the trail was level and smooth; but darkness was falling quickly, making it difficult to see the trail and its heading. *I can't stay here for the night. The wind is too strong and the chill is deep.*

He stopped and released a lengthy sigh. After a few moments of reflection, he resigned himself to a frigid night and slipped his knapsack off. Leaning against a tree, he remembered the starry night on the mountaintop before his descent to Dimen Castle. Tonight, however, no stars blessed his eyes and no fire warmed his soul. He stared off into the woods imagining a ray of hope.

Imagination. That's all it was. Or was it? He was too numb to know the difference. It was just a flicker. *It was a flicker!* Through the woods, Fritz could barely see a dim flickering light. His eyes grew wide with anticipation. He grabbed his sack and took off. Stumbling over downed trees and rocks, Fritz frantically ran on, determined to make it to the source of light.

All at once, it was gone. The light was gone. It couldn't have been his imagination. It was real. He saw it. *It was there!* Or was it?

Whether it had been real or imaginary, he decided to walk in the direction, or perceived direction, of what had been a ray of hope. His walk was now calm, unlike the stumbling scurry he had engaged in just moments before. He carefully felt his way with his hands and feet, hoping to avoid another stumble.

After a few near misses, he stopped to take in an old familiar smell that tugged at his resolve to keep going. It was burning wood. *Oh, what a warm smell.* He increased his pace a bit, aware of obstacles nonetheless.

He approached the cabin with a cautious hope. The smoke from the chimney gave him just cause to believe someone was home. Giving little thought to the hazards of waking up its residents, Fritz put his cold knuckles to the door.

Inside, his knock was heard.

"Hoff, do you hear that?"

"Hear what?" No sooner were the words spoken than Hoff did hear the knocking.

"No one would be at our door this time of night without good cause. Not out here in the wood," said Liebe. Hoff rose to check.

"Who is it?"

"I am sorry, sir. I am cold and need a place to stay for the night." Hearing the voice through the locked door, Hoff decided to open it. In stumbled a cold and weary stranger.

Liebe, putting on her robe, exclaimed, "For heaven's sake, Hoff! He's cold, and probably hungry. I will make some tea." Hoff led the young man to a chair by the fireplace and draped a woolen blanket over his shoulders.

"Who are you, and what are you doing on Seekers Mountain in weather like this and at this time of night?" questioned Hoff.

"Hoff, give him a chance to warm up before badgering him with questions." Liebe handed a cup of hot tea to the frigid young man.

After a few sips of tea, Fritz turned to the couple and softly said, "Thank you." Hoff turned and looked at Liebe. Without another spoken word, they knew. Liebe rose to get some extra bedding. Together she and Hoff made a makeshift bed next to the fireplace.

"No need to talk now. There will be plenty of time for that in the morning. Get some sleep," Hoff said warmly.

It took only moments of staring at the fire for Fritz to fade into sleep, a very deep sleep. No dreams. No fears. No cold. Only warm restful slumber.

Hoff and Liebe moved quietly in the morning. Hoff carefully put more logs on the fire. Liebe put bacon on the stove. They smiled as they glanced at each other. They had helped many travelers in their years on Seeker Mountain. This was a young one.

The crackling smell roused Fritz. "Good morning!" Liebe said cheerfully.

"Good morning," replied Fritz.

"Breakfast will be ready in a few minutes. Perhaps you would like to freshen up? You may use the bathroom down the hall to the left."

Looking in the mirror, Fritz saw a dirty, weathered face. It had been a long journey, but now he was near the journey's end. *Very near.*

After cleaning up, he returned to the common room that combined a living room, a dining room, and a kitchen. The great room's high ceiling was supported with timbers. The fireplace was grand, made from large stones, probably gathered from the mountainside.

"Have a seat here." Hoff and Liebe brought breakfast plates to the table and sat down with him.

"Our names are Hoff and Liebe," said Hoff as he passed the bacon. "And you are?"

"My name is Fritz Streuner."

"How long have you been on your quest?"

"Quest?"

"Yes, your journey."

"Oh. It was going to be a short two-week visit to Dimen Castle, but it turned into a year-long trek. I am almost home. My journey will soon be over."

"Oh? Soon over?"

"Yes, I am ready to be done with my travels."

"You know," said Hoff, as he sat back in his chair, "we have met many a traveler who was on their way home. At least, so they thought. It is interesting how that can change."

"Not me, I accomplished what I set out to do, and now I am ready to go home."

Breakfast was restoring, not to mention incredibly delicious. Fritz helped clear the table, and walked over to the window to look out at the surroundings. The view was distorted. "You won't see much through that thick ice," Hoff said.

"Ice?"

"Why, yes. During the night, we had a massive ice storm. About two inches accumulated in this area," replied Hoff.

"But I need to leave. I want to get home before the first snowfall."

"It appears as though you will not be going anywhere for at least a few days. You are more than welcome to stay here with us."

Fritz continued to look through the ice at the distorted images. Trees appeared twisted. The mountain he had come across was in an upheaval. A squirrel moved across the deck railing, changing shape as it hopped. Hoff stood next to Fritz. "Isn't it interesting how the images are distorted?" After a pause, he continued, "Life can be that way, Fritz."

"What do you mean?"

"Sometimes, we are sure that we understand what we see. We think we see things as they really are. The problem is that life and its experiences cover our eyes with ice, as it were, distorting what we see."

"For instance?"

"Well, since you asked, how about your perception that your journey is almost over? Could that be a distorted image?" Fritz looked at him intently. Hoff gently continued, "I just ask you to consider the possibility."

5.01

Spiritual Refraction

We have come quite far in our wandering. Together we have explored the strange nature of our existence, the limited dimensional perspectives we so easily label *consistent* and *complete*, and nature's overarching fractal structure whereby everything resembles and touches everything else in the cosmos. Yet there are a few more concepts that deeply impact the images we attempt to piece together, the processes we use to establish higher dimensional perspectives, and the guidance we so desperately need to continue our processing. We begin with spiritual refraction and the images we have to work with.

Spiritual Refraction

It was a cool summer evening and I had just finished stirring the sugar into my tea. I carried the spoon over to the sink and tossed it into a glass bowl full of water. The spoon oscillated as it sank to the bottom, much like a leaf falling to the ground. As I gazed at the spoon, now settled in the bowl, I realized that it had deformed so dramatically that it barely resembled the spoon I had tossed into the bowl. The handle was now significantly curved upward and irregular in pattern. The head of the spoon was much broader than I had previously realized. It certainly was not the same spoon I had used to stir my tea.

Of course I knew what had happened. The glass of the bowl, combined with the water inside its curved walls, refracted the light coming at me from the spoon. There were several contributing factors that deformed the spoon. The first was the combination of mediums: glass and water. Every optical medium has an index of refraction, or a numerical value that describes the way light behaves as it moves through that medium. Light travels at a fixed velocity of 299,792,458 meters per second in a vacuum, but when light enters an optical medium, such as glass or water, it slows down. When light crosses the boundary between two different mediums, at an angle, the light rays bend. The result is the formation of a virtual image: one that appears to be at a location other than its real location.

The second contributing factor was the shape of the boundary. The glass bowl was curved, behaving like a lens, magnifying the image. In this case, it did not magnify it uniformly, but disproportionately, due to the irregular shape of the bowl, resulting in a warped virtual image.

The third contributing factor was the angle at which I was peering through the glass bowl. In the case of the spoon, I was looking through the walls of the bowl at a fairly steep angle, resulting in significant refraction of light and a very distorted virtual image.

In reality, there were more than two indexes of refraction at play that eventful evening. There were, of course, the indexes of the glass and water. But the light had to pass through more mediums than water and glass to hit my retina. It passed through air, my cornea, my lens, and the vitreous humor in my eye. All these mediums refracted the light from the spoon to form the final image on my retina.

Do we see anything that is not refracted, bent, or warped? The short answer is no. However, our brains are quite good at translating the resulting images into recognizable objects. We do it so much that we do not think about it. We accommodate to account for the refractions that warp what we see. Yet, they are virtual images.

Intentional Refractions

All views, regardless of their sophistication, are subject to refraction. The Greeks understood this, knowing that what we perceive as linear is not. They developed illusionary refinements to compensate. The columns in the Parthenon were intentionally shaped with a slight belly in the mid-portion, giving a linear perception to what would have appeared as columns with a skinny waist, given the height of the columns and the perspective of the onlooker.

We intentionally refract light with corrective lenses, such as glasses. Lenses and prisms are used in optical devices such as binoculars and microscopes to create magnified images. Telescopes enable us to peer into the night sky to observe stars, planets, and galaxies. Medical imaging is made possible via refraction. There are obviously numerous beneficial uses of refraction.

Misleading Refractions

Most of us have seen a mirage. I remember seeing one as a child and puzzling over why we never arrived at the water on the road ahead. I was simply told that it was a mirage, but did not understand the physics behind it until much later. The point is that the image was quite real, yet very misleading.

Why is the Sun so red and so large when it first appears in the morning, gradually shrinking and turning to bright white as the day progresses? Does it actually change its nature throughout the day? We know it does not, but it certainly appears to go through drastic changes, morphing from sunrise to sunset.

Such refractions are not limited to physical vision. Obviously, I would not have included these stories and descriptions if there were not more to the story. In spite of the fact that I had encountered what I now call *spiritual refraction* many times in my life, it did not become real to me until the spoon hit the bottom of the bowl.

Everything is Refracted

Everything we perceive, whether philosophical, theological, spiritual, or scientific, is subject to refraction. Everything passes through numerous mediums and subsequent refractions to arrive at its final destination in our neural networks. Furthermore, our brains work overtime to accommodate these refractions, plugging them into systems of understanding and belief, creating systematic, orderly, complete and consistent worldviews. These combined images can be quite real, yet they are virtual images.

Mediums

Some of the mediums we peer through are solid and steadfast. Refractions that result from such unchanging mediums may be 500 or 5,000 year-old refractions, but are refractions nonetheless. Some mediums, and their subsequent refractions, waffle, changing with trendy winds. Some are given to us, such as culture and tradition. Some we have sought out through education and self-improvement disciplines. Some we wish we could get rid of. Some we are grateful for. Some are quiet and still, giving steady clear images. Others are turbulent, yielding unrecognizable refractions. Yet even the best of mediums still refract reality.

Some mediums are quite sophisticated, though often manipulative and arrogant, to the point of believing in their necessity at the expense of clarity. Such mediums may include academia, intellectualism, social position, popularity, data, research, and approval by the masses.

Physical mediums, though tangible and quite real, affect our psychological, philosophical, and spiritual formulations. Included in these mediums are poverty, wealth, hunger, satiation, health, illness, climate, natural disasters, peace, and war, to mention a few. The impact of want and need are profound. The impact of excess is also profound. Both refract our perceptions. Each refracts our perceptions of the other.

Some individuals are utterly convinced that there is no such domain as a spiritual realm. Is that due to their particular *non-spiritual* mediums, or is it a function of the lack of a spiritual medium? It may be an issue of semantics. My personal insistence that the spiritual realm is quite physical, but hidden dimensionally, is comprised of a unique set of mediums.

Our religious upbringing, or the lack thereof, profoundly infiltrates our mediums. Traditions easily morph into very rigid religious mediums. Literalism and legalism are mediums that push us toward works-based religions and away from grace. They easily introduce other warping mediums such as inadequacy and guilt.

The densest and most opaque of all mediums is the human will. Ultimately, we will believe what we want to believe.

Mixtures

We each have a unique blend of mediums to peer through. Most mediums, if not all, are mixtures of culture, parenting, community, religion, family, self, traditions, friends, etc. I would *like* to think that my medium is a single piece of high quality, clear, crystal plate glass, providing a view with the least distortion. But it is not. There may be a thin sheet of it somewhere in the mix, but it is deeply submerged in the mixture that warps my view.

Many of us spend our lives working steadfastly at a perfect blend. We have become quite good at mixing them, so that we see what we want to see. However, we must not be so deceived as to think that our mixtures have any impact whatsoever on the truth. We only see refracted truth. Truth lies beyond our mediums.

Recognizing the mixed mediums that each of us deals with helps us to better understand Jesus' words regarding children. Children have few mediums to interfere with their perceptions of God and the world. Jesus said we must become like children to enter the kingdom of God.[538] Unfortunately their mediums also become distorted. No wonder Jesus said that it would be better for us to have a stone hung about our neck and be dropped into the sea than to distort a child's view by oppressing them with our mediums.[539]

We Are Mediums

Not only do we struggle to make sense of what we see through our mediums, but we are also mediums that influence the views of others. We are part of the mixture of mediums that others peer through to see God. We may be the only images of God that some people see. This puts an amazing responsibility on each of us. We are representations of the IICP. Are we skewed? Yes. Are we effective? We can be. But we can also be hindrances. Strangely, the best image of God we can provide is one that recognizes that we too peer through warped views, but are working steadfastly at clarifying our own perspectives.

Scripture as a Medium

I think you know by now that scripture holds a primary status in my medium mixture. Yet even scripture is subject to refraction. Scripture may be the best

---

[538] Mark 10:14.
[539] Matthew 18:6.

representation of the voice of God that limited and broken human beings can render, yet our spiritual refraction mediums not only influence our reading and interpretation of scripture, but also the writing of it. Even the best oral or written traditions come through many mixed mediums, refracting images again and again and again. Even if someone were able to convince me that the formulation of scripture was not impacted by the mediums of its authors, I cannot read scripture without warping it as it passes through my mixture of mediums.

Exegesis of scripture recognizes that the authors of scripture had mediums of their own. It requires studying the mediums of the times (culture, language, context, personality, etc.) to adequately interpret such texts. We cannot read scripture without peering through generations of mediums that contributed to the authorship of such scripture, let alone generations of mediums that contribute to our unique mixtures, through which we attempt to interpret the texts.

Community

How can we identify such mediums and their refractions? Once again we come full circle to the concept of *iterations*. We need multiple iterations, including multiple witnesses, to identify our refractions and discern what is accurate enough to follow. We have seen the fractal importance of community. Dimensionally, we have seen the necessity of acquiring multiple perspectives in order to form higher dimensional perspectives, *even if they are constructed out of refracted views*. We need such perspectives. We need community.

In Closing

The good news in all of this is that there would be no refractions without light. God is the light of the world.[540] Even as we distort God's image, at least it is the light we are distorting. What is more, God's grace extends beyond our mediums and our spiritual refractions. It extends beyond systematic theology. It extends beyond organized disbelief. Grace overcomes spiritual refractions.

---

[540] John 8:12.

5.02

Religion Revisited

I have argued extensively that religion is the natural outcome of human tendencies to deny or defy the infinitude of God. Religions are finite and exclusive. God is not bounded by our religious architecture, no matter how advanced or innovative it may be.

As we attempt to move away from such finite systems of belief, we often trade one idol for another. We focus so heavily on the *words* in our statements of faith, that we lose focus on the ultimate *Word*: God himself. Religion has missed the mark, and not by a slight error, not by a random error, but by a very large systematic error. Religion resembles Jesus' words: "Though seeing, they do not see; though hearing, they do not hear or understand."[541]

But, in my staunch rebuttal of religion, have *I* missed the mark? I believe I have, and here is why.

The GBF

It was not until most of the way through this project that I realized that when I criticize and argue against religion, pointing my fingers at its forms and failures, I indirectly reject the legitimacy and effectiveness of the incarnation of God: the God-become-flesh, the GBF.

The incarnation is the ultimate demonstration of God's desire to meet us *where we are*. He meets us in our limitations and in our religious forms. He used and uses our forms to live among us and in us. It is precisely because we are finite and need finite expressions of faith that God meets us in religion. *To argue over the forms of*

---

541 Matthew 13:13.

transformation and religious rituals is to deny the validity of the incarnation. God took on the form of humankind to meet the forms of humankind.

By assuming that God cannot use religious forms alien to us, we reject the infinitude of the incarnation. There are many peoples around the world who have hearts for God, but express this love through forms that are different from mine. To reject such forms is to reject the Arm who took on finitude on our behalf. Ironically, we who proclaim the incarnation, deny it by insisting that all religious forms must resemble our own. Is it not more sacred for Native Americans to perform the Ghost Dance, eat sacred mushrooms, and wade in the water, than to insist they deny their culture, post the Ten Commandments, and go to church, observing someone else's finitude?

Religion with Purpose

Religion with purpose lives humbly. To truly acknowledge the infinitude of God is to acknowledge how little we know. To acknowledge how little we know is to acknowledge the infinitude of God. The loop goes on.

Religion with purpose is a learning process.

Religion with purpose listens.

Religion with purpose thinks.

Religion with purpose recognizes that any position or belief, new or old, can turn idolatrous.

Religion with purpose works across drawn lines.

Religion with purpose acknowledges we only see in part (slices) and embraces this restriction with grace.

Religion with purpose acknowledges that God is God and *it* is not!

Religion with purpose acknowledges that we, by the very nature of our finitude, limit God.

Religion with purpose accepts God's grace for our finitude.

Coming Together

Religion with purpose serves yet another purpose: coming together to provide mutual support and encouragement for the wandering.[542] In so doing, we worship God *and* build up the fractal. Such encouragement provides strength to continue in discipleship and love. But we must do so in ways that respect the "solitude of the soul" and without coercing anyone to meet our needs.[543] God treats each of us with respect for our individuality; so we are to treat each other. Fractally, we are called to treat everyone with the same respect.

What Does God Require?

What does God require of us? To do justice, love mercy, and walk humbly with him.[544] It is really that simple. But whether or not we fully embrace the simplicity of being with God, God's mercy and grace continue to embrace us. God uses the finitude of religious forms to meet us.

---

[542] Colossians 3:16.
[543] Palmer, *Let Your Life Speak*, 92-93.
[544] Micah 6:8.

5.03

Compassionate Theology

What is God's mission? The prophet Isaiah beautifully summarized it: it is a mission to bring hope, freedom, healing, and forgiveness to the world.[545] But how is it to be accomplished?

Compassion

The Bible says, "The Lord is compassionate, abounding in love."[546] The Koran calls God *the merciful* and *the compassionate*.[547] Fractally, we are called to be followers and imitators of *Compassion*: we are called to *be* compassionate.[548] Jesus said the two greatest commandments are to love God and love our neighbors (albeit an expanded definition of neighbor!)[549] It is a call to live compassionately, to empathize with sufferers, to be caretakers of those unable to care for themselves, to go the extra mile. It comes from a transformed heart: one full of compassion. If you want to know how to change the world, scripture makes it perfectly clear: "Love never fails."[550]

To seek the truth is to be filled with compassion. The Dalai Lama understands this. In his book *The Art of Happiness*, he says, "I would regard a compassionate, warm, kindhearted person as healthy. If you maintain a feeling of compassionate loving kindness, then something automatically opens your inner door." Such behavior creates openness and facilitates communication, enabling us to relate to

---

[545] Isaiah 61:1-3.
[546] Psalm 103:8.
[547] Sura II:158.
[548] Ephesians 5:1.
[549] Mark 12:29-31.
[550] 1 Corinthians 13:8.

each other more easily.[551] This is how we are to live. When we have and express compassion toward all beings, then, and only then, is God fully expressed in us. There is no greater truth than compassion.

It is also through compassion that we extend truth in grace to others. Karl Barth said, "By this we shall be judged, about this the Judge will one day put the question, 'Did you live by grace, or did you set up gods for yourself and perhaps want to become one yourself?'"[552] Living by grace means more than accepting it. Compassion opens the valve for grace to flow to others.

Compassionate Expressions

What does compassion look like? Perhaps we need to start by looking at Jesus' description of what it does not look like. In a paraphrase by Richard Stearns, in his book *The Hole in Our Gospel*, Jesus said, "For I was hungry, while you had all you needed. I was thirsty, but you drank bottled water. I was a stranger, and you wanted me deported. I needed clothes, but you needed more clothes. I was sick, and you pointed out the behaviors that lead to my sickness. I was in prison, and you said I was getting what I deserved."[553]

In very revealing words, as reported by Jim Wallis of *Sojourners* magazine, a Native American at a New York conference on social justice, attended by theologians, pastors, priests, nuns, and lay leaders, said,

> Regardless of what the New Testament says, most Christians are materialists with no experience of the Spirit. Regardless of what the New Testament says, most Christians are individualists with no real experience of community. Let's pretend that you were all Christians. If you were Christians, you would no longer accumulate. You would share everything you had. You would actually love one another. And you would treat each other as if you

---

[551] Lama, *The Art of Happiness: A Handbook for Living*, 40.
[552] Barth, *Dogmatics in Outline*, 152.
[553] Richard Stearns, *The Hole in Our Gospel* (Nashville: Thomas Nelson, 2010), 59.

were family. Why don't you do that? Why don't you love that way?[554]

Our focus has turned on itself. We have lost sight of the two greatest commandments: love God and others. Without compassionate living we are chaos to God. Fractally, when we ignore the needs that surround us, we ignore God. When we ignore God, we ignore our own souls.

Compassionate Theology

God *is* love.[555] In a very real sense, theology is the study of love. If our theology is built on compassionate truth, it is true theology. If we love *all* humankind in word and deed, we are a part of God and his domain.

All the theological debates may be waged, all the academics may argue and publish, all the strange, dimensional, and fractal books may be sold, but if none of it is filled with compassion, it is nothing. Theology that is of God is not complex; it is simple: love God and love all humankind. That is it. If you want to be sure your theology never fails you: be compassionate. The details will take care of themselves.

---

[554] Wallis in Augsburger, *Dissident Discipleship: A Spirituality of Self-Surrender, Love of God, and Love of Neighbor*, 200.
[555] 1 John 4:8.

5.04

Continuous Wandering

As I look out the window and watch the leaves gently fall to the ground I am reminded that life is a cycle, a process, a journey. This principle permeates nature. And even if we pretend that our journeys are linear, still we are part of this cyclical journey, and it calls out to us to embrace it.

We have forsaken process for stability and satisfaction. We have forsaken the divine for brokenness. While religion has helped on occasion, it has also left us empty. Carl G. Jung, the Swiss psychologist, once said, "Christian civilization has proved hollow to a terrifying degree . . . Too few people have experienced the divine image as the innermost possession of their own souls."[556] We are detached from our roots in the divine.

So much landscape lies ahead, waiting to be traversed. Scripture tells us, "No one's ever seen or heard anything like this, never so much as imagined anything quite like it—what God has arranged for those who love him."[557] We must wander.

Wandering

In the words of an old spiritual song, "I'm just a poor wayfaring stranger. I'm traveling through this world of woe. Yet there's no sickness, toil nor danger in that bright land to which I go." The call to process and wander is a call to journey toward God and away from emptiness. When Jesus said, "I am the way," he implied

---

[556] Jung in O'Murchu, *Quantum Theology: Spiritual Implications of the New Physics*, 163.
[557] 1 Corinthians 2:9 The Message.

a journey [558]. He did not say, "I am the destination." It is the journey to God that brings fulfillment.

As we journey we leave behind footprints to help those who come after us. These footprints lead to more and more slices of God. These slices, blurred as they may be, facilitate seeing the substance of our beliefs. Karl Barth wrote, "Even dogmatics with the best knowledge and conscience can do no more than question after the better."[559] But as we seek and question this *better*, we lay foundations for those who come after us, to pick up where we left off, continuing the wandering.

A Sobering Encounter

As I was driving down the interstate one morning a number of years ago, feeling good about my wandering and the progress I was making on this project, I said, "So, Lord, what mystery do you want to reveal to me today?" In a heartbeat I heard a voice say, "That you do not have a better understanding of me." I was stunned. It was the first time I ever felt hurt by something God said to me. I thought, "What? I have spent the past 12 years reading, studying, contemplating, listening, and writing, and I don't have a better understanding?" He continued: "Is what you have developed new? Yes. Is it innovative? Yes. Has it helped you? Yes. Will it help others? Hopefully. Is it more appropriate at this point in time? Perhaps. But, is it better? No." This encounter was sobering.

Then, as I sulked and pondered, heading down the highway, it dawned on me that it *must* be the case if, as I have argued incessantly, God is infinite. Can I take my own medicine? God is infinite and I am not. Anything I come up with, compared with God's infinitude, cannot be better, only different. Relative to our finite reference frame it may *seem better*, but not relative to *Essence*. At that moment I prayed, "Father, forgive me for pretending to know so much." Letting go is so difficult to do. But it is freeing, so freeing. I can now honestly say that I do not have a better theology: I have less.

---

[558] John 14:6.
[559] Barth, *Dogmatics in Outline*, 11.

Longing to Know God

To me the most significant outcome of this project is a profound and growing desire deep within to know God. I have become keenly aware of the vastness beyond my little theological world, a vastness that cannot be written, that no mind or book can contain.

C.S. Lewis wrote, "Our longing to be reunited with something in the universe from which we now feel cut off, to be on the inside of some door which we have always seen from the outside, is no mere neurotic fancy, but the truest index of our real situation."[560] It is this hunger that drives my wandering. I cannot help but go back for more.

God Loves Me

After all the logic, mathematics, physics, and other analyses have come and gone, after everything has been said and done, only one thing stands out above the rest: God loves me. This is truth. It is the most profound of all truths. God's love is the simplest concept, and strangely the most complex. It is simple in that it simply is. It is complex in its refusal to be thwarted by any human reasoning; complex in its strange, dimensional, and fractal qualities. God's love is complex and simple. It *is*.

The Initial Question

I have never experienced the love and gentleness of God so vividly as that fateful Saturday when I spewed forth that dark question at God. It was the encounter that initiated this project. Do you remember the question? I walked out into the driveway, looked up to the sky, with teeth gritted, and said, "Who gave *you* the right to be God?"

I stood there in the driveway waiting to be struck by lightning. All of a sudden I heard the softest, most gentle voice, whisper two words in my ear: "I did." I stood there for a second, shocked, then erupted in tears. Those two words said it all. First of all, it was a very strange loop: God gave himself permission to be. The I Am *is* because the I Am *is*. What is more, this *I Am* is so eternal, so infinite, and so

---

[560] Lewis, "The Weight of Glory," 7-8.

secure, that it was not threatened by such a blasphemous question as mine and did not respond in anger and insecurity, but with deep compassion. I hope you, too, will find freedom in asking the difficult questions.

Closing or Opening?

Many times in our journeys we will arrive at places we have been before. We will cover and re-cover, learn and re-learn, traverse and re-traverse, continuously refining the loop. And even when we do not perceive the hidden meaning or understand the purpose, even when our journey seems redundant, if we walk with *Hope* and *Love*, we will one day see the ultimate meaning. For now, we continue to traverse these paths, wandering through old familiar territory, only to see new and brilliant scenery, views we missed on previous iterations. We go back, again and again and again . . .

5.05

The Narrative

The next few days in the cabin with Hoff and Liebe were days of contemplation. There were, of course, very few other things to do. His hosts were very caring and thoughtful, allowing him plenty of time to sit in solitude next to the fireplace pondering his journey.

The ice slowly melted. By the third day, enough had melted to permit Hoff to open the door onto the deck. Fritz put on his vest and stepped out into fresh air. The view was gorgeous. The mountain glistened as rays of sunlight penetrated the remaining ice. The distortion was gone. He saw the mountain for what it was. The squirrel was back, attempting to dig food out of a frozen birdfeeder. As it ran across the rail, its body and tail flowed like undulating waves of water.

Melting. It had taken place outside, and inside. The ice over his eyes was slowly giving way, providing a clearer view of his journey, the inadequacy of a very small journey. What previously seemed prolonged, now seemed quite short. The journey he had intended to take was simple, not complex, and not difficult to understand. Instead, he had been pushed outside his comfort zones on many occasions and forced to let go of his shortsighted objectives. He had been challenged to consider possibilities previously out of the realm of, well, the realm of common sense. In exchange, the journey had proven rich, much richer than he had hoped; he was rich with new friends, and full of maturing tensions. He was not disappointed; rather, he felt a sense of strength and an odd expectancy.

Continuing the journey presented another dilemma. If he were to continue, what guarantee would preserve his new crisp images? What if they, too, were distorted by remaining ice? Would there be further melting? And, more melting after that? Where, and when, would it end?

"Hoff," Fritz asked over lunch, "how do you know when the melting is done?"

Hoff let out a gentle sigh and said, "That is an incredibly important question, Fritz, and one that is difficult to answer. Perhaps, you must continue the journey to find out!"

That evening after dinner, the three of them sat around the fireplace. The room was silent, but not empty. Glances of warmth, and a wealth of thoughts flowed through the spaces between them.

Finally, Fritz broke the silence, "I have to go back."

"Back where?" asked Liebe.

Fritz looked her in the eyes and said, "Back to Dimen Castle. I want to know more. I want to understand. There are so many questions. I need time with Lord Zeitlos. Perhaps, he will be there this time."

"Did you not see him on your previous journey?"

"Yes, but I did not know at the time who it was that gave me directions."

"Will you know him the next time you see him?"

"Of course. I know what he looks like now."

"Do you?" asked Liebe with wide-open eyes.

Instantly, Fritz's mind went back to the portraits in the hallway at Dimen Castle. They were very different portrayals of the same person; so different, that he had wrongly assumed they were previous lords. "How, then, shall I know when I see him?"

Liebe set her knitting on the hearth and leaned forward in her chair. "Be always on the watch. He appears when least expected. Look everyone in the eyes, pondering the possibilities. Never stop seeking him. Never stop seeking to understand. You know by now that he is not to be contained by Dimen Castle."

During the night, Fritz restlessly pondered Liebe's words. They were rich, yet disconcerting. He truly wanted to see Lord Zeitlos again. But, would he be quick enough to recognize those eyes? Would Lord Zeitlos be a hunched over old man again? What other forms does he assume? Why does he challenge a seeker so?

In the morning, Fritz found a warm breakfast waiting on the table, but only one place was set. Beside the teacup was a note:

Fritz, stay as long as you need. We are heading south for winter. If you decide to go back to Dimen Castle, you will need to go west over the mountain, then head north. Seekers Bridge went down during the ice storm. Wish you well.

He walked over to the window and looked out over the mountains and Satisfaction Gorge. He was not satisfied. He could not go home. He would pack and leave for Dimen Castle after breakfast.

A few paces from the cabin, he turned and softly said, "Thank you. I hope we meet again, friends."

The air was cool, but the sun was warm to his skin. The slippery autumn leaves all but covered the ground. They made the climb a challenge, as they deceivingly obscured the rocky path.

As Fritz climbed, he thought of all the friends who had so graciously brushed some of his roughness away. How fortunate he was to have encountered such seasoned individuals!

Near the ridge, the rocky path that had demanded great attentiveness during the climb became smooth. The covering of leaves still made it a challenge to see. Autumn filled the air. Sunlight pierced the wood where it could, scattering light over the fallen leaves. The color was beautiful. It was almost as though . . .

"Uh!!!"

With his face in the leaves and dirt, and his shin thumping with pain he tried to gather his frazzled senses. He lifted his head, spit out the leafy dirt, and gazed back over his shoulder. If only he had been watching the path instead of the sunlight passing through the trees!

Rising slowly to his feet, he brushed off the debris and examined his leg. Blood ran down his shin. He pulled out a ragged kerchief and tied it around the wound. He consoled himself, knowing it would heal in time.

Looking up once again, he paid a glance to the obstacle that caused him injury. But the glance, without conscious effort, turned to fixation. It was just a rock. Or was it?

Perplexed, he knelt in the damp debris next to the rock. No simple geological fracture produced its sheer faces, for there were signs of artistic effort in its smooth facets and sharp edges. He brushed away the leaves and dirt to reveal an inscription that read,

Listen!

Is is not and IsNot is

Many are one

One is many

Seek to understand![561]

---

[561] S.F. Augsburger, *Slices of God: Strange, Dimensional, and Fractal Perspectives on God and the Cosmos* (Strange Loop Type I: Achronos Media, 2015).

Bibliography

Augsburger, David. *Dissident Discipleship: A Spirituality of Self-Surrender, Love of God, and Love of Neighbor.* Grand Rapids: Brazos Press, 2006.

Augsburger, S.F. *Slices of God: Strange, Dimensional, and Fractal Perspectives on God and the Cosmos.* Strange Loop Type I: Achronos Media, 2015.

Barth, Karl. *Dogmatics in Outline.* New York: Harper & Row Publisher, Inc., 1959.

Bell, Rob. *Velvet Elvis: Repainting the Christian Faith.* Grand Rapids: Zondervan, 2005.

Bible, The. *New International Version.* Grand Rapids: Zondervan Publishing, 2002.

Biography. "Analysis of Vincent Van Gogh's the Starry Night." http://lifeofvangogh.com/analysis-starry-night.html.

Bonhoeffer, Dietrich. *The Cost of Discipleship.* New York: Touchstone / Simon & Schuster, 1995.

Borg, Marcus J. *The Heart of Christianity: Rediscovering a Life of Faith.* New York: HarperCollins Publishers, 2003.

Britannica, Encyclopedia. "Occam's Razor." http://abyss.uoregon.edu/~js/glossary/occams_razor.html.

Brown, Devin. *A Life Observed: A Spiritual Biography of C.S. Lewis.* Grand Rapids: Brazos Press, 2013.

Chesterton, G.K. *The Everlasting Man.* San Francisco: Ignatius Press, 1993.

———. *Orthodoxy.* Colorado Springs: WaterBrook Press, 2001.

———. *St. Thomas Aquinas / St. Francis of Assisi.* San Francisco: Ignatius Press, 2002.

Cobb, John B. *God and the World.* Eugene: Wipf & Stock Publishers, 1998.

———. "Process Theology," http://www.religion-online.org/showarticle.asp?title=1489

Cole, K.C. *The Universe and the Teacup.* Orlando: Harcourt Brace & Company, 1997.

Connor, James A. *Pascal's Wager: The Man Who Played Dice with God.* New York: HarperCollins Publisher, 2006.

Dawkins, Richard. *The God Delusion.* New York: Houghton Mifflin Company, 2006.

Donne, John. *Devotions Upon Emergent Occasions.* 1624.

Edgework. "Finding God Abroad." http://www.edgework.ca/weeklyedgework94.html.

Elder, Robert Finch and John. *The Norton Book of Nature Writing.* New York: W. W. Norton & Company, 1990.

Faughn, Raymond Serway & Jerry. *Physics.* Austin: Holt, Rinehart and Winston, 2006.

Geometry, The Center For. "The Projective Plane." University of Minnesota,
    http://www.geom.uiuc.edu/zoo/toptype/pplane/.

Giorbran, Gevin. "Stephen Hawking and the Time Has No Boundary Proposal."
    http://everythingforever.com/hawking.htm.

Greene, Brian. *The Elegant Universe: Superstrings, Hidden Dimensions, and the Quest for the*
    Ultimate Theory. New York: W.W. Norton & Company, 2003.

———. *The Fabric of the Cosmos: Space, Time, and the Texture of Reality.* New York:
    Random House, Inc., 2004.

Hauerwas, Stanley. *With the Grain of the Universe.* Grand Rapids: Brazos Press, 2002.

Hawking, Stephen. *A Brief History of Time.* New York: Bantam Books, 1996.

Hennacy, Ammon. *The Book of Ammon.* Salt Lake City: Self Published, 1965.

Hofstadter, Douglas R. *Gödel, Escher, Bach: An Eternal Golden Braid.* New York: Basic Books,
    1979.

———. *I Am a Strange Loop.* New York: Basic Books, 2007.

John B. Cobb, Jr. "Process Theology." http://processandfaith.org/writings/article/process-
    theology.

Lama, His Holiness The Dalai. *The Art of Happiness: A Handbook for Living.* New York:
    Riverhead Books, 1998.

———. *The Universe in a Single Atom: The Convergence of Science and Spirituality.* New
    York: Morgan Road Books, 2005.

Lawson, Hilary. *Closure: A Story of Everything.* London: Routledge, 2001.

Lee, Duk. "In Pursuit of a Formula for Beauty." *Ambassador Magazine*, 2012.

Lewis, C.S. *Mere Christianity.* New York: HarperCollins Publishers, 1952.

———. "The Weight of Glory." *Theology / SPCK Publishing*, 1941.

Manning, Brennan. *The Ragamuffin Gospel.* Sisters: Multnomah Publishers, Inc., 2000.

Marinari, E. "Numerical Evidence for Spontaeously Broken Replica Symmetry in 3d Spin
    Glasses." *Physical Review Letters* 76, no. 5 (1996): 843-46.

McLean, Don. "American Pie. Reprinted by Permission of Hal Leonard Corporation.", 1971.

———. "Vincent. Reprinted by Permission of Hal Leonard Corporation.", 1971.

McManus, Erwin Raphael. *An Unstoppable Force: Daring to Become the Church God Had in*
    Mind. Loveland: Group, 2001.

McNeal, Reggie. *The Present Future: Six Tough Questions for the Church.* San Francisco:
    Jossey-Bass, 2003.

Merali, Zeeya. "Back from the Future." *Discover Magazine*, 2010.

Merton, Thomas. *The Seven Storey Mountain.* Orlando: Harcourt, 1948.

NOVA. "Hunting the Hidden Dimension." In *NOVA*: PBS, 2011.

O'Connor, J.J. "Klein Bottle." http://www.gap-system.org/~history/Biographies/Klein.html.

O'Murchu, Diarmuid. *Quantum Theology: Spiritual Implications of the New Physics*. The Crossroad Publishing Company, 2004.

Oakes, John. "Why Did God Wait to Send Jesus." http://www.evidenceforchristianity.org/index.php?option=com_custom_content&task=view&id=4786.

Ollenburger, Ben. *A Mind Patient and Untamed: Assessing John Howard Yoder's Contributions to Theology*. Telford: Cascadia Publishing House, 2004.

Ollenburger, Ben C. *A Mind Patient and Untamed: Assessing John Howard Yoder's Contributions to Theology, Ethics, and Peacemaking*. Telford: Cascadia Publishing House, 2004.

Palmer, Parker J. *Let Your Life Speak*. San Francisco: Jossey-Bass, 2000.

Peterson, Eugene H. *Leap over a Wall: Earthly Spirituality for Everyday Christians*. New York: HarperCollins Publishers, 1997.

Picasso, Pablo. "Picasso Response to Criticism." http://cubism-picasso.blogspot.com/.

Polkinghorne, John. *Science and Religion in Quest of Truth*. New Haven and London: Yale University Press, 2011.

Poythress, Vern Sheridan. *Symphonic Theology*. Phillipsburg: P & R Publishing Company, 2001.

Reimer, Todd. "The Creation: Norse Mythology." http://todd.reimer.com/norse/story.html.

Ridenour, Fritz. *So What's the Difference*. Ventura: Regal Books, 2001.

Rodwell, John Medows. *The Koran*. New York: Bantam Books, 2004.

Saxe, John Godfrey. "The Blind Men and the Elephant." http://www.wordfocus.com/word-act-blindmen.html.

Schaeffer, Francis A. *Genesis in Space and Time: The Flow of Biblical History*. Downers Grove: Intervarsity Press, 1972.

———. *How Should We Then Live?* Wheaton: Crossway Books, 1976.

Seton, Earnest T. & Julia M. *The Gospel of the Redman: A Way of Life*. Santa Fe: Seton Village, 1963.

Soelle, Dorothee. "Pre-Pain Theology Quote." http://www.clayfirecurator.org/2011/04/someone-said-w-david-o-taylor-art-of-lament/.

Stearns, Richard. *The Hole in Our Gospel*. Nashville: Thomas Nelson, 2010.

Strobel, Lee. *The Case for Christ: A Journalist's Personal Investigation of the Evidence for Jesus*. Grand Rapids: Zondervan, 1998.

Tolkien, J.R.R. *The Hobbit*. The Random House Publishing Group, 1996.

Tolle, Eckhart. *A New Earth: Awakening to Your Life's Purpose*. London: Penguin Books,
     2005.

Tozer, A.W. *The Knowledge of the Holy: The Attributes of God: Their Meaning in the Christian
     Life*. New York: Harper & Row Pubisher, Inc., 1961.

Tutu, Desmond. *No Future without Forgiveness*. New York: Doubleday, 1997.

Wikipedia. "Local Connectivity and Mandelbrot."
     http://en.wikipedia.org/wiki/Mandelbrot_set.

———. "Messianic Claimants." http://en.wikipedia.org/wiki/List_of_messiah_claimants.

———. "Theory of Forms." https://en.wikipedia.org/wiki/Theory_of_Forms.

———. "Vincent Van Gogh." http://en.wikipedia.org/wiki/Vincent_van_Gogh.

Willard, Dallas. *The Divine Conspiracy*. New York: HarperCollins Publishers, 1997.

Wright, N.T. *Surprised by Hope: Rethinking Heaven, the Resurrection, and the Mission of the
     Church*. New York: HarperCollins Publisher, 2008.

Young, William P. *The Shack*. Newbury Park: Windblown Media, 2007.

Appendix A

Biblical References

One God - Isa 42: 4-7, 22

Proof Texting - Isa 45:23-24

Shadows, Slices - Isa 51:12-16

Religion, Manmade, Shadows - Isa 59:9-10

No Awe, No Surprises - Jer 2:19

Innocent, Deceived - Jer 2: 35

Eyes to See, Ears to Hear, But Don't - Jer 5:21-23

Our Own Theology, Beliefs of Our Making - Jer 5:30-31

True Way vs. False Words and Teaching - Jer 7:1-11

False Wisdom, Deception - Jer 8:8-11

Self-Justification, Wickedness, Disobedience - Jer 11:15

Talk Faith, Not Of the Heart - Jer 12:2

False Prophets, Teaching, Today - Jer 14:11-14

False Prophets, Testing the Spirit - Jer 23:25-32

Oracles, Falsehood, Man's Ideas - Jer 23:36-40

Test of a True Prophet - Jer 28:8-9

Backs to God - Jer 32:30-35

Unsearchables, Ask - Jer 33:1-3

Call To Write - Jer 36:2

False Prophets, Destruction - Lam 2:14

Not Willing To Listen - Eze 3:4-7

Knowledge, Mysteries, Wisdom - Dan 2:20-23

Prayer for Understanding, Heard - Dan 10:12-14

Prophecy, Dreams, Visions - Joel 2:28

Criteria, Credentials, Whose? - Amos 7:14-16

False Prophets - Mic 3:5-11

Earth Filled With Knowledge, Glory of the Lord - Hab 2:14

Who Is Our Theology For? God or Us? - Zech 7:4-7

One God, Division - Mal 2:10

Rules Taught By Men - Mat 15:1-14

Manmade Traditions, God's Grace and Mercy - Mat 19:1-9

Logic of the Church, Play It Safe - Mat 21:23-27

Blind Guides, Vipers - Mat 23:13-36

Who Understands? - Mar 4:10-12

Four Winds, Four Corners of the Earth, Literal? - Mar 13:24-31

See but Not See, Hear but Not Understand - Luk 8:1-10

Disbelief, Understanding - Luk 24:25-27

Refusing One We Think We Worship - John 5:31-47

False Assumptions We Make - John 7:25-29

No Surprises Allowed, Know It All - John 7:50-52

Claimants of the Answers, Guilt by Seeing - John 9:35-41

Polity, Driving Force of Many, Flesh vs. Spirit - John 11:45-48

Thinking outside the Box, Just As Hard Today - John 12:27-34

Guide Us into All Truth, Prophetic Truth - John 16:12-15

Priorities, the Strangest Of Things Dictate - John 18:28

Prophecy, Not For Today? Joel 2:28-32 - Acts 2:14-21

Thinking We Know the Proper Order - Acts 10:44-48

Truth Suppressed by Wickedness, Churches Not Exempt - Rom 1:18-19

Without Excuse, Nature, Evidences - Rom 1:20

Disobedience, Approving Disobedience - Rom 1:32

Progressive Revelation, Progressive Understanding - Rom 16:25-27

Unity, Assumption - 1 Cor 1:10-17

Wisdom, Secret - 1 Cor 2:6-8

Understanding - 1 Cor 2:11-12

Theology, Survival - 1 Cor 3:10-15

Firm, Deceived - 1 Cor 10:12

Reflection, Poor, Dim - 1 Cor 13:9-12

Prophecy, Today - 1 Cor 14:1-5

Prophets, False - 2 Cor 11:1-15

No Other Gospel, Angels - Gal 1:6-9

Apostles, Human, Error, Preconceived, Legalism - Gal 2:11-13

Call to Process, Grow - Eph 1:17-18

Unity, Assumption - Eph 4:1-6

Unity - Eph 4:11-13

Scripture, Misuse - Eph 4:28

Imitate God, Call - Eph 5:1-2

Continuous Process, Not Static - Phi 1:3-6

Details, Too Much Concern - Phi 1:15-18

Process, Work out Salvation - Phi 2:12-13

Process, Continuous - Col 1:9

Unity, Assumption - Col 1:15-18

Mysteries Disclosed - Col 1:25-27

Unity, Complete Understanding, Mystery - Col 2:1-5

Philosophy, Hollow, Deceptive, Tradition, World - Col 2:6-8

Things Above, Mind - Col 3:1-3

Prophecies, Current, Hinder, Fire, Continuous - 1 The 5:19-20

Form of Godliness, Deny Power - 2 Tim 3:1-5

Prophecy, Today - Heb 1:1-2

Grow, Continuous - Heb 6:1-3

Strange Teachings - Heb 13:9

Wisdom, Ask - Jam 1:5-7

Listening, Doing - Jam 1:19-25

Holiness, Call - 1 Pet 1:13-15

Prepared, Defense - 1 Pet 3:15-16

Child of God, Know, Assurance - 1 John 5:1-5

Ignorance, Speech, Against, Lack of Understanding - Jude 8-10

First Love, Forsaken - Rev 2:4

Dead, Reputation of Being Alive, Deceived - Rev 3:1-3

Hot, Cold, Neither - Rev 3:14-18

Dare to Question, Academes, Galileo, Scriptural Assumptions - Rev 7:1

Dare to Question, Academes, Galileo, Four Corners - Rev 20:7-8

Strange References

Holy Ground - Exo 3:5

I Am That I Am - Exo 3:13-15

Strange Destiny - Exo 9:15-16

Do Not Break Any of the Bones, Passover, Symbolism - Exo 12:46

Strange Pillar of Fire And Light - Exo 14: 19-20

Strange Commandments, Unexpanded - Exo 19:1-17

Dressed Stones, Same as Sandals on Holy Ground - Exo 20:25-26

Forty Days - Exo 24:15-18

Attention to Detail, Tabernacle - Exo 25:1-26:4

Breast piece, Urim and Thumin - Exo 28:15-38

Equality - Exo 30:15

Creativity, Prophetic Gifts - Exo 31:1-11

Clean and Unclean, Figure and Ground - Lev 10:8-11

Reward for Obedience - Lev 26:3-7

Infinitude, God's Arm Too Short? - Num 11:21-23

Forty Years - Num 14:34

Sins Visited To Third and Fourth Generation - Num 14:13-24

Prophets from Other Peoples, Balaam - Num 22:1-13

Talking Animals, Donkey, Balaam - Num 22:21-35

Immutability of God, God Does Not Lie - Num 23:13-21

One God, Sovereign - Deu 4:32-40

Forty Days - Deut 9:25-29

Figure and Ground - Deut 11:26-28

Need For Blood, Even Heathen Know, God's Way - Deut 12:29-31

God's Way Only, Figure and Ground - Deut 12:4-14

Law, Not Expanded, Eye For Eye - Deut 19:15-21

Caring For the Underdog, Inverse Dynamics - Deut 21:15-17

Hung On a Tree, Symbolism, Foreshadowing Christ's Death - Deut 21:22-23

Healing Response, Globulin A, Naturopathic Medicine - Deut 22:6-7

Caring For the Poor, Healing - Deut 24:19-22

Building Relationships - Deut 24:5

Caring For Animals, Muzzling the Ox - Deut 25:4

Affected by the Disobedience of Others - Deut 29:18-19

Figure and Ground - Deut 30:15-18

Twelve Stone Column, Asymmetric - Josh 4:20-23

Holy Ground, Christophany, Impartial, Holy - Josh 5:13-15

Inverse Dynamics, Pick the Least - Judg 6:11-23

Let Baal Defend Himself - Judg 6:31-32

Inverse Dynamics, God's Way - Judg 7:1-8

God's Name Is Beyond Understanding - Judg 13:17-21

God's Mirror, Honoring God - 1 Sam 2:27-30

Words, God's or Ours? - 1 Sam 3:19-21

Nothing Can Stand Before God - 1 Sam 5:1-8

Inverse Dynamics, Saul - 1 Sam 9:18-23

Worthless Pursuits - 1 Sam 12:21

Obedience vs. Sacrifice - 1 Sam 13:9-14

Obedience vs. Sacrifice - 1 Sam 15:22-23

God Does Not Change His Mind, Infinitude - 1 Sam 15:27-29

Inverse Dynamics, Turn the Other Cheek - 2 Sam 16:5-14

Inverse Dynamics, God Looks At the Heart - 1 Sam 16:7-13

Music and Strange Spirits - 1 Sam 16:23

Whose Battle Is It? - 1 Sam 17:45-47

Not Lift a Hand against the Lord's Anointed - 1 Sam 24:5-7

Offer Not That Which Costs Nothing - 1 Sam 24:24

CPR? - 1 Kings 17:19-23

Grounding, Lightening? - 1 Kings 18:30-39

Inverse Dynamics, God in Quietness - 1 Kings 19:9-14

How Much Faith? Number of Jars - 2 Kings 4:1-7

Humble Yourselves, Forgiveness, Inverse Dynamics - 1 Chron 7:11-16

Seek God and He Will Be Found - 1 Chron 28:8-10

Earth and Heaven Can Not Contain God - 2 Chron 2:5-6

God's Mirror - 2 Chron 15:1-15

Why Do Wicked Prosper? - Job 21:7-16

What God's Presence Does to Humankind - Ps 5:4-6

Becoming Like a Child, Inverse Dynamics - Ps 8:1-2

Does God Exist? - Ps 14:1

God's Mirror - Ps 18:25-27

Effect of the Word - Ps 19:7-11

Inverse Dynamics, Meek - Ps 37:10-11

Care for the Weak - Ps 41:1-3

Mathematics of God, Infinitude of God - Ps 62:9-12

Animals and God, Heaven - Ps 84:3

Infinitude of God, Math of God - Ps 103:11-14

Death, Precious and Noticed To God - Ps 116:15-16

God's Word - Ps 119:105-112

God's Word - Ps 119:130

Infinity, Math of God - Ps 139:17-18

Mathematics of God, Infinitude of God - Ps 145:1-7

Inverse Dynamics, Humility, Exaltation - Ps 147:6

Mathematics of God, Infinitude of God - Ps 147:4-5

Keeping Statutes, Globulin A - Prov 3:1-2

Words Give Character Away - Prov 10:19

Globulin A - Prov 14:29-30

Globulin A - Prov 17:22

Equality of Man - Prov 29:13

Inverse Dynamics - Prov 30:24-28

Cyclical Nature of Knowledge - Eccl 1:9-10

Wisdom, Meaninglessness - Eccl 1:12-18

Cyclical Nature of Time - Eccl 3:15

Trinity, Three Stronger - Eccl 4:12

Strangeness of Wisdom - Eccl 7:12

Counter Intuitive Wisdom, Crime - Eccl 8:10-13

Strange Wisdom against Anger - Eccl 10:4

Inverse Dynamics - Eccl 11:1-2

Manmade Wisdom - Isa 5:20

Mathematics of God, Infinitude of God, Virgin Birth - Isa 7:14

Differences Will Vanish, Equality in Judgment, End Times - Isa 24:1-3

Compassion and Justice of God - Isa 30:18

The Word, Everlasting - Isa 40:7-8

Servant of the Lord, Savior, Not What We Expected - Isa 42:1-4

Got Forgets, Forgiveness - Isa 43:25

Creation Waiting Eagerly, Redemption, Romans 8 - Isa 44:23

Predestination - Isa 45:9-10

Palm, Hands, Love, Engraved - Isa 49:15-16

Savior, Need to Suffer, Resurrection - Isa 53:1-12

Thirsty, Power of the Word to Save - Isa 55:1-7

God's Word, Not Return Empty - Isa 55:10-13

Nature Sin, Separation - Isa 59:1-2

Salvation, Arm of God - Isa 59:15-17

Inverse Dynamics - Isa 61:7

Hardened Hearts - Isa 63:16-17

Separation from God, Math of God - Isa 64:6

Death in New Heavens and Earth, Reincarnation - Isa 65:17-23

Inverse Dynamics, Contrite Heart - Isa 66:2-4

Becoming What We Worship - Jer 2:5

Strange Mercy - Jer 3:12-13

Old Testament Inverse Dynamics, Boast in the Lord - Jer 9:23-24

Trust Not in Man, Trust in the Lord - Jer 17:5-8

Separation from God, Deceitful Heart, Lack of Understanding - Jer 17:9

Sovereignty of God - Jer 18:1-10

Laws of Nature, Fixed By God - Jer 33:25-26

Sarcasm of God - Jer 34:17

Truth Knows Lies, Lies Know Not Truth - Jer 43:1-3

Forgiveness, Faithfulness - Jer 50:20

Punish the Punisher - Jer 51:49

Hearts of Flesh vs. Hearts of Stone - Eze 11:18-21

Eyes to See, Ears to Hear, But Don't - Eze 12:1-2

Inverse Dynamics, GBF Prophecy - Eze 17:22-24

Inverse Dynamics, Repentance - Eze 18:25-27

Inverse Dynamics, Lowly Exalted, Exalted Brought Low - Eze 21:25-26

Do Not Mourn, Ezekiel's Wife Dies - Eze 24:15-18

Aliens Adopted, Palestinian Rights - Eze 47:21-23

Faith, Commitment unto Death, Salvation - Dan 3:16-18

Ezekiel Wheel - Dan 7:9

Revelation to Prophets - Amos 3:7

God's Mirror, Golden Rule - Obad 1:15

God of Mercy - Mic 7:18

Divided Loyalty, Worshipping the Stars - Zeph 1:5

Not by Might, by the Spirit - Zech 4:6

Evil Woman, My Dream - Zech 5:5-11

Offering to God What Is Not Good Enough For Man - Mal 1:6-8

Love through Pain, Refining - Mal 3:2-4

How Are We to Return? Robbing God, Blessing - Mal 3:6-11

Power of the Word, Temptation of Christ - Mat 4:1-11

Inverse Dynamics, Beatitudes - Mat 5:3-12

Prayer, Few Words - Mat 6:5-13

Fasting, Solitude, Humility, Joyful - Mat 6:16-18

Pay It Forward - Mat 6:19-21

Two Masters, Impossible - Mat 6:24

Judging, by Our Own Faults, Own Guilt - Mat 7:1-5

Don't Waste Words, Use Wisely - Mat 7:6

Law and the Prophets, God's Mirror - Mat 7:12

Inverse Dynamics, Inverse Pathways - Mat 7:13-14

Inverse Dynamics, Lose It to find It - Mat 10:37-39

Inverse Dynamics, Greatest, Least - Matt 11:7-15

Inverse Dynamics, Wisdom - Mat 11:25-26

Strange Light Yoke of Christ - Mat 1128-30

Figure and Ground, Beelzebub against Figure and Ground - Mat 12:22-36

Inverse Dynamics, Save It, Lose It - Mat 16:21-28

Inverse Dynamics, Faith of a Mustard Seed, Small Is Big - Mat 17:20

Inverse Dynamics, Become Like a Child, Greatest, Least - Mat 18:1-4

Inverse Dynamics, Children, Heaven - Mat 19:13-15

Inverse Dynamics, First, Last - Mat 19:30

Inverse Dynamics, Fairness, First, Last - Mat 20:1-16

Inverse Dynamics, Repentance, Show - Mat 21:28-32

Figure and Ground, Clothed In Righteousness or Not - Mat 22:1-14

Inverse Dynamics, Humility, Exaltation - Mat 23:1-12

Words, Never Pass Away, Infinitude - Mat 24:35

Holy of Holies, Entrance Gained - Mat 27:51-54

Figure and Ground, Whom Did Christ Come For?, Surprise - Mar 2:13-17

Figure and Ground, Atheists - Mar 3:20-30

Inverse Dynamics, Save It, Lose It - Mar 8:34-37

Inverse Dynamics, Greatest, Least - Mar 9:33-335

Figure and Ground, For Me, Against Me - Mar 9:38-41

Inverse Dynamics, Like a Child - Mar 10:13-16

First Will Be Last, Last Will Be First - Mar 10:29-31

Son of Man, Greatest Servant, Came to Serve, Not Be Served - Mar 10:35-45

Faith vs. Doubt - Mar 11:20-25

More Is Less, Less Is More - Mar 12:41-44

Spirit vs. Flesh, Weak, Strong - Mar 14:32-38

Surprise Even to Jesus, My God Why Have You Forsaken Me? - Mar 15:33-34

Virgin Birth, Impossible to the IICP? - Luk 1:26-37

Inverse Dynamics, Kings, Humble - Luk 1:46-56

Inverse Dynamics, Shepherds vs. Royalty - Luk 2:8-15

Assumption of Literal Genealogies, Abraham as Our Father, Ages - Luk 3:7-9

New Wine, Old Wine Skins - Luk 5:33-39

Legalism, Sabbath, Good vs. Evil - Luk 6:7-11

Inverse Dynamics, Blessings, Cursings, Now or Later? - Luk 6:20-26

Inverse Dynamics, Least, Greatest - Luk 7:24-30

Inverse Dynamics, Least Educated, Most Faithful - Luk 8:49-56

Let the Dead Bury the Dead, Don't Look Back - Luk 9:57-62

Hidden From the Wise, Revealed to Little Children - Luk 10:21

Figure and Ground, For Me, Against Me - Luk 11:23

Inverse Dynamics, Who to Invite - Luk 14:12-14

Inverse Dynamics, Valued By Man, Detested By God - Luk 16:14-15

Inverse Dynamics, Prayers, True Repentance - Luk 18:9-14

Inverse Dynamics, as a Child - Luk 18:15-17

Inverse Dynamics, Riches, Eye of the Needle - Luk 18:23-27

Inverse Dynamics, Less Is More - Luk 21:1-4

Inverse Dynamics, Greatest, Least - Luk 22:24-29

Strange Grace - Luk 23:39-43

Infinite Suffering, Infinite Price, Emmaus - Luk 24:25-32

Made Known in the Breaking of the Bread - Luk 24:33-35

Word Became Flesh - John 1:1-2

Dark Does Not Understand Light - John 1:3-11

Figure and Ground, Darkness and Light - John 3:19-21

Inverse Dynamics, Infidels Believe - John 7:45-49

Obedience Spawns Belief - John 8:31-32

Inverse Dynamics, Fools Wisdom - John 9:24-34

Inverse Dynamics, Seeing to Blind, Blind to Seeing - John 9:39

Prophesying Without Knowing It - John 11:49-53

Left Brain World - John 14:15-18

Christ's New Boyd - John 20:15-18

Blessed Are Those Who Believe Without Seeing - John 20:24-29

Strange New Body - John 21:6-14

Cyclical Nature of the Church - Acts 9:31

Strange New Body - Acts 10:39-41

Inverse Dynamics, Giving And Receiving - Acts 20:32-35

Need Each Other's Faith, Strange Loop - Rom 1:8-12

Strange Love, Inverse Dynamics - Rom 5:6-8

Strange Loop, One Act to Death, One Act to Life - Rom 5:18-21

Strange Grace - Rom 6:19-23

Figure and Ground, Sin and Death - Rom 7:7-13

Figure and Ground, Mind and Spirit and Flesh - Rom 8: 5-8

CS Lewis and Talking Animals - Rom 8:18-25

Infinite Initial Cause - Rom 11:33-36

Figure and Ground, Overcoming Evil with Good - Rom 12:21

Inverse Dynamics, Foolishness - 1 Cor 1:18-25

Inverse Dynamics, Foolishness, Shame, Wise - 1 Cor 1:27-29

Figure and Ground, Understanding - 1 Cor 2:14

Inverse Dynamics, Wisdom - 1 Cor 3:18-20

Inverse Dynamics, Persecution, Blessing - 1 Pet 4:12-16

Beast That Speaks, CS Lewis - 2 Pet 2:13-16

Figure and Ground, Walking, Darkness, Light, Fellowship - 1 John 1:5-7

Truth, Sin, Lie, In or Out, Forgiveness, Purify - 1 John 1:8-10

Figure and Ground, Light, Darkness - 1 John 2:9-11

Math of God, Strange Love - 1 John 4:7-12

Figure and Ground, From God or Not - 3 John 11-12

Second Death - Jude 12-13

The Word, Double Edged Sword - Rev 1:12-16

Second Death - Rev 2:11

Food, Idols, Sacrifice - Rev 2:18-25

Number, Completeness, 144, Symbolism - Rev 7:4

Number, Completeness, 144, Symbolism - Rev 7:9

Premillennialism, Amillennialism, Escape, Deception - Rev 7:11-14

End Times, Nuclear, Volcano - Rev 9:1-19

The Two Witnesses - Rev 11:1-12

Number of the Beast - Rev 13:11-18

Premillennialism, Amillennialism, Escape, Deception - Rev 14:6-13

Dimensional References

Lost Dimensions, Lost Access - Gen 3:20-24

Slices of God, Moses Sees God - Exo 33:12-23

Seeing a Slice of God, Impact on Moses - Exo 34:29-35

God's Face Shining on Us - Num 6:22-27

Cloud of God, Pillar of Fire - Num 9:15-23

Narrow Sighted, Need of Expansion - Deut 4:15-20

Freewill - Deut 4:25-31

The Lord Is One - Deut 6:1-9

Circumcise Hearts, Expansion - Deut 10:16-22

Circumcise Hearts, Expansion - Deut 30:1-6

Freewill and Choice - Josh 24:15

Seeing Slices, Balaam's Prophecy of Christ - Num 24:15-19

Messianic Prophecies - 1 Sam 2:34-36

God Looks on the Heart - 1 Sam 16:7-13

Translation of Bodies, Like Jesus And Phillip - 1 Kings 18:9-15

Double Portion, Chariots of Fire - 2 Kings 2:9-12

Open My Eyes, Dimensional Sight - 2 Kings 6:15-17

We Are Shadows, Slices - 1 Chron 29:14-18

Earth and Heaven Can Not Contain God - 2 Chron 2:5-6

Slice of God, Cloud in Desert - 2 Chron 5:13-14

Slice of God, Glory of the Lord - 2 Chron 7:1-3

Dimensional Dialogue - Job 1-42

Seeing and Perceiving God, Difficult to Impossible - Job 9:10-11

Who Can Fathom, God's Dimensions - Job 11:1-9

What God Has Done, Not Why, There Is a Difference - Job 12:7-12

Shadows - Job 12:22-25

God's Wisdom, Our Limited Wisdom - Job 15:1-13

Religious Debates, Futility - Job 16:1-3

Both Sides Refusing to Budge, Arguments - Job 18:1-3

Fatal Assumption, Wicked and Punishment - Job 20:1-7

Teaching God - Job 21:22

Glimpse of God, Cannot See - Job 23:8-12

Argument Not Resolved, No Winners - Job 32:1-3

Wisdom Not Limited to the Old - Job 32:4-9

Side-Stepping Dimensional Principles - Job 32:10-14

God's Words Do Not Have to Make Sense in 4d - Job 33:8-14

Do Not Reduce God to Our Understanding - Job 34:10-14

The Sin of Insisting We Understand - Job 34:31-37

Can We Influence God by Manmade Beliefs? - Job 35:1-10

God Is Faithful - Job 36:1-7

Who Do You Think You Are?, Man's Limitations - Job 38:1-23

Shadows of God - Ps 17:6-9

God Is Dimensional - Ps 18:1-3

Shadow of God, High and Low - Ps 36:5-9

Shadow of God - Ps 57:1

Shadow of God - Ps 63:6-8

Skies Opened, New Dimensions - Ps 78:23-25

Freewill - Ps 86:5-7

Freewill - Ps 86:15-17

Time Dimensions, Compare to 2 Peter 3:8-9a - Ps 90:4

Shadows of God - Ps 91:1-2

Time, Age of Man - Ps 103:15-18

Prophecy of Christ - Ps 110:4

Prophecy of Christ - Ps 118:22-24

Statutes Last Forever, Expanded But Not Abolished - Ps 119:152

Where Is God?, Omnipresence - Ps 139:7-10

Election, Foreknowledge - Ps 139:13-16

Darkness Is Not Dark to God - Ps 139:11-12

Omniscience of God - Ps 139:1-6

God's Time Compared With Ours - Ps 144:3-4

Love of God to All - Ps 145:8-20

Prophecy of Christ, Compare With Isaiah 61:1-3 - Ps 146:7-147:3

Sovereignty of God - Prov 16:9

Sovereignty of God - Prov 19:21

Expansion Began In the Old Testament - Prov 21:3

Expansion Began In the Old Testament - Prov 25:21-22

Prophecy of Christ - Isa 9:2-7

Prophecy of Christ - Isa 11:1-9

Prophecy of End Times - Isa 24:18-25:9

Prophecy of Christ - Isa 28:16-17

Prophecy of Christ, Also John, Comfort Ye My People - Isa 40:1-6

Dimensions of God - Isa 40:18-26

Ancient of Days - Isa 43:13

First and Last, God and Time - Isa 44:6-8

God's Foreknowledge - Isa 48:3-7

Timelessness of God - Isa 49:1-4

God's Thoughts, Higher Dimensions - Isa 55:8-9

Dimensional Expansion in the Old Testament - Isa 58:1-9

Sabbath, What Christ Fulfilled, Expanded - Isa 58:13-14

Ultimate Dimensional Expansion - Isa 60:15-22

Before You Call, God Will Answer - Isa 65:24-25

Dimensional Expansion in the Old Testament, Extended to Imagination - Isa 66:18

Timelessness of God, Knowledge of Us - Jer 1:5

Hints of Old Testament Expansion, Circumcision of the Heart - Jer 4:4

Hints of Old Testament Expansion, Circumcision of the Heart - Jer 9:25-26

Prophecy of GBF - Jer 23:5-6

Omnipresence of God - Jer 23:24

Expansion, Law on Our Hearts - Jer 31:33-34

GBF, the Ultimate Expansion - Jer 33:17-18

Punish the Punisher - Jer 51:49

Shadow of God - Lam 4:20

Old Testament Expansion, Idols of the Heart - Eze 14:1-5

Against Calvinism - Eze 18:1-4

Prophet, Engineer, Gearhead - Eze 40-42

Expansion in the Old Testament, Quoted by Christ - Hos 6:6

Expansion in the Old Testament, Rend Your Hearts Not Your Garments - Joel 2:12-14

Free Will in the Old Testament - Amos 5:4-6

Expansion in the Old Testament, Justice, Mercy, Humility - Mic 6:6-8

Prophecy of GBF, Bethlehem - Mic 5:1-5

Dimensions of Rule - Zech 6:1-8

Spiritual Blindness, No Depth of Field, No Dimensional Expansion - Zech 11:15-17

Prophecy of GBF, Pierced - Zech 12:10

Predestination - Mal 1:2-5

Sanctifying Offspring - Mal 2:13-16

Slice, Always Present, Never Leave - Deu 31:6

Expansion Foreseen - Jer 31:31-34

Mixing of Faiths and Astronomy, Wise Men from the East, Who Were They? - Mat 2:1-2

Faith and Works - Mat 3:7-10

Fulfillment of Righteousness, Expansion of Righteousness - Mat 3:13-17

Motive of Action, Compare with Mat 6:1-4 - Mat 5:14-16

Announcement of Expansion - Mat 5:17-20

Expansion of Murder - Mat 5:21-22

Expansion of Adultery - Mat 5:27-28

Expansion of Divorce - Mat 5:31-32

Expansion of Oaths - Mat 5:33-37

Expansion of an Eye for an Eye - Mat 5:38-42

Expansion of Love for Enemies - Mat 5:43-48

Motive of Action, Compare with Mat 5:14-16 - Mat 6:1-4

Summation of the Law and Prophets, Confucius - Mat 7:12

Faith and Works - Mat 7:21-23

Jesus Did Not Abolish the Law, Example - Mat 8:1-4

Centurion, Man of Faith vs. Non Resistance, What Jesus Did Not Say - Mat 8:5-13

Jesus Quotes Old Testament Expansion - Mat 9:10-13

Snakes and Doves - Mat 10:11-16

Expansion of the Sabbath - Mat 12:9-12

Faith of a Mustard Seed - Mat 17:14-20

Number Three, Strong Band, Chord, Stool, Wisdom - Mat 18:19-20

Prophecy of Christ Fulfilled - Mat 21:1-5

Kingdom Given to Fruit Bearers - Mat 21:42-46

Who Is the Christ, Who Came First?, Timelessness of Christ - Mat 22:41-46

Who Is Quoting Whom?, David vs. Jesus - Mat 27:45-50

Trinity Mentioned - Mat 28:16-20

Jesus Did Not Abolish the Law, Example - Mar 1:40-45

Expansion of the Sabbath, Everyday Expanded to Sabbath - Mar 2:23-28

Expansion of the Sabbath, Doing Good or Evil - Mar 3:1-6

Expansion of Brothers and Mothers - Mar 3:33-35

Expansion of Hand Washing to Heart Washing - Mar 7:5-8

Election - Mar 13:20-23

Expansion Early On In the Life of Jesus - Luk 4:23-29

Expansion of the Sabbath - Luk 6:1-5

Expansion of Love for Enemies - Luk 6:27-36

Hearing Implies Doing - Luk 6:46-49

Expansion of Brothers and Mothers - Luk 8:19-21

Amillennialism vs. Premillennialism, the Kingdom, the Resurrection - Luk 9:27

Godhead, Father and Son - Luk 10:22

Expansion, Giving, Pharisees, Neglecting Justice - Luk 11:42

Prince of Peace Brings Dimensional Division, News Flash! - Luk 12:49-53

Amillennialism vs. Premillennialism, Announcing the Kingdom within - Luk 17:20-25

Free Will vs. Election, Save Whom?, The Lost - Luk 19:1-10

Election, Free Will, Both - Mat 22:14

Free Will - Mar 8:34

Higher Dimensional Treasure - Luk 12:32-34

Dimensional Reduction, Incarnation - John 1:14

Born Again, Higher Dimensional, Higher Plane - John 3:1-8

Living Water, Expanded to Eternal Life - John 4:10-14

Those Who Are Dimensionally Expanded Can Worship God - John 4:19-24

Dimensionally Expanded Food - John 4:27-38

God Is Always at Work, So Is Christ, Sabbath? - John 5:16-18

Slices of God, Father and Son Doing the Same!!!!!!!!!!!!!!!!!!!!!!!!!!!!!! - John 5:19-23

Become Expanded to Do Expanded Work - John 6:28-29

Free Will and Election in the Same Breath, Jesus - John 6:36-44

Call to Dimensional Expansion - John 6:25-27

Flesh and Spirit in Different Dimensions - John 6:60-64

Election - John 6:65

Example of Jesus' Expansion - John 7:1-8

Knowing Comes from Doing - John 7:14-19

Outside Our Dimensions, Jesus - John 7:32-34

Higher Dimensional Water - John 7:37-39

Following Dimensionally - John 8:12

People Cannot Handle Dimensional Expansion - John 8:13-20

Dimensional Freedom - John 8:33-38

Hearing and Dimensional Expansion - John 8:42-47

Timeless, Expanded Vectors, I Am, Jesus - John 8:48-59

Jesus, an Added Dimension to the World - John 9:1-5

Father and Son, One - John 10:22-30

Klein Bottles, Christ and the Father - John 10:37-38

I Am the Resurrection - John 11:17-26

Dimensional Blindness - John 12:37-40

Free Will - John 12:46

Porthole, Higher Dimensions - John 14:5-6

Klein Bottles, Christ and the Father - John 14:8-14

Three Klein Bottles, Christ, the Father, Us - John 14:19-21

One Slice at a Time - John 16:5-7

Sin, Righteousness, Judgment, Dimensional - John 16:8-11

Relativity of Time, A Little While - John 16:16-24

Slices, Father, Son - John 17:1

Election - John 17:2-10

Slice Subjected to Space and Time, GBF - John 17:5

Election - John 17:12

Glory, Oneness, Timelessness - John 17:20-24

Higher Dimensional Kingdom - John 18:33-37

David Saw Ahead - Acts 2:22-31

Higher Dimensional Thinking - Acts 5:33-39

Uncircumcised Hearts and Ears - Acts 7:51-53

Translation of Phillip - Acts 8:34-40

Dimensional Expansion, Clean Vs. Unclean - Acts 11:1-10

Dimensional Expansion, Who Can Be Saved - Acts 11:15-18

Expansion of the Law - Acts 13:38-41

Election - Acts 13:46-48

Lower Dimensional Thinking - Acts 15:1-4

Freewill - Acts 17:24-28

God in the Flesh, Dimensional - Rom 1:1-6

Dimensional Reduction through Sin, Idolatry Is Attempted Incarnation - Rom 1:21-28

Expansion of Law - Rom 2:12-13

Dimensional Expansion, Circumcision of the Heart - Rom 2:17-29

Non-Expansion vs. Expansion - Rom 3:20-26

Expanded Law into Faith - Rom 3:27-31

Abraham, Expanded Faith - Rom 4:1-3

Dimensional Battle - Rom 7:14-25

Freewill - Rom 8:28-30

Lower Dimensional Adversaries Can't Touch Higher Dimensional Beings - Rom 8:31-39

Abraham's Children, Expanded - Rom 9:6-9

Election - Rom 9:10-24

Fulfillment of the Law, Christ - Rom 10:1-4

Freewill - Rom 10:5-13

Freewill - Rom 11:17-24

Prophesying, Seeing Dimensions Beyond - Rom 12:1-8

Authorities - Rom 13:1-7

Fulfillment of the Law, Love - Rom 13:8-14

Strong and Weak, How Expanded Are You? - Rom 14:1-8

Dimensionally Expanded, Law, Righteousness, Peace, Joy - Rom 14:13-18

Saved, Being Saved, Continuous - 1 Cor 1:18

Time, Beginning - 1 Cor 2:7

Election, Salvation of Family Members - 1 Cor 7:12-16

Worship, Expanded - 1 Cor 14:13-17

Tongues, Prophecy, Who Is the Audience - 1 Cor 14:22

Difficult to Expand, Paul, Women, Silence, Sequential, Pharisee - 1 Cor 14:33-35

Expansion, Letter to Spirit, Paul, Attempt - 2 Cor 3:1-6

Expansion, Spirit, Freedom - 2 Cor 3:12-18

Expansion, Seen to Unseen, Temporal to Eternal - 2 Cor 4:16-18

Spirit, Guarantee, Foreshadow - 2 Cor 5:1-5

Expansion, In Christ, New Creation - 2 Cor 5:16-19

Expansion, Tithe - 2 Cor 9:6-11

Difficult to Expand, Paul, Women, Silence, Concrete Sequential, Pharisee - Gal 1:11-17

Personality Types, Peter to Jews, Paul to Greeks - Gal 2:6-10

Difficult to Expand, Paul, Women, Silence, Concrete Sequential, Pharisee - Gal 2:11-13

Klein Bottle, Christ in Us, We in Christ - Gal 2:19-20

Expansion, Paul, Signs of - Gal 2:15-16

Law, Give It Up, Move on - Gal 3:3-5

Fruit, Singular, Nine Dimensional, One Entity - Gal 5:22-23

Election, Predestination - Eph 1:11-14

Time, Ages, Expansion at End - Eph 1:19-21

Expansion, Law, Paul - Eph 2:11-18

Wide, Long, High, Deep, Dimensional - Eph 3:14-21

Limited Expansion, Paul - Eph 6:9

Humility, Incarnation, Slice Coming to Earth, Embodiment - Phil 2:1-11

Christ, Full Representation, Fullness of Deity - Col 2:9-12

Shadows, Slices, Things to Come - Col 2:16-19

Proof of Calling, Election - 1 The 1:4-5

Free Will - 2 The 2:1-12

Free Will - 1 Tim 1:12-17

Expansion, Partial, Incomplete - 1 Tim 2:9-15

Free Will - 1 Tim 4:1-8

Time, Beginning, Reduced Dimension of Time - Tit 1:1-3

Free Will, All Men - Tit 2:11-14

Rebirth, New Dimension - Tit 3:1-8

Free Will - Heb 3:7-11

Free Will, Responsibility - Heb 4:1-2

Timelessness, Before and After, Backwards, Reversal, Vectors - Heb 4:7-11

God's Vision, Infinite Dimensions - Heb 4:12-13

Timeless, Slices, Christologies - Heb 5:1-10

Free Will, Fallen Elect - Heb 6:4-12

Immutability, Changeless God, Changeless Purpose - Heb 6:16-20

Timeless, Slices, Christologies - Heb 7:11-17

Expanded Law - Heb 7:18-19

Shadows, Slices, Tabernacle, True Tabernacle - Heb 8:1-6

Expansion Foreseen - Heb 8:7-13

Shadows, Expansion, Law - Heb 10:1-4

Free Will - Heb 10:19-25

Faith, Higher Dimensions - Heb 11:1-2

Seeing Higher Dimensions, Future, Prophetic - Heb 11:13-16

Expanded Prophet, Moses - Heb 11:26-28

Cloud of Witnesses, Higher Dimensions, Seeing Lower Dimensions - Heb 12:1-3

Slice, Always Present, Never Leave - Heb 13:5

Slices Change, Higher Dimensional Images Do Not - Heb 13:8

Expansion, Sacrifices - Heb 13:15-16

Slices Change, Higher Dimensional Images Do Not - Jam 1:16-18

Law, Foreshadow of Expansion, Many Slices, One Sin Breaks All Law - Jam 2:8-11

Mercy, Judgment, Mercy over Judgment - Jam 2:12-13

Faith, Works - Jam 2:14-24

Wisdom, Dimensions - Jam 3:13-18

Free Will, Election, a Dance, Dimensional - Jam 4:7-8

Foreknowledge, Election - 1 Pet 1:1-2

Christ, Chosen before Creation - 1 Pet 1:17-20

Born Again, Higher Dimensional, Higher Plane - 1 Pet 1:22-25

Fruit, Singular, Eight Dimensional, One Entity, Peter's Version - 2 Pet 1:3-9

Free Will, Election, in One Passage - 2 Pet 1:10-11

Prophecy, Higher Dimensional Vision, Past, Present, Future - 2 Pet 1:19-21

Time, Warp, Thousand Years, One Day - 2 Pet 3:8-9a

Free Will, Desire All to Come - 2 Pet 3:9b

Expansion, New Commandment, Darkness, Light - 1 John 2:7-8

Sin, Three Dimensional - 1 John 2:15-17

Expansion, Ultimate, See Him, Will Be like Him - 1 John 3:2-3

Love, Dimensions - 1 John 3:11-20

Love Is Dimensional, God Is Love, God Is Dimensional - 1 John 4:8

Love Is Dimensional, God Is Love, God Is Dimensional - 1 Cor 13:4-7

Expansion, Ultimate, Imperfect Vanishes when Perfect Comes - 1 Cor 13:9-10

Three Testify, Water, Spirit, Blood - 1 John 5:6-12

Alpha, Omega, Dimensions - Rev 1:8

Porthole, Tree of Life, Higher Dimensions - Rev 2:7

Food, Higher Dimensional, Israel in Desert - Rev 2:17

Slices Of God, Dimensions of God, Seven - Rev 4:1-6

Slices Of God, Dimensions of God, Seven - Rev 5:6-10

Time, Heaven, Conversion, One Half Hour Approximately 21 Years - Rev 8:1

Overcoming, Blood, Testimonies - Rev 12:7-11

Tree of Life, Porthole to Higher Dimensions, Rivers as Wormholes - Rev 22:1-5

Wash, Robed, Tree of Life - Rev 22:12-14

Free Will, Dimensional Proclamation - Rev 22:17

Fractal References

Negative Fractal, Worshiping Creation - Deut 5:1-21

God's Mirror, to Each His Own - 2 Sam 22:25-28

Repeated Numbers, 666 - 1 Kings 10:14-16

Messianic Symbolism, Solomon - 1 Kings 10:23-25

Prophets Anointing Prophets, John and Jesus - 1 Kings 19:15-21

Adoption as Sons, Like Paul in Romans - Neh 8:15-17

Beatitudes Shadowed - Ps 9:7-10

Resurrection Shadowed - Ps 16:9-11

Who Is Quoting Whom?, David vs. Jesus - Ps 22:1-2

Who Is Quoting Whom?, David vs. Jesus - Ps 31:1-5

Broken Bones - Ps 34:19-20

Repeated Prophecies, Footstool - Ps 110:1

Christ's Words Shadowed in the Old Testament - Prov 19:17

Images and Slices in the Old Testament - Prov 27:17-19

Images and Slices in the Old Testament - Prov 30:15-19

New Testament Principle in the Old Testament - Eccl 9:10

Sins and Color - Isa 1:18-20

Twin Towers - Isa 30:1-33

Types of Christ, Samaritan Woman - Isa 12:3-6

Following Babylonian Captivity, Future as Well - Isa 14:1-2

Satan and Nations - Isa 14:12-15

Blind and Deaf, Then and Now, A New Thing - Isa 42:18-22

New Thing Then and Now - Isa 43:16-21

Idolatry, Still Doing It, Blindness - Isa 44:9-20

House of Prayer, Now Extended to Our Bodies - Isa 56:3-8

Idolatry, Still Doing It, Blindness - Isa 57:5-13

Repeated Theme, Year of Jubilee, GBF Fulfillment - Isa 61 1-4

Bride Theme - Isa 62:5

Two Sins, Repeated Today, Forsaken God, Created Their Own - Jer 2:11-13

Idolatry, Abortion, Repeated Today - Jer 7:30-34

No Shame, No Repentance, Repeated Today - Jer 8:12

Marriage Theme in the Old Testament - Jer 31:31-32

Twin Towers, Hope in the End - Jer 49:4-6

Lost Sheep, Bob Dylan - Jer 50:6

Today's Sitcoms - Jer 51:17

Images Common to the Old Testament and Mandelbrot - Eze 1:15-18

Sacrificing Children, Abortion - Eze 16:20-22

Standing In the Gap, Still Looking - Eze 22:30-31

America? - Eze 23:28-34

Twin Towers? - Eze 28:1-18

The Good Shepherd, the GBF - Eze 34:11-16

Seek Good, Not Evil - Amos 5:11-14

Jonah and GBF, Three Days - Jonah 1:17

America?, House of Man vs. House of God - Hag 1:3-6

House of God, Temple in Body - Hag 2:6-9

Old Testament Types and Symbols, Things to Come, Shadows, GBF - Zech 3:8-9

Many Nations Adopted, God's People - Zech 2:11

Two Anointed Ones, More Than Two? - Zech 4:11-14

Flesh-Eating Bacteria - Zech 14:12-15

Elijah Coming Back, GBF?, One of Two Witnesses?, Repentance - Mal 4:1-6

Fascination with Numbers - Mat 1:17

Fascination with Numbers, Forty Days - Mat 4:1-11

Body Metaphor - Mat 5:29-30

Direct Dynamics, God's Mirror - Mat 6:14-15

Metaphors from Nature, Do Not Worry - Mat 6:25-34

Fascination with Numbers, 144,000 - Mat 10: 26-31

Direct Dynamics, Acknowledgement - Mat 10:32-33

Direct Dynamics, Reception - Mat 10:40-42

Jonah and GBF, Three Days - Mat 12:38-42

Brothers and Mothers - Mat 12:46-50

Parables, Sower - Mat 13:1-9

Parables, Yeast - Mat 13:31-32

Parables, Net - Mat 13:47-50

Multiplying Fish and Bread - Mat 14:13-20

Multiplying Fish and Bread - Mat 15:32-39

Signs from Nature - Mat 16:1-4

Yeast of the Pharisees - Mat 16:5-12

God's Mirror, We Are that Mirror - Mat 16:13-20

Elijah Coming Back - Mat 17:10-13

Direct Dynamics, Welcoming a Child, Welcoming Christ - Mat 18:5-6

Members of One Body, One Fractal - Mat 18:7-9

Other Faithful Worlds? - Mat 18:10-14

Fascination with Numbers, Forgiveness - Mat 18:21-22

Direct Dynamics, Forgiveness - Mat 18:32-35

Levels of Calling, Degrees of Sacrifice, Proportional Rewards - Mat 19:21-30

You Will Drink from My Cup! - Mat 20:20-23

Commandments, Greatest, All Others Branch from Two - Mat 22:34-40

Jerusalem, Chicks under Wings - Mat 23:37-39

You, Now and Later, Multiple Fulfillments - Mat 24:1-14

Generation, Race, People, Multiple Fulfillments - Mat 24:32-35

Direct Dynamics - Mat 25:28-30

Direct Dynamics, the Least of These - Mat 25:37-46

Body of Christ - Mat 26:26-30

Direct Dynamics, Live by the Sword, Die by the Sword - Mat 26:47-54

Multiple Fulfillments, Psalm 22:18 - Mat 27:32-35

Water and Spirit - Mar 1:1-8

Fishers of Men - Mar 1:14-20

New Wine, Old Wine Skins - Mar 2:18-22

Parables, Sower - Mar 4:1-9

Lamp Stand - Mar 4:21-23

Direct Dynamics, God's Mirror - Mar 4:24-25

Parables, Mustard Seed - Mar 4:30-34

Spread the News - Mar 5:18-20

Fish and Bread Multiplied - Mar 6:37-44

Yeast of the Pharisees - Mar 8:14-21

Direct Dynamics, God's Mirror - Mar 8:38

Welcome a Child and Welcome Christ - Mar 9:36-37

Multiple Fulfillments, Psalm 118:22-23 - Mar 12:1-11

Gospel Preached to All Nations, Multiple Times, Matrix Must Be Complete - Mar 13:1-13

Use of Scripture against Satan - Luk 4:1-13

Jesus Reading Isaiah 61 - Luk 4:14-19

Direct Dynamics, God's Mirror, Judging - Luk 6:37-38

Listening, Accepting, Rejection - Luk 10:16

Responsibility for Past Wrongs Done by Others, Passed on - Luk 11:47-51

Direct Dynamics, God's Mirror, Justice - Luk 12:47-48

Kingdom of God, Mustard Seed, Yeast - Luk 13:18-21

Giving Up Everything, Ownership - Luk 14:31-33

The Days of Noah - Luk 17:26-37

Direct Dynamics, God's Mirror, Justice - Luk 19:26-27

Stones Crying out, Someone along the Fractal Will Cry out - Luk 19:38-40

The Stone the Builders Rejected, Psalm 118:22 - Luk 20:14-18

House of Prayer - Luk 19:45-48

Signs of the Times, Multiple Fulfillments, One Base Fulfillment in Future - Luk 21:5-19

Signs of the Times, Generation, Race - Luk 21:25-36

Meaning of the Passover - Luk 22:14-16

Christ's Body and Blood, Communion - Luk 22:17-23

First Order Fulfillment, Isaiah 53:12 - Luk 22:31-37

Children Born of God - John 1:12-13

David's Words Repeated Fractally - John 2:12-17

Destroy this Temple, Raise In 3 Days - John 2:18-22

Bread of Life, Fractal Use - John 6:25-35

Fractal Use of Prophecy, Isaiah 54:13 - John 6:45-47

Bread of Life, Fractal Use - John 6:48-51

Eat the Flesh, Old Testament Priests Eating the Sacrifices, Communion - John 6:52-59

Streams of Living Water, Flows Fractally - John 7:37-38

Other Sheep to Be Included - John 10:11-18

Seed Dying and Producing Many Seeds - John 12:20-26

Fractal Belief - John 12:42-46

Propagate Feet Washing - John 13:12-17

Acceptance, Father, Son, Believer - John 13:20

Fractal Love, Jesus' Example - John 13:34-35

Likeness of Father and Son - John 14:7

Numerous Fractal Teachings - John 15:1-20

Repeated Model, Oneness - John 17:11

Repeated Knowledge - John 17:25-26

Repeated Fulfillments, Psalm 22:18 - John 19:24

Fractal Fulfillments, Ex 12:46, Num 9:12, Ps 34:20, Zech 12:10 - John 19:28-37

Becoming Christ-like, or Christ's - John 20:19-23

All the Things Christ Did, Exhaustive - John 21:25

Multiple Fulfillments, Peter Quoting David, Ps 16:8-11 - Acts 2:22-31

Your Children, and Those Far off - Acts 2:36-39

Times of Refreshing, More Than One - Acts 3:17-19

Coming of the Holy Spirit, Multiple Ways, Multiple Times - Acts 8:14-17

Tongues of Fire, Related to Ezekiel and Daniel, Fire around God's Throne - Acts 2:3

Fractal Fulfillments, Isa 6:9-10 - Acts 28:26-27

Need Each Other's Faith - Rom 1:8-12

Direct Dynamics, Judgment's Mirror - Rom 2:1

From One to Many, Grace, So it is to be with Us - Rom 5:15-17

Baptized into Christ's Death - Rom 6:1-14

Marriage Theme - Rom 7:1-6

Suffer with Christ, Inherit with Christ - Rom 8:12-17

Redemption Permeates Creation - Rom 8:18-25

Mind of Christ, Possess - 1 Cor 2:15-16

Seed, Gardner - 1 Cor 3:5-9

God's Temple - 1 Cor 3:16-17

What Belongs to Whom? - 1 Cor 3:21-23

Boasting, Yeast, Malice - 1 Cor 5:6-8

Bodies, Members of Christ, Temples - 1 Cor 6:12-20

Analogies, Ox, Seed, Flock, Milk - 1 Cor 9:7-12

Head of Whom? - 1 Cor 11:3

Communion - 1 Cor 11:23-26

Same Lord, Many Gifts - 1 Cor 12:1-11

One Body, Many Members - 1 Cor 12:12-31

Head, Christ, over Everything, Fills Everything - Eph 1:22-23

One Body, Many Gifts - Eph 4:7-13

Imitate God, the Call - Eph 5:1-2

Wives, Husbands - Eph 5:22-30

Armor of God - Eph 6:10-18

Imitators, Models - 1 The 1:6-7

Use of Scripture - Heb 2:5-8

Idea, Desire, Sin, Death - Jam 1:13-15

Faith, Works - Jam 2:25-26

Tongue, Taming - Jam 3:1-12

Patience, Like a Farmer - Jam 5:7-9

Living Stones, Christ, Us - 1 Pet 2:4-8

Suffering, Like Christ - 1 Pet 2:20-21

Noah, Flood, Ark - 1 Pet 3:20-22

Shepherds, Examples - 1 Pet 5:1-4

Walk as He Walked, Claims - 1 John 2:3-6

Antichrist, Antichrists - 1 John 2:18-23

God, Heavens, Heavenly Bodies, Earth, Sea, Inhabitants - Rev 10:5-7

Multiple Fulfillments, Prophecy, 1 Hour Is 42 Years - Rev 17:1-18

Multiple Fulfillments, Twin Towers - Rev 18:6-24

Conclusionary References

Do Not Forget, Refresh Regularly - Deut 4:9

Life or Death, the Commission - Deut 30:11-14

Be Courageous, Meditate on the Law - Josh 1:1-9

Calling of Samuel, Repeated Callings, Not Giving Up - 1 Sam 3:1-14

Biology, Wisdom of Solomon, More than Theology! - 1 Kings 4:29-34

My Redeemer Lives! - Job 19:23-27

God's Sarcasm - Job 38:21

Justifying Ourselves at God's Expense - Job 40:1-14

Ultimate Confession, What the Church Must Do - Job 42:1-6

Be Silent Before God - Ps 4:4-5

The Words of My Mouth, Meditation of My Heart - Ps 19:12-14

Be Still and Know That I Am God - Ps 46:10

Doorkeeper in God's House - Ps 84:10-12

Hide His Words in Our Hearts - Ps 119:9-16

Study God's Word - Ps 119:125-128

Peace Comes From God's Word and Law - Ps 119:165

Unless God Builds Your House and Theology It Is In Vain - Ps 127:1-2

Fear God - Eccl 12:13-14

Swords to Plowshares - Isa 2:1-5

Peace in the Process - Isa 26:3-4

Compassion and Justice of God - Isa 30:18

Strength from the Lord - Isa 40:28-31

Ultimate Mission, Not Theological Arguments, GBF Mission, Our Mission - Isa 61:1-3

What God Wants, Obedience, Inside and Out - Jer 11:1-5 -

Seek Me with All Your Heart, I Will Be Found - Jer 29:10-14 -

Singleness of Heart, God's People - Jer 32:36-41 -

GBF Not Serving As High Priest, When Hell Freezes Over - Jer 33:19-21 -

Signs of a True Prophet - Eze 33:33 -

Going Further and Deeper, Discontent for the Normal, Expect Surprises - Eze 47:1-5 -

Blessings for the Wise and Leaders of Righteousness - Dan 12:1-4 -

Plumb Line Is Set, What Will the Church Do? - Amos 7:7-8 -

Mountain of the Lord, Swords to Plowshares - Mic 4:2-5 -

Be Silent, the Lord Is in His Holy Temple, Listen - Hab 2:20 -

Rejoicing in God My Savior, Barren Trees, No Fruit or Sheep - Hab 3:17-18 -

Help My Unbelief - Mar 9:14-24 -

Direct Dynamics, God's Mirror, What We Think We Have! - Luk 8:16-18 -

Don't Lose Sight of What Is Important - Luk 10:17-20 -

Fear Whom? - Luk 12:1-7 -

Worry - Luk 12:27-31 -

Example of All Three, Strange, Dimensional, And Fractal - John 3:1-8 -

Example of All Three, Strange, Dimensional, And Fractal - John 10:7-10 -

Reminders by the Holy Spirit - John 14:25-27 -

No Favoritism with God - Acts 10:34-35 -

Finishing the Race, Completing the Tasks - Acts 20:24 -

How to Pray, Holy Spirit Helps - Rom 8:26-27 -

Every Tongue Will Confess - Rom 14:10-12 -

Don't Function on the Basis of Doubt - Rom 14:22-23 -

No Eye Has Seen What Awaits - 1 Cor 2:9 -

Boast in the Lord, Not Theology - 2 Cor 10:12-18 -

Press On to the Goal - Phili 3:12-14 -

Peace, Guard Hearts - Phili 4:2-9 -

Set Minds, Things above - Col 3:1-4 -

Pray, Continuous - 1 The 5:16-17 -

Steadfast, Sound Doctrine - 2 Tim 4:1-8 -

Equipped, Read, Study - 2 Tim 3:10-17 -

Do Not Refuse God, Shaking Earth, Shaking Heavens - Heb 12:25-29

Worthy Is the Lamb - Rev 5:11-12

White Horse, Faithful Rider - Rev 19:11

Appendix B

Koran References

No God But One: No Trinity - Sura V:77

Hatred for Joining Other Gods with God - Sura V:85

"The Creator: ""We""" - Sura VII:10"

The Holy Spirit? - Sura XVI:104

"We" Breathed of "Our" Spirit into Mary's Womb - Sura LXVI:12

Conclusionary References

Seeking First God - Sura II:106

A Faithful God - Sura III:189-192

A Believer: Hears and Obeys - Sura IV:48-49

Resignation to God: The Better Religion - Sura IV:123

Believers: Trust In the Lord - Sura VIII:2

Humble Yourselves and Pray! - Sura IX:11

It Is God Who Holds all Things Together - Sura XVI:81

The Light of the World - Sura XXIV:35